197

D0208096

Rev
2020

XENOPHON AND THE HISTORY OF HIS TIMES

XENOPHON AND THE HISTORY OF HIS TIMES

John Dillery

London and New York

First published 1995
by Routledge
11 New Fetter Lane, London EC4P 4EE

Simultaneously published in the USA and Canada
by Routledge
29 West 35th Street, New York, NY 10001

Typeset in Garamond by
Florencetype Ltd, Stoodleigh, Devon

Printed and bound in Great Britain by
TJ Press (Padstow) Ltd, Padstow, Cornwall

British Library Cataloguing in Publication Data
A catalogue record for this book is available from the British Library

Library of Congress Cataloguing in Publication Data
Dillery, John.
Xenophon and the history of his times/John Dillery.
p. cm.
Includes bibliographical references and index.
1. Xenophon–Political and social views.   2. Xenophon. Hellenica.
3. Greece–History–Peloponnesian War, 431–404 BC.   4. Greece–
History–Spartan and Theban Supremacies, 404–362 BC.
5. Imperialism.   6. History–Philosophy.   I. Title.
DF229.D55   1995
938′.007202–dc20   94–30021

ISBN 0–415–09139–X

For my parents
Marita and Edward Dillery
(Exodus 20.12)
and for my wife
Sara Myers
(Proverbs 19.14)

CONTENTS

PREFACE AND ACKNOWLEDGEMENTS

I have written this book from the conviction that Xenophon's longer historical works, the *Hellenica* and *Anabasis*, have a great deal to tell us about how one thoughtful man of unusually wide experience attempted to make sense of the history of his times. The perspective it takes is not adversarial, as though Xenophon was a witness who was either unable to tell us the things we wish to know, or was unwilling; rather, this book takes account of what he wanted to tell us, and suggests reasons why he might have felt that way. It does not censure, it explains. My chief concern has been twofold: first, to place the discussion of the *Hellenica* and *Anabasis* in the larger context of Xenophon's entire corpus, in order to see with greater clarity the structures of his thought; and second, to look at how his contemporaries or near-contemporaries grappled with issues that also come up in his work. Thus I hope that a better understanding of how Xenophon viewed his world will emerge, as well as an awareness of how his thinking was like and unlike those who lived at about the same time he did. The period Xenophon covered in his historical writing was a crucial one, not only for Greek political–military history, but also for Greek intellectual history, in which ideas that can be recognized, roughly speaking, as 'Classical' or even 'Archaic' were being gradually modulated and changed into ones we might style 'Hellenistic'.

I have followed throughout the Oxford Classical Texts (OCT) of Xenophon's works. All translations are my own. I have tried to transliterate Greek terms precisely; however, when a word has a more recognizable Latinized form, I have used it.

This study began as my doctoral dissertation at the University of Michigan (1989). I have completely revised and updated the work, and have considerably broadened its scope. I would like to thank, first, my doctoral committee, especially for their suggestions for improving my discussion and making it less a thesis and more a book: Ludwig Koenen, Rudi Lindner, David Potter and Ruth Scodel. I owe a special debt to Ludwig Koenen, a great scholar of antiquity whom I was most fortunate to have as my teacher, and to David Potter, my keenest critic and most generous friend. I would also like to thank the Institute for the Humanities at the University of Michigan and its director, James Winn, for the award of a timely fellowship that helped me make significant progress on the writing of the book. A generous leave granted by the Department of Classical Studies at the University of Michigan enabled me to finish the project.

A number of individuals have assisted me at various stages. Toni Raubitschek gave me early words of encouragement when my ideas were still in the thesis stage. I presented some of the arguments of this book at annual meetings of the American Philological Society and the Classical Association of the Middle West and South, and would like to thank the audiences on those occasions for their suggestions. Robin Lane Fox generously took the time while on a visit to Ann Arbor to discuss with me at length matters pertaining to chapters 3, 7 and 8. In matters more generally Xenophontine I have been helped by conversations with Ariel Loftus and Andy Meadows. Sabine MacCormack read drafts of chapters 1, 7 and 8, and made many helpful suggestions, showing interest in the whole project throughout its composition. Elspeth McIntosh and Peter Krentz read a draft of the entire book and suggested significant improvements; I cannot thank them enough. Ellen Bauerle, Sara Myers, David Potter and Jeremy Taylor read the proofs and saved me from numerous errors. Warm thanks are also due to Richard Stoneman, Caroline Cautley and Kim Richardson at Routledge. Needless to say, I alone am responsible for any shortcomings that remain.

Finally, some thanks of a different kind. The dedication of this book records two debts. First, I would like to mention my wife, Sara Myers; her kindness and tolerance have supported me throughout the writing of this book; I could not have written it without her. My parents, Marita and Edward Dillery, have helped me throughout my education; their care and encouragement have meant everything to me; the debt I owe them I can only partially express and can never adequately repay.

ABBREVIATIONS

For ancient Greek texts I have followed throughout the abbreviations to be found in the ninth edition of Liddell and Scott's *A Greek–English Lexicon* (1940); in the case of Isocrates, however, I have identified his work by short abbreviations of title rather than by number, and my abbreviations of Xenophon's works do not always follow *LSJ* (see list below). The few Latin texts I have cited are abbreviated according to Lewis and Short's *A Latin Dictionary* (1879). For modern works cited in the Bibliography, I have followed the abbreviations found in the issues of *L'Année Philologique*. Certain works have been cited in the discussion itself, and are abbreviated as follows:

CAH	*Cambridge Ancient History* (1928–), Cambridge: Cambridge University Press.
DK	H. Diels and W. Kranz, eds (1951–1952) *Die Fragmente der Vorsokratiker* (6th edn), Berlin: Weidmann.
FGrHist	F. Jacoby, ed. (1923–1958) *Die Fragmente der griechischen Historiker*, Berlin and Leiden: E.J. Brill.
Giannantoni	G. Giannantoni, ed. (1990) *Socratis et Socraticorum Reliquiae* 4, Naples: Bibliopolis.
GVI	W. Peek, ed. (1955) *Griechische Vers-Inschriften* 1, Berlin: Berlin Akademischer Verlag.
Harding	P. Harding, ed. (1985) *From the End of the Peloponnesian War to the Battle of Ipsus*, Translated Documents of Greece and Rome 2, Cambridge: Cambridge University Press.

LSJ   H.G. Liddell and R. Scott (1940) *A Greek–English Lexicon* (9th edn), Oxford: Oxford University Press.

P.Oxy.   *The Oxyrhynchus Papyri* (1898–), London: The Egypt Exploration Society.

RE   A. Pauly, G. Wissowa and W. Kroll, eds (1893–)*Real-Encylopädie der klassischen Altertumswissenschaft*, Stuttgart: Alfred Druckenmüller.

SVA   H. Bengtson, ed. (1975) *Die Staatsverträge des Altertums* 2 (2nd edn), Munich and Berlin: C.H. Beck.

Tod   M.N. Tod (1948) *A Selection of Greek Historical Inscriptions* 2, Oxford: Oxford University Press.

Voigt   E.-M. Voigt, ed. (1971) *Sappho et Alcaeus Fragmenta*, Amsterdam: Athenaeum.

West   M.L. West, ed. (1972) *Iambi et Elegi Graeci* 2, Oxford: Oxford University Press.

XENOPHON'S WORKS CITED

Ages.   *Agesilaus*

An.   *Anabasis*

Ap.   *Apologia Socratis*

Cyr.   *Cyropaedia*

Hell.   *Hellenica*

Lac.   *Respublica Lacedaemoniorum* (*Constitution of the Spartans*)

Mem.   *Memorabilia*

Oec.   *Oeconomicus*

Poroi   *Poroi*

Smp.   *Symposium*

Part I

BEGINNINGS AND ENDS

INTRODUCTION

Xenophon's *Hellenica* is a narrative account of a particularly bloody and confusing period of Greek history. It is also a document recording one man's understanding of what happened in his lifetime. The assessment of whether and to what degree the work succeeds as a work of history has often been done before. It is the second issue that forms the topic of this book. How did Xenophon understand the history of his times? How can we reconstruct his view? Did others – Xenophon's contemporaries – think about their world in similar ways?

PRELIMINARY REMARKS

By the end of 411 BC the second phase of the Peloponnesian War was heading towards the end of its third year.[1] By the middle of 410 the first oligarchic coup at Athens had collapsed, and soon would come the see-saw naval combat in the Aegean that would culminate ultimately in Lysander's defeat of the Athenian fleet at Aegospotami. The century concluded with peace and another oligarchic revolution at Athens, and then a brief dynastic war in Persia. Throughout Athens' former empire the Spartans were stepping in, and soon were championing the freedom of the Greeks of Asia Minor. Alarmed, the Persian king sent emissaries to Greece to help foment war against the new imperial Hellenic power. The Corinthian War followed, producing no real military winners, although Sparta managed to emerge supreme thanks to the so called King's Peace she brokered with her former enemy Persia (387/6). Sparta's ascendancy lasted only for a few years as it was soon shaken from within by a series of ill-advised aggressions against states that were at least in theory protected by the Peace. These actions alienated her old enemies Thebes and Athens, who rose again as formidable powers; indeed

3

Athens formed a new maritime alliance in response to growing Spartan ambitions. Again there was war; Sparta and Thebes faced each other at Leuctra and Sparta came out the loser (371). The world had changed, and now Thebes was the leading power of Greece; Sparta continued to be humiliated by numerous Theban invasions of the Peloponnese. Eventually the two powers squared-off again, this time at Mantinea, and again Sparta was defeated (362), though Thebes was dealt a serious blow by the loss of her ablest general, Epaminondas.

Seldom before in the history of the Greek world had power proved so labile. Two hegemonies had fallen, and the third, that of Thebes, was soon to give way to Macedon, and all this in less than fifty years. Warfare was almost a constant feature of life during the period. Cities seemed continually to realign themselves in a series of alliances and confederations. And, in fact, new cities were born (Messenia), and in place of cities new ways of concentrating power even came into being in certain areas (the Arcadian and Aetolian leagues, c. 370 and shortly before autumn 367 respectively, Tod 137). The world of the independent and aggressive *polis* was not to last for long.

It is precisely this crucial period, from 411 to 362, that Xenophon covers in his *Hellenica* or 'Greek Affairs'. Although others wrote contemporary treatments of this phase of Greek history, or at least parts of it, only Xenophon's has come down to us intact. For the work of Ephorus and Theopompus we have to look to later quotation and excerption. Additionally, papyrus has preserved very valuable fragments of an unknown historian, the so-called Oxyrhynchus historian. Otherwise, we have mostly names of individual historians and nothing more.

For some years comparisons between Xenophon and the scanty remains of his contemporaries have shown that the *Hellenica* is not a completely satisfactory account. It betrays distortions due to his personal biases, especially in favour of Sparta and against Thebes, as well as glaring omissions of fact and other structural shortcomings. For many readers Diodorus Siculus, a first-century compiler who made use of Ephorus for the same period covered by Xenophon's *Hellenica*, has become the better place to turn for a narrative treatment; the argument is often made that since it seems Ephorus was himself using the excellent work of the Oxyrhynchus historian, Diodorus is the ultimate beneficiary and should be preferred. But this tendency to dismiss Xenophon has met with resistance,[2] and recent work has gone even further to correct the excesses of his critics.[3] But while not the failure he is sometimes considered to be, few would want to overlook the serious problems of Xenophon's history. A fair but by no means innocent view has developed.

As a more balanced assessment of the *Hellenica* emerges it seems an especially opportune time to consider the thinking that lay behind Xenophon's narrative. What were the forces that he considered decisive in shaping the history of his age? How does he go about explaining what happened? Does his history have an overarching point? In order to get at answers to these questions, we need to look at how Xenophon thought, how he conceived of his world; and to do this we must look beyond the *Hellenica* to the many other works, historical and otherwise, that he wrote. Indeed, one of the main contributions this book makes to the study of Xenophon is to link the study of the *Hellenica* to the rest of his corpus, and further, to see as best we can how his contemporaries explained events and how these explanations compare with Xenophon's. As such, this discussion aims at studying the *Hellenica* both as a text which documents the events of Greek world from 411 to 362, but which is also a document itself of the intellectual history of the same period. In this sense the present book concerns Xenophon and the history of his times.

READING THE *HELLENICA*: TWO GENERAL ASSUMPTIONS

The relevance of significant persons and events

Guiding my discussion of the *Hellenica* has been the assumption that crucial to any understanding of it is appreciating the influence that three separate men had on Xenophon, as well as a handful of significant events from his lifetime. I believe that whether or not he was a genuine student of Socrates, Xenophon thought of himself as his follower; and further that what he thought about right and wrong behaviour, and about the divine's governance of the world, he believed he learned from the philosopher. I think that the younger Cyrus, under whom Xenophon served when that man tried to wrest the throne of Persia from his brother, also exerted a profound influence over him; specifically, he probably formed many of his notions regarding good leadership from the Persian prince, even if the real man did not measure up to these ideals. The last person to influence

Xenophon's thinking was King Agesilaus of Sparta. Xenophon served under him as well, and like Cyrus, Agesilaus helped to distil in his mind what it took to be a good leader of men; he came also to symbolize for Xenophon the excellence of the Spartan way of life. However, in addition to these positive examples, Agesilaus also became the focus of Xenophon's critique of Spartan failure in the years following the King's Peace. While he was personally devoted to him, and indeed wrote an encomiastic biography of him after his death, this did not stop Xenophon from using Agesilaus as an explanation for a general pattern of decline at Sparta that was precipitated by her ambitions as an imperial power. Nothing was probably more difficult for Xenophon than the criticism of his friend and patron (it was probably through Agesilaus' agency that Xenophon received an estate near Olympia after the Corinthian War), but nothing testifies better to his attempt to understand the history of his age, even if imperfectly accomplished.

Rather than perceiving complex chains of causation working through time, Xenophon relied on signal, benchmark events to interpret the history of his age. The defeat of Athens in the Peloponnesian War was his first introduction to the fall of an empire – something he would witness later in connection with Sparta, and a topic that would absorb much of his attention throughout the *Hellenica*. The tyranny of the Thirty at Athens in the year immediately following the conclusion of the war was also instrumental in shaping his notions regarding the decline of regimes. The tyrants of Athens taught him the perils of autocratic rule; and while he may not have understood this lesson completely at the time, when he saw similar mistakes being committed by Sparta at the international level years later, the memory of their rule proved a ready model of explanation. The death of Socrates at the hands of the restored democracy convinced him of the inherent weakness of democratic government; although he does not deal with this event in the *Hellenica*, we can tell from his introductions to his *Memorabilia* and *Apology* that it troubled him deeply and demanded some sort of explanation. Important, too, was Xenophon's participation in the famous March Up Country or 'Anabasis' by the ten thousand Greek mercenaries originally in the service of Cyrus. While he may not have been quite as important or successful as he depicts himself in his *Anabasis*, this episode from his life added further to his understanding of good leadership. But at a more general level, it also planted in his mind notions of panhellenism, as well as ideas concerning what contributed to his conception of the ideal community, his utopia. The Spartan seizure of the citadel of Thebes in 382 in contravention of the King's Peace was arguably the most important event for Xenophon that happened in his lifetime. It was the clearest expression of Sparta's self-destructive imperial policy and accounted in his mind for her punishment by the gods on the battlefield of Leuctra a little more than ten years later at the hands of the Thebans. Finally, the battle of Mantinea, at which Sparta was defeated a second time by Thebes, shook his confidence in the meaningfulness of history itself, for as he says at the end of the *Hellenica*, the conflict was not decisive in producing a clear winner but contributed only to the further confusion of Greek affairs. In the few years that remained left to Xenophon the lesson of Mantinea became clear to him; it was probably in the wake of this battle that he saw with a clarity only hindsight can provide the folly of Spartan imperialism and indeed of imperialism in general. It was surely with this realization in mind that, at the very end of his life, he was struggling to bring about a *rapprochement* between Athens and Sparta.

The relevance of comparisons made from Xenophon's entire corpus and from his contemporaries

While readers in antiquity understood him to be both a historian and a philosopher, and were not averse from treating these two aspects of his overall achievement together,[4] modern scholars have shown a marked tendency to keep Xenophon the historian apart from Xenophon the philosopher;[5] and even when they are linked together, the connection is invariably drawn to show that he was a bad practitioner of both.[6] But not to have the rest of Xenophon's corpus firmly in mind when looking at the *Hellenica* is a grave mistake. If, in light of the problems posed by the divinely sent dreams at the beginning of Book 7 of his *Histories*, Herodotus had written elsewhere what he really thought concerning divine agency, would we not read it when discussing the reasons for Xerxes' invasion of Greece? Or if, in connection with his evaluation of the leadership of Pericles in Book 2 of his *History of the Peloponnesian War*, Thucydides had discussed separately how an exceptional commander could affect the course of history through his rule, would we not consult it? This is precisely the opportunity we have with Xenophon. As Arnaldo Momigliano acutely noted, he is the only historian from antiquity to rival Tacitus in the range of writing that came from his pen.[7] It simply does not make sense to ignore or insufficiently appreciate the value of this range of material when looking at problems associated with the *Hellenica*; with Xenophon we are uniquely placed to see the historian's methods of explanation and argument, his procedures for evaluation and judgment – all these being issues of great importance for any historiographic critique – in contexts other than his main historical work. Ideas regarding Sparta, panhellenism, good leadership, the exemplary paradigm, and the working of the divine in human history, ideas that play such important roles in the *Hellenica*, are often treated in greater detail elsewhere by Xenophon. And before throwing these notions about in a discussion of the *Hellenica*, we should come to terms with how paradigmatic history worked in Xenophon's mind; what it meant for him to be a panhellenist; precisely what was the nature of his pro-Spartan bias; and what kind of power did the gods possess in his worldview. Accordingly, in this book full use is made of the *Memorabilia, Cyropaedia, Agesilaus* and *Constitution of the Spartans*, not to mention the *Anabasis*, which I see as especially important to an understanding of *Hellenica* as a whole and in particular Books 3–4.

Marc Bloch wrote eloquently of the essential 'solidarity' between the past that the historian is attempting to recount and the present he is living in; that no historian can make sense of his past without structures of thought that derive from his own time.[8] And indeed, it is precisely this link that makes any historian's account both a treatment of the past and simultaneously a historical document itself, something I briefly alluded to above (p. 5). One of the most important tasks facing any student of a historian from antiquity is to try to see how his narrative reflects the intellectual climate of his day. The best way we can go about doing this is by comparing the historian with contemporary texts. Naturally comparisons between Xenophon and his contemporaries have often been made before, but frequently they have been drawn for the narrow purpose of pointing up his failures. In this book I have frequently noted points of comparison and contrast not only with Xenophon's contemporary and near-contemporary historians (especially Ephorus and Theopompus), but also with other writers, ranging from Aeneas the Tactician, to Isocrates, to Plato. Additionally, I have also made occasional use of inscriptions (chiefly from Athens) to help create a backdrop for appreciating

Xenophon's thinking. Indeed, I have been particularly concerned to show how the *Hellenica* may or may not reflect attitudes that were current in his day. To the extent that this can be done we can perhaps catch a glimpse of how people in general may have reacted to the monumental changes that occurred in the Greek world during the period covered by the *Hellenica*.

THREE SPECIFIC PROBLEMS

Xenophon the 'continuator' of Thucydides

It was widely believed in antiquity that Xenophon attempted to complete Thucydides' *History of the Peloponnesian War*.[9] This view gains some credence when it is noted that the *Hellenica* begins, roughly speaking, where Thucydides' account leaves off in the autumn of 411, and further that there seem to be formal similarities between the first part of the *Hellenica* (1–2.3.10; more on this division below) and Thucydides' history.[10] However, we need to be wary: much of the material that is thought to support the view that Xenophon was trying to finish his predecessor's work may well be later insertion; and even if it is not, there are other reasons to remain cautious before accepting that this was Xenophon's plan.[11]

The possibility that Xenophon may have tried in some formal sense to 'fill out' Thucydides' history, however, has encouraged many to make a general comparison between the *Hellenica* and the work of Thucydides, with the predictable result that Xenophon has been found an unworthy successor, and further, scarcely deserving of the title 'historian' at all. To be sure, the legacy of Thucydides, probably more than any other factor, has led to the sharp criticism of Xenophon. A glance at the modern evaluation of the Oxyrhynchus historian supports this suggestion: in him we have 'a worthy successor', and his work is thought to be of the first order. Yet such a process of evaluation is problematic for three reasons. In the first place it encourages us to look for Thucydides in Xenophon, rather than attempting to make sense of what Xenophon says in his own terms. Second, the comparison with Thucydides obscures the possible influence other historians, and indeed other non-historical writers, might have had on Xenophon's historical thinking. And finally, a related difficulty though on a larger scale, the comparison involves us ultimately in holding Xenophon up to our own standards of historical research, for as has recently been argued,[12] when we say that an ancient historian does not measure up to Thucydides, often we are really saying that he is not a modern historian. Such an analysis is obviously vitiated by the fact that it is patently anachronistic, that it assumes a great deal about Thucydides' methods which is at least open to question, and that it privileges modern historical writing with a status few would want to grant it without considerable hesitation and consideration.[13] In general I believe that the 'Thucydides-continuation' question takes our attention away from understanding what Xenophon himself tried to say and how he thought about the history of his age.

Indeed, the continuation issue has tended to obscure the fact that Xenophon's history does not have a proper beginning. Granting that in some general sense only Xenophon sought to take up the narrative of the Peloponnesian War left incomplete by Thucydides, this is not a sufficient explanation to account for why the *Hellenica* does not have a preface. It is highly unusual for any work from antiquity, not just a history, to lack some sort of introduction. Theopompus and Ephorus both had extensive introductions to their histories; and, in fact, Xenophon himself was not otherwise averse to prefacing most of his other works with some type of carefully worded opening statement (though it should be noted that his *Anabasis* also lacks a formal prooemium).[14] Furthermore, in the *Hellenica* itself there are a number of passages that contain the elements of a historiographic programme, which is to say the very sort of thing one might expect at the start of a history.[15] The omission of an introductory statement is a radical departure from earlier tradition in Greek historical writing; although the second-century AD critic Lucian can imagine a history without one, he makes it clear that it was very unusual, if not actually unprecedented (*Hist. Conscr.* 52–53). Going back to Hecataeus of Miletus (late sixth and early fifth century) at least (*FGrHist* 1 F 1), there was a tendency for the writer to distance himself from his predecessors at or near the beginning of his work.[16] What may have been Xenophon's model for omitting a preface to the *Hellenica*, and why did he do so?

One example of an omitted preface is the Epic Cycle – the epic poems that 'fill out' the whole story of Troy left incomplete by the *Iliad*. In particular, the *Aethiopis* lacked an introduction and, as the *Hellenica* in relation to Thucydides' history, it joined up with a variant last line of the *Iliad*.[17] Xenophon no doubt was familiar with these poems; I should hasten to add too that, like Herodotus (2.117, 4.32), he probably knew that they were not part of Homer's work.

Hence, he had a ready model for a continuation as well as an awareness that the continuation would be recognized as a separate work.
And before this parallel is dismissed on the grounds that it comes
from a different genre, it should be remembered that Homer was
widely thought of as a chronicler of the past; indeed, Xenophon has
a character from his *Symposium* describe the contents of his poetry
in much the same terms as Xenophon thought about the value of
his own historical work (*Smp.* 4.6; cf. *Hell.* 5.1.4). I should point
out, however, that the situation regarding Homer and the Cycle is
not precisely parallel with Thucydides and Xenophon's *Hellenica*;
the *Iliad* was in some sense regarded as complete, whereas
Thucydides' history clearly was not.

Assuming that Xenophon was not unfamiliar with the possibility
of continuing a well-known work and hence with not including a
preface, it is still important to ask why he followed this plan. This
is a difficult issue and the suggestions one proposes must necessarily
remain speculative. At one level Xenophon was surely attempting to
associate the *Hellenica* in some very general sense with the work of
Thucydides. But by the same token, inasmuch as all the histories we
know of that were written before had prefaces, Xenophon may also
have been trying to create a unique place for the *Hellenica* in the
tradition of Greek historical writing, showing it to be a text unlike
anything that had been done before, including Thucydides' history.
It may also be that Xenophon did not want an introduction because
he felt that the *Hellenica* did not have one overarching topic; introductions to histories are places where typically the historian states
his theme – the conflict between the Greeks and barbarians for
instance, or the war between Athens and Sparta – and he may have
believed that his work was not unified by a single, central issue.
Indeed, there is something to be said for the related suggestion that
the beginning of the *Hellenica* lacks a formal preface for the same
reason that the end of the work does not have a conclusion.[18] In the
belief that the history of his age did not have a final culmination or
meaning, Xenophon may have deliberately avoided an introduction,
inasmuch as it would have demanded, among other things, that he
explain what was important about the recent past and how it
explained the present and future, something he may well have been
unable to do.

The composition of the *Hellenica* and its historiographic implications

Xenophon as a continuator of Thucydides involves us in the issue of composition of the *Hellenica*, an issue that I need briefly to discuss as well. Problems of composition – that is, attempting to determine under what circumstances and precisely when, or rather for how long, a work was written – seem to dog the vast majority of texts from antiquity. And while they are favourite chestnuts for philologists to try to crack, they seem only to send non-specialists running for cover. It should come as no surprise, then, that the *Hellenica* has its own composition problem.

Composition problems are important because they bear directly on issues involving what an author could have known when he wrote his work, and consequently what meaning or message he may have wished to convey to his audience. This is especially true of contemporary histories written over long periods of time. To get beyond these generalities, though, I can do no better than to quote Dover on the issues involved in the composition of Thucydides' *History of the Peloponnesian War.*

> There are three ways of writing the history of a war which is fought during one's own lifetime. One way is to wait until it is over; the task then differs, in the nature of the evidence available, from that of writing the history of a war remote in time, but the principle is the same. The second way is to keep a kind of diary and eventually put the entries together in the right order without revision. The third way also involves the keeping of a diary, but the recorded material is revised later and *subordinated to a considered design for the work as a whole* [my stress].[19]

The third scenario Dover imagines is the most important. The ancient historian may revise much of his already written material in light of important events that happen towards the end of his career, events that provide a framework of judgment or the foundation for a meaningful 'design' that informs his entire work. It is good to remember here that Bloch confessed that although he had written about 'wars and battles' he did not really know the meaning of victory and defeat until he had experienced those things personally.[20] A comparison will help to clarify what is at stake. The obituary of Pericles, which Thucydides gives immediately following the leader's last speech, refers to the end of the war and so must have been written at least in part after the war was over (2.65.12). On the other hand we know from Thucydides' preface that he started writing an account of the war from its outset (1.1.1). Consequently, some revision must have taken place. In this particular case, Thucydides, with the knowledge that Athens lost, and further in the belief that the city's defeat was due more to its own ill-advised decisions and internal troubles than to other factors (2.65.12), very probably went back to Pericles' speeches and inflected the politician's words, as he presented them, with an admonitory and indeed prophetic tone, that is in words advising against the very actions which in his mind at least led to Athens' failure in the war; perhaps he even wrote them up for the first time at this late stage.[21]

The problem of the composition of Xenophon's *Hellenica* has exercised the minds of scholars for some time, and I do not intend to review its entire course here; rather I will mention the parameters of the debate and then indicate my own views on the matter. Essentially there are two camps: the 'unitary' position which claims that the work was written at one time, and the 'analyst' position which maintains that it was written at different points in Xenophon's lifetime; the 'analyst' position further subdivides according to differing opinions as to where and how many divisions there are in the work. To start with the 'analysts' first, it was long ago felt that the first two books of the *Hellenica* seem different in perspective from the last five – that we see things through Athenian eyes first, and that the orientation changes to a Spartan one beginning with Book 3.[22] As one might imagine, the ancient testimonia that assert that Xenophon attempted to complete Thucydides' history of the Peloponnesian War were brought in to support the division.[23] But not satisfied with a break somewhere in or at the end of Book 2, some scholars posited another division in the longer second portion of the history at or near Xenophon's account of the King's Peace which brought to a close the Corinthian War.[24] The analyst position was further buttressed by work from an unrelated quarter: in an attempt to date the dialogues of Plato, the *Hellenica* was enlisted to help establish an outside chronology roughly contemporary with the philosopher; particle usage was thought to support the tripartite division of the work.[25]

From the nineteenth century on, however, the 'analyst' position had its critics. The employment of particle usage for the determination of composition boundaries was disputed;[26] historical arguments were made challenging the existence of a break after the King's Peace;[27] and recently, the precise nature of the 'Thucydides-continuation', whether regarded as regular narrative or in fact as some sort of summary, has been problematized.[28]

My own position regarding the composition question falls in between the extreme 'unitarians' and 'analysts'. It seems to me to be correct that the statistical analysis of particle use in the *Hellenica* should not be dismissed;[29] based on it most recent scholars seem to agree that a break should be assumed at or near 2.3.10 and that this first portion is early.[30] A second break in the *Hellenica* is more difficult to justify; the evidence yielded by dividing the history at 5.1.36 and measuring the frequency of certain particles in *Hell.* 2.3.11–5.1.36 and 5.2.1–end is not statistically significant.[31] But this leaves 2.3.11–end unexplained as to when it was written. The narrative itself goes down to Mantinea in 362. We know that Xenophon was at work at least on 3.5.25 after 381; furthermore we know that he was at work on 6.4.37 some time after 357/6 but before 353.[32] Beyond these facts we cannot proceed with certainty. It seems reasonable, however, to make the following suggestions. Early in his career (I do not know exactly when) Xenophon began writing the *Hellenica*, not with a view to imitating Thucydides precisely and so to supplement the latter's work, but to complete what was the most famous contemporary narrative history of his day as best he could. When many years later he continued the *Hellenica* beyond the Peloponnesian War, the influence of his predecessor – whatever it may have been – was even less pronounced.[33] This second suggestion is supported by the work of I. Bruns, H.R. Breitenbach and P.J. Rahn.[34] These scholars focus their attention on those places in the *Hellenica* where Xenophon seems to acknowledge the existence of 'Thucydidean' rules for writing history – concentration on *dapanemata* (expenses), *mechanemata* (strategic plans) and *kindunoi* (great danger or changes of fortune in war). As they point out, these 'rules' are cited only to be dismissed, as though Xenophon was indicating his independence from Thucydides.

The reader will notice that I have not provided dates for the two periods of composition for the *Hellenica*. Perhaps the first part (1–2.3.10) was finished soon after Xenophon's return to Greece (394). The second (2.3.11–end) was clearly completed only after the battle of Mantinea (362); what is more, I believe, as do many others, that the bulk of this, the major portion of the *Hellenica*, was composed from start to finish in this same period. This position raises an extremely important issue that constitutes the third special problem associated with the *Hellenica* as well as the subject of the first chapter.

The evolution of Xenophon's thought and the spirit of revision in his later work

I would like to return to Dover's observation regarding the ways an extended contemporary narrative history can be written. As I indicated above, the most reasonable, and it seems the more typical model of composition, is for a historian to keep a record of events throughout the period with which he is concerned and then at some later point to 'subordinate' his account to 'a considered design for the work as a whole'. In the case of Xenophon, determining what is the 'considered design' or 'point' of the *Hellenica* is an especially important but also an especially difficult task.

Throughout his life Xenophon was devoted to certain principles: panhellenism and a very militarily oriented notion of perfect community life, both inspired by his time with the ten thousand Greek mercenaries; a belief that good leadership was the critical factor in determining the success of an army or a *polis*; that the divine was an essentially providential force working for good in human history. Above all he was an ardent admirer of Sparta; indeed, for a long time he believed that in Sparta these other issues would find expression: pious and disciplined Sparta, especially under the leadership of Agesilaus, would liberate the Greeks of Asia and bring order to the whole of the Hellenic world after years of strife. And indeed one gets the sense in the *Hellenica* that Greek history is really coterminous with Spartan history. For much of the 390s and the early 380s Xenophon looked at his age very much from this Spartan perspective and kept his record accordingly. When, however, in the years following the ratification of the King's Peace, Sparta seemed to abuse her authority, doubts formed in Xenophon's mind. These doubts were given further weight by the city's failure at Leuctra, and were positively confirmed by Mantinea. In the wake of that battle Xenophon could see the self-destruction of the Spartan hegemony very much in terms of what had happened to the regime of the Thirty Tyrants at Athens some forty years before. His world was shattered; indeed, the chaos that characterized the last period of his life left him terribly confused. His long-held beliefs seemed invalidated by the events of his own day. Thus, correspondingly, we can see a radical revision in some of his other work: both the *Cyropaedia* and *Constitution of the Spartans* contain passages that suggest Xenophon was rethinking his ideas regarding the efficacy of good leadership, the excellence of the Spartan way of life and his most cherished notions regarding what constituted ideal community life.[35] No doubt much of the material of the second portion of the *Hellenica* was subordinated to this pessimistic view late in Xenophon's life.[36]

But this is not the whole story. Xenophon's very last work, the *Revenues* or *Poroi*, is an essentially optimistic work. It contains numerous recommendations for the Athenians on how to sustain and even increase the resources of their state without resorting to hegemonic war against other Greeks.[37] Speeches found towards the end of the *Hellenica* given by Athenians and by Spartans and their friends lead me to believe that he had developed a similar view regarding Sparta. Indeed, at the very end of his life I believe Xenophon had become very much a man of 'the loyal opposition' to Sparta, a man intimately conversant with the workings of that *polis* and essentially sympathetic to it, but not blind to the reasons for its recent failures. He wanted to see both Athens and Sparta join in developing a new sort of benign leadership in the Greek world.

Thus the 'considered design' of the *Hellenica* is a complex one, containing as it does a pronounced pessimistic component, as well as an element of optimism. But rather than continue these introductory comments further, I would like to turn to a detailed consideration of the pessimism of the work and what contributed to this feature of Xenophon's historical vision.

1

XENOPHON, HISTORY AND ORDER
The battle of Mantinea

XENOPHON AND MANTINEA

Between the so-called King's Peace of 387/6 and the peace of 362/1, no fewer than three and possibly four general peaces were arranged among the Greek states, in addition to numerous bilateral and multilateral treaties. This profusion of settlements eloquently underscores the fact that in the first half of the fourth century the Greeks were almost continually at war with one another.[1] All of the early common accords were negotiated at the court of the great king of Persia (thus the name 'King's Peace'). This was not because the Persian dynasts regretted the violence of continuous Greek internecine war, but rather because, since the latter phases of the Peloponnesian War, their policy aimed at keeping at least a rough balance of power maintained throughout the Greek world. The substance of these pacts was always the same: the Greeks promised to respect the sovereignty of all states, both large and small, on the mainland, and the king promised to use force against any who broke this clause. The price of this guarantee was that the Greeks were forced to acknowledge the king's authority over their brethren in Asia Minor.

In 362/1, however, the cycle of hegemonic war and peace brokered by the Persians seemed to have come to a halt. We learn from an inscription from Argos (Tod 145 = *SVA* 292, now regrettably lost) that in that year an envoy from Persia came to the Greeks, apparently to ask them to participate in the satraps' revolt against the Persian king, Artaxerxes II.[2] The envoy found the Greeks observing a common peace negotiated by themselves, without the intervention of Persia. What is more, it was made clear to the envoy that while the Greeks had no interest in fighting a war with the

17

Great King so long as he kept to himself and did not attempt to set them fighting with one another, they would defend themselves should he attempt to play his old game of pitting Greek against Greek. It may have seemed to an outside observer that something like a lasting and real peace had been settled in mainland Greece. Add the presence in Egypt of the Spartan king Agesilaus who was helping to disrupt Persian control there and the same observer may have considered 362/1 a watershed year in which peace was finally secured between the various Greek states and serious internal dissension had begun to appear instead more frequently in the territory of the Great King.

But this imaginary observer would have been wrong. After only one year the Greek world saw hostilities renewed (Diod. 15.94.1) and would soon be convulsed by the Social War and the aggressions of Phocis. Furthermore, on the eve of his return to Sparta from Egypt, Agesilaus died after his efforts were spent fighting not in a panhellenic war against the Persians, but in a struggle between rival Egyptian dynasts. Additionally, the revolt of the satraps was suppressed in 352. Troubles would only continue for Greece, through the rise of Philip, the reign of Alexander and well beyond. In fact, if our observer had looked more closely at the circumstances of 362/1 he would have realized that, despite the peace, there were indications that problems would continue. In the first place Sparta, whether voluntarily or not, was not a participant in the new peace; because of her insistence that the Messenians did not constitute a state (another way of saying that Sparta was still the rightful authority over the Messenians), the Spartans either stood back from the peace (Plutarch *Ages.* 35.3–4, Diod. 15.89.2) or were refused participation (Polybius 4.33.9). Hegemonic ambition had not gone away; indeed it lay behind much of the conflict that followed shortly after 362/1, beginning with Athens' bitter Social War. As for Agesilaus' campaign in Egypt, his behaviour there, especially his betrayal of his first overlord Tachos, showed his actions for what they really were – an attempt to net Sparta badly needed revenues for mercenaries back in Greece: scarcely a panhellenic crusade.[3] The problems that had characterized the Greek world before 362/1 would carry on for years: lack of constructive leadership and cooperation, and the persistent struggle for the domination over other Greek states. And the vulnerability this situation produced for all Greece, for so long exploited by the Persians, was by the time Xenophon was writing already being manipulated by Philip of

Macedon, who had taken Amphipolis in the winter of 357/6. Xenophon could see the danger.

Xenophon realized that 362/1 was not a watershed in the history of Greece. Writing the bulk of the *Hellenica* sometime in the 350s,[4] he concluded his account with an appraisal of the military action that helped to precipitate the peace of 362/1. The battle of Mantinea was fought in the summer of 362 between the Spartans and Thebans and their respective allies. In his summation of the battle Xenophon states that after Mantinea the opposite (*to enantion*) happened from what everyone expected: 'inasmuch as nearly all of Greece had come together and was deployed, there was no one who did not think that if there was to be a battle the victors would rule and the vanquished would become subject' (7.5.26). But the battle was indecisive. Although a tactical victory for the Thebans in the heart of Laconia, the battle claimed the life of Thebes' ablest general, Epaminondas, and the Thebans could not exploit their costly success. God, Xenophon claims, so brought it about that both sides claimed victory by setting up trophies and both admitted defeat by requesting the return of their dead under truce. Furthermore, as Xenophon makes clear, neither side's material resources were increased as a result of the battle (7.5.27). Instead of determining the next hegemon of Greece, Mantinea decided nothing; or, as Xenophon puts it, 'there was confusion and still more disorder in Greece after the battle than before'. With this observation Xenophon turns the task of writing about subsequent events over to another.[5]

Xenophon did not have to end the *Hellenica* where he did. As noted above, he was in all likelihood at work on his history in the decade *following* Mantinea and so could have included events subsequent to the battle (in fact he himself draws notice to some of them in the *Hellenica*). He could have chosen to take the *Hellenica* down through the campaign and death of Agesilaus, events he actually treated elsewhere in his biography of the Spartan king. He may have found it fruitful to parallel Sparta's loss of empire with Athens' in the Social War. The early successes of the Phocian general Onomarchus followed by his defeat and death in the Crocus Field in the Third Sacred War would have formed an admirable illustration of the inevitability of divine justice, one of Xenophon's favourite topics (that is assuming Xenophon lived through the spring of 352). But Xenophon recorded none of these things.

A clue to why Xenophon ended the *Hellenica* with his disquieting evaluation of Mantinea can, I think, be deduced from the almost personal sense of frustration and anxiety which underlies the concluding paragraph. Since he says that all men (*pantes anthropoi*) expected Mantinea to be decisive and that no one thought otherwise,[6] we can assume Xenophon was one of those confounded by the outcome of the battle. Indeed, one gets the sense that Xenophon wanted Mantinea to be conclusive and was disappointed that it was not. This disappointment may have stemmed at a personal level from the fact that Xenophon's own son Gryllus died in the campaign leading up to this battle, a battle which Xenophon implies might as well not have been fought. Furthermore, Xenophon could see clearly that no one city was confirmed as the leader of Greece; in other words, there was no new ordering of Greece and her resources, without which the Greeks could not launch an effective panhellenic crusade against the Persians, one of Xenophon's long-cherished hopes.

MANTINEA, EPHORUS AND THE NOTION OF THE EPOCH

In order to shed further light on Xenophon's evaluation of Mantinea, I would like to look briefly at the account of the battle provided by Ephorus, the universal historian from Cyme in Asia Minor and a younger contemporary of Xenophon. Ephorus had a reaction similar to Xenophon's when he considered the impact of Mantinea on Greek affairs. If we can assume that much of Diodorus' account of Mantinea is largely that of Ephorus,[7] then we can say that he too notes that the preliminaries to the battle raised expectations that it would decide who was to be the hegemon of Greece: 'immediately the Spartans and Mantineans appeared, and all prepared themselves for the contest for all and summoned their allies from all quarters' (Diod. 15.84.3). In the same vein, Ephorus styles the battle itself 'a contest for the whole of Greece' (Diod. 15.85.1). And if these two passages were not enough to suggest that Ephorus regarded Mantinea as a battle that might very well have proved to be epoch-making, he also asserts that more troops, better generals and more gallantry were found in this conflict than in any other before in the history of wars between the Greeks (15.86.1). But like Xenophon, Ephorus notes that despite the indications that Mantinea would be decisive, the battle did not produce a clear winner: both the Spartans and the Thebans claimed victory (15.87.2). The two historians differ in their treatments of the aftermath of Mantinea at two points. In the first place Ephorus, writing continuous history down to 341, naturally records the peace negotiations which followed the battle while Xenophon does not. Additionally, while Xenophon characterizes Greece after Mantinea as being in a state of confusion and turmoil (*akrisia* and *tarache*), Ephorus sees the Greeks 'wearied' (*kataponoumenoi*) by a series of conflicts (15.89.1). While I think that Xenophon's choice of words derives from an understanding of the world that is specific to him, it seems that both historians are saying that the battle should have been conclusive in deciding the future of Greece but was not. In a sense both Xenophon and Ephorus felt they lived in a time that confused them and frustrated their attempts to understand it.[8]

That Mantinea was seen as a potentially epoch-making battle that in the event changed nothing is a point of immense importance. From the very earliest stages of Greek thought, there is evident a tendency to recognize and enshrine moments regarded as decisive for the shaping of history. So already in the *Iliad* Homer drew attention to the sailing of Paris' ships for Greece (5.63–64) and the despatch of Patroclus by Achilles to intercept Nestor during the fighting by the ships (11.604) as the 'beginnings of evils'; and indeed without Paris' abduction of Helen there would have been no Trojan War, and without Patroclus' return to combat and his subsequent death there would not have been the tragedy of the *Iliad*. Among the Greek historians in particular the ability to isolate those moments which define a historical epoch goes back to Herodotus. Like Homer, and indeed possibly in imitation of him,[9] Herodotus considers the ships which the Athenians sent to the Ionian revolt in 499 'the beginnings of evils for both the Greeks and barbarians' (5.97.3). While it is no doubt right to say that this statement does not capture the variety of Herodotus' history of the Persian wars,[10] the passage does reflect 'the narrative impulse itself, the impulse towards "closure" and the sense of an ending ... retrojected to become "explanation" ':[11] Herodotus finds it natural to mark the sailing of the ships under Melanthius as a watershed forming the divide between the history of Greece before and after the Persian conflict. Similarly Thucydides, in words reminiscent of Homer and Herodotus,[12] has the Spartan Melesippus say upon leaving Attica, an action which marked the formal beginning of the Peloponnesian War: 'this day will be the beginning of the greatest evils for the Greeks' (2.12.3). Perhaps an even closer parallel to what Mantinea was expected to be can be found in Thucydides' evaluation of the

21

failure of the Sicilian expedition at 7.87.5–6.[13] There Thucydides stresses that it was the greatest *ergon* or episode of the war and indeed all of Hellenic history – this because the disaster sealed Athens' fate (cf. Thuc. 2.65.11) and so in a sense was the 'projected' end of the greatest conflict in world history (cf. Thuc. 1.1). Thucydides' mention (5.26.1) of the demolition of the Long Walls at Athens also clearly marks an end. Thus while his history may seem technically incomplete, Thucydides had formed a complete view of the war.[14] Similarly Polybius, writing at least 200 years after Xenophon, could view the history of the entire Mediterranean basin as united into an organic whole, literally a 'body' (*soma*), by Roman power (1.3.4) – drawing on a notion of unity perhaps derived from earlier Hellenistic historiography.[15]

Mantinea may well have portended a similar conclusiveness for Xenophon and Ephorus. Indeed, at least one other historian, Anaximenes of Lampsacus, brought his history to a close with the battle (*FGrHist* 72 T 14 = Diod. 15.89.3). We do not know how he treated it; he may well have styled it the event which marked the close of Sparta's hegemony once and for all, although the attention he seems to have given to the death of Epaminondas would align him more with the accounts of Ephorus and Xenophon.

This capacity for privileging certain events, especially battles, was not restricted to Homer and the historians. The Athenian people held festivals in memory of the battles at Marathon, Salamis and Plataea.[16] What is more, this penchant for marking decisive episodes could even result in the assimilation of several discrete episodes to one momentous event: as has recently been shown, the battle of Marathon in Aristophanes' *Wasps* 1071ff. became a *locus* for all the important events of the Persian Wars.[17] The desire to mark temporal boundaries could in fact obliterate the divisions of history.

THE *HELLENICA*: FALSE ENDS
AND BEGINNINGS

What, then, are we to make of a history that seems to draw attention to the fact that the episode which marks its end was itself inconclusive, 'contrary to the expectations of all'? The above discussion suggests that it was natural for Xenophon to look for a conclusion to his work, and that he thought (at least before the battle) that Mantinea would be just such a moment of 'closure' or the end of an era in Greek history. That Xenophon did not find

Mantinea epochal is perhaps the most important feature to notice about the *Hellenica*.[18] Indeed, to understand Xenophon's historical writing it is crucial to find out why the *Hellenica* ends (or rather does not end) the way it does. It was not out of a sense of duty or modesty that he turned the writing of history over to another. Nor did lack of insight or ability prevent him from finding an appropriate coda for his work. Since he mentions events in the *Hellenica* that happened some years after Mantinea it is not reasonable to assume that the imminence of death made him end his history on such a disquieting note of incompleteness (compare the case of Thucydides). The end of the *Hellenica* ends the way Xenophon intended it to do. Consequently it is fair to assume that he wanted to communicate something through the way he brought his history to a close, and it is essential that we investigate what it is.[19]

We are aided in this task by other moments recorded in the *Hellenica*, sections that can also be understood as false beginnings or ends; that is, episodes that Xenophon characterizes as the beginnings or ends of significant enterprises or even chapters in Greek history that are later shown not to be definitive.

Xenophon tells us that in 396, prior to departing for Asia Minor to liberate the Asiatic Greeks from the Persian yoke, Agesilaus stopped at Aulis to perform a sacrifice, just as Agamemnon had done prior to setting out for Troy. The Boeotians learned of what Agesilaus was doing and prevented him from completing his sacrifice (3.4.3–4). Given that Agesilaus' campaign did not achieve what was hoped for, the interrupted sacrifice seems a foreboding of failure (see below, p. 116).[20] What does Xenophon gain by telling the story of Agesilaus' sacrifice at Aulis? He does not report the episode in his encomiastic biography of the king. It seems that Xenophon could have left the story out and the reader would still have understood that ultimately Agesilaus did not accomplish what he set out to do. The point of including the detail about Agesilaus' attempted sacrifice at Aulis is obviously to set up an implicit comparison between Agesilaus and Agamemnon. In his panhellenic zeal, Isocrates also understood Agamemnon as the first crusader against the barbarian east (*Panath.* 77). But a comparison between Agamemnon and Agesilaus can only have the effect of drawing attention to the scale of Agesilaus' *unfulfilled* plans for his campaign in Asia: it was to have been nothing short of a second conquest of the *barbaroi*. This suggestion of unrealized hope makes all the more bitter Agesilaus'

23

eventual recall to Greece to fight Sparta's enemies at Coronea. The point of this beginning that promises more than was achieved is to make more powerful our sense of disappointment that Agesilaus' panhellenic venture was thwarted by in-fighting among the Greeks.[21]

Another boundary that divides era from era, and which subsequent events show to be false, comes at the end of Book 2 of the *Hellenica*, where Xenophon details the end of the tyranny of the Thirty at Athens and the restoration of the democracy. Xenophon reports that after the last remaining pocket of oligarchic resistance was eliminated at Eleusis the Athenians swore not to remember the injuries they had inflicted on one another in their recent civil strife, and he assures the reader that 'even to this day both factions take part in government together and the *demos* abides by its oaths' (2.4.43).[22] Only two pages later, however, Xenophon informs the reader that in response to a Spartan request for soldiers to participate in a campaign to defend the Greeks of Asia, the Athenians sent out some of those who had been in the cavalry under the Thirty tyrants, 'considering that it would benefit the *demos* if they went abroad and died' (3.1.4) – a plan not at all in keeping with the spirit if not the letter of the agreement. Given that only a year separates the agreement reached between the Athenians and the oligarchs at Eleusis (*SVA* 215) and the start of the Spartan expedition under Thibron it may seem to some that Xenophon wrote the second passage later and simply forgot or neglected to amend his statement regarding the Athenians' fidelity to their oaths.[23] But since most students of the *Hellenica* assume that both passages fall into the same compositional unit this explanation does not seem valid. That an inconsistency is felt between the two passages must be admitted; reading about the people's calculation and malice so shortly after the display of their generosity of spirit cannot but make us question the sincerity of their original oath. It may be that Xenophon is trying to suggest that the Athenian *demos* is destructively fickle; and indeed he makes just such a point elsewhere in connection with the notorious trial of the generals of Arginusae (1.7.35). It may also be that Xenophon wishes to draw attention to the specific crime of *de facto* if not *de iure* oathbreaking, a topic in which he has a keen interest.[24] But whatever the motivation, we have in these two passages another place where a seemingly settled condition (the amnesty at Athens) is almost immediately disrupted, and old animosities allowed to surface.

24

There is one more example of the destabilization of a temporal boundary that was designed to set the limits of a significant historical period. While it may be correct to rule out ancient testimony, the presence of an abrupt beginning in place of a proem and some other superficial features of the *Hellenica* as proof that Xenophon intended to imitate the history of the Peloponnesian War left incomplete by Thucydides on his death, he did, it seems, attempt in some general way to complete it. Thucydides clearly envisioned the end of the Peloponnesian War to be the capitulation of Athens and the tearing down of the Long Walls (5.26.1). If we can reasonably assume that Xenophon was in some sense picking up where Thucydides left off (though not attempting to complete the work in Thucydidean fashion), then I think we can also assume that he had his eye on 5.26.1 when he reported the end of the war in the *Hellenica*: 'after these things Lysander sailed into the Piraeus, the exiles returned and with great zeal they tore down the walls to the music of flute-girls, expecting that day to be the beginning of freedom for Greece' (2.2.23). There are two very important points to note in connection with this passage. In the first place Xenophon makes the demolition of the Long Walls both an end and a beginning; Thucydides considers the event only the formal end of the Peloponnesian War. It is Xenophon who adds the detail that people believed it to be (*nomizontes*) the beginning of freedom for the Greeks. Second, Xenophon does not bring the *Hellenica* to an end with 2.2.23. Even assuming a major break at 2.3.10 (a common and probably correct assumption), there are still about forty lines of text (OCT), not including those thought to be interpolations,[25] between 2.2.23 and the (first?) end of the *Hellenica*. In this admittedly brief space Xenophon manages to mention the establishment of the Thirty at Athens, the aggressions of Lycophron in Thessaly, the tyranny of Dionysius in Sicily and Lysander's reduction of Samos. In connection with Samos, Xenophon records that Lysander forced the islanders to capitulate, permitted the freeborn to keep the clothes they were wearing, confiscated everything else and handed the island over to the restored Samian oligarchs and a board of ten (cf. Diod. 14.3.4–5).[26] Even if we believe that Xenophon had a basic predisposition in favour of the Spartans and conservative or even oligarchic government, the language of Xenophon's description of the settlement of Samos, as well as the reference to autocratic government in Sicily and Thessaly, will not allow us to believe that he viewed these states as enjoying freedom (the echo between 'freeborn' Samians leaving their city with one *himation* and the 'freedom' of the Greeks is particularly telling).[27] Furthermore, it is difficult to imagine Xenophon putting a positive interpretation on the activities of the Thirty at Athens, writing from a vantage point sometime in the 390s or later. Additionally, the *Hellenica* does not end at 2.3.10, and the remainder of the history shows that those who thought that lasting peace and freedom were at hand when the walls fell at Athens were naive fools. Even if we assume that Xenophon believed that the universal freedom of the Greeks was at hand when he wrote 2.2.23 (and I do not think we are entitled to do so), the question arises: why did he leave the passage in his history when his own account of subsequent events showed the hopes of 404/3 to have been in vain?

Perhaps Xenophon meant the reader to draw just such a conclusion; indeed, the simplest explanation is to assume that the text is as Xenophon wanted it to be. If the above interpretations of Agesilaus' attempted sacrifice at Aulis and the amnesty at Athens are correct, then it is possible that in his treatment of the end of the Peloponnesian War Xenophon was attempting to characterize it too as a 'false' historical boundary – in this instance the hoped-for but unrealized end of powerful hegemons imposing from outside government on independent city states. It could not be denied that the destruction of the Long Walls really did constitute the end of the war – it left no doubt that Athens was utterly defeated. But by including the expression of hope that the same event also marked the beginning of freedom for Greece (something he knows to be incorrect), Xenophon creates the possibility for disappointment; and indeed as he lets us see, disappointment comes almost immediately with the mention of tyranny in Thessaly, Sicily, Athens and Samos. It is as if we can see in the close juxtaposition of the hope for freedom and those passages which suggest its demise Xenophon's own recognition that the true nature of Greek inter-state relations was a 'continuum', a chronicle of on-going strife resulting from the impulse of more powerful states to impose their will on weaker ones, a chronicle moreover that had different protagonists but always the same unmistakable dynamic.[28] Seen in this way, *Hell.* 2.2.23 helps in the interpretation of Xenophon's evaluation of Mantinea. Just as people thought (*nomizontes*, 2.2.23) that the destruction of the Long Walls would herald a change in Greek affairs, so too everyone thought (*oieto*, 7.5.26) that Mantinea would produce a decisive winner or hegemon. Both times the popular expectation was proved wrong. At the end of the Peloponnesian War, the maintenance of a state's sovereignty was no better off after Athens' surrender. After Mantinea, Xenophon reports, there was even more disorder in Greece than before. That means he thought that there was disorder in Greece before Mantinea.[29] He was an acute enough observer of his own day to recognize that not only was Mantinea not the decisive battle it was supposed to be but also the very fact that it settled nothing revealed a profound truth about the Greek world during the second half of the fifth and the first half of the fourth century: disorder was the typical condition of Greece. No clear-cut hegemon ever had emerged or (and this was the important inference) *ever would emerge*. This was a shattering realization for a man committed to panhellenic ideals and to order in every facet of his world. It was also an enormously disturbing one insofar as historians must in a sense rely on 'ends' to provide the 'meaning' of larger patterns of historical change.[30]

XENOPHON AND DISORDER

What precisely did Xenophon mean when he said that there was even more confusion and disorder in Greece after Mantinea? To get an answer to this question we have to look not only throughout the *Hellenica*, but also to other works in his corpus. A picture will emerge of Xenophon as a man devoted to the principle of order and equally fearful of disorder.[31] Indeed, it will be seen that the subject of order and ordering (*taxis*) often comes up in his writing, and in connection with a variety of human enterprises: the household, the army, the city and the chorus. And while Xenophon discusses order in a variety of contexts, one theme will emerge which will go a long way towards shedding light on the end of the *Hellenica*. A 'disordered' Greece meant that its potential for good or usefulness, seen primarily from a panhellenic perspective, was not being realized due to infighting among the Greeks.

The case of the *Hellenica*

At 7.5.27 of the *Hellenica* the concept of disorder is applied to the whole of Greece; so also at 5.2.35 where Xenophon is speaking of the Corinthian War. At 2.4.42 Xenophon has the Athenian democrat Thrasybulus encourage the oligarchic forces 'not to cause disturbance but use the ancient laws', where the idea of disorder is clearly descriptive of civil strife. Fundamentally, however, Xenophon's understanding of order and disorder comes very much from the world of the army – not surprising in a military man.[32]

A pattern at once emerges from an examination of the military engagements described in the *Hellenica*: order, and a range of accompanying notions (preparedness, obedience, caution), tend to be found in the ranks of the victorious, while disorder is often cited as the chief reason for failure on the battlefield.[33] As Xenophon himself puts it in the *Anabasis*, 'good order (*eutaxia*) seems to provide safety while disorder (*ataxia*) has already destroyed many' (3.1.38). Indeed, order and disorder can serve as a kind of short-hand: it is enough for Xenophon to say in his description of the battle of Notion (407), 'the Spartans fought in formation (*en taxei*), the Athenians scattered about in their ships, until the Athenians fled having lost fifteen ships' (1.5.14). Explanations based on details such as numerical superiority or topographical advantage are secondary. Perhaps only the quality of leadership rivals order and discipline as a prognosticator of victory.

A glance at four separate military actions recounted in Book 4 of the *Hellenica* will show how Xenophon associated military discipline with military success. At 4.8.17 he reports that the Spartans, anxious about the hostility of the Persian satrap Struthas, sent out in 391/0 an expedition against him commanded by Thibron. According to Xenophon, Struthas notes that his Spartan counterpart sends out his men in a disorderly (*ataktos*) and over-confident manner. We learn that Struthas then sends a large and compact (*suntetagmenous*) cavalry unit against the vanguard of the Spartan force, few and disordered (again *ataktos*). Thibron is killed along with several of his men and the survivors flee or remain in the Spartan camp, never having received their marching orders. The major difference between the two armies, indeed what seems to decide the battle in favour of the Persians, is the loose order of the Spartan troops and the tight formation of the Persian. In this instance the lack of battlefield order is the fault of poor leadership. A surprise attack on unsuspecting troops can have the same results. At 4.8.35–39 we learn of Iphicrates' successful ambush of the Spartan Anaxibius and his soldiers: waiting for the Spartans to be stretched out in marching formation, on uneven ground and on a narrow road, Iphicrates attacks and achieves total surprise, winning a complete victory.[34] Anaxibius knows that his doom is certain from the outset of the ambush, for he sees that his men are poorly deployed for combat and are in a state of panic (4.8.38). Enemy tactics can also lead to a loosening of the ranks and disorder: the peltast's basic tactic, aimed at luring the heavier hoplite into pursuit and consequently breaking formation, is an example of this, and the battle of Lechaeum near Corinth (390) is a textbook case as described by Xenophon (4.5.15). Lack of preparation and hastiness also result in failure, such as the men of Phlius suffered at the hands again of Iphicrates sometime around 390 (4.4.15).[35] Whatever the precise reason (and the examples could be multiplied) disorder in the ranks is an almost infallible predictor of defeat in the *Hellenica*.

Conversely, order in camp and on the battlefield – in particular density of formation as opposed to looseness – is an indicator of excellence and a pledge of future success for Xenophon. A good example of both order and disorder at work is Xenophon's account of Leuctra (371), the battle that shattered Sparta's military preeminence and heralded the meteoric rise of Thebes in the 360s. In an otherwise problematic description[36] two features emerge that prove decisive in Xenophon's mind for determining the outcome of the battle: the density of the Theban formation (*hathrooteron*, 6.4.9; 6.4.12) and the confusion in the Spartan ranks caused by their own poorly trained cavalry (6.4.13).

The paired accounts of Mnasippus and Iphicrates in the Corcyraean campaign, also in Book 6, prove the same point (see below, pp. 164–171). Mnasippus, a bad commander, meets with disaster when the enemy in tight formation (*hathrooi*, 6.2.20) falls upon his own men who have lost order while attempting a difficult battlefield manoeuvre (6.2.21). Iphicrates' fleet, on the other hand, is endlessly drilled until it becomes a fine-tuned squadron able to execute complex tactical formations (6.2.27–30). Xenophon's admiration for the discipline of Iphicrates' force is noteworthy. Since Mnasippus manages to get himself destroyed before the Athenians arrive, the reason for including an account of Iphicrates' mission to Corcyra is removed (it should be pointed out that he does capture some enemy ships there). As if sensing that his account of Iphicrates' preparations will lead some to question his reporting, Xenophon feels compelled to apologize to the reader for his apparently pointless digression on Iphicrates' expedition (6.2.32). Nonetheless he cannot resist only one chapter later again expressing his admiration; commenting on the swiftness with which Iphicrates' vessels go into action upon sighting hostile Syracusan ships, Xenophon remarks, 'their speed was worthy of marvelling at' (*axia . . . theas*, 6.2.34). This point has significant implications for Xenophon's understanding of order, and consequently his evaluation of Mantinea: order (and the virtues it produces) in fighting men is not only praiseworthy, it is something to appreciate like a wonderful structure or a memorable deed (almost a Herodotean *ergon*). Xenophon uses the phrase 'worthy of wonder' only at one other place in the *Hellenica*, in his description of Agesilaus' training of his army at Ephesus in 395 (see below, pp. 86 and 113). Agesilaus sets up special athletic contests for each unit of the army, while the city teems with armourers, smiths and all types of military suppliers, all helping to create an image of 'a workshop of war';[37] Agesilaus personally leads his men from the gymnasium to sacrifices at the great temple of Artemis. The picture Xenophon creates of Agesilaus' army at Ephesus combines the historian's 'ideal aims and occupations of man':[38] hard physical training, careful material preparation, religious observance – all activities which Xenophon values highly and which turn up elsewhere in his corpus in association with ideal communities.[39] The sight of Ephesus is obviously very near to Xenophon's heart: 'for where men worship the gods, practise the arts of war and study obedience, how is it not likely that everything there is full of good hope?' (3.4.18). The tricolon reserves the best for last: obedience, without which military discipline and order are impossible.[40] In fact, Xenophon's description of the camp at Ephesus is entirely characterized by order (*taxis*), from the physical ordering and regimentation of the soldiers in their separate exercises to the cultivation of discipline by all the men, a picture of a model fighting unit. And indeed 'picture' is the right word to describe the effect of Xenophon's portrait because it is written in a way which imagines a reader who sees the camp (*paren horan*, 3.4.16; *axian theas*, 3.4.17; *idon*, 3.4.18).[41]

The accent on the visual in the description of Agesilaus' army at Ephesus suggests that Xenophon believed that order had an aesthetic – it could literally be perceived, and what is more, it was beautiful; indeed, as Plato makes Socrates say in the *Republic*, the correct love is of the *orderly* and the beautiful (403a).[42] Order meant more to Xenophon than simply military success. Indeed, the concept of order is central to Xenophon's entire way of thinking, not just his historical writing. In order to establish this point we must look outside the *Hellenica* to some of Xenophon's other works.

Order and the Socratic works of Xenophon

Perhaps the most convincing evidence for the profound importance of order for Xenophon comes from two of the so-called Socratic works, the *Memorabilia* and the *Oeconomicus*. At 8.3 of the *Oeconomicus*, Socrates' friend Ischomachus is recounting a conversation he had with his wife on the subject of ordering their household. Ischomachus suggests to his wife 'nothing is as useful (*euchreston*), or as beautiful (*kalon*) for human beings as order (*taxis*)'. Ischomachus' proof is drawn from the world of dance:

> for a chorus is composed of men; whenever they perform independently of each other, a certain confusion (*tarache*) results and something ugly to look at (*theasthai aterpes*), but whenever they perform and chant in an orderly manner (*tetagmenos*), at the same time these same men seem both worthy to observe and hear (*axiotheatoi, axiakoustoi*).

Ischomachus goes on to cite at length also the disadvantages and strengths respectively of the disorderly (*ataktos*, 8.4) and the well-disciplined (*tetagmene*, 8.6) army.[43] The important point to take note of is the value put on order. Potentially good dancers not only fail to please without order, when in a state of disorder they are actually ugly; or in the case of soldiers, disorder renders them not only ineffective as a fighting force but even easy to conquer for the enemy and shameful and useless in the eyes of friends (8.4; cf. *Cyr.* 8.1.2). A parallel passage from the *Cyropaedia* illustrates this point well. At 2.2.26 of that work, Cyrus the Great encourages his subordinates to fill their ranks with men selected on the basis of military excellence and not because they are from their own native lands. To support this point Cyrus notes that 'a house cannot be run well by using bad slaves, but even lacking slaves altogether it is less likely to run into difficulties than one disordered by wicked slaves'.

Even at a very mundane level order makes items good or useful (*kalon, chreston*). So in an extraordinary passage later in the same chapter of the *Oeconomicus* mentioned above, Xenophon has Ischomachus praise all manner of humble objects (sandals, cloaks, linens, bronze vessels, tableware, even pots and pans, 8.19), and conclude: 'indeed, from this all things appear better (*kallio*) when they are arranged in order (*kata kosmon*); for each of the instruments appears as in a chorus, and the middle space between all of them seems beautiful, out of the way of the positioned items' (8.20).

Order is so important for Xenophon because it imbues those people (in the case of the chorus or army) or items (as in the household) with the capability for good to realize that potential. Indeed, this discussion in the *Oeconomicus* on the virtues of order began because Ischomachus' wife was unable to find something her husband had asked for: disorder had prevented the use of a desired good.

The notion that order is the necessary condition for something with the capability for good to be used properly is also important in the *Memorabilia*.[44] At 3.1.7 Socrates agrees with a young man interested in a military career (perhaps Xenophon himself) that the good commander, in addition to providing for his army, must also know how to deploy it effectively (the art of *to taktikon*); he continues:

> for there is an enormous difference between an ordered and a disordered army, just as stones and bricks and wood and tile, when cast down without order, are not at all useful, but when the things susceptible neither to rot nor melting (the stones and the tile) have been laid down below and above, and the bricks and wood in the middle, just as they are put together in house construction, then they become a thing worth a great deal – a house.

As we saw with the example of the chorus and the army in the *Oeconomicus*, so here with the army and the house (cf. *Cyr.* 2.1.27), items which can produce good will not do so until they are ordered. What is more, disorder not only prevents them from being useful, it makes them potentially dangerous. This point is especially clear when applied to hoplite tactics, as the young man observes: with the best men in front and rear (like the roof and foundation of a house), there is less chance of panic and a rout (3.1.8; cf. *Cyr.* 6.3.25 and *Oec.* 8.8).

While Xenophon has no difficulty comparing the activities of dancing, house management and warfare, this grouping should not be understood to indicate that he viewed all these enterprises equally. In the *Cyropaedia* Xenophon has Cyrus the Great endorse the virtues of order in the house for precisely the same reason Ischomachus urges his wife to impose *taxis* upon their household: order permits you to find what you need when you need it (8.5.7). But in the same passage Xenophon also notes that Cyrus 'thought that the good order of military units was by far more important (*kallion*)' than household management (thought of as *kalon*). The priority Cyrus accords order in the army over order in the household reflects Xenophon's recognition of its importance in all spheres of human activity, but even more so in those enterprises where most was at stake. Warfare is clearly one such enterprise. Many of the passages cited above show that Xenophon's articulations of the merits of order come up frequently in connection with the disposition of troops. In fact one would not be far off the mark to assert that Xenophon's understanding of order and organization was essentially military (see below, p. 86).[45]

But there is at least one area of human experience where Xenophon believes order is even more important, indeed even subsuming order in the army: the society of the *polis*.[46] So much is made clear in the meeting of Socrates and Pericles the Younger at *Mem.* 3.5. Pericles despairs that his city has lost its respect for honouring elders, physical training, obedience and harmony; indeed, on this last topic he notes that the Athenians take more delight in treating each other spitefully than the rest of the world. In such a condition Pericles fears that a terrible and irreversible calamity will befall Athens (3.5.16–17). In a remarkable passage, Socrates tries to counter Pericles' gloomy assessment by drawing notice to those activities in which the Athenians participate that still demonstrate order. Socrates encourages Pericles,

> never think that the Athenians are ill with a sickness beyond cure. Do you not see how they are orderly (*eutaktoi*) in their naval matters, and in their gymnastic exercises how they obey their supervisors in an orderly way (*eutaktos*), and how they heed their instructors in the choruses no worse than any one else?

Socrates' cure for Athens' ills, the loss of traditional virtues and, it seems (3.5.18), especially civil strife, is somehow to restore to prominence order and discipline which at that time were only in evidence in those activities that must have it to succeed – military formations, athletic exercises and the chorus. As Karl Joël once observed, the essence of *Mem.* 3.5 may well be summed up by the phrase *eutaxia soizei poleis* – 'good order saves cities' (John Stobaeus 3.271 (Wachsmuth)) – a sentiment attributed to Crates and deriving from the Cynic tradition as articulated by Antisthenes, a slightly older contemporary of Xenophon and a thinker who had a significant influence on him.[47]

The paramount importance of order in the city, especially in the maintenance of harmony and the suppression of *stasis* or discord, is touched upon elsewhere in the *Memorabilia*. In another discussion with another young Athenian, Critobulus, this time on the subject of friendship (*philia*), Socrates anticipates his friend's difficulty on the subject of 'gentlemen' (*kaloi te kagathoi*) who despite their good qualities hate one another. Socrates observes, 'it confuses you [literally: disorders your thinking, *tarattei*] that you often see men who both do good and keep away from shameful things, instead of being friends, fight with one another and treat each other more cruelly than men of no worth' (*Mem.* 2.6.17). Socrates detects that Critobulus is troubled by the fact that the very best people in Athenian society, far from recognizing the worth of their social peers, treat them worse than their social inferiors; in a sense Plato's *Lysis* considers the same problem (see especially 213a–b). Such an apparent contradiction brings into question the authenticity of the excellence such men are thought to possess. Xenophon has put his finger on something; he has no quarrel with good-natured rivalry, an ancient aristocratic value (*Lac.* 4.2 and 4.5; cf. Hesiod's good strife (*eris*) *Op.* 17ff. and Soph. *OT* 879–881; cf. Johnstone (1994)), but he sees *stasis* as a particularly destructive manifestation of *tarache*. As we saw above in connection with housebuilding and household management, for Xenophon disorder consists in not being able to make use of items which have the capacity for good. Discord, the evil to which Socrates is referring at *Mem.* 2.6.17, results when men who are otherwise good cannot make use of one another in a constructive way, due to factionalism. It is worth remembering that Thucydides characterized the bloody civil war (*stasis*) at Corcyra in 427 as a disruption of order – a breakdown of law, religion, community and finally basic human decency. Indeed, it seems that for Thucydides whenever the very fabric of human society was most in peril because of atrocity or disaster, disorder (*tarache*) was present (in addition to Corcyra (3.79.3), note also the plague at Athens (2.52.4), and the murder of schoolchildren at Mycalessus (7.29.5)).[48]

In response to Socrates' observation that the strife among good men is deeply troubling, Critobulus extends the application of *stasis* beyond the behaviour of individuals within one city to the behaviour of cities towards each other. Critobulus says: 'and not only do individuals behave in this way [that is in *stasis*] but also cities that especially (*malista*) cultivate noble things and that least of all approve of wicked things are often (*pollakis*) hostile towards one another' (*Mem.* 2.6.18). The emphasis again is on not just any cities doing harm to one another but (as with individual men of one state) specifically *good* ones. Critobulus' characterization of this situation as *stasis* is important towards understanding Xenophon's views of disorder and consequently the aftermath of Mantinea. While it may seem natural to us to style the nearly continuous warfare among the Greek city states, from the end of the Peloponnesian War to the Macedonian conquest, as civil strife or even civil war, that was not at all the case for the ancient Greeks themselves: they certainly considered themselves connected by important institutions (see especially Herodotus 8.144.2), but not at all a 'nation'.[49] *Stasis* was a term, even for Thucydides, which could only be applied to division and violence within a state; it was not normally descriptive of hostility between states. For Xenophon to have Critobulus represent conflict between good *poleis* as a kind of *stasis* was very bold; it suggests that the historian believed that there was (or ought to be) a bond of unity among at least the noble cities of Greece. Consequently *tarache* at the level of inter-state relations may well mean for Xenophon the condition that results when *poleis* that otherwise cultivate good things (*ton kalon*) are interfering with each other in the realization of their potential for good.

When Xenophon spoke of disorder after the battle of Mantinea he meant, among other things, a general uncertainty and anxiety in the air after the conflict. Many parallels from contemporary or near-contemporary literature echo this sentiment.[50] Indeed, in one of his own works written at about the same time as the latter part of the *Hellenica* Xenophon uses *tarache* in precisely this sense (*Poroi* 5.8). Of course at *Hell.* 7.5.27 the word is accompanied by *akrisia*, or lack of decision. Mantinea did not produce a hegemon; its outcome did not constitute a determination or *krisis*.

But Xenophon also had something quite specific in mind when he wrote the final words of the *Hellenica*. Understood as a *stasis* among the cities of Greece, indeed as an obstruction in the way of corporately achieving the greatest good, just as dancers, soldiers or the materials of a house do when well organized, *tarache* may well stand for Greek disunity in Xenophon's mind. And in his recognition that there was yet more disorder and disunity in the Greek world after Mantinea than before, we can see Xenophon's discovery that inter-state strife was endemic to Greece and would never go away.

CONCLUSION

To judge from the testimony of both Plato and Xenophon, discussion of the 'ordered world' or cosmos was not uncommon in their day: both refer to the speculations of wise men regarding the whole of the ordered universe (*Gorgias* 508a; *Mem.* 1.1.11).[51] Indeed, the notion of *kosmioi* or 'ordered aggregations', from collections of atoms to collectivities of humans, is central to Democritus;[52] Critias styles the life of primitive man as *ataktos* (DK 88 B 25.1); and, evidently, *kosmos* and *taxis* were favourite terms of Gorgias, as a glance at the proem of his *Helen* suggests.[53] Order was an important concept. According to Plato, the true philosopher turns away from the troubles of human life and gazes instead at eternal and unchanging order (*tetagmena*, *R.* 500b–c), while the tyrannized soul does what it least wishes and is full of confusion (*tarache*, *R.* 577e). On a more mundane level Aeneas Tacticus, an exact contemporary of Xenophon, could begin his work on the defence of fortified positions with a discussion of the right disposition of troops (*suntaxis*, 1.1), and could stress the need throughout his treatise of unanimity (*homonoia*) in a besieged city.[54] From the most elevated to the most humble of intellectual enterprises, order and its disruption were common topics.

In particular, in the area of religion, the notion of order underwent a fascinating and significant evolution during the period of Xenophon's lifetime. In the archaic period the divine could be a powerfully disruptive and disordering force. Hesiod refers to the absolute power of Zeus in his hymnic opening to *Works and Days*, and specifically to his ability to reverse the human order (5ff.). In a similar vein Solon recognizes that sometimes the man who tries to act prudently is thwarted whereas the ne'er-do-well is handsomely rewarded by the gods (Solon 13.67–70 (West)). Indeed, as Herodotus has Solon say at Croesus' court in Lydia, 'the divine is completely jealous and disruptive (*tarachodes*) regarding the affairs of men' (1.32.1).[55] While it is true that this belief in the divine as capricious and a force of disorder in human life continued into Xenophon's period,[56] an alternative and opposite understanding developed. For in places Xenophon asserts that the gods were the guarantors of order. As Cyrus exhorts his sons on his deathbed, 'the gods are immortal and all-seeing and all-powerful; they keep this order (*taxis*) of all things undamaged, ageless, flawless, indescribable in its beauty and magnitude' (*Cyr.* 8.7.22; cf. *Mem.* 1.4.8, 13). For Xenophon it is man who disorders (*atakton*) his world by acting contrary to his nature, and it is the gods who in the interest of maintaining order punish him (*Oec.* 7.31). Similarly in the myth told by the stranger in the *Politicus* of Plato, the point is made that it is God who brings order to the world (*katakosmoumenos*), which when left unsupervised lapses into disorder (*tarache*, 273a–d). And Socrates in the *Philebus* states that it was the opinion of earlier men that the universe 'is governed by reason and a wondrous regulating intelligence' (*Phlb.* 28d). At a time when it became scarce in political, civic and social life the gods became the wardens of order.

Despite passages that seem to illustrate Xenophon's belief in the divine as protector of order, however, one can also find in the *Hellenica* vestiges of the old archaic view of the gods as arbitrary or vengeful powers. So, echoing Hesiod's hymn to Zeus at the beginning of the *Works and Days*, and indeed following an already established historiographic tradition, Xenophon has Jason, the strongman of Thessaly, observe 'often God delights in making the small great and the great small' (6.4.23). That Xenophon himself endorsed this view is suggested by the fact that Jason is himself brought low at the height of his powers,[57] assassinated in an episode described only a few pages after his observation on the mutability of human fortune (see below, p. 174). Another passage from the *Hellenica* presents the archaic view on the divine perhaps even more clearly. When during a battle at the walls of Corinth, Argive troops are unexpectedly delivered vulnerable and in a panic into the hands of their Spartan enemies, Xenophon considers the event divinely motivated precisely because of the unforeseen circumstances that gave the Spartans total victory. As Xenophon remarks in a carefully crafted sentence, 'for them [the Spartans] to have delivered into their hands a mass of enemy troops panicked, stunned, exposing their unprotected side, not one of them turning to fight but rather all assisting in every way their own destruction, how could one not think such an episode divine (*theion*)' (4.4.12). It seems the gods can be responsible for sudden windfalls and unexpected reverses. Or to put it another way, the gods are responsible for what appears 'incomprehensible', an event which defies human explanation or accounting (cf. Hdt. 9.100.2). But before we conclude that 'the divine' or 'the god(s)' in Xenophon are simply the precursors of the later Hellenistic understanding of randomness in history (*tuche*),[58] it should be noted that when an event is accounted for by divine agency in the *Hellenica*, the old and the new view of the divine are simultaneously invoked. On the one hand the historian tacitly admits that an event is beyond his own understanding. However, attributing the outcome of an event to the gods also enables Xenophon to provide *some* explanation, that only in the world of the gods can the said event be explained.

Mantinea was just such an event for Xenophon.[59] He expected it to be decisive and it was not. The gods had made it so. Xenophon's disappointment is easy to discern between the lines. The continuous warfare of his entire lifetime produced no secure leader, no order in Greece; in fact the battle which was hoped to be the culmination of this never-ending struggle helped Xenophon to see that not only was Mantinea indecisive but, in a certain sense, there would never be a decisive engagement. It must have been a deeply bitter realization: as suggested above, Xenophon was a man devoted to the principle of order, yet his age was disordered and confused and would not stop being so as far as he could tell in 362. No more important point can be made about the *Hellenica* than that the bulk of it was probably composed after Xenophon had come to this realization, and that in consequence a deep pessimism is to be understood shaping the historian's judgment at every turn.[60] Indeed, this pessimism must be recognized as the backdrop for all the other historiographic issues of the *Hellenica*. In a way the history of Greece from the end of the Peloponnesian War to the battle of Mantinea and beyond simply did not make sense to Xenophon. But what were Xenophon's ideas about Greek unity and ideal community that were in a sense subverted by the battle of Mantinea? To arrive at a possible answer to this question we must look at his *Anabasis* and the campaigns of the Spartans in Asia after the Peloponnesian War.

Part II

UTOPIA AND PANHELLENISM: XENOPHON, THE *ANABASIS* AND THE SPARTANS IN ASIA

2

XENOPHON, UTOPIA AND PANHELLENISM

During the part of their journey which took them along the southern shore of the Black Sea, the ten thousand Greek mercenaries, or 'Cyreans' as Xenophon calls them,[1] halted for a while near the city of Cotyora, roughly halfway between Trapezus and Sinope. At this place, as he tells us, Xenophon had a remarkable vision:

> at this time, as Xenophon saw the many hoplites of the Greeks, as he saw the many peltasts, bowmen, slingers and cavalry, and all made expertly capable through experience, as he saw them there on the shore of the Black Sea where so great a military force could not have been put together without considerable expense, it seemed to him to be a good idea to add land and power to Hellas by means of the soldiers founding a city. And it seemed to him that it would be a great city when he reckoned up the number of soldiers themselves as well as those who dwelt around the sea. And for the accomplishment of these things he held a sacrifice.
>
> (*An.* 5.6.15–16)[2]

While this plan came to nothing – indeed it caused Xenophon some embarrassment before his comrades-in-arms – and hence could presumably easily have been passed over in silence, its presence in the *Anabasis* helps to connect Xenophon to two issues which were important in the intellectual and political climate of his day – panhellenism and utopian thinking. At one stroke Xenophon wanted to convert the army he served with into a *polis*, indeed a great *polis*, thereby adding to the power of Greece. But while 5.6.15–16 helps to align Xenophon with some of the concerns of his time, his utopian and panhellenic interests were, unlike those of his contemporaries, grounded in real experience, specifically the

41

experience he gained from the march of the Ten Thousand back to the Greek world from the heartland of the Persian empire (the *anabasis*, or more properly *katabasis* – 'the march *back*'); his ideas about these matters are not detached 'thought-experiments' which are used in the service of other, often unspoken intellectual projects. Xenophon's utopian leanings often find their clearest expression in military models for society, and in many ways these models prefigure later historical developments, especially from the period of Alexander and his Successors. His panhellenism also has its roots in military thinking and consequently is similarly unusual, entailing views which derive from his personal experience with the Ten Thousand. In the chapter which follows I will offer a sketch of fourth-century panhellenism and utopianism; I will then compare these with Xenophon's views as they are found in the *Anabasis*. The resulting discussion will help not only with the understanding of the *Anabasis* (Chapter 3) but will also help with working through problems connected with notions of ideal society and panhellenism found in the *Hellenica* – the topics of Chapter 4.

THE BACKGROUND: UTOPIA AND PANHELLENISM IN THE LATE FIFTH AND EARLY FOURTH CENTURIES

The terms 'panhellenism' and 'utopia' are notoriously slippery, and using them to describe trends in Greek intellectual history is a perilous business requiring considerable caution. In the first place, at the lexical level, it could be argued that neither word is appropriate to a study of the culture and society of fourth-century Greece – 'utopia' is a sixteenth-century AD neologism of St Thomas More, and 'panhellene', while it is found before the late fifth century, did not really apply to the set of beliefs commonly associated with the term (cf. Thuc. 1.3.2–4).[3] Furthermore, both words are quite elastic, each permitting a range of associations that make it sometimes difficult to establish precisely what they mean. But it does seem fair to say that there was a marked preoccupation in the fourth century with the modelling of ideal societies and with the exploration of ways in which all the Greeks, or at least some combination of them, could in some sense unite or act in concert to achieve specific ends; in support of this claim one need only think (respectively) of Plato and Aristotle, Gorgias and Isocrates. But some scholars would with some justification take issue with the claim that panhellenism and utopianism first made their appearance in the late fifth and early fourth centuries; indeed, it has been objected that both panhellenism and utopian thinking could already be found in the Greek world in the archaic period.[4] Phaeacia in Homer's *Odyssey* has a utopian air about it (see esp. *Od.* 7.117ff.), a land where the inhabitants do not need to work, and live in a remarkably ordered and regulated community – indeed, it is interesting to note in this connection that Lucian (*VH* 1.3) cites the *Odyssey* as the beginning of a tradition of utopian fantasy writing that includes Iambulus among others (see below, p. 52). The Golden Age in Hesiod (*Op.* 110–120; cf. Diod. 5.66.6) also suggests that the projection of ideal states of human life was not unique to the fourth century.[5] Likewise, the case for panhellenism before the age of Xenophon is also strong: Greek shrines, popular by the early eighth century and continuing to be so long after the fourth, were truly panhellenic ventures (cf. e.g. Ar. *Lys.* 1128–1134);[6] amphictyonies or loose alliances of Greek cities constituted to address specific problems go back to the First Sacred War (c. 590);[7] according to Herodotus, already in the sixth century thinkers were contemplating federations of Greek states in Asia Minor (Bias of Priene and, earlier, Thales of Miletus, Hdt. 1.170); further, the Greeks of Asia were organized along ethnic lines (Hdt. 1.142–151); and, of course, more than anything else the Persian Wars demonstrated that some Greeks could act cooperatively and with a real sense of unity against a common foe (see in this connection the celebrated passage in Herodotus, 8.144; cf. 9.7α–β). But panhellenism could mean different things to different people. It ought not be forgotten (though it sometimes is) that even after the oath and battle of Plataea the language of panhellenism continued on in the Hellenic (later the Delian) League, the purpose of which seems to have been to take the war back to Asia (see e.g. Plutarch *Cim.* 8.2) and to free the Greeks who lived there (see esp. Thuc. 3.10.3).[8] Whether the Athenian empire was popular or not, at some points Athens was pursuing panhellenist objectives and at other points not. Furthermore, it was ostensibly for the same panhellenic reason, freeing the Greeks, that the Spartans declared war on Athens (Thuc. 2.8.4).

These clear manifestations of panhellenic and utopian thinking before Isocrates and Xenophon prompt a useful question: what made late fifth- and fourth-century panhellenic and utopian speculation so different from similar currents in earlier Greek thought? E.R. Dodds has provided a helpful starting point:

When we pass from the fifth century to the fourth we enter a perceptibly different atmosphere. There is no falling off in creative energy: the fourth century produced the greatest philosophers and the greatest orators of Antiquity; it invented new art forms, prose dialogue and domestic comedy; it witnessed great advances in mathematics and astronomy. Yet it is hard to deny . . . that something at least of the old confidence has been lost. The feeling of insecurity expressed itself in a variety of ways. Men looked over their shoulders to a supposedly more stable past, to what they called 'the ancestral constitution', or beyond that to a state of primal innocence no longer to be found save among remote peoples . . . Alternatively, the dream could be projected as a blueprint for the future, one of those 'rational Utopias' of which Plato's Republic is only the most famous example. Utopias of this kind are less a sign of confidence in the future than of a dissatisfaction with the present; their authors seldom have much to say about the practical steps by which Utopia is to be achieved.[9]

A lack of 'confidence', a feeling of 'insecurity', 'dissatisfaction with the present' all suggest that the writers of the period were aware in some way of a systemic failure of organized society in Greece, that they perceived profound inadequacies in the existing political structures of their day.[10] While many factors contributed to the mobilization of the utopian and panhellenic imagination at the end of the fifth century, perhaps the single most important was the Peloponnesian War. Few modern historians would want to dispute Thucydides' claim that the Peloponnesian War was up to that time 'the greatest disturbance which had ever happened to the Greeks' (1.1.2; cf. Gomme (1937) 120–121), and that 'sufferings befell Greece in the course of it such as there had never been before over a similar length of time' (1.23.1; cf. Hdt. 6.98). The world which had experienced the earlier forms of panhellenism and utopia – the world that revered Homer, witnessed colonization as recently as 445 (Thurii)[11] and that periodically gathered at Delphi and Olympia – this world of the *polis* had been shattered by the material destruction of whole cities (e.g. Plataea, Melos) and the widespread disruption of normal civic life caused by the war (cf. Thuc. 3.82–83 on the revolution in Corcyra).[12] As Thucydides puts it, 'thus every form of wickedness (*kakotropia*) happened in Greece because of the social disturbances' (*staseis*, 3.83.1).

44

In order to get a better handle on fourth-century utopianism and panhellenism, I should like to take up some of the specific manifestations of 'anxiety' listed by Dodds in his description of the intellectual climate of the time. One of the categories of utopian thought Dodds mentioned was 'a state of primal innocence no longer to be found save among remote peoples'. This kind of admiration from a distance of foreign peoples – 'others' – goes back, as I mentioned, to the Phaeacians of Homer, and in historiography, probably to Hecataeus and certainly to Herodotus: the latter has in his history not only positive accounts of races familiar to the Greeks (the Egyptians, Babylonians, Persians, Scythians), but also remote people who, unlike most dwelling on the margins of the world, are exemplary in their justness;[13] people such as the long-lived Ethiopians whose king in his negotiations with the agents of Cambyses makes off-hand criticisms that are applicable not only to the Persians but also the Greeks (greed, lying; Hdt. 3.21–23.4). But while these earlier authors meant this special class of *barbaroi* to stand in contrast to the Greeks as a kind of implicit commentary on certain shortcomings of Greek society, this criticism was never meant as a fundamental indictment of Greek life; there was never ultimately any question in Herodotus' mind that Greek civilization was inherently superior. This type of idealization of distant barbarians was carried on in the fourth century rather mechanically by Ephorus in his description of the Scythians (*FGrHist* 70 F 42) 'who observe the most just of customs'.[14] But note that Ephorus feels he must make this observation to counter the reports of 'others' who concentrate on the Scythians' savagery.[15]

Theopompus, in his deployment of the fantastic barbarian utopia, adds a new and important element. In his *Thaumasia* he recounts the meeting of King Midas of Phrygia and Silenus (*FGrHist* 115 F 75). The latter explains that in reality Europe, Asia and Libya are islands and that beyond the circuit of Ocean is a boundless continent that supports all forms of large animals and humans twice as large as 'the ones here' and who live twice as long. Many great cities are found there,[16] and they observe customs completely contrary to those in 'our' world; from these cities he singles out two for special mention: Machimos or 'Wartown' and Eusebes or 'Pioustown'. The people of Pioustown live in continual peace and abundant wealth, getting their fruits from the earth without plough or ox, farming or sowing. They pass their lives free from sickness and end them laughing and happy. 'Thus', writes

Theopompus, 'they are indisputably just, since not even the gods refrain from visiting them.' On the other hand the people of Wartown are, predictably, the most belligerent: they spend all their time in arms, fighting and raiding their neighbours with the result that they rule 'many nations'. Most often they die in war, struck down by stones or wood (they are not vulnerable to iron); less frequently they die naturally, having spent all their lives in illness. Although they have an abundance of silver and gold, they consider the latter less valuable than iron. Evidently the people of Wartown once launched an enormous expedition to 'our' world and came first to the Hyperboreans. Learning from the Hyperboreans that they were regarded as the most fortunate of the inhabitants of this world, the Wartowners, who find them a despicable race, decide to go no further and return.

Theopompus informs us that to this story Silenus added 'a still more remarkable thing'. Among the inhabitants of the continent separated from our world are a people called the Meropae (cf. Homeric *merops*, an epithet used only of humans). At the furthest reaches of their land, in what is like a cavern covered by neither light or darkness but bathed in a foul red air, lies a place called Anostos ('No Return'). In No Return flow two rivers, one called the river of Pleasure and the other of Sorrow; and beside each river grows a tree. If someone eats the fruit from the tree beside the streams of Sorrow, 'they shed so many tears that they spend their whole lives in mourning until they die'. Those who eat from the tree beside the river of Pleasure give up all their desires (even if they happen to be in love with someone), and by stages they become younger: they pass from old age to ripe maturity, from maturity to youth, from youth to childhood and from childhood to infancy, 'and after that they disappear'.

Silenus' story, especially the first part, can be connected both to earlier accounts of strange and distant people living in a sort of latter-day Golden Age (chiefly Herodotus),[17] as well as to later Hellenistic stories concerning wonderful and exceedingly pious tribes, often from the East (accounts of India and the Indian Ocean as found in Onesicritus, Iambulus and Euhemerus).[18] Longevity, contempt of gold and freedom from disease are a few of the features that make Theopompus an important transitional figure in the history of what may perhaps be called 'ethnographic utopia'.[19] A unique and discordant note, however, can be heard in the story of the people of Wartown and their expedition to the Hyperboreans.

Their dismissal of the most fortunate people of this world reflects a structure of thought that can be traced back at least to Heraclitus:[20] when he wanted to stress the difference between gods and humans, he introduced a third element (apes) and assumed the humbling correlation that apes are to us as we are to the gods (DK 22 B 82–83). Similarly the logic of Theopompus suggests that if the people from the true continent regard the most fortunate people of our world as miserable and worthy of their contempt, then we must be in a very sorry condition indeed! But Theopompus builds on this traditional triadic explanation: those who condemn this world's best are themselves the worst of the 'other', utopian world; what is more, their opposite numbers, the people of Pioustown, destabilize the logic of the comparison by being so good that the gods enjoy their company. All this compounds the awful condition of humans in this world.

The problematizing of the explanatory triad raises the even more vexing issue of the second panel of Silenus' story, the land of No Return at the edge of the territory of the Meropae. The whole of Silenus' *logos* has been thought to be Theopompus' own creation.[21] On the other hand it has been pointed out that the story of Midas' capture and interview of Silenus seems to have been a fairly wide-spread tradition, making its appearance in Herodotus (7.26; 8.138.3) and Xenophon (*An.* 1.2.13), as well as Roman authors such as Cicero (*Tusc.* 1.114). Since the first part of Silenus' story is closer to conventional pictures of fantastic people dwelling on the edges of the earth, I would like to believe that this element is derivative and the second is original to Theopompus.[22] Be that as it may, the story of the chasm and the rivers of No Return clearly parallels the first story of Pioustown and Wartown: it too concerns a pair of opposites, good and bad, where the respective residents (or consumers) experience very different fates – the people of Wartown and those who eat from the fruit of Sorrow experience unimaginable grief, and those of Pioustown and those who eat from the tree of Pleasure experience equally wonderful bliss. Or do they? It so happens that Plutarch reports the same story as Theopompus and he provides the detail (perhaps expanding and so interpreting the version that Theopompus produced) that Silenus told Midas that 'the best thing for all men and women was not to have been born' (*Mor.* 115E), an old and familiar Greek adage that dovetails nicely with the fate of those who are reduced to nothingness after eating of the fruit of Pleasure. But even without external testimony to help with interpretation, we can see for ourselves that the great joy promised in Theopompus' land of No Return for those who eat from beside the tree of Pleasure is really *obliteration*. Is this the best that humans can hope for – the best existence is non-existence?[23] If this interpretation of the fate of those who eat from the tree of Pleasure is correct, then, by extension, doubts are cast on the corresponding view of the people of Pioustown. It may be that Theopompus, in his apparent subversion of the second utopia, is also destabilizing the first and so in a sense is challenging the very production of utopian visions.[24] One thing seems certain, that Theopompus' utopia is an allegorical indictment of war, and a pessimistic one at that: the Wartowners enjoy considerable power, but they lead a wretched life.[25] Furthermore, insofar as war was believed to be a constant and essential feature of political life, Theopompus seems to have levelled a much more searching criticism at the Greek world than those presented by earlier utopias located on the fringes of the earth. Theopompus, writing sometime in the middle of the fourth century, did not have far to look to find 'Wartowners'. This sort of penetrating and comprehensive criticism of his own era is a distinctively fourth-century element.

Another type of utopia which Dodds mentions as characteristic of the fourth century is the 'blueprint for the future', or 'rational utopia'. At least as early as Herodotus' account of the conspirators' debate over the form Persia's constitution would take (3.80–83), the notion that the form of government could be changed and that, furthermore, there was a theoretically perfect type of government must have been circulating in the Greek world, probably thanks in large part to the older sophists.[26] Indeed, it seems fairly certain that a rich discourse of speculation regarding the origins of human society was going on in the second half of the fifth century,[27] and it is not hard to imagine these debates turning to utopian as well as to strictly anthropological topics. With the foundation of Thurii in southern Italy, we catch a glimpse of two fifth-century utopian designers at work – Protagoras of Abdera and Hippodamus of Miletus. If the testimony of Plato can be relied on, Protagoras was one of those thinkers mentioned above who were engaged in the debate about the origins of civilization, especially with the question of the beginning of excellence in civic life (*Prt.* 320c–322e = DK 80 C 1). It was Protagoras who was supposed to have framed Thurii's constitution.[28] Evidently Hippodamus designed the plan of the city on a grid system, as he had done for the Piraeus, the port of Athens (cf. Xenophon *Hell.* 2.4.11).[29] Aristotle tells us (*Pol.* 1267b–1268a) that he was an eccentric town-planner who 'discovered the division of cities' (by which is probably meant the rational division of cities into precincts), and furthermore 'was the first among men not in government to attempt to say something about the best constitution'. According to Aristotle, the main feature of Hippodamus' ideal state of ten thousand citizens was that they were divided into three classes – craftsmen, farmers and soldiers. This idea of division into class and specialization of duties was to become a common feature of later Hellenistic utopias. The polity of Euhemerus, for instance, is especially close in this regard.[30] His Panchaeans are also divided into three classes – priests, farmers and soldiers, with artisans forming a separate service class attached to the priests (Diodorus 5.45.3). Some time after Hippodamus, but probably also in the fifth century,[31] Phaleas of Chalcedon came up with a plan for a polity whose distinguishing feature was the equal distribution of wealth, a detail that also shows up in later ethno-utopias.[32] And as Aristotle's association of Hippodamus and Phaleas with Plato suggests (*Pol.* 1261a–1264b, 1266a–1269a), there are obvious affinities between their utopias and Plato's Kallipolis as described in the *Republic*, having as it does both division into classes specialized for certain tasks as well as the abolition of money – a reform similar in its effects to the equal distribution of wealth (*R.* 422a).

The notion of division is important because, as Plato suggests, each class looks after the need it is best suited to address (*R.* 421b–c). That is to say, the greatest happiness of humans is realized only in a collectivity (519e). To this notion is related the most common explanation for the origins of human society: need. Protagoras, Plato and Aristotle all believed that humans first formed communities out of need for essential mutual benefit: for Protagoras it was for the formation of a common defence against predatory animals; for Plato it was for the provision of the basic requirements of life (food, shelter, clothing); for Aristotle humans formed collectivities out of the need to procreate.[33] Of course, the idea that the good of the individual was dependent on or in an inferior relation to that of the community is reflected in the very earliest periods of Greek literature.[34] Hector, in his defence of Troy, embodies the spirit of self-sacrifice for the greater good of his community (see, e.g., *Il.* 6.441–446, 12.243),[35] and the refrain that it is a beautiful thing 'to die for one's country' is not uncommon in archaic and later poets (Homer *Il.* 15.494–499, Tyrtaeus 10.1–2 (West), Aeschylus

Th. 1011) and is certainly the implied if not stated theme of epitaphs for fallen soldiers (e.g. *GVI* 1–51).

More useful for an understanding of Xenophon's utopian thinking because of temporal proximity, certainty of influence and similarity of view is Thucydides, specifically the vision of Athens as articulated by Pericles.[36] While it is true that Athens is 'somewhere' and not 'nowhere' and hence is not strictly a utopia, nonetheless the picture of Athens constructed by Pericles in Thucydides' history contains strong utopian elements. The city which we see in the Funeral Oration especially, with its adherence to the rule of law, its ideal citizenry and its magnificent and open culture (a *koinen polin*, Thuc. 2.39.1), is as much a utopia as any other ideal city[37] – indeed, it is a city to fall in love with (Thuc. 2.43.1, a very odd notion to a Greek). But even more than this vision of Athens as a superior city – 'an education for all Greece' (Thuc. 2.41.1) – the notion of the transcendence of the community over the individual expressed by Pericles in his third and last speech links Thucydides squarely with the tradition of 'blueprint' social utopias we have been discussing. In this speech, Pericles clarifies and defends his views on how the Athenians should fight the rest of the war with Sparta. Citing their anger directed at him for the recent setbacks the city has suffered, Pericles refers to a guiding principle behind his strategy:

I believe that the city when flourishing in its entirety helps private individuals more than when in the case of single citizens it fares well but as a whole stumbles. For a man faring well in his own regard is nonetheless destroyed when his homeland is destroyed, whereas doing badly in a flourishing city he is far more likely to be saved. Seeing that a city is able to bear the disasters of individuals while the individual is incapable of enduring those of a city, is it not essential for everyone to defend the city and not to do what you are doing now? Shocked by your personal losses you are throwing away the safety of the commonwealth (*tou koinou tes soterias*), and you blame me for having recommended going to war and yourselves for having agreed.

(Thuc. 2.60.2–4)

In his obituary of Pericles which immediately follows this speech, Thucydides declares that the Athenians did not follow his advice and essentially defeated themselves by letting their personal interest take priority over the interests of the state (Thuc. 2.65.12).

Consequently it is fair to assume that Thucydides endorsed the views expressed by Pericles in his last speech; indeed, he found the idea that the well-being of the state must come before the well-being of the individual so compelling that he seems to have let it shape his understanding of the progress of the entire war.[38] While this belief clearly has its origins in earlier Greek thought (as suggested above), it was one thing for Pericles to recommend self-sacrifice on the battlefield and quite another to suggest that the interests of the individual should be subordinated to those of the city. This was a radical notion. The ideal of the 'quietist' who minded his own business in his effort to make his own household flourish was a strong one at Athens,[39] as Pericles' earlier denunciation of the 'useless man', the *apragmon*, testifies (Thuc. 2.40.2). And in fact many of the passages that have been adduced as parallels for Thucydides 2.60.2 occur in contexts that make it reasonably clear that the idea of the state having priority over the individual in matters of security and well-being was not a common one.[40]

Perhaps the most significant parallel to Thucydides 2.60.2 is Democritus DK 68 B 252:

> one must consider the affairs of the city as far more important than the rest, that they be conducted well, and one must not be ambitious beyond what is reasonable nor give oneself power beyond the limits of what is useful for the community. For the well-conducted city is itself great prosperity (*orthosis*), and everything is in this, and with this preserved all is preserved, with this lost all is lost.[41]

The similarities between this passage and Thucydides 2.60.2–4 are obvious and striking. In the first place the central concept of prosperity is described in both passages by the idea of 'straightening' (*polin orthoumenen*, Thuc.; *polis megiste orthosis*, Democr.); second, both passages speak of the total dependence of the individual upon the city in terms of common safety or salvation (*tou koinou soterias*, Thuc.; *toutou soizomenou panta soizetai*, Democr.). But the Democritus passage also goes beyond the words Thucydides gives to Pericles. Democritus speaks of divisiveness which comes about not because of personal loss blinding one to the demands of the common good (the situation Pericles is addressing), but because of ambition, and specifically a love of conflict or rivalry (*philonikeonta*). Furthermore, Democritus' passage also contains a notion of balance and propriety (*epieikes*) that is missing from Thucydides.

The demands particular to the circumstances of Pericles' speech (a hostile crowd reeling from serious setbacks early in the war) account for these differences; it would have been inappropriate for him to go into the kind of detail Democritus does given the fear and impatience of his audience. But, on the whole, Democritus and Thucydides show remarkable similarities in thinking. Perhaps the most important is their organic understanding of the city and their attendant concern for unanimity within the *polis*.[42] Thucydides, like Plato later in the *Republic*, is comfortable speaking of the individual and the city as though categorically the same in terms of their behaviour (3.82.2; cf. 1.144.3); furthermore he understands the city as susceptible to growth and decay (e.g. 2.64.3).[43] As is well known from his discussion of the Corcyrean revolution (3.82–83), he regards internal discord or *stasis* as a disease which has a definite pathology like the plague.[44] Likewise, Democritus viewed the city as an 'organic unity'[45] which thrived when its citizens, both rich and poor, were 'of the same mind' (*homonoous,* DK 68 B 255).[46] Indeed, for Democritus, likemindedness or *homonoia* was the necessary precondition for a city achieving great things such as the defeat of an enemy in war (DK 68 B 250). Like Thucydides, Democritus considered *stasis* a destructive force, and civil war an evil that befalls both the winners and losers (DK 68 B 249).

The 'blueprint' utopias of Xenophon's time and later were often conceived as organic unities. Furthermore, a common and essential component of these ideal states was precisely this notion of concord or harmony brought about by likemindedness. So, in his exchange with Thrasymachus in the first book of the *Republic*, Socrates stresses that 'injustice and hatred produce civil wars (*staseis*) and internecine conflicts, while justice produces *homonoia* and friendship' (*R.* 351d). And later 'Iambulus' notes that in his model society there is no *stasis*, and *homonoia* is valued highly. In the very next paragraph as it is preserved in Diodorus, we learn further that among the people of this utopia lives a wondrous creature that has a remarkably plural array of external organs (four eyes, four mouths), but a unitary interior nature; its blood, we are told, acts as a type of glue that can restore severed members to the body (Diod. 2.58.1–4): it is what one might call 'the *homonoia*-animal' – an objectification almost into a fetish of the notion of concord that demonstrates the centrality of the concept to utopian thinking.

The principle of *homonoia* is an important one to monitor.[47] While the term is found only twice in Thucydides, these occurrences are instructive: both are found in association with Athenian politics, specifically issues connected with the tyranny of the Four Hundred (8.75.2, 8.93.3).[48] These passages suggest that for Thucydides like-mindedness and lack of discord are concepts that apply only to the internal politics of a city: for Thucydides the notion of inter-*polis* affairs being in some sense governed by a sense of concord or harmony is literally inconceivable.[49] Similarly Democritus thought of *homonoia* only in terms of intra-*polis* matters,[50] and this was probably the norm.[51]

With certain of the sophists, however, this restriction on the application of *homonoia* was removed, and with this change we can conveniently turn to the question of panhellenism. While Dodds left this category of utopian thinking out of his summary of the intellectual crisis of the fourth century (see above, p. 44), he elsewhere traced the beginnings of those radical thinkers who sought to extend the concept of concord from relations within the state to relations between states.[52] Gorgias of Leontini was one of the first to apply the term *homonoia* to concord among all Greeks, not just citizens of a single *polis*:[53] he spoke about *homonoia* among the Greeks in an oration delivered at the panhellenic sanctuary at Olympia (DK 82 B 8a), and in his Funeral Oration delivered at Athens he lamented the warfare among the Greeks, observing that 'trophies commemorating victory over barbarians demanded hymns, those over Greeks dirges' (DK 82 B 5b; cf. the words of his student Isocrates, *Pan.* 158). As this fragment suggests, the crucial element in panhellenic *homonoia* is collective action against 'the barbarian', specifically the Persians; concord was not so much envisioned as a permanent condition among the Greeks but rather as a necessary preliminary to or result of all-Greek war against Persia. Some thinkers pushed the notion of unity even further and proposed that all of humanity, Greek and barbarian, was in actual fact linked by common natural bonds: Hippias of Elis imagined an intellectual kinship that surpassed the claims of convention (Plato *Prt.* 337c–d); Xenophon reports that he viewed some laws as binding on all humankind (*Mem.* 4.4.19);[54] and Antiphon the Sophist claimed that 'by nature we are all constituted in every way alike, both barbarians and Greeks' (DK 87 B 44 fr. B col. 2).[55] This sort of thinking was probably found only on the intellectual fringe. Indeed, it was probably a stretch for most writers (let alone the putative 'man on the street') to extend the notion of unity beyond the factions within an individual *polis*. Even those who did on one occasion speak of *homonoia* among the Greeks could on another use the term to mean concord among citizens of a single *polis*: so for example Lysias in his Olympic Oration could (appropriately) advocate the unity of the Greeks against external threats such as Persia and the tyrannical rule of Dionysius of Syracuse (33.6), while in his Funeral Oration he could (equally appropriately) speak of the noteworthy *homonoia* of the Athenians (2.18).[56] Aeneas Tacticus, an exact contemporary of Xenophon writing in the second quarter of the fourth century, probably represents the more common understanding of *homonoia*:[57] he devoted an entire treatise to the topic of maintaining unanimity *within* a besieged city.[58]

ISOCRATES, *HOMONOIA* AND PANHELLENISM

In its advocacy of diverting hostility and warfare away from the Greek world and into a cooperative invasion of the Persian empire, panhellenism, with its emphasis on concord among the Greeks, is a special type of utopia, quintessentially fourth-century in spirit. But despite the fact that the concept had broad influence, it is linked to one champion, Isocrates, another contemporary of Xenophon and originally his fellow demesman.[59] Isocrates' thinking on the matter, however, was not simple, nor did it remain static or undergo no change throughout his remarkably long career.

The best place to start an investigation of Isocrates' thoughts on panhellenism and *homonoia* is with the *Panegyricus*, an oration published in 380 and aimed at all Greeks. Arguing that the Greeks should abandon discord and war among themselves, and that they should instead seek peace in which they all might live more securely, Isocrates sums up his position towards the conclusion of his speech:

> my thoughts concerning these matters are simple and straight-forward: it is not possible to enjoy secure peace until we make war in common on the barbarian, nor is it possible for the Greeks to be of one mind (*homonoesai*) until we gain our profits from the same source and venture risks against the same enemy. When those things happen, and the shortages in essential supplies are no more – shortages which dissolve friendly associations, turn bonds of kinship into hatred and lead all men to war and civil strife – it cannot but happen that we shall have concord (*homonoesomen*) and enjoy the true

feelings of good will towards one another. For the sake of these things it is imperative that we remove war as quickly as possible from Greece to the continent [of Asia]; thus we would profit from this one good result from the dangers we have undergone among ourselves, if it should seem a good idea to us to make full use of the experiences we have gained from these conflicts against the barbarian.

(*Pan.* 173–174)

Here in this passage are conveniently almost all the hallmarks of Isocrates' thought: concord (*homonoia*) among the Greeks, war against the Persians, alleviation of poverty in Greece, good will. We may establish the logical sequence of all these ideas as follows: war is an endemic condition among the Greeks because in an effort to provide for themselves they continually take from one another in ceaseless warfare; once all the Greeks seek the material resources they need from the same external source – that is to say the barbarians – true peace and concord will result. The essence of Isocrates' proposal for peace in the Greek world is built on an age-old hellenic view of the nature of friendship: 'count my friends your friends, and my enemies your enemies'.[60] The innovative or at least uncommon element in Isocrates' thinking is to apply the concept to inter-state relations.

Passages like *Panegyricus* 173–174 have encouraged many to see in Isocrates a 'preacher of hellenic unification', a visionary whose ideas regarding Greek unity were ahead of his time and were eventually brought to reality first by Philip of Macedon and then Alexander the Great.[61] But such an interpretation of Isocrates has been shown to be mistaken.[62] Setting aside the question whether the Macedonian conquest of Greece and the League of Corinth can be considered positive steps towards the improvement of Greek political life, the uncritical acceptance of Isocrates the 'Panhellenist' tends to oversimplify his views, glossing over those passages that problematize the message thought to be found in his work. Indeed, if we look elsewhere in the *Panegyricus* we can see that Isocrates' advocacy of panhellenism is not as straightforward as it seems.

Early on in the oration, at chapters 16–17, he observes that in reality all Greece is under the control of either Athens or Sparta, and their governments reflect this division (not a new idea: see Thucydides 3.82.1 and cf. Xenophon *Hell.* 6.3.14);[63] hence if anyone wants to accomplish more than just oratorical display, he must persuade the two leading powers to 'share equally with each other, dividing their hegemonies and, those material advantages which they seek for themselves at the cost of the Greeks, these they should get from the barbarian'. While there are superficial similarities between this passage and *Pan.* 173–174, *homonoia* seems in actual fact to have been for Isocrates concord between the hegemons of Greece, namely Athens and Sparta: evidently once these powers agreed to share the control of Greece, war against Persia and concord among the Greeks would result. What is more, because of the abuse he heaps on Sparta later in the same oration, combined with the laudatory and at times disturbingly selective review he provides of Athens' achievements as a hegemon in the fifth century,[64] it seems clear that Isocrates is really justifying a new Athenian hegemony based on the prestige of the city's past, its cultural preeminence (note *paideusis*, 50) and military (especially naval) power. Even when he seems to condemn Athens' naval supremacy, it is in actual fact praise for Athens as well as criticism of Sparta (cf. *Panath.* 53).[65] Isocrates was not an advocate of the unification of Greece in some new political ordering but a partisan of Athens who tried to win for his city as much authority as was possible in the volatile conditions of the first two quarters of the fourth century. But even if we take Isocrates at his word and assume for the moment that he meant what he said when he dismissed in the *Panegyricus* any proposal for settling Greece's ills that did not include Athens and Sparta as leaders (16–17), the argument that the best way to achieve universal concord throughout Greece was by maintaining a dual hegemony is patently self-contradictory: *homonoia* implies cooperation, whereas hegemony implies coercion. The logical impossibility of Isocrates' position in the *Panegyricus* underscores his basic commitment not to promote concord among the Greeks but to advance the interests of his native Athens.

That Isocrates' real loyalty lay with his city and not a confederation of Greek states is further suggested by the support he offers in the *de Pace* of the King's Peace, the very agreement he had denounced so vehemently in the *Panegyricus* (115–124).[66] Essentially Isocrates was seeking at this time (c. 355) to minimize Athens' losses after the Social War, and in the Peace he saw an opportunity to ensure the independence of the Greek cities (*de Pace* 16). Again the preservation of his *polis* is his primary objective. While it is true that at §82ff. he denounces sea power, he still wants Athens to be a cultural hegemon. When later still he reverted in the

Philippus to his former policy of war against Persia, this time with Philip as the supreme commander, he again made it abundantly clear that his primary interest was first and foremost the well-being of Athens (*Phil.* 9).[67] Moreover, he not only encouraged Philip to reconcile the four leading states of Greece (30), he also warned him, albeit in a veiled fashion, not to try to coerce them (35–38); indeed, Isocrates declares that leadership won through *eunoia* (good will) is far better than that won through force (*kata kratos*, 68), and characterizes Philip's ambitions against the Greek states as rumour, thereby subtly condemning the policy of interference in the affairs of the *poleis* (73). Due to her naval power, Athens, predictably, emerges as Philip's most important ally (57ff.).[68]

Isocrates was not the radical idealist of Greek unity he sometimes is imagined to be. He was an advocate of his *polis*, and while political and military exigencies made him change what precisely he proposed, he inevitably put the interest of Athens before all else. And this should not surprise us. The true panhellenists and internationalists were (as suggested above) very much in the minority. While Greeks could no doubt recognize that there were common bonds of language and religion between themselves, their regional and especially their *polis* loyalties were simply too strong for them to entertain seriously notions of national unification. So potent was this regional loyalty, in fact, that men like Isocrates, when confronted with the ten thousand Greeks who marched with Cyrus, saw not panhellenic champions but indigent opportunists in search of gain (*Pan.* 146);[69] their success was held up not as a positive example of what Greeks could accomplish against the Persians but a negative one. Indeed, Isocrates' later plans to launch a panhellenic crusade of conquest and colonization of Persia were aimed in large part at settling the troublesome poor of Greece in Asia, something which was hoped would reduce the threat of the ever-increasing numbers of itinerant mercenaries (*Phil.* 120–122; cf. *Pan.* 182).[70] No, for Isocrates the Ten Thousand were a paltry force that exposed weaknesses a larger and more professional army could (he hoped) easily exploit (*Pan.* 146–147).[71]

Seen in light of the circumstances of his time, Isocrates was not unusual. Although ancient testimony suggests that 'the freedom of the Greeks of Asia' could mobilize panhellenic action, modern scholars have concluded that the slogan and concept really only came into circulation *after* the freedom of the Asiatic Greeks had been bartered away to Persia under the terms of the King's Peace[72]

– a settlement that essentially ratified Sparta's hegemony as champion or *prostates* of the Peace. Furthermore, even the most generous critics of the Second Athenian Confederation have to admit that what started as a league to ensure the 'freedom and autonomy' of its member states ended in revolt and war[73] – and this is not to mention those associations of states whose adherence to the principles of the independence was much less defined, if present at all (the Peloponnesian and Boeotian leagues). Panhellenism, while quintessentially Greek in outlook, was actually an impossibility given the realities of Greek inter-*polis* life.[74] Or was it?

3

XENOPHON'S *ANABASIS*
Panhellenism and the ideal community

Xenophon's *Anabasis*, written after the battle of Leuctra in 371,[1] contains something of all the currents of thought discussed above. It shows the influence of panhellenic thought and utopian thinking in all its varieties; it also contains elements of exotic ethnography as well as early intimations of biography. The most important component of all of these, and the one that seems sustained throughout the work, is the view of the Ten Thousand as a model society, a 'blueprint' utopia in action. This understanding of the Greek mercenaries as members of an evolving, then decaying community comes into sharpest focus when set beside the panhellenic elements of the *Anabasis*. In the following chapter I will explore first the panhellenism of the *Anabasis* and then turn to a consideration of the Ten Thousand as an ideal community. This two-part discussion will help lay the groundwork for an examination of the notion of paradigm found in the *Hellenica* in Chapter 4.

THE *ANABASIS* AS PANHELLENIC TEXT

The march of the ten thousand Greek mercenaries from Babylon to the Black Sea and Hellespont earned them almost instant celebrity. Their exploits were recounted by two and possibly three historians shortly afterwards – Ctesias, Sophaenetus (a veteran of the march) and Ephorus' source (either Sophaenetus or perhaps the Oxyrhynchus historian).[2] Additionally, as mentioned above (p. 57), rhetors like Isocrates could refer to them as if their accomplishments were widely known; certainly later writers like Polybius (3.6.10–11) and Arrian (*An.* 1.12.1–4) treated the Ten Thousand as if their fame was beyond question. Like moderns, these later authors saw in the expedition a revealing precursor of Alexander's conquest of the East.

Seen in this light, it is not difficult to understand how the activities of the Ten Thousand could be seen as panhellenic.

At a detailed level, there are several telling passages in the *Anabasis* which suggest the panhellenic orientation of the work. A number of stock-in-trade images of the Persians simultaneously suggest and justify the certain success of Greek military action against the barbarian East.[3] So, for instance, we see at one point Persian troops driven into battle 'under the lash' (3.4.26; cf. Hdt. 7.56 and 7.223), suggesting their servility and essentially cowardly nature. We also have a reference to *proskunesis* or 'paying homage', a feature of Persian life that was also illustrative for the Greeks of the easterners' basic lack of freedom (cf. Isocrates *Pan.* 151).[4] The reference comes from a speech of exhortation to the Ten Thousand by Xenophon himself, and the passage expresses neatly the connection in the Greeks' mind between freedom and military superiority: referring to the Greek repulse of the invasions of both Darius and Xerxes, Xenophon observes, 'as proof [of our ancestors' success] it is possible to see their trophies, but the greatest proof is the *freedom of the cities* in which you were born and raised; for you worship (*proskuneite*) no man as supreme ruler (*despoten*), rather you worship the gods' (3.2.13). Military success is one proof; freedom, represented by not revering any man as a god, is a better proof still that Greek and barbarian are radically opposed.[5] Indeed, so thoroughgoing is this panhellenic understanding of the Persians as morally and therefore militarily inferior, that even they are made to recognize their own inherent weakness when compared to the Greeks: as Cyrus the Younger admits to the commanders of the Ten Thousand on the eve of Cunaxa,

> O Greek men, not because I lack barbarian soldiers have I made you my allies, but because I consider you better and stronger than many barbarians; for this reason I added you to my force. Be sure then to be men worthy of the freedom that you possess and because of which I consider you blessed. For know well that I would prefer to have freedom than all I now own and much more than that. I who will explain to you so that you know into what sort of contest you are going. The mass [of the enemy] is vast, and they advance with great shouting; should you withstand these things, regarding the rest, *even I feel ashamed* at what sort of men you will find the inhabitants of this country to be.
>
> (1.7.3–4)

A finer panhellenic broadside against the barbarian, especially with its accent on the numerical superiority of the Persians in contrast to the freedom of the Greeks, could not be found (cf. Isocrates *Pan.* 150 and, interestingly, Xenophon *Cyr.* 8.1.4); and by putting it in the mouth of an 'easterner', Xenophon, as does Herodotus in the famous banquet of Thersander at Thebes (9.16ff.), gives the point an authority that surpasses that spoken by a Greek – the remarks become 'autoethnography'.[6]

These passages, and others like them, are not only descriptions of Persian society, they are also collectively a call to panhellenic action.[7] The very success of the Ten Thousand and the weaknesses their march reveals in the social and military structure of the Achaemenid realm are presented in the *Anabasis* in part to suggest the certain conquest of Persia by some future expedition. Xenophon himself encourages such an interpretation when he comments on the speed with which Cyrus pressed his march into the interior of Persia:

> and it was possible for one looking carefully at the empire of the King to see that in quantity of land and men it was strong, but in terms of lengths of roads and the scattered disposition of its forces it was weak, if someone speedily prosecuted the war [against it].

> (1.5.9)

This is precisely 'panhellenist big-talk', designed it seems to precipitate action. An intriguing antecedent for it may be found in the meeting between King Cleomenes of Sparta and Aristagoras of Miletus (Hdt. 5.49–51). The speech is best thought of as 'big-talk' insofar as the retreat of the Ten Thousand, however remarkable it was in terms of the difficulty of terrain and the hostility of barbarous peoples, did not really reveal any serious weaknesses in the structure of the Persian empire.[8] Xenophon, however, liked to think that it did and even suggests that the King was correspondingly driven to destroy the Greeks to 'set an example' (note esp. 2.4.3 and 3.1.18).

The passage from the *Anabasis* which best illustrates contemporary panhellenist views is from the speech of exhortation mentioned briefly above (p. 60), delivered shortly after the original commanders of the Greeks were treacherously seized by the satrap Tissaphernes.[9] Xenophon tries to instil courage in the troops by pointing to the situation of the Mysians, a powerful and autonomous tribe living in the north-western sector of the Achaemenid empire. Noting that the

Great King would be more than happy to provide the Mysians with guides in order that they leave his land, Xenophon declares,

> I think he would be three times as pleased to do these things for us, if he saw we were making preparations to stay. But I am afraid that if once we learned to live life without having to work and spending our time in luxury, consorting with the beautiful and impressive wives and daughters of the Medes and Persians, just as the Lotus Eaters we will forget the return home. It seems to me to be both reasonable and just first to try and return to Greece, to our kinsmen, and demonstrate to the Greeks that willingly they are poor (*hekontes penontai*), since it is possible for them to see those who now live as free citizens there in harsh circumstances having returned from here rich men.
>
> (3.2.24–26)

Here we see quite clearly the programme advanced by men such as Isocrates: the weakness of the Persian empire and the settlement of Greece's poor in the East. The suggestion that the Greeks are willingly poor is related to the crucial difference between their freedom and the Persians' servitude already mentioned above (p. 60); the idea goes back to Herodotus (e.g. 9.82) and is found especially in contexts where Spartan freedom and discipline are stressed (cf. Theopompus *FGrHist* 115 F 22).[10] But despite these clear indications of the passage's alignment with the central tenets of panhellenism, there is a problem in Xenophon's words that complicates a simple interpretation. While the threat of permanent settlement will frighten the King into aiding the Greeks in their return, note too that settlement in the East is characterized as a threat *also to the Greeks*: like the famous Lotus Eaters of the *Odyssey* (9.94ff.) Xenophon fears that the Greeks will be seduced by the good living of the Persians, specifically by their women, and decide to settle in Asia. There is a suggestion here that the Greeks will in some way lose their identity, that in losing their desire to return home they will lose their 'Greekness'. At least in this passage, then, the most ambitious panhellenic accomplishment of defeating the barbarian and colonizing his land is also conceived of as 'anti-hellenic' insofar as it entails the obliteration of Greekness itself.

The tension felt at 3.2.24–26 between settlement in Persia and return to Greece underscores what I believe to be a central problem of the *Anabasis*: for Xenophon there was not one panhellenism but two competing panhellenisms, represented in the first instance by the need to return to Greece and second by the desire to found a new city in Asia. Superficially, the 'second' panhellenism looks like the Isocratean programme of colonizing troublesome mercenaries far away from the Greek homeland. In fact, it is quite different. Xenophon's interest in the settlement of Greeks in Persia extends beyond trying to solve the societal and political problems of Greece; he is keenly interested in the Ten Thousand *as a community*, and the question of its permanent realization as a *polis* is but one of the issues on which he focuses his attention. Indeed, the *Anabasis* is not just the story of the Ten Thousand's successful return to the Greek world, it is also a study of the evolution and decay of what was an ideal Xenophontic community or a utopia.

THE *ANABASIS* AS UTOPIAN TEXT

In the preceding section I considered how Xenophon's *Anabasis* could be seen as a panhellenic text, primarily in connection with the Isocratean brand of that vision. But as I tried to demonstrate, panhellenism in some form had existed as a concept for a long time before Isocrates and Xenophon, and it meant different things to different people. It should not surprise us, then, if we should find that Xenophon developed his own views in addition to and possibly as a replacement for the sort of things Isocrates and others were saying. In the *Anabasis*, panhellenism also takes the form of an inquiry into the workings of an ideal community, the Ten Thousand, so that in a sense panhellenism and utopianism coincide. As we will see, however, the history of the expedition is divided into phases, and charting Xenophon's thoughts on the progress of the community of soldiers is essential.

It is impossible to establish with certainty precisely why Xenophon wrote the *Anabasis*. No doubt it was intended in part to inspire the hope of military action against Persia, despite the problems I have outlined above. Some have argued that he also wrote it as an *apologia* or defence of his conduct:[11] Xenophon may have been negatively portrayed in another version of the march, that by Sophaenetus, and felt the need to defend himself; furthermore, as I have noted above, the Ten Thousand were sometimes characterized as little better than brigands and Xenophon may have wanted to counter that accusation as well (note esp. 6.4.8; cf. Isocrates *Pan.* 146).[12] Additionally, his service with Cyrus the

Younger, an enemy of Athens (3.1.5, 5.3.7), as well as his subsequent collaboration with the Spartans, may have led to his exile from his native city and thus to an attempt by him to account in some way for his actions.[13] But while there is nothing to prevent us from seeing the *Anabasis* as both *apologia* and panhellenic call to action, the aspect of the account which may have meant most to him was the presentation of the Ten Thousand as an ideal community. As I hope to show below, Xenophon's experience on the march first as participant and then as leader brought him into intimate contact with the dynamics of community life, both successful and unsuccessful, and this experience forged many of his later ideas regarding what constituted good and bad forms of political life.[14] Indeed, one can see from the rest of his corpus that studying the causes of success and failure of government held a special fascination for him: to judge from the introductions to the *Cyropaedia* and the *Constitution of the Spartans*, he often thought about the question of what contributes to stable and effective government (note the telling similarity of language, *ennoia poth' hemin egeneto, Cyr.* 1.1.1; *all' ego ennoesas pote, Lac.* 1.1);[15] indeed, it can fairly be said that Xenophon treated the topic throughout his career (*Hieron, Agesilaus*, portions of the *Hellenica*, the *Poroi*). Nowhere in the *Anabasis*, however, does he state that the Ten Thousand were a perfect community. Rather, he lets us see them evolve gradually into a remarkably cohesive civic and military collectivity that just as gradually dissolves. The suggestion of its excellence is in the presentation, the index of its success being its continuing survival despite great odds (at least as Xenophon presents them), and the sign of its failure the eventual break-up. He traces a tendency; he does not articulate a clear programme.

It is both important and convenient to distinguish the different phases through which the Ten Thousand evolve in the course of their march; there are subtle and less subtle differences between each phase, making it a mistake to generalize about the character of the army and apply to the entire history of its life what is true of only a part of it. In fact one of the most common descriptions of the Ten Thousand is 'mobile *polis*', but this identification really fits only one of the phases well.[16] This division of the Ten Thousand into stages or periods permits a more precise understanding of what Xenophon thought were the army's greatest strengths and weaknesses.

In the first phase the Ten Thousand are brought together by Cyrus and function only as a mercenary force, until the capture of their commanders by Tissaphernes after Cunaxa and the awkward truce which followed the battle. The second phase is marked by the redefinition of the Ten Thousand after the loss of their commanders as a new structure devoted exclusively to survival in the face of external danger and to a return to the Greek world; in this phase the greatest unity of the Ten Thousand is achieved. In the third phase, the Ten Thousand experience serious internal divisions regarding what the chief goals of the army should be while operating at the fringes of the Greek world (the southern coast of the Black Sea). In the final phase the unity of the army disintegrates, and elements of the original Ten Thousand are absorbed by Spartan forces led by Thibron. In the discussion that follows, I will examine each phase in connection with a set of interrelated questions: to what degree do the Ten Thousand at any given stage exhibit a strong sense of unity and concord; what sort of division of tasks and command structure are present; what are the objectives of the group, and are they the same for everyone? In this way Xenophon's own views on what makes up an ideal community will become clear and points of contrast and comparison with the thought of his age will be established.

The Ten Thousand as mercenary force (*An.* 1–2)

Having detailed the grounds for Cyrus' dispute with his brother Artaxerxes, Xenophon turns his attention to an account of the assembly of the Greek mercenaries. The recruitment of the Ten Thousand is done primarily by individual Greeks who not only raise the units but remain in command of them during the campaign as generals or *strategoi*.[17] This is an important point, for while they seem to achieve operational unity and cohesion quite rapidly, something which is best seen in their parade and mock attack before the Cilician queen Epyaxa (note her wonder at the order of the Greeks, as well as Cyrus' admiration for their ability to instil fear in his own native troops, 1.2.18), early in their march to Cunaxa serious divisions occur precisely along the lines of their recruitment. This propensity to split up and quarrel is seen most dramatically when the companies of two commanders, Menon and Clearchus, almost come to blows and actually form into battle lines opposite each other after one of Menon's men is summarily punished by Clearchus (1.5.11–17). That the companies think first of themselves and then of the larger group is also suggested by Menon's desire to be the first to cross the Euphrates and thus win Cyrus' admiration and generosity (1.4.13–17).[18] The Ten Thousand are not really a single army but a collection of several independent units, each with its own commander.[19] Thus it is interesting to note that when 'the soldiers' of the army refuse at one point to go forward, suspecting that they are marching against the King, Clearchus does not try to force them all into continuing, only his own men (1.3.1); and when he calls an 'assembly' (*ekklesian,* 1.3.2), to persuade them, it is made up of his men only. In the course of his speech to his men, Clearchus makes a telling observation which reveals precisely what the status of each unit in the Ten Thousand was at this stage:

> but since you do not wish to obey me, I will follow you and I will obey whatever is required. For I consider you to be my homeland, my friends and my allies; with you I believe I will be honoured wherever I happen to be, but without you I do not think I will be able either to help a friend or ward off an enemy.
>
> (1.3.6)[20]

Although this speech is part of a trick Clearchus has designed to lure the soldiers back into Cyrus' service, his statement is basically true:[21] Clearchus depends on his men for the maintenance of his status in the Greek world – he is an exile from Sparta (1.1.9 and 1.3.3) and so has no country, and more importantly, his friendship is only meaningful for Cyrus insofar as he is able to maintain control of his men.[22] The speech makes clear that there is a reciprocal relationship between the commander and the commanded. When Xenophon tells us that Clearchus' appeal was so persuasive that more than two thousand men from two other companies joined his ranks, he is pointing out something unusual (1.3.7; cf. 1.4.7); the troops' loyalty was first and foremost to their immediate commander.

At the battle of Cunaxa itself, the Ten Thousand are deployed in their contingents with their generals in command (1.8.2; cf. 1.2.15). While some operational changes were made in the course of the march that probably entailed the reconfiguration of troops from different commands into one unit (the peltasts, 1.8.5), the reassignment of soldiers was very unusual;[23] the only mission of consequence reported by Xenophon prior to Cunaxa is the escort of Epyaxa to her home and the reconnoitring of the Cilician gates, both performed by Menon and his men – a single unit (1.2.20–21, 25).

A change in command structure does occur after the death of Cyrus at Cunaxa. In the immediate aftermath of the battle two commanders (Clearchus and Proxenus) deliberate as to what should be done (1.10.5), and 'the Greeks' (the entire army is meant) are described as holding discussions and deciding the next steps (1.10.17). Soon, however, Clearchus emerges as the general with the most authority due to his considerable combat experience (2.2.5; cf. 2.6.1): he calls the meetings of the officers (2.2.3, 2.3.8), and it is he who responds to the complaints of the soldiers which are directed to him and the other commanders (2.4.2–5). Clearchus had enjoyed a privileged position in the army while Cyrus was alive (he was the only Greek present at the secret trial of the traitor Orontas, 1.6.5, and he was the one to whom Cyrus shouted his orders before Cunaxa, 1.8.12),[24] so that his eventual position as the supreme general probably seemed a logical step after Cyrus' death. His power was not, however, absolute: although he called the meetings of the officers, he could not ignore what they said, and more importantly, before his capture at the camp of Tissaphernes he is reported as seeking the loyalty of the whole army, a situation which implies that the mercenaries still felt their first loyalty to their immediate commanders (2.5.29).

At this, the earliest stage, the Ten Thousand have two concerns: pay and provisions.[25] While Cyrus only distributes pay to the troops once, and even then it is more than three months overdue (1.2.11), he promises no less than three increases (1.3.21, 1.4.13, 1.7.7).[26] The first two increases are the result of pressure applied by the mercenaries as Cyrus' real plans become clearer and the scope of their commitment becomes considerably enlarged; the third, a promise of a golden crown for each soldier, comes on the eve of Cunaxa as a final incentive. Certain individuals are given bonuses as rewards for noteworthy service (Menon, 1.4.17; Silanus, 1.7.18). No doubt most of the Ten Thousand were motivated chiefly by the hope of such extra pay and the expectation of booty if the campaign against Artaxerxes proved successful (cf. 1.7.6–7).[27] The Ten Thousand are completely dependent on Cyrus for provisions. The army seems to have been maintained directly, either by requisitions of food in friendly or abandoned territory (e.g. 1.4.19, 1.5.4) or by being permitted to plunder in hostile territory (1.2.19).[28] Sometimes the troops purchased food from markets (1.5.10), probably with money provided by Cyrus. In periods of shortage they were driven to hunt or forage for themselves (1.5.1–3, 1.5.6), although it seems that Cyrus had a wagon-train loaded with emergency supplies (1.10.18).[29] After Cyrus' death, matters became much more difficult for the Greeks. In the immediate aftermath of Cunaxa, they had to make do as best they could, being forced to slaughter their draught and pack animals (2.1.6). During the uneasy truce with the King they are guided to villages where they are either permitted to requisition supplies (2.3.14) or seize them (2.4.27). In the negotiations it is agreed that the Greeks will be guaranteed the opportunity first to buy food and only when that is not possible to take it (2.3.26–27).[30] As Clearchus himself stresses, the Ten Thousand depend completely on the Persians for their food supply (2.5.9).

In terms of long-range objectives, return to Greece is the soldiers' only goal. In his impassioned and deceptive speech before his own contingent in which he declares his ultimate loyalty to his troops, Clearchus assures his men that 'no one will say that I, having led Greeks against barbarians, abandoned them and preferred the friendship of the barbarians' (1.3.5).[31] Such talk not only earns him the respect of the men under his command, it also brings into his camp (as I have mentioned) more than two thousand from two other units. Return is a complicated matter, however, for the Ten Thousand. In another address he encourages his men to decide whether to remain or to go: while remaining entails no special risk, he warns that marching back will involve problems of provisioning, and that Cyrus will prove a dangerous adversary (1.3.11–12; cf. 2.2.11). Xenophon tells us that Clearchus is secretly working to return his men to Cyrus' control (1.3.8), and in fact in the debate which follows his speech, soldiers acting as his agents draw attention to the difficulty of returning to Greece both by proposing impossible schemes for marching back through Persia and then objecting to those plans (1.3.13–19). These remarks underscore the practical problems of returning to the Greek world, but they also reveal that the Ten Thousand are divided between those who seek above all else to return to Greece and those who want to remain with Cyrus and profit by doing so. At any rate Cyrus seems to recognize that the Greeks are divided when he promises just before Cunaxa that he will make those Greeks who decide to return the envy of their friends, but asserts also that he is sure that many will want to stay, adding that those who do will be masters of vast territory (1.7.3–4, 7).[32]

The Ten Thousand as heroic community (*An.* 3–4)

The capture of the generals and the murder of all the others who went to the headquarters of Tissaphernes precipitate a crisis among the Ten Thousand; as Xenophon asserts shortly afterwards, the Persians broke the truce and seized the Greek commanders, assuming that without leaders the Ten Thousand would collapse as a fighting force (3.2.29). And indeed, immediately following the capture, the Greeks are reported as having fallen into 'profound helplessness' (*pollei aporiai*, 3.1.2), surrounded as they are by the enemy and far from home. Many are so despondent that they are unable even to eat or to light fires, and they lie instead on the ground wherever they happen to be, sleepless out of longing for their 'homelands, parents, wives and children whom they thought they would never see again' (3.1.3): it is a picture of an army completely demoralized. As Xenophon characterizes them, the Ten Thousand almost have to be reconstituted as an army again, their command structures rebuilt and their goals redefined.

The aims of the army change between phases one and two. In the period after the loss of the generals, the soldiers do not fight for pay and for the most part are not driven by a hope of profit from booty (although Xenophon does mention this as a possible motive at 3.2.39). Indeed, to become a more mobile force the troops destroy some of their own equipment (3.3.1; cf. 3.2.27) and later give up some of their own property (4.1.12ff.). Finding provisions for the army is still difficult, though during this phase of their journey they seem to have fewer difficulties than before; most of their march is through hostile territory. The soldiers take what they need (cf. 3.1.19ff., and see 2.5.9 and Isocrates *Pan.* 148), and only once do they experience extreme shortage (4.7.3; see also 4.1.9).

In his important speech to the troops shortly after the seizure of the generals, Xenophon articulates a new goal for the Ten Thousand: *soteria* or safety. The shift in purpose from the first to the second phase of the march is clearly signalled when he notes, 'before you showed yourselves brave men in Cyrus' quest for the throne, now when the contest is for your survival (*soterias*) it is much more fitting that you be better and braver' (3.2.15). The importance of the concept *soteria* is suggested in the beginning of the same speech when the word takes on literally magical force:[33] the first time Xenophon mentions it someone in the audience

sneezes, an omen which precipitates an elaborate vow of games in
honour of Zeus *Soter* (Zeus 'the Saviour') as soon as the Greeks
reach safety; the word is then repeated when Xenophon resumes
his address (3.2.8–10).[34] At one level *soteria* means simply survival.
So, at the conclusion of the same speech Xenophon identifies
three *separate* goals that might possibly motivate the Ten Thousand
– desire to return home, desire to live and desire for riches (3.2.29)
– a distinction that suggests that *soteria* can mean precisely 'staying
alive'. Survival for Xenophon, however, meant not just living but
living honourably and free from the control of the enemy (3.1.43,
3.2.3). But at another level the notion of 'safe-return', specifically to
homes in Greece, is also clearly meant when reference is made to
surviving. Thus, when Chirisophus, the Spartan who replaces
Clearchus as general, declares to an emissary of the King that return
to Greece is the only goal of the Ten Thousand, the Persian understands this to mean *soteria* (3.3.3–4), an extension of meaning that
is common in Greek.[35] And on another occasion Xenophon can
encourage his men to capture strategic heights and thereby get the
army out of danger by shouting 'now, men, consider that you are
struggling for Greece, now you are trying to reach your children and
wives, and by labouring a little now we will make the rest of our way
without conflict' (3.4.46): immediate survival and return to Greece
could sometimes be linked together.

One of the most dramatic changes between the army of the first
phase and the army of the second is its sense of unity. Before, the
units were kept separate and functioned independently, under the
command of their own leaders; indeed, at times they almost fought
one another. None of this divisiveness is present in the second
phase; in fact at the command level there is almost complete
unanimity, with Xenophon reporting only one disagreement
between himself and Chirisophus (4.6.3; however cf. 3.3.11 and
4.1.19), the major decision makers among the leaders of the army.
As Xenophon realizes, the goal is survival, and the survival of the
individual depends on the survival of the whole, or as he puts it, 'we
are all in need of common safety' (3.2.32). The story of the Ten
Thousand's march northward from the Zapatas river is characterized
at almost every turn by cooperation between all the units of the
army, as it must maintain contact and provide mutual support
through difficult terrain – terrain that precisely tests unit integrity:
river crossings, heights, essential passes. The best illustration of this
mutual defence and cooperation comes during the march through

the mountainous territory of the Carduchi: with Chirisophus in charge of the vanguard and Xenophon in charge of the rear, the two continually thwart attempts by the enemy to outmanoeuvre and destroy the forward or rearmost units by swift, cooperative counter-marches, leading Xenophon to observe, 'and thus always they were helping one another and very carefully looked after one another' (4.2.26). In this second phase of the evolution of the Ten Thousand, the unity of the army reaches a high point, largely because there is universal recognition that unity is tantamount to survival. The concept was certainly not new: in the *Iliad*, Agamemnon is made to observe that the majority of men who look after one another survive; cowards do not (*Il.* 5.531).[36]

Another major difference between phases one and two, and one that is most important for my discussion, is an increasing focus on the leaders of the army and the almost total disappearance of the regular soldiers: while we see general assemblies of the army in Books 1 and 5–7, there is only one reported in 3–4, the one in 3.2 at which Xenophon delivers his inspirational speech.[37] And while there may not have been any more meetings for Xenophon to report, as the next part of the march required decisive action and not deliberation, nonetheless this fact does not explain the absence of common soldiers in other contexts. The leaders of the Ten Thousand, and Xenophon in particular, are not only prominent in this portion of the *Anabasis*, they dominate the action of the narra-tive. Indeed, in one of the very earliest examples we possess, and possibly for the first time in Greek historiography, the presentation of the individual and his activities are the primary means by which the historian communicates information about the past. One may quibble, noting the portraits of individuals in Thucydides especially; but even the cameo appearances of Pausanias and Themistocles do not constitute a continuous mode of presentation for Thucydides; rather they are digressions from a narrative more interested in what *states* do.[38] By contrast, even military matters are presented subjec-tively in the *Anabasis*.[39] The domination of leader-figures is espe-cially true of the actions reported in Books 3–4, where we enter the world of the individual officer, and in particular the world of Xenophon the Commander.

The obituaries of Cyrus (1.9.1–31) and the captured generals (2.6.1–30) provide early clues that the *Anabasis* is a historical work built around the characters of individuals.[40] In providing such passages, Xenophon may have looked more to popular literary models than the examples provided by the still very young discipline of historical writing; some have even suggested that the nearest parallel for the portraits of the generals and their contrasting traits is Euripides' *Suppliants* (860ff.).[41] Be that as it may, when we turn to the events of phase two of the Ten Thousand, we enter the world of the individual who shapes history.

We sense this nowhere more forcefully than the point when, having detailed the despair in the army after the loss of the generals, Xenophon introduces himself into the narrative with an elaborate story-teller formula akin to our 'once upon a time there was a . . .' (see below, p. 229): 'there was in the army a certain Athenian, Xenophon, who went on the expedition neither as a general nor a captain nor a soldier; rather Proxenus, his old guest-friend, sent for him from home' (3.1.4). This introduction is remarkable in two ways. First, because Xenophon had included himself in the narrative before this elaborate entrance: he was the one who provided Cyrus with the password 'Zeus Soter and Victory' before the battle of Cunaxa (1.8.15–16; cf. above, n.34). Second, the introduction prepares the way for the lengthy explanation of Xenophon's presence in the army of Cyrus, a passage which is almost without parallel in the *Anabasis* in terms of the detail it provides (only his account of life at Scillus and the obituaries of the generals approach it; the obituary of Cyrus is longer). The story concerns, of course, Xenophon's meeting with Socrates, his consultation of Delphi and his eventual decision to join up with Proxenus and the other Cyreans (see below, p. 182). The account is found where it is because Xenophon wants to suggest that his decision to go on the campaign with Cyrus was a momentous one, not just for himself, but, as events would soon prove, for the army as well. The importance of the individual agent in relation to the affairs of the greater community, here the Ten Thousand, is unmistakable. The story-teller introduction functions, as it does elsewhere in Xenophon, to suggest the fortuitous nature of a moment of great historical importance, since the modest, inconspicuous manner of introducing the subject has the effect of drawing notice to it.[42]

Xenophon follows up the story of his decision to go on the expedition with yet another passage which suggests that he considers his own role crucial to the survival of the Ten Thousand: he reports that during the crisis of morale he went to sleep and had a dream that his father's house was struck by a thunderbolt and completely illuminated (3.1.11). The very fact that he reports his dream shortly before he takes on great responsibility and before the army begins its march back to safety confers great significance on Xenophon himself and on the events which follow. In the first place, as with Agamemnon's dream in the *Iliad*, portentous dreams do not come to anyone, but only to the most important (cf. Nestor's words, *Il.* 2.76–83).[43] Second, as in the *Iliad*, the reporting of the dream functions as a signpost, signalling that a major turning point in the course of the narrative is coming up.[44] And in fact, Xenophon heightens the importance of his dream by creating a sense of uncertainty about its predictive powers; he comments that at the time he was uncertain whether to interpret the dream as a positive or negative communication from the divine, and he adds: 'what sort of thing it is to see such a dream is possible to determine from the things that happened after it' (3.1.13).

As if reporting his dream did not highlight his role enough, Xenophon continues to focus our attention on his thoughts during the crisis. He reports that after waking from his dream he came to his senses and exhorted himself to action, beginning with the words *ti katakeimai* – 'why am I sitting idle' (3.1.13) – perhaps an adaptation from the language of military exhortation represented best by poets such as Callinus and Tyrtaeus.[45] Following the exhortation he gives to himself, he summons the captains of Proxenus' contingent and stirs them to action. At his suggestion (3.1.24) they call together the officers from the rest of the army (3.1.32), whom Xenophon also inspires; he also recommends that they call a general meeting of the troops to encourage the rank and file soldiers to fight on (3.1.39); the troops gather at an assembly (3.2.1), and again Xenophon delivers the key speech (3.2.8ff.). In a sense then, as Xenophon recounts it, his dream set in motion a chain of events that culminates ultimately in the decision of the entire army to fight on, making him the vital initiator of action.[46] In retrospect the question he left open as to the proper interpretation of the dream is answered: the dream foretold good things insofar as it mobilized Xenophon, and in so doing, the rest of the army.

These passages from the beginning of Book 3 signal that much of the focus of the subsequent narrative will be on the actions and decisions of Xenophon. However, while they suggest that Xenophon will be the principal initiator of action they ought not to obscure other indications early in the book that it will be the individual officer, not always Xenophon himself, who will figure most prominently. Indeed, the very fact that much of the command structure of the army had been destroyed, and that consequently there was an acute need for new leaders to step forward, allows Xenophon to draw special attention to individuals and away from the army as a whole.

In his speech to the surviving officers mentioned above, Xenophon articulates the decisive role the commanders and their subordinates are to play in the march through enemy territory. The speech also explains why Xenophon will place so much emphasis on the officers in this portion of the narrative. In the first place he tells them that the soldiers look to them for morale: 'if they see you down-hearted, all will become cowardly, but if you are clearly making preparations against the enemy and exhorting the rest, you know well that they will follow you *and try to imitate* you' (3.1.36). The officers are models who set the standards of behaviour for the rest of the army: this thought is not a particularly original one, and similar statements can be found elsewhere in Xenophon's corpus (see, e.g., *Cyr.* 3.3.53).[47] The next sentence, however, is crucial to an understanding of his perception of the officer in Books 3 and 4 of the *Anabasis*:

> But, you know, it is probably also appropriate that you some-what surpass [the average soldier]. For you are generals, you colonels and captains: when there was peace, you had the advantage over them in money and honours; and now when there is war it is right that you reckon yourselves to be better than the mass and that you do the planning for them and toil in their place, whenever that is necessary.
>
> (3.1.37)

There is little that separates the thinking of this passage from the exhortation of Sarpedon to Glaucus in the press of battle in the *Iliad* (12.310–321): you, as the social superiors of the common soldiers, must take on responsibilities proportionate to the advantages you enjoy; indeed, you must think for them and, if necessary, act for them. This being Xenophon's understanding of the proper function of the officer corps, it is no wonder that in this phase of the army's evolution, when circumstances force important decisions at lower levels in the chain of command, he views the actions of the Ten Thousand primarily as the actions of its officers, the individual unit commanders. As he goes on to say, the leaders of any enterprise are the ones who make it worth anything, and this applies to military matters especially (3.1.38; see above, p. 28): 'good order seems to provide safety while disorder has already destroyed many'. In particular, he expects that the officers will be able to change the very character of the army, converting the men from an attitude of 'what will they suffer next' to one of 'what will they do next' (3.1.41). Xenophon clearly attributes the will to act to the officer corps, for without them the army would, in his eyes, remain stranded after the capture of the generals and eventually be destroyed (cf. 3.1.13).

Throughout the narrative of Book 4, Xenophon stresses the value of individual officers, particularly in the detachment Xenophon was commanding:[48] officers volunteer for special duty (e.g. 4.1.27–28, 4.6.20), their deaths are carefully recorded (e.g. 4.2.7, 4.7.13–14) and their bravery is noticed (e.g. 4.2.21).[49] Most of all, though, we sense the progress of the army through Books 3 and 4 by means of individual acts of heroism or decision-making that punctuate the march. Often, of course, the episodes of decision-making involve only Xenophon and Chirisophus or Xenophon and a group of officers; the army for its part seems to become secondary (note above, p. 71, where the complicated movement of troops becomes simply the movement of 'Chirisophus' and 'Xenophon' (4.2.26)).[50] But a very good illustration of how the activities of other individual officers either stand in for or take the place of the activities of the army can be found at 4.7.8ff. Just days away from sighting the Black Sea, the army gets held up by a mountain tribe, the Taochi, who have fortified their village and occupied the neighbouring heights from which they roll down stones onto any Greek who approaches. At this juncture, Xenophon tells us, one Callimachus of Parrhasia 'devised a plan':

> he ran out two or three steps from the tree under which he was hiding; whenever the stones came down, he would quickly run back . At each of his sorties out more than ten wagon loads of stones were used up. But Agasias, when he saw that the entire army was observing what Callimachus was doing, and fearing that he would not be the first to run across to the place, without summoning his comrades Aristonymus (who was close by) or Eurylochus the Lusian nor indeed anyone else, he dashed out and passed everyone. Callimachus, when he saw him run by, took hold of the edge of his shield; at this point Aristonymus the Methydrian ran past them and after him Eurylochus the Lusian: for they were all trying to lay claim to military excellence and used to vie with one another. Thus in their rivalry they seized the village.

> (4.7.10–12)

What is remarkable about this passage is the degree of detail, the focus on the rivalry of the men involved (cf. 5.2.11) and especially the fact that all of this activity not only wins fame for the officers but also contributes directly to an accomplishment of major importance for the whole army. The report of individual as opposed to collective action does not form an excursus from the main narrative; it constitutes the main narrative. It is individual heroism, not the achievement of the army, that is the stuff of Xenophon's account.[51] The reconstructions of Ephorus' narrative provide little scope for the notice of personal achievements outside of the brief biographies which probably accompanied the first appearance of important individuals in his account.[52] We must turn to the fragments of Theopompus, whose *Philippika* was obviously dominated by one individual, and Philistus, who evidently had provided many scenes of praise and blame (*FGrHist* 556 T 16a), to find anything similar to Xenophon. I should note in passing, however, that heroism is probably not to be found much in Theopompus at least; rather it is villainy (see below, p. 136).[53] To be sure, the prominence which individual officers have in *Anabasis* 3–4 is no doubt due to Xenophon's interest in the qualities of good leadership, but this is only a partial explanation; he is also concerned to represent the Ten Thousand at this point in their march as a quasi-epic army or 'Warrior-band'.[54]

Xenophon's admiration for this phase of the Ten Thousand is not unrelated to the larger issues of utopianism and panhellenism. It is in this portion of the *Anabasis* that we find some of the more overtly panhellenic features already mentioned, such as Xenophon's reference to settlement in Asia (3.2.23ff.) and the barbarians under the lash (3.4.25), as well as others, such as the sack of a satrap's camp (4.4.21; cf. Hdt. 9.82). Undoubtedly panhellenic as well, though simultaneously barbaric, is Xenophon's appeal to his men just before reaching the sea to vanquish the Colchians who were blocking their way: 'men, these people whom you see are alone now in preventing us from getting to where we have struggled to be; these people, if it were somehow possible, we ought to devour raw' (4.8.14) – an exhortation that has a good Homeric pedigree, but which nonetheless represents a startling inversion of Greek and barbarian custom at the very point when the Ten Thousand finally reach the Greek world. But perhaps most important of all the panhellenic passages is the most celebrated scene from the *Anabasis*. When the Greeks finally catch sight of the sea from Mt Theches, they embrace one another; and then the soldiers, without being commanded, erect a massive trophy (4.7.25–26). Over whom specifically did they triumph? This is not at all clear; it had been sixteen days since their last engagement with barbarians (the Chalybes), and in it they had not fared well (4.7.15–21). Indeed, the trophy is best understood as a monument to the Ten Thousand's triumph over all the barbarians they met insofar as it was proven by their successful march to the sea: in a sense the entire campaign is crowned as a panhellenic venture.

Simultaneously, however, the scene on Mt Theches celebrates the unity of the Ten Thousand (perhaps symbolized by the spontaneous embracing), and the success which that unity brought. In a technical sense one cannot call the Ten Thousand at this point a utopia, for it did exist and was not an idealized projection of an alternative society. Nonetheless, there are utopian features which are felt here thanks to Xenophon's nostalgic memorialization. So, for example, he would have us believe that there was complete unanimity in the command and the ranks during this phase of the march, but there are good indications in the *Anabasis* itself that there was not (on the quarrel between Xenophon and Chirisophus, see above, p. 70; note also desertion of post or complaint about duty, 4.2.20, 3.4.47). He will later imply that no serious setbacks occurred on this leg of the march (5.4.16–18, see below, p. 81), and this too is not completely true (3.3.7–10, 4.7.15–16). With the possible exception of one or two instances (4.3.10ff., 4.2.21, but see above, n.49), there are no examples of individual enterprise or bravery on the part of common soldiers, and this seems highly improbable. But a unified, very successful and largely officer-grade army is what Xenophon wants us to see, an army of comrades united as an organic whole and aided by a significant but nonetheless supporting cast of anonymous troops. I do not mean to suggest that Xenophon was entirely conscious of the overall effect of his characterization of the army at this point; rather, the characterization is achieved subtly through a mode of presentation and language that contrasts sharply with other phases of the Ten Thousand.

The Ten Thousand as *polis*: utopia and dissension (*An.* 5–6)

A set of profound changes takes place in the army of the Ten Thousand after they reach the sea and the margins of the Greek world, in each of the major areas I have so far examined: their command structure, their goals, their sense of unity. What is more, whereas Xenophon's own views (insofar as they were represented) largely coincided with the general feelings of the army in the earlier phases, in the third phase they diverge; and in this divergence we are well placed to gain an appreciation of his own unique ideas about panhellenism and ideal community.

The command structure of the Ten Thousand throughout the second phase was very much 'top-down', that is to say the common soldiers had little input in deciding what the army did; decisions had to be made at the command level as each new crisis was encountered. But once the immediate danger of the enemy and the difficult terrain are behind them, the ultimate power of decision gravitates back towards the soldiers where it was in the first phase. In fact, the very first matter that is reported at the start of phase three is a general assembly (Xenophon does not report who called it), held to discuss 'the remainder of the journey' (5.1.2); since 'the soldiers' roar approval at Leon's suggestion that, like Odysseus, they forgo marching and sail home (5.1.3), we can assume that it was a general assembly. Other meetings of the entire army are reported or assumed at 5.4.19, 6.1.25, 6.2.4, 6.4.10, 6.6.11 and 6.6.29,[55] two of which are convened without the approval of the officers (6.1.25 and 6.2.4). The assembly of all the soldiers has the authority to receive foreign dignitaries and to negotiate with cities (5.5.7ff., 6.1.14); further, it can decide to do away with the board of generals and select a supreme commander (6.1.17–19), pass legislation regarding the conduct of individuals and appoint juries to handle breaches of army law (5.7.34), and can delegate persons to convey to others the army's demands (6.2.6). As for the generals and the other officers, they of course retain control in combat situations (e.g. 6.5.1) and act as liaisons between the army and external authorities (6.6.19–20); it seems that any executive decisions that need to be made are taken by the board of generals 'by majority vote' (6.1.18). As a replacement for the board, the post of supreme commander is created, as mentioned above, obviously with considerable powers; nonetheless, the position is thought of as ultimately subordinate to the will of the soldiers whose idea it is (6.1.17ff.). Even Xenophon, who is not an official holder of the post (he was the army's first choice but refused the offer), and who wields significant unofficial authority (see esp. 6.5.14ff.), is for all that frequently unsuccessful in seeing his plans carried out (most notably 5.6.19, see below, p. 185). Contributing to the weakness of the supreme command is the fact that the first holder of the post died within days of assuming it (6.2.12). But if the army is ever at a loss or in need of guidance, officers do have the power to summon the soldiers to an assembly and urge a certain course of action (6.4.10, 6.6.11). Furthermore, rivalry among the officers for distinction in battle continues (5.2.11). For the most part, however, the officers function in an advisory capacity, akin to a probouleutic council (see esp. 6.1.3–14), and their recommendations are not always followed (5.1.14). In summing up the location of authority in the Ten Thousand in this phase, it might be fair to say that the ultimate power of decision rests with the assembly, although the troops are not always aware of this fact and pay considerable attention to the advice of the officers; at an operational level, and especially in crisis situations, the commanders of the army continue to exercise executive control.

As in phase one, the most pressing short-term goal is the provision of food. It becomes a difficult matter for the Ten Thousand largely because they are often in theoretically friendly territory and cannot plunder (at least not initially), but must rely instead on being given access to markets and on distributions of food by neighbouring cities. At Cotyora they are forced to pillage both the land of the Paphlagonians and the people of the city because they were not given the chance to buy food (5.5.6), an action which Xenophon defends by noting that friendship and hostility was determined for the Ten Thousand by whether they were offered the chance of acquiring food, not by nationality (Greek or barbarian, 5.5.14–16). However, even if a city does provide food it is no guarantee that the army will not become hostile: although Heraclea sends the army a gift of grain, wine, oxen and sheep (6.2.3; cf. 6.5.1), the troops nonetheless become belligerent and demand exorbitant sums from the city (6.2.4ff.), theoretically to cover the costs of further provisioning (although see below, p. 88). Despite their efforts at plundering (which are frequently unsuccessful: see esp. 5.2.13ff., 6.4.24ff.), as well as at more peaceful ways of acquiring food, the Ten Thousand do experience severe shortages (see esp. 6.4.22 and 25 where they have to sacrifice draught animals, having run short of sheep).

The Ten Thousand seem to have only two long term-goals in phase three: personal profit and return to Greece. Importantly, safety from the enemy or from the natural perils of the march is no longer a major concern. In a sense, then, the army returns to the basic objectives of phase one. Xenophon himself provides the clearest information regarding the shifting hopes of the soldiers after they reach the southern coast of the Black Sea. At 6.4.8 he explains why they refuse to go near the beautiful Port Calpe peninsula, fearing that they would be settled there:

> for most of the soldiers had sailed out for this service not out of want but because they heard about Cyrus' excellence, some even bringing men, others spending money, and others still who had run away from their parents, and some who had left behind children, so that having accumulated wealth for them they might return again, hearing also that the others in Cyrus' company were doing very well indeed. Being such men they were desiring to return safe (*soizesthai*) to Greece.
>
> (6.4.8)

While this passage refers only to those who had come from Greece, we can attribute the same motives to those who were already in Cyrus' company; after all, they seemed to be profiting handsomely from service with Cyrus and were in all likelihood drawn to him precisely because they expected opportunities for enrichment.[56] The portrait of the average soldier was no doubt in part designed to counter the claims, such as those found in Isocrates' *Panegyricus* (146), that the Ten Thousand were desperate brigands in search of booty (see above, p. 57).[57] But even allowing for some anxiety on Xenophon's part to characterize the men of the Ten Thousand as solid citizens, it is clear that making money from the campaign was a chief interest of the soldiers, and that this goal was combined with returning safely to Greece. This connection becomes even clearer when the troops decide to appoint a supreme commander who would make the acquisition of plunder easier: as Xenophon explains, 'since they thought they were near Greece, even more than before it came into their heads how they might acquire something and return home' (6.1.17). In the event, as Xenophon himself knew well, very few of the Ten Thousand later showed any particular zeal to get home to Greece. Many stayed on in Asia until 395.[58] While he allows for the Greeks to have had thoughts of plunder before, Xenophon seems to be suggesting that the very prospect of return to Greece brings with it a desire on the part of the soldiers for quick material gain. Greece and greed are somehow connected. Xenophon presents Timasion the Dardanian as an ardent and vocal supporter of return to Greece and nothing else (even though he was not from the mainland but from the Troad). While he says to the troops, 'it is not right to think about remaining, men, nor to consider anything more important than Greece' (5.6.22), we know that he was bribed to say this by Greeks from Sinope and Heraclea who were eager to see the Ten Thousand leave their territory.[59]

The Ten Thousand's interest in plunder would not by itself be all that remarkable – after all, they were similarly motivated in phase one – were it not the case that invariably in this portion of the *Anabasis* interest in gain is associated with insubordination and action taken independently from the rest of the army. Xenophon himself anticipates this crucial theme of phase three in his speech to the troops at the beginning of Book 5. After the departure of Chirisophus to arrange the transport of the Ten Thousand by sea, Xenophon, having dealt with the issue of taking precautions during foraging (*ta epitedeia porizesthai*, 5.1.6), turns to the problem of plundering (a separate enterprise, *epi leian ekporeuesthai*, 5.1.8). His advice is simple: 'I think that it is best that anyone about to venture out speak to us [the commanders] and report where he is going' (5.1.8). Despite this advice, there are numerous unauthorized plundering forays in phase three and they all end in disaster. The first one Xenophon reports is instructive. At 5.4.16ff. he tells of the story of a group of Greeks who accompany friendly barbarians in a raid on some nearby villages. He goes out of his way to state that 'they had not been ordered by the generals but [went] for the sake of robbery'. The mission fails; several Greeks are killed, their bodies are mutilated by angry villagers and the survivors flee back to the Greek camp. Noting that the Ten Thousand took it badly that the fool-hardy mission both emboldened their enemy and involved the flight of Greek troops even though they were very numerous, Xenophon pauses to provide a telling detail: referring to the retreat of the troops he says, 'this [the Greeks] had never done on the expedition' (5.4.18). He singles out this raid as the first instance where men from the Ten Thousand were forced to retreat despite appearing in strong numbers: while previous raids had on occasion been almost as unsuccessful, though admittedly without mutilation (cf. the attack on the Drilae in 5.2), this incident is set aside for special censure because the Greeks were defeated, and more importantly, they were defeated because they were insubordinate and allowed their greed to dictate their actions.

Even more helpful for illustrating the perils of greed and independent plundering is the example Xenophon makes later in another speech of the actions of one Clearatus, a captain or *lochagos* (5.7.14ff.):

> Clearatus the captain, having discovered that [the place] was small and unguarded because [the villagers] considered themselves to be our friends, marched out against them during the night in order to sack it, even though he had spoken to no one of us [the commanders]. He had planned that if he took this place he would not return to the army, but get on board a ship on which there happened to be comrades of his sailing by, and having in mind that if he got possession of something, he would sail away from the Pontus. And his comrades from the ship agreed to these things with him, as I now know. Then having summoned as many as he managed to persuade, he led them to the place. But on his way there it became daylight, and the villagers gathered from their fortified positions, shot at them and struck them down, killing Clearatus and many of the rest, but some of them did flee back to Cerasus.
>
> (5.7.14–16)

A textbook case: greed leads to an unauthorized raid on a friendly village which turns into a disaster when the natives repel the attack and kill several of the Greeks. Indeed, Xenophon uses this and a subsequent episode involving the unauthorized and shameful murder of ambassadors from the same village (5.7.17ff.) to make the point that independent action is not only dangerous for those who undertake it, it is also dangerous ultimately for the army as a whole. If matters go on the way they are, he claims, and individuals continue to chase away and kill ambassadors and launch raids on their own for the sake of plunder, then the army will lose its authority to make war and peace with whomever it desires (5.7.27). And as Xenophon presents it, the consequences of that situation, where there is essentially no authority at all, are very grim indeed: denouncing lawlessness and the forces which erode community life, he declares,

> if this situation is a good one, then let it gain your approval so that, with things being in such a state [of anarchy], a person may provide for protection on his own and try, while holding on to deserted higher ground, to pitch his own tent. But if such actions seem to belong to wild animals and not to human beings, consider a way to stop them.
>
> (5.7.31–32)

Anarchy means for Xenophon the complete dissolution of the Ten Thousand and the subsequent descent into bestial life for everyone in the army. Hence the consequences of greed that lead to independent action and the challenging of authority are not trivial but concern the very identity of the Ten Thousand as Greeks; it is a commonplace in Greek ethnographic ideology for them to be contrasted with men who live like beasts (cf. the Libyan tribes in Herodotus who live in the area populated by wild beasts, 4.174ff.). In fact just such a people, the Mossynoeci, were encountered by the Ten Thousand shortly before Xenophon's speech, 'the most barbarous people' the Greeks encountered on their march (the only ones of such savagery reported in the *Anabasis*), in large part because they confused public and private actions (5.4.34).[60]

The view of panhellenism (or rather 'hellenism') which we get in these passages is very different from the one we get, for instance, in Isocrates and which shows up in the *Anabasis* in other places (see above, pp. 59–63). Unity is truly panhellenic; it is the urge to plunder and then return home, conventional panhellenic goals which in Xenophon's eyes have 'anti-hellenic' or at least 'un-hellenic' consequences. And in fact earlier in Book 5, when he was trying to make an example of the failed and unauthorized attack on the Mossynoeci (see above, p. 81), he encourages the troops to show to the friendly barbarians that they are better, and to the hostile ones that they will not be fighting against undisciplined soldiers (*ataktois*), as they did before (5.4.21); in other words, obeying one's orders and staying at one's post – that is, not splitting off but rather remaining together – will separate Greek from barbarian. Unity and being Greek are again connected.

I have anticipated somewhat my discussion of Xenophon's thoughts during this period and how they contrast with the majority of the Ten Thousand. While the army was primarily interested in returning to Greece and in personal gain, Xenophon was committed to maintaining the unity of the Ten Thousand above all else; this is of course entirely consistent with his views throughout the *Anabasis* – as far back as 3.2.32 he had insisted on a 'common salvation' for the Ten Thousand (see above, p. 70). As I have already noted, at the very beginning of Book 5 he advocates the maintenance of the command structure and the unit cohesion of the Ten Thousand (5.1.5ff.). Time and again in phase three he tries to convince the army that staying together is the goal which subsumes all others.

No section of the *Anabasis* better illustrates Xenophon's understanding of the significance of unity in contrast to the rest of the army than 5.6. The chapter begins with an ambassador from Sinope, Hecatonymus, speaking before a meeting of the army. He states that it would be impossible for the Ten Thousand to go by land through Paphlagonia, owing both to the natural barriers of the area and the people who live there; he recommends instead that they sail along the coast from Cotyora to Sinope and thence to Heraclea (5.6.3–10). Though suspicious, the soldiers agree with Hecatonymus and decide to travel by sea (5.6.11). But before the meeting breaks up and the embassy returns to Sinope, Xenophon adds some cautionary words:

> O men of Sinope, the soldiers have chosen the way which you recommend. The matter stands as follows: if there will be enough boats so that not a single man is left here, then we will sail; if, however, some of us will be left behind and others will sail, we will not get on board the ships. For we know that wherever we have power we are able both to save ourselves (*soizesthai*) and to acquire provisions; but if we are caught being weaker than our enemy, it is perfectly clear that we will be in the place of slaves.
>
> (5.6.12–13)

This passage contains a number of significant points arranged in priority of importance. In the first place, it is clear that unity is more important for Xenophon than return, for if the entire army is not embarked on the ships then he feels the whole enterprise should be called off. Second, and related to the first point, he puts the highest value on the Ten Thousand remaining unified as a fighting force. He first implies hyperbolically that with one man left behind, the effectiveness of the army will in some way be compromised, and he argues that the ability to exercise power independently of other authorities is the key to the Greeks' survival; with that ability diminished, he asserts, the Ten Thousand might as well be slaves – yet another way of saying 'non-Greek', insofar as being a slave, like being a savage, entailed for them the negation of their identity as Greeks.[61] To recap, then, in Xenophon's eyes for the Ten Thousand to remain free and consequently Greek was contingent on being able to defend themselves, and having the power to defend themselves was contingent on remaining unified. From his point of view the lure of returning home, particularly without being careful about the way that would be achieved, was paradoxically one of the greatest threats to the unity of the Ten Thousand.

It is in the context of this line of thinking that we must approach Xenophon's utopian vision that immediately follows the dismissal of the Sinopian embassy. I quoted the passage at the beginning of chapter 2 (see p. 41) and will repeat it again here:

> at this time, as Xenophon saw the many hoplites of the Greeks, as he saw the many peltasts, bowmen, slingers and cavalry, and all made expertly capable through experience, as he saw them there on the shore of the Black Sea where so great a military force could not have been put together without considerable expense, it seemed to him to be a good idea to add land and power to Hellas by means of the soldiers founding a city. And it seemed to him that it would be a great city when he reckoned up the number of soldiers themselves as well as those who dwelt around the sea.

> (5.6.15–16)

Xenophon tells us that after this vision, without having spoken to any of the soldiers and with only the prophet (*mantis*) Silanus in attendance, he 'sacrificed with a view towards obtaining these things' (5.6.16).[62] We learn then that Silanus, out of a desire to return as quickly as possible to Greece with the considerable sum of 3,000 darics which Cyrus had given him (see 1.7.18), told the troops that Xenophon wanted to found a city there on the Black Sea and create for himself a name and power. When they find out about Xenophon's plans, some favour them but most do not (5.6.17–18). To make matters more difficult for Xenophon, two more unscrupulous officers, Timasion of Dardanus and Thorax of Boeotia, inform certain merchants from Heraclea and Sinope who happen to be in camp of Xenophon's plan; although they make demands for pay in the interests of the whole army they are sure to gain privately if the extortion works (5.6.19; cf. 5.6.21).[63] They claim that Xenophon is urging the men to settle wherever they wish in the surrounding territory, or, if they prefer, to sail home (5.6.20).

The two lines of inquiry with which I started this chapter meet in this passage: panhellenism and utopia. Xenophon himself describes the plan as being of advantage to the whole of the Greek world: 'it seemed to be a good idea to add land and power to Greece by means of the soldiers founding a city'. Furthermore, it involves the establishment not just of anyone but specifically the soldiers of the Ten Thousand, that is to say mercenaries, in a permanent settlement; it is very important that Xenophon is made to seem the founder or *oikistes* of a colony through the sacrifice he offers,[64] for it aligns this passage with the views of those best represented by Isocrates who argued that complete panhellenic victory entailed not just the defeat of the Persians but also the colonization of their land by Greek mercenaries (note above, Isocrates *Phil.* 120–121, p. 57).[65]

The utopian aspects of this passage, while perhaps a little less obvious, are more important for the present study than the panhellenic, insofar as they connect directly to attitudes that are central to Xenophon's own way of thinking. This utopian vision, while it concerns the foundation of a city, is essentially military in conception. Indeed, the idea comes to him when he takes note of two things about the army: first, its location on the coast of the Black Sea where it was otherwise difficult and costly to assemble a fighting force; and second, the quality of the army in terms of preparedness earned through hard experience. The very fact that Xenophon's imagining of a city is inspired by military realities is itself significant for, as I have suggested elsewhere (p. 33), much of his thinking about the ideals of human organization and achievement derives from his experience as a soldier. It has been argued that from the beginning of the fourth century the influence of military matters on social and civic thinking increases dramatically, putting Xenophon squarely at the beginning of that tendency.[66]

Xenophon's notice of the quality of the army suggests a line of interpretation that will help us understand his purpose in including the account of his plan to found a city. He noticed similar virtues a few years later in a Spartan army encamped at Ephesus in the spring of 396, and, fortunately for us, he made the reasons for his admiration clear in his description of it (*Hell.* 3.4.16–18 = *Ages.* 1.25–27; see below, p. 113). Xenophon singles out for praise the fact that the soldiers are drilling in their separate units – the hoplites, cavalry, peltasts and archers;[67] further, he marvels at the material preparedness of the army, noting that the entire city had become a 'workshop of war', devoting its energies to producing the equipment the troops required; he even confesses that the sight of King Agesilaus leading the men in a religious procession from the gymnasia to the great temple of Artemis would produce stirring emotions in the observer (I think we are meant to understand Xenophon himself). Indeed, as he explains, 'where men worship the gods, practise the arts of war and study obedience, how is it not likely that everything there is full of good hope?' (*Hell.* 3.4.18). Polybius read this passage and remembered it.[68] Evidently what impressed him about it, and what he used in his own description of New Carthage as another 'workshop of war', were both the material preparation of the troops under Scipio and the fact that each unit was training in its own place (Plb. 10.20.7). It is precisely a sense of preparedness and operational distinctness which we get at *Anabasis* 5.6.15 – the troops are trained, not by drill masters but by experience, and they are divided up into their various unit types. The army at Cotyora was also a 'workshop of war', a finely tuned collectivity or organic unity.

However, in two ways the Ten Thousand were not like the Spartan army encamped at Ephesus. They showed no particular piety – it was Xenophon who performed the sacrifice to determine whether the Greeks should stay and later actually had to defend having done this before the troops knew what was going on (5.6.28ff.). Nor were they cultivating a strong sense of obedience or discipline; indeed, they were becoming increasingly less disciplined. What Xenophon saw in the army near Cotyora was the potential for greatness as a city. In the difference between what he hoped for and what really happened we can see him make perhaps the most important point of the *Anabasis*.

Earlier, Xenophon had spoken of the dangers of settlement in Asia; he feared that the Greeks would be seduced by the good living of the East and consequently lose their Greekness (3.2.25; see above, p. 62: even if the reference to 'Lotus-eaters' is meant to be 'witty' or 'joking', that does not diminish the implied threat).[69] Essentially, earlier in the march, founding a city in Asia meant not returning to Greece. What is the necessary consequence of founding a city at this point in the history of the Ten Thousand? Modern studies of utopias suggest a useful line of approach: no utopia can be fully understood without pairing it with its 'contradiction', drawn from what is perceived as the 'real world', the 'opposition' that the utopia is meant to 'neutralize' by showing what happens when it is inverted.[70] Xenophon imagined founding a city on the coast of the Black Sea as a response to forces he felt were bringing about the destruction of the Ten Thousand.

The forces Xenophon saw at work in the Ten Thousand were greed, a growing propensity towards independent action and eventually ethnic divisiveness. The regrettable incident involving the Mossynoeci has already been discussed (p. 81); so too the story of Clearatus, which comes immediately after the account of Xenophon's vision of the city and the soldiers' reaction to it. As I have noted, both episodes stress how greed drives the men to act without authorization and independently from the rest of the army, and that in so doing they bring danger to themselves and the army as a whole. And, of course, in the account of the vision itself, personal greed scuttles the plan – or rather it is characterized as the chief reason for its failure: while we know that Silanus on the one hand and Timasion and Thorax on the other are acting out of a desire to secure gain only for themselves, we see them cruelly pervert Xenophon's words and attribute to him personal ambition in wanting to found a city. But as the episode of the raid on the Mossynoeci suggested, the lure of gain attracts not only unscrupulous individuals. The soldiers in the ranks are also driven by greed.

As I have already mentioned, interest in material gain encourages the soldiers to change the command structure of the Ten Thousand, from a board of generals to a supreme commander. Finally, and most importantly for this discussion, troublemakers among the Achaeans and Arcadians – especially two, Callimachus and Lycon, men who had been singled out for their heroism before – manage to convince the soldiers to try to extort ten thousand Cyzicene staters from the city of Heraclea and to appoint Chirisophus and Xenophon to act as envoys to deliver their ultimatum. When the two commanders refuse, the soldiers send out Callimachus, Lycon and one other (Agasias) to convey their demands, a move which has the effect of putting Heraclea on the alert. When confronted by the determined resistance of the Heracleots, the troublemakers blame Chirisophus and Xenophon for the city's reaction and encourage the Arcadian and Achaean troops in the army to split off from the rest. Citing their reluctance to serve either under a Spartan or an Athenian, and arguing that although they constituted more than half the army they felt that they were not sufficiently rewarded, the ringleaders urge the Arcadians and Achaeans to leave their units and band together to try to secure some gain for themselves. This the soldiers do, and the army is broken into three parts. The newly formed Arcadian and Achaean force immediately turns to plundering the region around Port Calpe and is surrounded by hostile Thracian tribesmen; at the head of one of the other two divisions, Xenophon rescues them and marches back to Port Calpe where the remaining third element of the original force is also encamped.

As the site of the reunification after the disastrous experiment of splitting up into three separate units, Port Calpe is extremely important in Xenophon's narrative. Here many of the internal tensions and contradictory goals of the Ten Thousand converge and are seen with great clarity. On the one hand, as if acknowledging their earlier folly in agitating for the division of the army, the senior Arcadian commanders succeed in convincing the whole army to pass a resolution forbidding anyone even to mention breaking up the unity of the army under penalty of death (6.4.11) – a motion similar to one they had passed earlier on Xenophon's advice (5.6.33). But despite this resolution, no more than a few days later two thousand men go out to forage in nearby villages with the authorization of the new supreme commander, Neon of Asine. While they are spread out gathering supplies, they are attacked by the cavalry of Pharnabazus, and five hundred are lost (6.4.23–26).

In addition to the persistent problem regarding unity and division, the tension between return and settlement also surfaces at Port Calpe. While the soldiers cannot wait to continue their journey home (6.4.8; see above, p. 80), and only with great reluctance abide by the negative portents warning them to stay put for a while (6.4.16 and 20), Xenophon has yet another vision of founding a city and converting the Ten Thousand into a *polis*. While he does not explicitly state that he wished to settle the army on the Calpe peninsula, he reports rumours to the effect that he was forming such a plan (6.4.14; cf. 6.4.7 and 6.6.3-4), and more importantly he describes the site in unmistakably utopian terms, leaving little doubt that these rumours were correct;[71] indeed at one point, in his voice as narrator, he observes that the peninsula 'was suitable for settling ten thousand men' (6.4.3)![72]

The Cotyora and Port Calpe episodes come before and after the gravest internal crisis of the Ten Thousand – the break-up of the army and the departure of over half its original strength (cf. 6.2.10). The Cotyora vision in a sense anticipated the troubles which followed, for it is presented as Xenophon's response to precisely those destructive forces which eventually led to the mutiny of the Achaeans and Arcadians. In the language of utopian analysis, the vision created unity and discipline where in fact those qualities were absent. What, then, can we conclude from the episode at Port Calpe? The suggestion of another utopian plan to found a city, together with the soldiers' insistence that the army do nothing else but make its way home, demonstrates that the forces which brought about the break-up of the army are still very much around, even though measures have been taken to counter them. That the army is really no closer to understanding that it is unity, not return, which should be its chief goal, is proven by the unfortunate foraging expedition authorized by Neon. Although the Greeks do take their revenge on their enemy (6.5.25–32), the army is only temporarily repaired.

This suspicion is confirmed at the end of phase three when the army is almost declared outlaw by the Spartan Cleander (6.6.9). While Xenophon makes it clear that the riot of the army which gets them into trouble is really the result of justified anger at the scoundrel Dexippus (6.6.5; cf. 5.1.15), he also emphasizes that the army is dangerously susceptible to sudden and ill-timed spasms of violence. When we see the Spartan commander eventually come to terms with the Ten Thousand, following the Dexippus affair, and actually promise to lead them back to Greece (6.6.34), we know better than to expect these good feelings to last and the promises to be kept.

Indeed, it comes as no surprise that in phase three, when the unity of the army begins to fracture, we see not only the two utopian visions of Cotyora and Port Calpe, but also Xenophon's nostalgic description of his estate at Scillus (5.3.7–13). Ostensibly an explanation of how he continued to honour the memory of Artemis of Ephesus, the vignette, which details Xenophon's life long after returning to Greece as a country squire living on a farm near Olympia, seems oddly placed and insufficiently motivated by the narrative. But perhaps the quiet and ordered life we see in this bucolic description is a capsule or miniature of the life he had hoped to lead as a prominent settler leader in Asia. Scillus, like Cotyora and Port Calpe, is described in glowing terms – a place blessed by nature. And although this spot was settled by Xenophon, it too ultimately became a lost vision.

The end of the Ten Thousand (*An.* 7)

The final phase of the Ten Thousand is relatively simple to outline. The army becomes precisely the sort of dangerous band of marauders that so frightened men like Isocrates and Aeneas Tacticus. As Xenophon presents it, this happens as the command structure of the army continues to change and the same tensions that were present in the previous phase become even more apparent: executive power gravitates away from a board of generals and towards one supreme commander (Xenophon), but this authority rests precariously on the consensus of the army which can at times become controlled by the whims of mob rule. Indeed, at one point they riot and threaten to sack the city of Byzantium (7.1.15ff.). While return home and pay do come up as topics, the need for a secure supply of provisions pushes other concerns into the background; it even determines where the army marches (7.3.5–6). Thus when they vote to join up with Seuthes, the Thracian chieftain, it is the offer of provisions which attracts them, and the possibility of pay is thought of as a *heurema* or unexpected windfall (7.3.13).

Phase four marks the end of the Ten Thousand, as they lose their ability to act independently and eventually become absorbed by the Spartan army operating in Asia (7.8.24). Even before the soldiers become part of the army under Thibron, they spend a fair amount of time in the service of Seuthes. But even more telling for signalling the end of the Ten Thousand than their enlistment in the armies of Seuthes and the Spartans, is the actual break-up of the army. As individual commanders form different plans as to what should be done next, and itinerant *condottieri* woo the soldiers with promises of riches (Coeratidas, 7.1.33), some men sell their weapons and sail away or 'mingle into the cities' (7.2.3), while others find themselves separated from the army because of illness and are actually sold into slavery (400 altogether, 7.2.6) – the very thing Xenophon had warned against earlier. Departures on an individual basis, as well as *en masse* (800 under Neon, 7.2.11), together with misfortunes such as sale into bondage, reduce the army's strength to about 6,000 men by the conclusion of the *Anabasis* (7.7.23). As a final irony, the army that had crossed over to Europe to serve with Seuthes sails back to Asia, even though it had struggled for so long to return home, and Xenophon who had long advocated maintaining the unity of the Ten Thousand leaves the army twice (7.1.40, 7.8.11), the second time to secure for himself a small fortune by kidnapping a Persian nobleman. While it is probably asking too much to believe that Xenophon intentionally portrayed himself negatively in this the final scene of the *Anabasis*, one cannot resist noting that the episode represents the very kind of independent action aimed at profit that he earlier so often deplored.[73]

Anabasis: conclusions

The *Anabasis* is not a day-by-day chronicle of the events surrounding the march of the Ten Thousand. It is unified by an important theme:

the growth and decline of the Ten Thousand as a community. What can Xenophon's purpose have been in writing up his personal history of events that happened about thirty years before? What does the *Anabasis* tell us?

It was not a particularly new idea to think of a large body of soldiers as a city; Xenophon might well have got the idea from reading Thucydides, who in his seventh book has Nicias make the famous observation before the beleaguered Athenian forces, 'for men constitute a city, not walls or ships empty of men' (Thuc. 7.77.7).[74] Or the concept may have been familiar to Xenophon because it was a common and traditional identification (cf. Hdt. 8.61.2). A close parallel to his way of thinking can be found in a paraphrase of the sixth-century poet Alcaeus by Aelius Aristides: 'it is not stones or wood or the art of builders which make up cities, rather, wherever there are men who know how to save themselves, there you will find both walls and cities' (Aristid. *Or.* 46.207 (2.273 Dindorf) = Alcaeus 112 Testimonia (Voigt)).[75] This passage is particularly apt because the defining quality which makes soldiers into a city is the ability to save themselves, precisely the goal which Xenophon stresses over and over in the *Anabasis*. Indeed, he suggests that without the unified effort to secure the safety of all the soldiers in the army, the men will be reduced to barbarity and slavery – something which, in the event, did happen to at least four hundred of the Ten Thousand. Early on in the *Anabasis*, safety for Xenophon seems to mean what it does for most of the men of the army: a safe return home. However, as the soldiers' interest in material gain increases as the army draws closer to the Greek world, his notion of salvation gravitates more towards settlement in Asia and the preservation of the unity of the Ten Thousand.

If we use the unity of the Ten Thousand and their ability to save themselves as a measure of their status as a community, we run into a curious problem. With frequent meetings of the assembly of soldiers, a probouleutic council and executive officers, as well as diplomatic relations with other sovereign states, one might think *a priori* that the period when the army is most like a city is phase three. It is useful to remember at this point that Xenophon was not the only one who saw the Ten Thousand as a mobile *polis* – Isocrates did too (*Arch.* 71ff.). But it is precisely during the third phase when the unity of the army begins to be eroded and its ability to defend itself seriously challenged for the first time, particularly when the men are divided into three separate groups. Xenophon's point may well be that the mobile *polis* which we see in the third phase is a democratically run city in *all* aspects. The army not only looks like a city in terms of its organizational structure; it also reveals the flaws that a conservative man like Xenophon would naturally see in a community dominated by the *demos*, with the common soldiers being led astray on a number of occasions by unscrupulous officers functioning much like 'demagogues' (e.g. Timasion and Thorax, Clearatus, Callimachus, Lycon and Agasias). It is an odd and telling irony that what may be the first clearly negative instance of the term 'demagogue' is found in the *Anabasis*, where it is used by Spartans to describe Xenophon's leadership of the army (7.6.4).[76]

If we cast about the narrative of the *Anabasis* for a community that answers most nearly the description of the *polis* as a collection of men who know how to defend themselves, we are drawn towards phase two of the Ten Thousand. It is during the march north to the Black Sea that the army is most successful and most unified: units come to each other's aid, decisions are made rapidly and the army's progress is constant – the most serious threat comes not from tribesmen but from a snowstorm in the mountains of Armenia. But while it is safe to say that the army at this point looks most like one made up of 'men who know how to save themselves', in another sense it is not *polis*-like at all (and I do not mean necessarily a democratic *polis*). The organizational structure of the army is quite simple, consisting of supreme commanders and almost immediately below them the unit leaders. With one exception the soldiers never meet in assembly, and in fact they do not figure in the narrative very much at all. The army has no diplomatic contact with external authorities except barbarian tribesmen. The salient feature of phase two is the prominence of the army's leaders, beginning with Xenophon, but extending down to the activities of the *lochagoi* or captains. The action of the narrative is driven by their deeds, not those of the army.[77] If an antecedent is sought for the second phase of the Ten Thousand, it is probably best seen in the heroic band of warriors.[78]

Xenophon's greatest loyalty was towards phase two of the Ten Thousand, even though he possessed more power in phases three and four. His preference was for the community of warriors, not the community of citizens – the visions at Cotyora and Port Calpe, both clear reponses to the division which so characterizes phase three, tell us that. If it is true that in the Greek world there was a constant tension between identifying the army as a city and the city as a collection of soldiers,[79] if it is true, furthermore, that any large group of Greek soldiers would invariably organize themselves into a entity which shared significant features with civic life,[80] then I think it is safe to say that Xenophon preferred to see the essentially military nature of community life, not the essentially political structures inherent in all armies.

This conclusion has quite profound implications. When Xenophon wrote up his experiences with the Ten Thousand some thirty years later, after 371 and the loss of his estate at Scillus, he was an exile both from his native land and his adopted home; he probably moved to Corinth where he finished out his days, watching the erosion of Spartan authority as Thebes launched a series of invasions of the Peloponnese which would culminate in the death blow dealt Lacedaemon at Mantinea in 362. Xenophon lived in an 'interstitial' position, a place not limited by the normal boundaries of society, a place where he might have seen deep structures and patterns of living and so formed an understanding of his world that 'transcended' his world.[81] From his recollections, Xenophon came to regard normal *polis*-life as somehow flawed, inherently unstable because of the divisiveness that seemed to come with it. His own experience suggested to him that a looser association of men led by capable and charismatic leaders was much more successful. His proof of this superiority of a quasi-epic 'band of heroes' over the *polis* was panhellenism: the rejoicing on Mt Theches capped a great achievement, the survival of ten thousand Greeks in the savage heartland of the Persian empire. In a paradoxical way it was when the army moved into the fringes of the Greek world that things began to turn sour for them and the conventional panhellenic goals of conquest and safe return combined with greed to destabilize the unity of the Ten Thousand. Isocrates is a useful contrast. His utopia was of an Athens flourishing as she had done in the fifth century; his panhellenism, which entailed the conquest of Persia and the settlement of mercenaries in Asia, was in reality a tool to bring security to his native city. Ultimately, as I tried to suggest above (p. 62), these goals were incompatible. With Xenophon, on the other hand, we see a rare congruence of utopia and panhellenism – an ably led band of warriors operating in the heart of the Achaemenid realm. While Isocrates' panhellenism was oriented around the *polis*, Xenophon's was oriented around the individual.

That in reality the Persians may not have been overly concerned with the Greek mercenaries (see above, p. 61) is not important.

What is important is that Xenophon raised the Ten Thousand to the status of panhellenic champions and ideal society; and, as we shall see, the memory of the Ten Thousand exercised a significant influence over his estimation of later expeditions to Asia, as well as more fundamental notions regarding ideal communities and ideal leaders – the subjects of the next three chapters.

THE BROADER CONTEXT

Before turning to Chapter 4, it is important to look at the *polis* of the *Anabasis* and what it meant to Xenophon, taking advantage in some cases of comparative texts. At the very beginning of their march, when still under the command of Cyrus, the Ten Thousand encounter a number of cities which Xenophon describes as 'inhabited, flourishing and great' (1.2.6–7, 1.2.20; cf. 1.4.1 and 4.7.19). It has for some time been argued that this strange refrain comes from the same geographical tradition that lay behind Herodotus' famous promise to treat cities 'both great and small alike' (Hdt. 1.5.4) in his effort to demonstrate the mutability of human fortune.[82] But while one can certainly see how the collocation of 'flourishing' (*eudaimon*) and 'great' (*megale*) is accounted for by this reference to a relatively common turn of phrase,[83] it does not explain the apparently otiose term 'inhabited' (*oikoumene*). The word is, however, important; indeed, it is enough for Xenophon to describe several cities in the same section of the *Anabasis* as only 'inhabited' (1.2.10–14, five cities altogether). Hence we can conclude that establishing whether a city was 'inhabited' or better 'settled, lived in' was a point worth making in his mind. What does this word add to the traditional pairing of *eudaimon* and *megale*, or in the case of those cities identified simply as *oikoumene*, what does it mean by itself?

In the first place, it is important to note that Xenophon does not use the term exclusively of cities; other forms of human habitation can also qualify as *oikoumene* (villages, 6.4.6). Perhaps more importantly, though, notions of greatness can be attached to cities that are no longer inhabited. During their march north along the eastern bank of the Tigris river, the Ten Thousand came to two impressive and deserted sites, the probable locations of ancient Nimrud and Nineveh (3.4.7–10).[84] It is possible that Xenophon is attempting to add a new component or criterion to the evaluation of cities: before he can pass a complete judgment on a *polis* he must see the inhabitants conducting their day-to-day lives; only then can he say what kind of community it is, having first determined how it is ordered.[85] It is perhaps useful to recall at this point that in his summation of the virtues of the people of Athens, Pericles is made to say 'we inhabit the greatest city' (Thuc. 2.64.3). Similarly Xenophon, while he was more than willing to concede on the basis of the ruins of Assyria's leading cities that they were once powerful, could not make a complete evaluation based on their physical dimensions alone, however imposing they may have been; the many villagers he reports as huddled in the old walls of Nimrud (3.4.9) alert us to the absence of organized civic life, and Xenophon does not even call Nineveh a city, rather a 'fortress' (3.4.10). Perhaps he also had in mind Thucydides' caveat against judging cities by their physical remains (Thuc. 1.10.1).

In this connection it is worth reconsidering Xenophon's utopian vision at Cotyora (5.6.15–16). The number of men in the army, together with the inhabitants of the region, lead him to believe that the city he imagines founding would be a 'great' one (*megale*). About five hundred years after Xenophon wrote the *Anabasis*, Arrian, who considered himself a second Xenophon,[86] adapted the vision at Cotyora in his own account of Alexander the Great's foundation of Alexandria in Egypt:

> and having come to Cenobus, and having sailed down round Lake Mareotis, Alexander disembarked where now the city of Alexandria stands, named after him. And it seemed to him to be an excellent place on which to found a city and that the city would be a flourishing (*eudaimona*) one. Then a yearning for the task seized him and he himself laid out the lines of the city, determining where it was best to build the agora and temples, however many there would be and of whichever gods, both Greek ones and of Egyptian Isis, and he determined where the wall that would encircle the city should stand. And for the accomplishment of these things he held a sacrifice.
>
> (Arrian *An.* 3.1.5)[87]

Whatever Alexander's real motives were in founding Alexandria,[88] it is clear from Arrian's version that it was the attractions of the place that excited him: it is the future buildings and spaces of the city that captivate him. Xenophon also notes the location of Cotyora, but only in terms of its remoteness – a place normally difficult to gather so many Greek soldiers. It is rather the prospect of freezing the Ten

Thousand in time and settling them that really captures Xenophon's imagination. And it is precisely this impulse to preserve the social order and discipline of the Ten Thousand that is related to his interest in settlement and administration (*oikesis*). Although one may object that at Port Calpe the place had obvious attractions for Xenophon, there too it must be remembered that preserving the unity of the Ten Thousand was the primary inspiration for the vision.

A passage from the *Cyropaedia* helps to clarify why precisely Xenophon was interested in the society – the inhabitants – of a city as well as its outward signs of prosperity in evaluating its achievement. At the very beginning of Book 8, the captain Chrysantas extols the virtues of discipline. He addresses Cyrus and his companions and urges them,

> consider what hostile city would be captured by disobedient soldiers, what friendly one would be protected by them; what sort of army made up of insubordinate men would obtain victory; how could soldiers be more prone to defeat in combat than when each begins privately to make plans regarding his own safety; moreover what good would be accomplished by men who do not obey their betters; what sort of cities would be lawfully administered (*oikeseian*) or what houses saved; how would ships reach where they had to go?
>
> (*Cyr.* 8.1.2)

Just as disobedient soldiers are unable to accomplish anything of note without discipline, so a city cannot be administered well if it does not have obedient citizens. Not only does this assertion tell us a great deal about Xenophon's views on the value of obedience (see above, pp. 32–33), it also implies that the character of a *polis'* inhabitants, not its buildings or resources, constitutes the litmus test. This passage from the *Cyropaedia* compares the poorly administered city full of bad citizens with an army composed of men who think only of their own safety. As I have argued above, this situation is precisely the one Xenophon describes in phase three of the Ten Thousand: the army meets with its first serious setbacks and begins to disintegrate when the soldiers think more of their own safety than of that of the entire army. But why then would Xenophon want to freeze the army at this stage and settle them on the Black Sea? Such an establishment or *oikesis* would not presumably create a 'flourishing' or 'great' city, to borrow his own language. As I mentioned above,

I think we should view both the vision at Cotyora and Port Calpe as responses to problems Xenophon perceived in the army. In true utopian fashion, they are yearnings for what was not present.[89]

The quality, number and location of the Ten Thousand inspired Xenophon at Cotyora to want to found a city. What he hoped to achieve by doing so is clear: 'it seemed to him to be a good idea to add land and power to Greece by means of the soldiers founding a city'. Some forty-five years after Xenophon wrote these words, in 325/4 at Athens, a continuous record of naval matters for that year describes a similar plan. The Athenians had voted to send out a colony to the Adriatic under the command of Miltiades of Lakiadai, very probably a descendant of the famous victor at Marathon. In the course of detailing the measures proposed to help expedite the readying of a fleet, the inscription partially preserves the reasons the expedition was sent out:

> in order that there be for the *demos* for all time their own port and grain depot; and, with their own naval base established, that there be a guard against the Tyrrhenians; and in order that Militiades the founder and the colonists be able to make use of their own naval force; and in order that both Greeks and barbarians sailing the sea may also be able to sail into the anchorage of the Athenians, keeping their boats and the rest of their possessions in safety, knowing that . . . [this part of the inscription breaks off]
>
> (Tod 200.217–32; cf. Harding no. 121)

Here surely we have a case of men under the command of a single leader attempting to win control of 'land and power' by establishing a community in a foreign land. But despite the reference to Greeks and barbarians, the Athenians were not motivated by altruistic reasons to establish an outpost in the Adriatic. They had become alarmed the year before that their access to grain supplies had become jeopardized by the depredations of pirates and the potential interference of Alexander;[90] the effort was, in other words, designed to safeguard Athens' interests.[91] This fact should not surprise us; what is interesting, however, is how this plan brings the radical nature of Xenophon's vision at Cotyora into relief. He imagined no one city to be the beneficiary of the new *polis* on the Black Sea, but the whole of Greece. Xenophon's vision transcended the normal boundaries of the *polis*.

4

THE LEGACY OF THE TEN THOUSAND?
Xenophon's vision and the Spartans in Asia

Xenophon's involvement in military adventure in Asia Minor did not come to an end with the final dissolution of the Ten Thousand. Along with many others from the army, he became part of a Spartan effort there that lasted five years (399–395). It would be strange, I think, if he did not think back on his earlier experience with his mercenary comrades while serving in the Spartan army, viewing the second expedition in light of what the first achieved. Indeed, it must have been natural for Xenophon to think back on what contributed to the success of the Ten Thousand and what caused them trouble, and to apply these same lessons to his evaluation of what the Spartans did in Asia Minor. He knew that Greeks could defeat the Persians in battle even when they were heavily outnumbered; he knew furthermore that their worst enemy had not been their opponents but themselves; finally, he believed that Greeks could, under able leadership, even settle new cities in the Persian hinterlands. In what follows I would like to examine briefly Xenophon's treatment of the Spartans in Asia Minor viewed from a panhellenic perspective – not the armchair panhellenism of an Isocrates, but a panhellenism born from the real experience of having served successfully with a band of Greeks drawn from throughout the hellenic world, a heroic army (or so he liked to think of them at their best) that held its own against the Persians and barbarian tribesmen.

Xenophon's account of Agesilaus' expedition to Asia Minor is at first full of hope and promise.[1] The reaction of the Persians[2] and Agesilaus' own statements of his plans[3] suggest that the Spartan king contemplated a march into the heart of the Persian empire. In Xenophon's account, the plan is frustrated by Persian gold distributed among Sparta's enemies (3.5.1–2) who, by threatening an invasion of Laconia, force the Spartans to recall Agesilaus (4.2.1–8).[4] Sparta is made to appear the frustrated champion of hellenic liberty in Asia, the victim of the Great King's gold and his Greek accomplices.

The probability that Xenophon was an eyewitness to the events in Asia, and the apparent pro-Spartan quality of his presentation,[5] have led scholars to doubt seriously his reliability as an historian. Since the consensus of scholarly opinion is that the Spartan presence in Asia was really the result of her imperialist interests rather than her commitment to the protection of the Asiatic Greeks,[6] the nature of his work is explained by his having been blinded by 'panhellenist big talk'.[7] Wilful misrepresentation of the truth is seldom ascribed to him,[8] but his pro-Spartan sympathies are held to be sufficient to produce unwitting distortions of fact.[9] This view would have us believe that there are no serious criticisms of Spartan foreign policy in Asia in *Hellenica* 3 and 4. But, although Xenophon's account is on the whole positive, a number of passages do not fit this popular assessment. Indeed, when Xenophon's narrative of 3 and 4 is set beside his own *Anabasis* and *Agesilaus* and the account of the same period by the unknown author of the *Hellenica Oxyrhynchia*,[10] serious questions arise regarding the prevailing view of Xenophon as the blind eulogist of Sparta and King Agesilaus.

It will be my contention first that Xenophon purposefully recalls the memory of the Ten Thousand at the beginning of Book 3 in order to establish them as a model for panhellenism against which the subsequent Spartan expeditions can be measured, and furthermore, if we measure the Spartan efforts by the expectations suggested by the *Anabasis*, they are disappointing; second, that comparison of the account of the battle at the river Pactolus near Sardis found in Xenophon's *Hellenica* and the *Hellenica Oxyrhynchia* suggests that since the latter represents the battle as being of greater significance, then Xenophon (as an eyewitness or close to first-hand knowledge) either represents the truth and rejected the source for the Oxyrhynchus historian, or, if he did not write the truth and the Oxyrhynchus historian did, then he reduced the scale and significance of the conflict; and third, that the comparison of Xenophon's encomiastic biography of Agesilaus with the relevant passages in the *Hellenica* turns up a number of telling omissions and expansions.

RECALLING THE TEN THOUSAND

It was pointed out some time ago by De Sanctis that the 'tone' and 'colour' of *Hellenica* 3 and 4 resembled the *Anabasis*;[11] the observation tended, however, to subordinate thematic and structural similarities between the works to arguments for the early composition of Books 3 and 4. Others have also noted similarities, but no significant conclusions have been drawn.[12] However, there are important thematic continuities and contrasts between the *Anabasis* and *Hellenica*.

In the *Anabasis*, official participation by Sparta in the campaign of Cyrus is considerable, and sizeable numbers of Peloponnesians serve privately with him (*An.* 1.1.6; note, however, Clearchus was an exile from Sparta, *An.* 1.1.9).[13] But after Cyrus' death, in the later books of the *Anabasis*, the Spartan authorities in Asia Minor are at times even hostile to the Ten Thousand. So, Cleander declares them enemies and bars them from land allied to Sparta (*An.* 6.6.9); Anaxibius, the *harmost* or military governor of Byzantium, so angers the Ten Thousand that they threaten to sack his city (*An.* 7.1.7–17); and finally Thibron is rumoured to be intent on executing Xenophon if he should happen to fall into his hands (*An.* 7.6.43). This opposition to the Ten Thousand probably resulted from Sparta's desire not to collaborate with the enemies of the Great King.[14] The *Hellenica* provides a somewhat different picture of Spartan involvement in Cyrus' campaign:

> So the revolution at Athens ended. After this Cyrus sent messengers to Sparta and asked that they render him the sort of service he had done them in the war against the Athenians. The ephors thought his request was just and ordered Samius the nauarch at that time to help Cyrus in whatever way he asked; and Samius eagerly did what Cyrus requested, for having his own fleet he sailed together with the fleet of Cyrus to Cilicia and rendered Syennesis, the ruler of that area, unable to oppose Cyrus as he proceeded against the King. How Cyrus gathered an army and, having it, marched up country against his brother, and how the battle [of Cunaxa] was fought, and how Cyrus died there, and how after that the Greeks [in his service] made their way safely to the sea, Themistogenes the Syracusan has described.
>
> (3.1.1–2)[15]

Although the Spartan contribution to the early stages of Cyrus' insurrection was not negligible, by singling it out as he has done here, Xenophon makes the campaign of the Ten Thousand seem like a Spartan operation.[16] Furthermore, he does not indicate that the Spartans consistently harried the Ten Thousand after Cyrus' death. Xenophon thereby accomplishes two things. In the first place, he makes the Spartans seem sympathetic allies of the heroic Ten Thousand, and establishes a link between them by the summary of the events detailed in the *Anabasis*. Second, he brings Sparta's interest in resisting Persian control of Asia Minor to the fore, thereby making their new commitment of resources seem a logical extension of their earlier efforts, instead of a radical shift in their policy of cooperation with the Persians.[17] This opening paragraph also introduces a general theme that will be felt throughout the record of Sparta's activities in Asia Minor: Cyrus claims aid from the Spartans proportionate to that which he gave them during the Peloponnesian War. Friendship and hatred, the observance and the violation of personal obligations, will be major threads running throughout.

Further themes are advanced in the second paragraph of Book 3:

When however Tissaphernes, who had proved his worth to the King in the war against his brother, was sent down [to the coast of Asia Minor] as satrap of the lands he held before as well as the territory that had been under Cyrus, immediately he ordered all the Ionian cities to declare themselves his subjects. These cities, wishing to be free and at the same time fearing Tissaphernes, because they had chosen Cyrus while he was alive instead of him and were not then receiving him into their walls, sent ambassadors to Sparta and asked that since the Spartans were the leaders of all Greece (*pases tes Hellados prostatai*) they ought to take care of the Greeks in Asia, in order that their land not be destroyed and in order that they remain free. In response the Spartans sent out to them Thibron as harmost.

(3.1.3–4)

This passage makes Tissaphernes, not Artaxerxes, the instigator of the attempt to subject the Ionian cities.[18] This makes Tissaphernes, the villain of the *Anabasis*, the chief antagonist in the Ionian War. Second, the Greeks' plea for Spartan help is also an acknowledgement of Sparta's preeminence in the years following the Peloponnesian War (*pases tes Hellados prostatai*: cf. *An.* 6.6.9). But with preeminence, the passage suggests, comes the obligation to protect. And this duty seems only reasonable for a state that styled itself the 'protector of Greek freedom', both in Greece proper and in Asia Minor.[19] Indeed, it has been suggested that the terms of the appeal are meant to look back to the Persian Wars:[20] *proestate tes Hellados* (Hdt. 5.49.2).[21] On the earlier occasion the Spartans did not lend material help; now the situation is different. It could not be guessed from Xenophon's description of the Spartan reaction to the plea that only a few years before she had acknowledged the king of Persia as master of Ionia.[22] The net effect of both passages at the beginning of Book 3 is to create the expectation of a monumental conflict between Sparta, as champion of the Greeks in general and those of Asia in particular, and Persia, the oppressors of the Asiatic Greeks.

Thibron's expedition, the first of three Spartan campaigns in Asia, is made up of several different states. The nucleus is one thousand *neodamodeis*, or emancipated helots from Sparta, and four thousand Peloponnesian allies. To this is added a contingent of Athenian cavalry, sent by the people on a mission from which it is hoped they will not return (3.1.4; cf. above, p. 24).[23] On arrival in Asia more troops are levied (3.1.5). Xenophon explains their willingness to serve: 'all the cities then obeyed whatever a Lacedaemonian man commanded' (3.1.5): the Ionian enthusiasm for Sparta confirms her status as the champion of all the Greeks, both those of Greece and of Asia.[24] Finally, the survivors of the Ten Thousand join up.[25] Thibron has modest aims at first because of his inability to match the Persian cavalry, a problem which would face future Spartan campaigns; he plans only to protect his immediate surroundings (3.1.5). With the addition of the Ten Thousand, his ambitions grow, and he succeeds in winning over the cities controlled by the descendants of famous Medizers;[26] mention at 3.1.6 of Demaratus (see Hdt. 6.70) and Gongylus (Thuc. 1.128) directs the reader's attention to the events of the Persian Wars and cannot but help to establish a connection between the glorious history of the fifth century and the present Spartan undertakings. But, in his first encounter with real opposition at Larisa Aegyptia, Thibron fails. The ephors at Sparta then order him to march against Caria;[27] while at Ephesus, on his way to Caria, Thibron is replaced by Dercylidas, and at Sparta he is condemned and flees into exile. Xenophon provides the explanation: Ionians had brought a charge that he had allowed his troops to plunder allied lands (3.1.8, and see also 3.1.10 and 3.2.1).

Thibron's expedition must have been a disappointment for Xenophon;[28] much of the blame for plundering the lands seems to have fallen on the shoulders of the Ten Thousand (3.2.6). This was an old charge that Xenophon fought against in the *Anabasis* (recall the scene with Cleander; see above, p. 90). Later in Book 3, Xenophon presents an officer of the Ten Thousand who argues that any blame for the plundering should be placed at the feet of the supreme commander who allowed it to take place (3.2.7); there is good reason to believe that the officer is Xenophon himself.[29] The problem of greed and leadership, a central theme in the *Anabasis*, has carried over to Thibron's command; he has not shown himself capable of managing.[30] Some have suspected that Xenophon had a private grudge against Thibron, and so explain his failure as a result of his incompetence;[31] others claim that Thibron's dismissal had more to do with Lysander's fall from power.[32] Whether these theories represent what happened is uncertain, but it remains clear that Xenophon has been careful to underline the fruitlessness of his expedition.[33] A cursory examination of his campaign reveals that he only goes on the offensive when he has the Ten Thousand with him, and all his successes are bloodless, involving cities already willing to come over to the Spartans.[34] His failure comes when he attempts to besiege a hostile city, and the only aggressiveness his army shows is against friendly territory.

We learn a great deal about Dercylidas, Thibron's replacement, in Xenophon's introduction to his campaign. He must have been unusual by Spartan standards: 'Dercylidas came as commander to the forces, a man who seemed to be especially cunning (*mechanetikos*); and in fact he was nicknamed "Sisyphus"' (3.1.8).[35] Dercylidas is a cunning strategist, and he bases his plan of action on a shrewd assessment of the relations between the two western satraps; observing that Tissaphernes and Pharnabazus were suspicious of each other, Dercylidas makes an agreement with Tissaphernes (3.1.9), presumably an armistice, and marches against Pharnabazus (3.1.9). Here the Persians' strategy against the Greeks is turned against them:[36] exploit the differences within the ranks of your enemy.[37] But Xenophon is careful to include the detail that Dercylidas had a private grievance with Pharnabazus, and so perhaps provides what he thinks is the real motive for his actions. At some time during the end of the Peloponnesian War,[38] during the period of Persian and Spartan cooperation, Pharnabazus denounced Dercylidas for disobedience or insubordination (*ataxia*),[39] and as a result Dercylidas was made to stand guard for an entire day (3.1.9). So, Xenophon writes, on account of these things he was delighted to proceed against Pharnabazus (3.1.9). Here again is the motif of private friendship and enmity, both in Dercylidas' choice as to which satrap to proceed against, and in the disagreement between the satraps themselves. Moreover, the personal history of Dercylidas which Xenophon provides presents some noteworthy facts about him: his motive in attacking Pharnabazus is personal, he has a chequered past and he is described as ambitious.

The first phase of Dercylidas' expedition is marked by the rapid recovery of Greek cities recently conquered by the hyparch Mania, a Dardanian woman, with a Greek mercenary army. On a single day the Aeolic cities of Larisa, Hamaxitus and Colonae are won back (3.1.16). Then the cities Neandria, Ilium and Cocylium are persuaded to become allies of Sparta in response to an agent of Dercylidas who urges them to be free (3.1.16). The explanation for these surrenders and alliances is close at hand: the Greeks who guarded the cities were not loyal to the man who killed Mania and took over her subsatrapy, her son-in-law Meidias (3.1.16). The city of Cebren offers the first real resistance to Dercylidas: it is in a strong position, favourable omens are not forthcoming at Dercylidas' sacrifices and a rash sally by one of his lieutenants (a Sikyonian) prompts Dercylidas to attack prematurely (3.1.17–18). But the capitulation of Cebren eventually follows the pattern of the other cities; the Greek mercenaries prefer to be with Greeks rather than barbarians (3.1.18). Dercylidas' next targets are Scepsis and Gergis, the heavily fortified towns where Mania kept her treasuries (3.1.15). Taking advantage of Meidias' unpopularity with Pharnabazus and his own subjects, Dercylidas marches unopposed into Scepsis and gives the city back to its citizens (3.1.21). On handing control of the city over to its inhabitants, Dercylidas urges them 'as Greeks to live as free men' (3.1.21), a remark that reminds us of the Spartans' mission to Asia. No such fine sentiments are to be found in Dercylidas' capture of Gergis. He wrests control of the city from Meidias with an argument that justifies his sobriquet Sisyphus: by demonstrating that all the lands of Meidias formerly belonged to Mania, and that Mania in turn was a vassal of Pharnabazus, then, Dercylidas claims, all the lands of Meidias were in fact Pharnabazus' and were therefore subject to seizure, insofar as Pharnabazus was an enemy of Sparta! He gains control of the treasury and remarks to his officers that now they had enough money to pay for an army of 8,000 for a year (3.1.28).

Dercylidas' success, the capture of nine cities in eight days, is remarkable. It is all the more impressive when it is remembered that he campaigned without doing harm to Sparta's allies, as Thibron had done (note 3.2.1). He crowns the first year of his campaign with another triumph. Fearful of Pharnabazus' cavalry, he scores a diplomatic victory by negotiating a truce with him (3.2.1). Unaware of his material advantage, the satrap is primarily concerned with the defence of his *oikesis* – a concern that will also be exploited in the case of Tissaphernes.

After Dercylidas' successful campaign in the Chersonese (3.2.2–10), which, taken together with the detachment of the Troad from the control of Pharnabazus, meant that the bridgehead from Europe to Asia Minor was secure, the Ionians go directly to Sparta to suggest that they concentrate their efforts on Caria, Tissaphernes' *oikesis*; if it is threatened, they argue, then Tissaphernes will leave the Ionian cities alone and let them be autonomous (3.2.12).[40] In reponse to the Asiatic Greeks' request, the Spartans order Dercylidas to attack Caria. But while he marches there, the combined forces of Tissaphernes and Pharnabazus march into Ionia; this forces Dercylidas to march back to Ionia. While on his march back, Dercylidas happens upon the massed Persian armies of Tissaphernes and Pharnabazus. A miscalculation on Tissaphernes' part, however, saves the day for the Greek army. Although Dercylidas' army is weakened from within by the desertion of Ionian troops (3.2.17),[41] Tissaphernes imagines that the whole opposing force is of the quality of the Ten Thousand, and so, not wishing to fight, he sues for a treaty with Dercylidas against Pharnabazus' advice (3.2.18). We know better; Dercylidas' army is in disarray, both because of his lack of preparation and because of desertion.[42] With the armies withdrawn from the field, the commanders negotiate a truce. When asked what would be necessary for peace, Dercylidas defines the Spartan terms: the Great King must allow the Greek cities to be 'autonomous' (3.2.20). In what must be a reference to the Greek cities of Asia,[43] Dercylidas reintroduces the slogan from 3.1.3. The utterance again reminds us of Sparta's purpose in going to Asia – to free the Greeks.

Dercylidas seemed to have achieved a great deal. The Ionian cities had been secured temporarily against Tissaphernes' threats and a significant portion of Aeolis had been detached from Pharnabazus' satrapy. Furthermore, Sparta's intention of preserving the freedom of the Asiatic Greeks had been made forcefully clear. But what exactly did he do? Essentially he waged a diplomatic war against a petty tyrant (Meidias), capitalized on his enemies' fears and miscalculations and blundered into a truce.[44] No significant show of arms has taken place. Xenophon wants us to see that Dercylidas' army in some sense did not measure up to the Ten Thousand.[45] And there is a good reason for this. The next Spartan commander in Asia will be King Agesilaus; regardless of how great Dercylidas' victories are made to seem in Xenophon, they cannot be allowed to overshadow the arrival of the true panhellenic crusader and inheritor of the legacy left by the Ten Thousand. Unlike Thibron, Dercylidas succeeds, but not so much as to upstage Agesilaus. Rather, his triumphs lay the groundwork for Agesilaus' campaign; the bridgehead between Europe and Asia had been secured, a successful strategy had been adumbrated (keeping the satraps divided and attacking their bases of operation) and a potential difficulty had been anticipated (Persian cavalry strength). Xenophon is setting us up for the great conflict between East and West; it seems that the realization of the hopes suggested by the march of the Ten Thousand is finally to be realized.

With the appointment of the new king Agesilaus to the command of the army in Asia,[46] along with the greater allocation of troops to the area, Xenophon records the increased commitment of Spartan interest in a successful conclusion to hostilities there.[47] In describing Lysander's reasoning for attempting a major expedition to Asia, Xenophon raises again for us the memory of the Ten Thousand as a model for action: 'Lysander, believing that in naval matters the Greeks would be vastly superior, and as regards infantry taking to heart how the men who marched inland with Cyrus survived (*esothe*), he persuaded Agesilaus to undertake the command in Asia' (3.4.2). Clearly Xenophon is trying to suggest that Agesilaus' expedition to Asia was expected to be the realization of the hopes of the Greeks that had been inspired by the achievements of the Ten Thousand. This is further supported by the fact that Xenophon is the only historian to record Agesilaus' desire to sacrifice at Aulis (3.4.3–4), a profoundly symbolic act that suggests that the campaign was to rival the first conflict between East and West, namely the Trojan War. That the Thebans prevented the ritual from being properly performed sounds an ominous note (see below).

The command of a Greek army in Asia provided Agesilaus with the best possible opportunity for demonstrating his panhellenism.[48]

Indeed, if Xenophon is the Spartan sympathizer and eulogist of Agesilaus he is so often made out to be, then it seems likely that we ought to see these biases especially in his account of the king's campaign in Asia. But Xenophon frequently misses chances to lionize Agesilaus, and to such a degree that one can detect his own disappointment in the progress and result of the expedition. The suggestion that Xenophon was personally disappointed with the progress of the Spartan efforts in Asia Minor raises a difficulty for reading the *Hellenica*. Xenophon the historian, writing later, must be kept separate from Xenophon the participant. To argue that we are encouraged to experience Xenophon's growing disappointment is admittedly problematic. But that his narrative tends to point up the ways in which Agesilaus' campaign fell short of panhellenist ideals that Xenophon the participant no doubt had at the time, will, I hope, be clearly demonstrated.

As soon as Agesilaus arrives in Asia, Tissaphernes sends a herald to him to ask what his purpose is in coming to Ionia; Agesilaus' response is noteworthy: he replies that cities in Asia ought to be autonomous, just as they are back in Greece (3.4.5).[49] Again the standard of Greek freedom in Asia is raised;[50] but the point is also made that the cities of Greece are in Agesilaus' mind autonomous. While it is probably a mistake to find any intentional irony here on Xenophon's part,[51] the remark does stand in sharp contrast with what we have just seen in Sparta's treatment of Elis and in her treatment later of many other Greek states. At this point in the narrative, Xenophon stretches the boundaries of verisimilitude and allows Tissaphernes and Agesilaus to hold a brief dialogue, even though he has just told us that the satrap was communicating through a messenger. In reply to Agesilaus' declaration that his only purpose in coming to Asia was to free the Greeks, Tissaphernes offers to strike a truce in order that he might go to the Great King and report Agesilaus' demands. Agesilaus shrewdly replies that he is willing to observe a truce so long as Tissaphernes is not trying to deceive him (3.4.5). Evidently in the conversation that follows (unfortunately lacunose) the two men exchange oaths through messengers sent to each party – a procedure nearer to how the two men actually communicated. This small scene takes on immense symbolic importance when we learn that immediately following the ratification of the truce, Tissaphernes breaks his oath (3.4.6). When he learns that Tissaphernes has actually been spending his time gathering his army together for an attack, Agesilaus informs the satrap that he owes him a debt of gratitude insofar as his behaviour as an oathbreaker has ensured that the Spartans will have the gods on their side (3.4.11). At the very start, then, of Agesilaus' campaign in Asia, the reader is reminded of the treachery of the Persians, and that of Tissaphernes in particular; importantly, the reader is told that the gods will be acting as the Greeks' *summachoi* (allies), a claim Xenophon himself also makes in the *Anabasis* after Tissaphernes' treacherous seizure of the generals (*An.* 3.2.10). This alleged participation of the divine in Agesilaus' expedition elevates the campaign above the previous Spartan efforts and rounds out our picture of it as a noble undertaking: all is in place for the true panhellenic crusade.[52]

THE BATTLE OF THE PACTOLUS

But we soon run into a problem. In describing Agesilaus' finest hour in Asia, the battle near Sardis in 395, Xenophon seems to introduce negative colouring. Strangely, the *Hellenica Oxyrhynchia* and Diodorus preserve a greater victory for Agesilaus than is found in the *Hellenica*. Whether Xenophon has reported the truth and the *Hellenica Oxyrhynchia* has magnified what happened, or whether Xenophon has purposefully reduced the real scale and significance of the battle, in both cases he seems to be fashioning his history in a manner contrary to what is commonly thought to be his sympathy for Sparta and Agesilaus. This is a complex and crucial point that deserves special attention.

The publication of the *Hellenica Oxyrhynchia* in 1908 precipitated a number of questions.[53] Second only perhaps to the authorship problem in generating debate is the account of the battle near Sardis in 395. P (the designation given by scholars to the unknown author) and Xenophon offer profoundly different versions of what is probably the same battle.[54] The accounts are often taken as a test-case for reliability, and Xenophon frequently comes off the worse.[55]

P's account of the battle near Sardis was apparently the source for Diodorus, working from an adaptation of P in Ephorus.[56] Hence we are able to reconstruct the preliminaries of the battle that are fragmentary in P from the account in Diodorus.

P

11.2 Agesilaus moves his army into the Caustrian plain (*Ka*[*us*]*tri*[*ion pedion*] = Diod. 14.80.1, *to Kaustrion pedion*), staying close to the mountains,[57] hoping to anticipate (*phthasas*) some movement of the enemy. *11.3* Tissaphernes follows with an army of cavalry and infantry.[58] Agesilaus, aware of his inferior numbers, takes some measure, to which the barbarians respond. Some combat seems to take place when the Persians see the Greeks, probably involving Persian cavalry and light troops attacking the rear of Agesilaus' marching column. Agesilaus forms up his men into a square (*ex]othen tou plin[thiou* = Diod. 14.80.1, *eis plinthion suntaxas*), deploying the Greek soldiers by regiment. When Tissaphernes sees the Greeks he manoeuvres again. Both armies are by now near a river (*ton potamon*).[59] *11.4* The focus shifts back to Agesilaus and preparations seem to be made until nightfall (*tes nukt[os*). At night Agesilaus picks some number of hoplites and peltasts (Diodorus has 1,400 total, 14.80.2) and puts them under the command of a Spartiate, Xenocles (indisputable, *]Xenoklea [S]partiaten*). He orders Xenocles to advance ahead of the army and deploy in an ambush (in a copse? Diod. 14.80.2, *eis tina dasun topon*). At daybreak, Agesilaus moves off (*anastesas ha[ma tei he]merai*) and is attacked by the enemy in the rear and flank, by now a customary manoeuvre (*hos eiothesa[n*), while other enemy units follow in disorder behind. *11.5* Xenocles, on his own initiative (*ho de X[e]nokles epeide kair[on hup]elaben*),[60] breaks out of his ambush and attacks the Persians at a run. As the Persians catch sight of the charging Greeks they flee through the plain. Agesilaus, seeing the Persians in fear and disorder, sends more light troops and the cavalry to help the ambushers pursue the enemy. *11.6* They are unable to catch up with the enemy and break off their pursuit, having killed about 600.[61] They march on the enemy camp and plunder it, including some possessions of Tissaphernes. *12.1* After the battle Agesilaus marches on Sardis. He spends three days in the environs of the city, during which time he returns enemy dead under truce, sets up a trophy and plunders the entire land (*tous nekrous huposp[on]dous apedoken tois p[o]lemiois kai tropaion este[se] kai ten gen hapasan e[porth]esen*). He then marches towards Phrygia.

Xenophon

3.4.20 Agesilaus informs his troops that he intends to march towards the most difficult land by the shortest route. *3.4.21* Tissaphernes believes that Agesilaus is trying to mislead him and that he intends in actual fact to invade Caria.[62] Hence he deploys his infantry there and sends his cavalry to the Maeander valley. Agesilaus marches directly on Sardis, not Caria. For three days he advances unimpeded by the enemy and plunders the land. On the fourth day he makes contact with enemy cavalry. *3.4.22* The enemy commander (*not* Tissaphernes who was at Sardis while the battle took place, 3.4.25) orders the leader of his baggage train to cross the Pactolus river and make camp. Sighting the Greeks spread out through the plain, they kill some of them. Agesilaus responds by sending some of his cavalry to help. The Persians react by drawing up into battle formation. *3.4.23* Agesilaus, realizing that he has the advantage because the Persians are unsupported by infantry, sacrifices and leads out a combined force of hoplites and peltasts against the Persians, with his remaining cavalry in the van. *3.4.24* The Persians resist the cavalry but soon give way, some falling into the river, others fleeing. The Greeks follow them and seize their camp. Agesilaus surrounds the camp and secures many goods, seventy talents and some camels. We learn later (3.4.25–29) that Agesilaus meets with Tissaphernes' successor, Tithraustes, accepts some money and leaves for Phrygia.

In the debate regarding which account is to be preferred the central issue has been credibility.[63] The problem is still currently being debated, but the issue goes back to Georg Busolt.[64] The lines of argument have been drawn as follows. Busolt and his supporters have argued that when any two accounts of the same event diverge, the differences are to be explained as the result of an inclination to overstatement, insufficient observation, defective knowledge of a participant, tendency to reorganize, and outright invention.[65] They argue that whether Xenophon was a participant or not, his military expertise and knowledge of the area are to be kept in mind, and that the very details which P's advocates hold up as proof of his superiority are to be suspected.[66] Attention particularly centres on P representing Agesilaus as marching in a square, a manoeuvre which the Ten Thousand learned was disastrous;[67] hence they conclude that the detail is a fabrication on the part of someone who did not know his military science.[68] The second observation Xenophon's defenders like to make is that if the battle was as P described it, then Xenophon failed to lionize his hero when he had the chance;[69] the dangerous march to the environs of Sardis, if really harried by the Persians, would have resembled the march of the Ten Thousand, and Xenophon would have made something of it.[70] Moreover, the battle itself in P involved careful planning (the ambush), was against the combined Persian infantry and cavalry and Tissaphernes was himself present. The conclusion drawn from all of this is that Xenophon is to be preferred, and that P has either created detail to establish credibility, or has uncritically relied on a bad source. P's supporters point to the noticeable lack of detail in Xenophon,[71] that he was probably not at the battle and that his tendency to glorify Agesilaus led him to distort the truth.[72] This position depends, of course, on the determination that P's account is of a less significant battle.

Rühl noted that trying to determine which version of the battle was grander is a subjective undertaking;[73] and, indeed, absolute certainty in finding out which account is closer to the truth is surely impossible.[74] A recent discussion of Agesilaus' campaign has argued that the destruction done was considerable and that some areas were so damaged that they did not recover.[75] I do not intend to argue for the superiority of one account over the other; I do take a position similar to the defenders of Xenophon, namely that P preserves the more significant battle. The critics of Xenophon have never successfully handled this issue.[76] As opposed to P, Xenophon does not have Tissaphernes at the battle nor is the entire army of the satrap engaged. These points are irrefutable, even considering the fragmentary nature of the papyrus. Furthermore, that Xenophon has the army of Agesilaus ravage enemy land before the battle unmolested, whereas P has it under constant attack on its march to the battle, is also undeniable. And, what has not been sufficiently appreciated, P has Agesilaus perform the acts of a victor, returning the dead under truce and setting up a trophy.[77] Finally, P has Agesilaus plunder the area around Sardis; Xenophon does not. This last point of difference is decisive; the consequence of the battle in P's version was that Agesilaus was able to march on the capital of the Ionian satrapy, Sardis, and devastate its outskirts. This would have been a considerable material and symbolic achievement (recall the Ionian revolt). Hence, I think that it is safe to say that Xenophon presents (which is not to say necessarily correctly) a smaller-scale battle than P.

Exception has been taken to this analysis. 'Quantitative measure' is not important to Xenophon; rather the account is designed to show Agesilaus as the ideal field commander.[78] The argument is made that the king shows adaptability when, having suffered a setback because of insufficient cavalry strength (3.4.13–14), he recruits a cavalry unit (3.4.15), trains it and makes his preparations carefully (3.4.16–19) and finally wins a cavalry victory over the

Persians; all this is thought to be designed to prove Agesilaus' persistence, adaptability and preparation.[79] While this is no doubt true, this argument does not adequately treat the details that are dismissed as merely 'quantitative': an engagement wherein the enemy commander is absent and 10,000 cavalry are present is of a different order from one in which the commander is present at the head of a combined army of cavalry and infantry.[80]

But this interest in incorporating the narrative surrounding the battle to help explain the role the Sardis campaign had in Xenophon's mind is a step in the right direction. The crucial passage is the camp at Ephesus, immediately before the account of the battle:

> After this, when spring arrived, [Agesilaus] gathered the whole army at Ephesus. Wishing to get it into shape he offered prizes to the hoplite unit that had the fittest men; he also offered prizes for the best cavalry unit, as well as awards for the light-armed troops and archers, whoever could perform best their special tasks. After this it was possible to see all the gymnasia full of men training, the hippodrome with riders, the javelin throwers and archers practising. Agesilaus made the whole city where he was staying worthy of wonder, for the marketplace was full of all sorts of horses and weaponry on sale, metal-workers, craftsmen, smiths, tanners and painters all preparing the tools of war so that one thought the city was truly a work-shop of war. One became inspired looking at it, first Agesilaus, then also the rest of the soldiers returning from the gymnasia with crowns on their heads and dedicating them at the temple to Artemis. For where men worship the gods, train in the arts of war and practise obedience, how cannot everything be full of good hopes there?
>
> (3.4.16–18; cf. *Ages.* 1.25–27 and see *Lac.* 12.5)[81]

Granted, cavalry are training here, and there is careful preparation on Agesilaus' part, but there is so much more.[82] This is a passage that goes far beyond simply showing Agesilaus' adaptability. This camp is an emblem of panhellenism, a picture of a world that Xenophon must have regarded as close to his ideal – a well-run, well-trained, pious army of Greeks fighting in Asia; these are finally the operations of the true successor of the Ten Thousand. Special attention should be paid to the rhetorical question at the end of the quotation: the hopes of Ephesus are first and foremost Xenophon's own, and it is really through his eyes that he invites us to observe the camp full of promise.

But, as Cartledge noted recently, 'everything may indeed have been "full of good hopes"; but hopes for what? No great and lasting benefit was to accrue from these admirably energetic preparations.'[83] That is precisely Xenophon's point. Ever since the publication of the London fragments of the *Hellenica Oxyrhynchia*, dissatisfaction has been felt with Xenophon's account of Agesilaus' actions near Sardis precisely because they seem to lack a purpose.[84] The *communis opinio* is that Agesilaus' expedition in Xenophon falls short of the preparations beforehand, whereas in P the success of the campaign is clear. What Xenophon's critics seldom ask, though, is whether he intended Agesilaus' campaign to seem 'ineffective' in comparison with its preparations; I believe he did. Indeed, some have noted that Xenophon was conscious of the fact that Agesilaus' campaign differed little from his predecessors'.[85] Whether that is true is not important; that this impression is given by Xenophon is very important. When the camp at Ephesus is set beside the battle at the Pactolus river, Xenophon's point becomes unmistakably clear: the hopes of Ephesus, Xenophon's hopes, were not realized.[86] It is vital that this point not be misunderstood; all this is not to say that Xenophon was openly critical of Agesilaus, only that he was personally disappointed with what happened.

THE *AGESILAUS* AND THE *HELLENICA*

It might be objected that the accounts in the *Hellenica* and the encomiastic *Agesilaus* are virtually the same; Ephesus, with its hopes, still comes before the battle, and the battle is (roughly speaking) the same. Since the *Agesilaus* is unreservedly an attempt to glorify the Spartan king, and since the accounts are so similar in Xenophon's two works, it would seem that the negative reading I am arguing for in the *Hellenica* is impossible. But there are major differences.[87] After the battle in the *Hellenica* the only information that we are given concerns the booty which Agesilaus eventually brings back to Greece. We are told of his whereabouts after the battle only when the satrap Tithraustes interviews him. The *Agesilaus* offers a very different picture.[88] Sensing that the enemy were arguing among themselves, Agesilaus marches on the outskirts of Sardis and plunders it (*eporthei ta peri to astu*, 1.33). He then makes a proclamation which amounts to a declaration of the principles of panhellenism:

'and he declared by proclamation that those in need of freedom present themselves as allies; and if there were those intent on making Asia their own, he declared that they should be present too to decide the matter with those intent on freeing her' (*Ages.* 1.33). This grandiose statement is followed by a remarkable montage of images:

> When no one came out to meet him, he continued to campaign knowing no fear. He saw Greeks who formerly were made to do obeisance now being honoured by those that had abused them; he made those who demanded to receive honours due only to the gods no longer able to look at Greeks square in the face; he made the lands of his friends safe from destruction and took so much plunder from those of his enemies that in two years he offered as a tithe to the god at Delphi more than one hundred talents.
>
> (*Ages.* 1.34)

This passage is no doubt part of the encomiastic fabric of the biography and could be read only as pro-Agesilaus and pro-Sparta propaganda; but more importantly, these words are also panhellenic,[89] and as such, perhaps, they reflect what Xenophon hoped would have happened after the battle at the Pactolus river. It is clear from the *Hellenica* that nothing like what we see in the *Agesilaus* actually happened. It is not important here which work was written first;[90] if the *Agesilaus* was, then Xenophon felt he could not include the panhellenic elements after the battle in the history because they did not happen; or, if the *Hellenica* was first, then, when he made his adaptation to the encomiastic genre, he could not bring himself to leave the narrative as it was with its suggestions of disappointment and failure, and so he made up the visions of panhellenic victory for the benefit of his recently deceased friend and benefactor.[91] If accurate, the first scenario is perhaps the most revealing; Xenophon could fabricate what he hoped for from Agesilaus' expedition when he wrote his encomium, but he could not when he wrote his history. On the other hand, he could not, and would not, be openly critical of his friend; but when his panhellenic dreams, formulated and brought close to reality during his service with the Ten Thousand, did not materialize, he could not hide the fact, even if it meant that it reflected badly, or at least not positively, on his friend.[92]

Further examination of the *Agesilaus* provides additional confirmation that Xenophon was prepared to cast Agesilaus as the panhellenic hero more forcefully in the encomium than in the history.[93] The preliminaries to Agesilaus' expedition to Asia as they are reported in the *Agesilaus* differ from those in the history. In the first place, unlike the *Hellenica*, there is no doubt that a Persian fleet is being assembled for an attack on Greece.[94] Accordingly Agesilaus, without the promptings of Lysander (absent from the encomium), promises to undertake the mission to Asia for reasons not explained in the *Hellenica*: he states that he will cross over to Asia to make peace, but if the barbarian wants war, to occupy his energies so that he cannot invade Greece (*Ages.* 1.7). This is precisely the purpose behind the panhellenic hope of taking the war to Asia such as we find articulated in Isocrates. So much is made clear by the response Agesilaus' enthusiasm receives:

> immediately scores of people cherished the same hope – to invade the Persians' land, since before they had crossed over to Greece; to be the first to attack rather than wait and fight a defensive war; to use up the resources of the barbarian rather than fight in defence of those in Greece. In sum it was thought best to make the contest one for Asia, not for Greece.
>
> (*Ages.* 1.8)

Here the Persian Wars and Agesilaus' expedition are explicitly equated, as though real vengeance for 490 and 480 had not been meted out until that moment. Given this context of the memory of the great wars between East and West, it is strange that the *Agesilaus* does not record Agesilaus' attempt to sacrifice at Aulis (3.4.3–4): if Xenophon saw the attempted sacrifice at Aulis as the inauguration of the second Trojan War,[95] he would have included it in the *Agesilaus*. He did not. The fact that the sacrifice was interrupted by the Thebans must have seemed inappropriate to the encomiastic context. No doubt this was because it involved Thebans who, one would expect, would not be mentioned much in Agesilaus' biography. But if Xenophon did not perceive the event as reflecting well on Agesilaus, why did he include it at all in the *Hellenica*? The simplest explanation is that we are meant to see that in addition to being an outrage committed by the Thebans, the sacrifice is also a failed sacrifice, one that suggests that Agesilaus' expedition will fall short of success.[96]

The conclusion of the account of the expedition of Agesilaus in Asia in the encomium also differs from that found in the history. In the *Hellenica*, Agesilaus is faced with a problem: most of his troops want to stay in Asia rather than go to fight fellow Greeks (4.2.5).

This contrasts sharply with the corresponding passage from the *Agesilaus*: there we learn that the Greeks of Asia are so loyal to Agesilaus they willingly follow him back to Greece in order to go to the help of Lacedaemon (*Ages.* 1.38). The passage from the *Hellenica* clearly reflects the soldiers' reluctance to fight other Greeks; the *Agesilaus* passage, on the other hand, obscures who the future enemy will be and concentrates our attention on Agesilaus' popularity. If the *Agesilaus* was written first, then one could imagine that, in making his adaptation of this passage from the *Agesilaus* to the *Hellenica*, Xenophon could not in good conscience describe the troops from Asia eagerly awaiting the chance to do battle with 'men not worse than themselves' (Greeks as opposed to Persians). If the *Hellenica* was earlier, then, in making the change to the biography of his friend, one could imagine that Xenophon felt he could not end Agesilaus' campaign on a sour note and ruin the portrait of Agesilaus as a panhellenist. In either case, Xenophon seems to have been keenly aware of what Agesilaus' departure from Asia meant: Agesilaus was no longer to fight Persians in Asia (what panhellenists should do), but Greeks in Hellas – a situation Xenophon must have found deplorable. Something of this disappointment and even anger no doubt lies behind his description of Agesilaus' return route through Greece as following in the footsteps of Xerxes (4.2.8).

Interestingly, in the *Agesilaus*, Xenophon makes the king share this sentiment: 'When news reached him that eight Spartiates and nearly ten thousand enemy had died in fighting around Corinth he was clearly not jubilant; rather he said "Alas Greece, for those who are now dead were enough while alive to defeat in battle all the barbarians" ' (*Ages.* 7.5).[97] This lament borrows from a panhellenist tradition dating back at least to Gorgias' Funeral Oration cited above (p. 53): 'trophies won from the barbarians demand hymns, those from Greeks, dirges' (DK 82 B 5b = Philostratus *VS* 1.9.5). When we turn to the same episode in the *Hellenica*, we find no such expression of sadness; in fact Agesilaus refers to the news of the battle of Nemea (what he is also referring to in the *Agesilaus* passage) as 'wonderful' (*kallista*, 4.3.2)! Granted, one can feel both sadness and delight at such a triumph for Sparta, and need not express both emotions in an historical account; but not to give expression to such an established panhellenic *topos* as the *threnos Hellenon* ('lament for the Greeks') either at the battle of Nemea or at Coronea reflects a profound difference of view between the history and the biography. And it is not as though Xenophon hesistated to report such sentiments in the

Hellenica; recall that another Spartan commander expressed his chagrin at Greeks fighting each other with Persian money when they should be attacking their ancient foe. Having waited for Cyrus to give him money for his men longer than he can tolerate, Callicratidas complains, 'saying that the Greeks are the most wretched of men because they fawned on barbarians for the sake of money' and vowed that 'if he returned home safely he would do his utmost to reconcile the Athenians and Spartans'; he then sailed away (1.6.7).[98] No such expression is ever attributed to Agesilaus in the *Hellenica*.

If we do turn to the *Hellenica* to get some idea of Agesilaus' views on inter-state relations among the Greeks, the interview between Agesilaus and the satrap Pharnabazus offers some illumination. When Pharnabazus, an example of the 'astute foreigner' who makes naive but probing observations of the Greeks,[99] complains of his treatment by the Spartans in Asia after he had shown himself a loyal friend and ally in the Peloponnesian War (4.1.32), Agesilaus responds with an explanation: among the Greeks even guest-friends must fight and kill one another when their respective cities are at war (4.1.34). This is an alarming admission from a man who was sometimes a friend to a fault.[100] Moreover, Agesilaus' explanation runs counter to the traditional Greek attitude towards *xenia*, best illustrated perhaps in Diomedes' speech to Glaucus at *Iliad* 6.215–231 where he asserts that bonds of friendship must still be honoured in war. Although Agesilaus' love of country is itself praiseworthy,[101] Xenophon in particular must have found Agesilaus' views troubling; as proven, after all, by his decision to follow Proxenus on the expedition of Cyrus, and later by his enduring affection for Sparta and Agesilaus, Xenophon often chose personal attachment over loyalty to state.[102] In a sense, Agesilaus' comment to Pharnabazus reflects his ambivalent attitude towards the problem of the competition between loyalty to state and loyalty to friends; sometimes he stresses the need to stand by one's friends, and at other times that the state must come before all other obligations (see below, pp. 208, 218, 233). If we set his remark at 4.1.34 in a larger context, it accounts for Sparta's catastrophic strategy later: 'the undisputed mastery of all Greece'.[103] Needless to say, the substance of this dialogue is not in the *Agesilaus*; it could not stand beside the enthusiastic panhellenic statements also found there and not in the *Hellenica*.[104]

Xenophon's account of the Spartans in Asia Minor offers a mixed picture that is difficult to make sense of. There are noteworthy successes – those of Dercylidas and especially those of Agesilaus. But there is also failure, notably Thibron, as well as missed opportunities: Dercylidas gained possession of a vast amount of money that enabled him to keep his army in the field for a year, and yet he did not achieve a military victory of consequence. More significantly, Agesilaus seems to have won temporary control of the lower reaches of the Maeander valley and even the Pactolus near Sardis and yet did not (according to Xenophon at least) press home his advantage. While the blame for the recall of Agesilaus must be placed on the enemies of Sparta back in Greece, they do not explain the disquieting and anti-panhellenic sentiments of Agesilaus when he prepared to return to Hellas. The hopes that had been raised by the Ten Thousand were certainly felt by Xenophon when he served with Agesilaus; the camp at Ephesus alone tells us that much. But the relatively insignificant battle that followed, and even more Agesilaus' ultimate recall to Greece and the subsequent history of internecine conflict there that was driven in large part by Spartan ambition, destroyed them.

Part III

IDEAL COMMUNITY, IDEAL LEADER: PARADIGM AS HISTORY

5

INTRODUCTION TO
THE PARADIGM
Phlius, the Thirty and the
model community

INTRODUCTION

How was Xenophon different from contemporary or near-contemporary historians? This is ultimately an impossible question to answer, as the other historians working during his time are preserved only in fragments (cf. Brunt (1980) and Pearson (1943)). However, in a couple of places in the *Hellenica* he seems to betray an awareness of a set of criteria used to determine the suitability of material for inclusion in the historical record (e.g. 2.3.56, 4.8.1, 5.1.4: on the last see below, pp. 197–198), implying that he knew there were others writing a brand of history quite different from his own. Indeed, in one passage he comes right out and says that he is knowingly going against the conventions of 'all historians': at 7.2.1 he defends the inclusion of a lengthy excursus on the city of Phlius in the period between the battles of Leuctra and Mantinea.[1] He writes,

> while these things were happening, and when the Argives had fortified the Tricaranum on the heights above for attacking Phlius, and while the Sicyonians were building a wall on their border at Thyamia, then the Phliasians were especially hard pressed and were running short of provisions. Nevertheless they remained loyal in their alliance [with Sparta]. Now all writers remember great cities if they do some excellent thing; but it seems to me that if a city though small performs many and excellent deeds, then it is even more appropriate to relate them.
>
> (7.2.1)

The principle that Xenophon is challenging here is that greatness as a power ought to determine the historical importance of a place; further, we can tell that he is straining to make this point because

Phlius, as he tells us himself elsewhere (5.3.16), was not a small *polis* but actually a fairly large one with a citizen body of 5,000.[2] This concern is consistent with his thought found in other works; as I suggested above (pp. 95–98) in connection with his evaluation of cities in the *Anabasis*, outward signs of power were not enough for him to judge the worth of a community.

The assumption that a 'great' city was deserving of record, whereas a small one was not, finds its earliest expression in Greek historical writing in the introduction of Herodotus' *Histories*. At 1.5.3–4, having discussed earlier explanations for the beginning of the conflict between East and West, he promises to indicate who he thinks started the troubles and then plans to move on, 'mentioning alike the small and great cities of men; for of the ones which were once great many have become small, and those which were great in my time were formerly small. Knowing that human fortune never remains in the same place I will make mention of both alike.' Of course what Herodotus is saying here is that he will monitor change – the rise and fall of states and persons, massive changes in fortune. But it is important to note that implicit in his thinking is the noteworthiness of greatness: although he promises to treat small cities as well, this is only because they either were once or would become powerful and hence worthy of attention; he is presumably not interested in small cities that remain small.[3]

Closer to Xenophon's way of thinking, but still fundamentally in line with Herodotus, is Thucydides' famous discussion of the size of the Greek expedition to Troy. Noting that it would be mistaken to judge that it must have been insignificant, given the size of Mycenae and other cities of that period, he offers the intriguing 'thought-experiment' of contemporary Athens and Sparta empty of inhabitants: on the basis of their physical proportions we would believe the former to be more powerful than the latter, and we would be in error. He concludes, 'it is not right to doubt, nor to consider the appearances of cities rather than their powers, but believe that the Trojan expedition was the greatest up to its time' (1.10.3). It seems that Thucydides is trying to allow for something more than just physical size to be the measure of greatness. Nonetheless, the central point of interest is establishing which cities were really great in terms of manpower as opposed to those which only seemed so; he is not advocating examining the powers of small cities.

If we want a closer antecedent for Xenophon's thinking at *Hellenica* 7.2.1, it is perhaps found in another passage from Thucydides. At

7.29–30 of his history he records the horrible atrocity at Mycalessus in which Thracian mercenaries under the command of the Athenian general Demosthenes massacred the entire population of that small Boeotian city, including (notoriously) the schoolchildren. The episode prompts a rare glimpse of Thucydides as more than the dispassionate observer of war as he passes judgment on the destruction that befell the city (cf. Herodotus on Chios, 6.27). What is important for this discussion, though, is the explanation he gives for including the story. Concluding his description of the atrocity, he notes, 'such were the things that transpired in connection with the disaster that befell Mycalessus, a disaster no less worthy to be lamented for its magnitude than any which happened during the war' (7.30.3). Thucydides feels the need to apologize for devoting attention to this side-light on the war; he does so by suggesting that the 'magnitude of suffering' was great, even if the city which suffered was not. While greatness still determines the historical worthiness of a subject, it is as the upper limit of neither physical size nor power but rather human suffering.[4] A new criterion based on the life of a city – or here, its death – is established.

Roughly contemporary with Xenophon's observation at *Hellenica* 7.2.1 and close to it in spirit is Theopompus' charming story of a certain Magnes who visited Delphi. It recounts how he went from Asia to the oracle to find out who honoured the gods most lavishly, believing himself to be the one. On being told (to his surprise) that one Clearchus of Methydrium was the one who best sacrificed to the gods, Magnes went to see the man for himself. Arriving at Methydrium he at first despised the place, 'being small and humble, believing that it was impossible for any of its citizens nor even the city itself to be able to honour the gods more splendidly or more beautifully than himself' (*FGrHist* 115 F 344). Predictably, when Magnes finds out from Clearchus how scrupulous and pious he is in the performance of his sacrifices to the gods, he learns that true piety is the result of an excellent character, not massive wealth – a sentiment Xenophon would no doubt endorse, and indeed one which he has Socrates articulate in the *Memorabilia* (1.3.3–4). What is important for this discussion, though, is Magnes' assumption that nothing of consequence could be achieved by Methydrium or any of its inhabitants because it was 'small and humble'. Confounding human perceptions of what is excellent or valuable is of course a commonplace in literature of all periods; in Greek historiography it is perhaps most familiar in the work of Herodotus. Indeed, there are

powerful resonances between the Croesus episode of Herodotus and
Theopompus' story of Magnes, especially in Croesus' belief that he is
the most fortunate of men and Solon's assertion that he was not.[5] But
it should be noted that the first reason Solon gives for Tellus' happiness is that his city was flourishing (*polios eu hekouses*, Hdt. 1.30.4),
and furthermore both Tellus and the brothers Cleobis and Biton are
not poor men and they come from large cities (Athens, Argos).
Herodotus is trying to show that the wealthiest man in the world is
not the most fortunate because the outward signs of his success are
not as stable as those of men of more modest means whose lives are
long and fruitful or short and glorious. Theopompus suggests that
the physical world is actually misleading, and that it is the world of
character, the moral world if you will, that must be considered.

Plato in the *Republic* is certainly in sympathy with this view. At
422e–423b Socrates attempts to convince Adeimantus that the term
polis is inappropriately applied to cities with accumulations of
wealth greater than Kallipolis, because in actuality they are made up
of a plurality of *poleis* – the rich and the poor, and further subdivi-
sions within these two groups. Arguing that if other cities are treated
in fact like agglomerations of several cities, and Kallipolis is wisely
governed, then

> [Kallipolis] will be great, and I do not mean in reputation, but
> truly great (*alethos megiste*), even if it possesses only a thousand
> defenders. For you will not easily find a single great city
> among either the Greeks or barbarians, although you will find
> many which are much bigger that seem to be as great.
>
> (Plato *R.* 423a–b)

Plato, too, seems interested in separating greatness of character or
moral greatness from physical or outward greatness – indeed, he
wants to detach the concept of greatness from size and reserve it for
moral evaluation alone.

Thus in his defence of including the trials and successes of Phlius,
Xenophon is moving precisely in the direction represented
by Thucydides on Mycalessus, Theopompus on Magnes and Methydrium and Plato on Kallipolis: greatness or noteworthiness is possible
for physically small places if they demonstrate excellence of character
(Kallipolis) or in some way exemplify human experience (Mycalessus).
This justification of historical worthiness based on exemplary or
paradigmatic quality is very important for understanding Xenophon's
place in Greek historiography and the degree to which the *Hellenica*

represents a shift from older fifth-century notions regarding the nature of history to those which characterize the writers of the later Hellenistic period. The next two chapters will focus on Xenophon's interest in paradigmatic history, both at the level of the community and the individual. Discussing first a model good community (Phlius) and a model bad one (the Thirty Tyrants at Athens), I will then move on to a consideration of Xenophon's treatment of three individual commanders found in the *Hellenica* – the paired descriptions of the Spartan Mnasippus and the Athenian Iphicrates, and the portrait of Jason of Pherae. But before turning to these passages it is important to consider briefly Xenophon's place together with Ephorus and Theopompus regarding the rise of paradigmatic history.

PARADIGMATIC HISTORY

Pseudo-Dionysius, writing some time after the first century BC,[6] records the famous statement that 'history is philosophy drawn from paradigms' (*Rh.* 11.2)[7] and attributes the thought to Thucydides, citing Thuc. 1.22.4: 'whoever will want to examine the clear truth of the past and of what will some day again be according to human nature, such things and things very like them, it will be enough if they find my history useful'. As Gomme wisely noted regarding this passage, the mention of 'the future' must be understood as relative to the historian, not the unknown future of a subsequent reader;[8] Thucydides is not claiming that his work should be viewed as a handbook for coming generations, a statement of a 'philosophy' for living life. In other words, Ps.-Dionysius was a bad reader of Thucydides. But his bad reading is nonetheless very illuminating. It suggests that there were some at least in antiquity who read history precisely as a guide for the conduct of their own lives and careers. Indeed (again I am following Gomme), Polybius for one believed that history had to have 'practical value', examples for statesmen and generals to follow,[9] and he modified Thucydides' methodological statement along the same lines as Ps.-Dionysius' understanding of the passage (Plb. 3.31.12–13). If Thucydides did not write para-digmatic history whereas Polybius did, where did it start? More importantly, what was it, and how do Xenophon's historical proce-dures and concerns compare to it?

While focusing on an individual for moral–didactic purposes goes back in Greek literature to Homer (e.g., Phoenix's story about Meleager, *Iliad* 9), and in historiography at least to Herodotus (see e.g., his final judgment on the death of Pheretime of Cyrene, 4.205), most scholars believe that Xenophon's contemporary, Ephorus, was among the first if not the very first to make education by examples from the past one of the primary goals of historical writing.[10] The suggestion is that it was Isocrates, Ephorus' teacher, who wanted to make history *mimetic* so that the reader would feel emotion through historical narrative (e.g. most famously at *Pan.* 168);[11] it is thought that in some sense Ephorus introduced explicit moral evaluation in keeping with this view. This suggestion seems a little too simplistic and straightforward, and our control over the historical writing of the fourth century is imperfect due to the fragmentary nature of much of what has survived (see above, p. 123). Nonetheless, we do have Polybius' critique of Timaeus and Ephorus from Book 12 of his history. Complaining that Timaeus unfairly charged Ephorus with rejecting rhetorical or epideictic writing, he notes that the older historian 'being remarkable throughout his entire enterprise in terms of speech, organization and thought is very clever in his digressions and statements of personal opinion and in general whenever he makes an additional comment (*epimetrounta logon*)' (Plb. 12.28.10 = *FGrHist* 70 T 23). Evidently Ephorus allowed himself to make personal comments in excurses or passages which Polybius considered 'superfluous' or 'additional'. What exactly were these *epimetrountes logoi*? Polybius gives us a good idea when passing judgment on historians who treated the career of Hieronymus of Syracuse. He notes that those who write specialized histories or monographs on particular topics,[12] as opposed to larger historical works, are compelled for want of material to be discursive and expand on matters which are not really worth recording; such an expansion he calls 'filling out books' and 'additional material in the narrative' (*ton anaplerounta tas bublous kai ton epimetrounta logon tes diegesios*, Plb. 7.7.7). Since Polybius is applauding Ephorus in contrast to Timaeus, we may assume that he found Ephorus' digressions timely and in proportion to the material covered.

These digressions were in all likelihood opportunities for praising or blaming individuals or events along the lines laid out by Polybius at 1.14.5:[13]

> when someone takes up the role of historian it is necessary to forget all [the normal loyalties of private life] and instead often praise and decorate with the highest laudations one's enemies when their deeds demand it, and censure one's closest friends

and blame so as to shame them, whenever the faults of their lives indicate this course.

This sentiment is clearly hyperbolic, but the hyperbole underscores the obligation, indeed the absolute necessity of the historian to *judge* the persons in his history. The picture we get of Ephorus from Polybius is of a historian who occasionally made charged editorial remarks about persons and events in the form of timely asides (*gnomologiai*) or fuller-scale digressions (*parekbaseis*).

Unfortunately, matters are not this simple. The view Polybius offers of the paradigmatic components of Ephorus' history do not square precisely with what we can glimpse from Diodorus Siculus;[14] this is not a trivial matter. Although Polybius was surely the better reader of his predecessors, Diodorus excerpted large portions of Ephorus' history for his own *Bibliotheke* and so had a more than passing familiarity with it. He informs us that Ephorus 'made each book of his history contain events according to type' or 'category' (*kata genos*, 5.1.4 = *FGrHist* 70 T 11),[15] and furthermore that each book was prefaced by a *prooemium* (16.76.5 = *FGrHist* 70 T 10). These testimonia would not in themselves be problematic, were it not for the probability that Ephorus' prefaces were places where this tendency to moral evaluation – praise and blame – was especially felt. It seems certain that in the prefaces Ephorus engaged in polemic against other writers of history, especially regarding the difficulty of obtaining accurate information because of the antiquity of the subject (F 9, 109, 110).[16] He also seems to have made what look like gratuitous moralizing platitudes about the human experience, such as the condemnation of music as a corrupting influence on humanity (F 8). Most importantly there is the evidence of the *prooemia* of Diodorus' own work. It is a matter of considerable debate how much, if at all, Diodorus was indebted to Ephorus (among others) for his prefaces.[17] While Laqueur's thesis that they are only very slight revisions of Ephorus' own *prooemia* is probably too extreme,[18] the fact that Diodorus' prefaces are interrupted precisely at the point where Ephorus would have given out as a source is compelling.[19] Moreover, despite slight differences in language between Diodorus and Isocrates, the type of thinking that we see in the preface to Book 15 of the *Bibliotheke*, for example, where Diodorus explains the collapse of the Spartan empire, is strikingly similar to that found in Isocrates, and this is no doubt due to Ephorus as an intermediate source.[20]

If the prefaces of Ephorus were primary locations of praise and blame, then it could be argued that the moral evaluations of Ephorus, far from being found in excurses or personal asides that were essentially extraneous, were actually found in prominent positions (e.g. the preface) and may have provided at least in theory the thematic unity of each book. However, such a characterization of an Ephoran book and its preface does not cohere well with Polybius' objection to additional narratives that are too narrowly focused: if Ephorus' books were circumscribed thematically by moral views expressed in the proem, would Polybius not have mentioned it? Perhaps not. It is probably the case that he did not regard the prefaces of Ephorus as 'additional' and hence regarded praise and blame as ways of organizing the material of the book: at 11.1a.2, he states that prefaces are 'useful' insofar as they 'lead the one who wishes to read to reflection, and call and stir readers to read'. Perhaps then Polybius and Diodorus were both right: Ephorus engaged in moral evaluation in prefaces but also at other points, especially in connection with the summation of men's careers.[21] And certainly the clearest and surest example of Ephoran moralizing comes from an evaluation of the career of Themistocles preserved on papyri (*P. Oxy.* 1610 frg.3–6 = *FGrHist* 70 F 191), and which incidentally is closely followed by Diodorus (11.59ff.).[22]

Xenophon, therefore, was not alone in permitting himself moments to praise and blame subjects in his history.[23] But even more importantly, it seems that this moral evaluation could form either an essentially unnecessary adjunct to the main narrative of a history (with Polybius), or it could be an important organizing principle around which a book is composed – not to mention an entire history such as Theopompus' *Philippika*. Xenophon elected to experiment with the latter approach, making moral evaluation of individuals in particular a central, not a marginal part of his history. Presentation of paradigms, both good and bad, of both communities and individuals, permits Xenophon not only to provide moral lessons but also to construct historical explanations, as those places and persons are made to represent larger truths about the past.

THE PARADIGMATIC COMMUNITY I: PHLIUS

It seems best to start with that community which Xenophon goes out of his way to insist on describing in his conscious departure from the main narrative of the *Hellenica* set up by 7.2.1, the 'small' *polis* of

Phlius. I will discuss later (pp. 209–214) how Xenophon uses this city in particular as an index of Sparta's growing imperialist policies after the ratification of the King's Peace of 386. Admittedly, this earlier role for Phlius does not cohere well with the Phlius of *Hellenica* 7.2. The explanation for this inconsistency seems at first to be relatively straightforward: due to Agesilaus' intervention earlier (5.3.25; see below, p. 211), the government at Phlius had changed to an oligarchy, thereby making it easier perhaps for Xenophon to single the city out for praise. To be sure, this makes his earlier, essentially sympathetic treatment of democratic Phlius all the more remarkable.[24] Before accepting this explanation, it should be noted that Diodorus challenges the truth of the central point of the digression: while Xenophon will make much out of the fact that Phlius remained loyal to Sparta despite enormous outside pressure in the years following the battle of Leuctra, Diodorus asserts that Epaminondas managed to bring the city over to his side (15.69.1). I simply cannot accept that Xenophon would make up something that was not true (omission is another matter), and that he fabricated Phlius' loyalty to Sparta during this period, at least in the first years following Leuctra[25] (although it is true that he reports later that Sparta permitted Phlius to abandon their alliance and reach a separate settlement with Thebes, 7.4.9–10). It is easier to believe that Xenophon exaggerated Phlius' loyalty when in fact the city, without formally renouncing ties with Sparta, was trying to mind its own affairs during the storms which the Theban invasions brought after Leuctra.

It is clear right from the very start of his digression on Phlius that the themes will be the Phliasians' loyalty, specifically towards Sparta, as well as their resilience and courage in the face of overwhelming odds (7.2.2–4). So much is evident from the summary Xenophon himself offers at the beginning of the next chapter: 'let so much be said about the Phliasians, how they were loyal (*pistoi*) to their friends and remained brave (*alkimoi*) in war, and how though short of everything they remained in the alliance' (7.3.1). It is no wonder that Xenophon underscores these virtues, for elsewhere they are ones he values highly (see below, p. 134, and note, e.g., *Mem.* 2.4 on friendship, especially in hard times, and *Mem.* 4.6.10–11 on courage). The excellence of the Phliasians is especially brought home in a set of vivid, short descriptions of them in action against their various enemies. In the summer of 369, the Thebans invaded the Peloponnese for the second time after Leuctra.[26] Xenophon tells us that while the Spartans and other allies were holding the pass at

Oneum (7.2.5; cf. 7.1.15), certain democratic exiles from Phlius persuaded the Arcadians and Eleans who were marching to join up with the Thebans to attack their native city.[27] With the help of a diversion as well as the cooperation of a group of confederates in the town, the exiles along with 600 'others' (mercenaries?) scale the wall of the city and seize the acropolis. Alarmed, 'the citizens' of Phlius (the oligarchic hoplites) struggle to pen the intruders in the citadel; simultaneously the Arcadians and Argives attack, and the fighting spreads to the walls and towers. Eventually fire drives the enemy from the towers and acropolis (7.2.5–9). The course of the battle resembles the fighting typical of factional disputes elsewhere in Xenophon and in other Greek historians (e.g. Corinth 4.4.1–14; cf. Thucydides on Plataea 2.2–5 and Corcyra 3.70–81): fighting in civic places (roof-tops, buildings), sudden and confused movements and countermovements of combatants, desperate hand-to-hand fighting.

While the episode is about *stasis* and faction, the success of the oligarchic citizens of Phlius implies that there was significant unanimity in the city (at least when the democrats were not included): as Xenophon's contemporary Aeneas Tacticus observed, there is no greater advantage to a city under siege than unanimity (10.20; see above, p. 54).[28] Xenophon seems to stress the *homonoia* of the Phliasians at the conclusion of the battle, after the enemy had fled: 'then it was possible to see the men congratulating one another for their deliverance (*soterias*) and the women bringing water and crying in their gladness. Indeed, truly on that day "mirth-in-tears" (*klausigelos*) took hold of everyone' (7.2.9). The universal joy and celebration of the Phliasians, including the women, underscores the fact that it was a common 'salvation' that was secured. A similar moment from elsewhere in Xenophon's corpus – and one that I have already discussed (p. 76–77) – is the famous scene from the *Anabasis* (4.7.21) when the Ten Thousand weep and embrace one another on the summit of Mt Theches after catching sight of the sea: another episode that marks the successful survival of a group against heavy odds.[29] And just as there are numerous heroic touches in that part of the *Anabasis*, so too in this scene the mention of 'mirth-in-tears' (*klausigelos*) calls to mind the famous scene in the *Iliad* of Hector and Andromache when the same mixture of emotions occurs (6.484). The resonance may be intended: Xenophon first uses the same word for 'weeping' from the *Iliad* scene, glosses the phrase 'weeping in joy' with the rare *klausigelos*, and emphatically reasserts (*tote ge toi onti*) that the use of the term was in this instance appropriate, suggesting that he has his eye on a noteworthy precursor as well as inappropriate applications of the word.[30] And in fact one ancient reader at least thought that Xenophon had the *Iliad* passage in mind.[31] If the reference is genuine, then Xenophon seems to be elevating the people of Phlius to the level of heroes and specifically that hero famous for his defence of his city (e.g. *Il.* 12.243) and his wife.

Although Xenophon details two more stunning Phliasian victories over superior invading armies, it is not finally their success on the battlefield that draws his special attention. In a brief paragraph in the middle of the excursus, he makes it clear why he has devoted so much attention to Phlius in the period after Leuctra:[32] 'and this worthy thing the Phliasians also accomplished; having taken alive the Pellenean proxenos, although they were short of everything themselves, they released him without demanding a ransom. How could someone deny that men who acted thus were noble and brave?' (7.2.16). It seems to me both strange and significant that, when the bulk of the digression concerns Phlius' achievements in war, Xenophon has reserved his most emphatic and generous praise for an action that has nothing directly to do with the battlefield. The willingness of the Phliasians to return the Pellenean and so remain faithful to the principles that were expected to govern Greek state relations, even in time of war (cf. Cyrus, *An.* 1.9.8; for the expected treatment of strangers in war see, e.g., the story of Pactyes, Hdt. 1.157–161), explains the term 'noble' (*gennaious*): Xenophon has someone use the term elsewhere in the *Hellenica* to describe the magnanimous behaviour of Athens towards her old enemy Sparta (curiously a Phliasian, Procles, 6.5.48), suggesting that he understood the term to be especially applicable when a state had the opportunity to take advantage of a situation in wartime but generously does not do so.[33] 'Brave' or *alkimos*, a poetic word with strong Homeric resonances, is, with the exception of Xenophon, exceedingly rare in fifth- or fourth-century prose.[34] 'Tyrtaeus' F 12 (West) is perhaps one of the clearest articulations of the precise meaning of the concept *alke* from which this adjective is derived: valour in war, especially in the context of defence, as apart from or (as the poet would have it) in opposition to more standard aristocratic virtues such as wealth or beauty.[35] Xenophon knows this meaning, as is clear from the *Oeconomicus* (6.10), where Socrates praises the side-effects of farming outside the walls of a city, one of which is to make people eager to defend the land they have so painstakingly cultivated; alternatively, he can employ the term to mean simply 'good at war' (so *Hellenica*

7.1.23). It is at first difficult to see how these virtues are not only illustrated by but especially illustrated by the Phliasians' release of the Pellenean.

If we look again at 7.3.1 (where the term *alkimos* is also used) the awkward application of the concept 'bravery' is explained, and in the process we gain a valuable insight into the whole digression on Phlius. As in 7.2.16, Xenophon lays great stress on the fact that the Phliasians conducted themselves with distinction in spite of suffering acute shortages of supplies (*panton spanizontes*, 7.3.1; cf. 7.2.16, *panton spanizomenoi*). Lying behind all of their virtues seems to be the ability to endure hardship; thus in the case of the Pellenean it was precisely their capacity to put up with hardship that permitted them to resist taking advantage of their prisoner, a virtue that simultaneously suggests that they would make very effective and valiant defenders of their city. It is worth noting in this connection that the Phliasians' self-control (*enkrateia*) drew Xenophon's notice earlier in the *Hellenica*, during the siege of Agesilaus (5.3.10). It seems that endurance, and by implication self-control, dominates Xenophon's understanding of the excellence of the Phliasians. Indeed, it is with this understanding of the source of Phlius' valour in mind that we are invited to consider the remainder of the excursus (7.2.17–23), an account of how the Phliasians, together with Athenian help, managed to secure a line of supply to Corinth when under repeated attack from their enemies. This entire section of the digression is offered as proof of 'how . . . on account of their patient endurance they preserved the trust they had with their friends' (7.2.17). Yet the subsequent episodes do not deal with Phlius' loyalty to her allies; rather, the stories are presented as proof that the Phliasians were capable of enduring hardship for the sake of an alliance (or by implication any other worthy cause).

Self-control and endurance, *enkrateia* and *karteria*, are central to Xenophon's understanding of human excellence. While these virtues are by no means unusual in Greek thought,[36] they do take on a special significance for the memorialists of Socrates and for Xenophon in particular.[37] To his way of thinking, as we learn from Socrates in the *Memorabilia*, *enkrateia* is 'the foundation (*krepida*) of virtue' (*Mem.* 1.5.4) because it literally emancipates a person from the tyranny of pleasures (*Mem.* 1.5.5; cf. 1.3.11, *Ap.* 16 and *Oec.* 1.19–23).[38] This is not a trivial matter for Xenophon: self-control alone permits a person to endure (*karterein*) the yearnings that are generated by the pleasures, so that when that same person does partake of them they have in a sense mastered them and can truly enjoy them (*Mem.* 4.5.9; cf. 1.3.5 and 1.6.5–6). What is more, self-control allows its possessor to learn and enjoy the good and noble pursuits: the proper care of the body, the management of one's house, the ability to be useful to one's friends and city, and to defeat one's enemies (4.5.10). That is to say, for Xenophon, self-control is the source of the other virtues, a point that goes a long way towards explaining why he seems to group so much of what he sees as praiseworthy about the Phliasians under their ability to endure hardship. It is as if once the possession of that virtue is demonstrated, all the others may be assumed.[39]

Xenophon was not alone in relying on a city's self-control as a measure of its success in war. Ephorus notes that when the Milesians did not live in luxury they defeated the Scythians and founded cities in the Hellespont and Black Sea; by the time of the Ionian revolt, however, they had become corrupted by pleasure and excess and their bravery (literally 'manliness', *andreion*) had vanished (*FGrHist* 70 F 183). While it is true that this explanation is not unique to Ephorus (Herodotus had understood the decline of Miletus in a similar way, see esp. 6.11–21), and furthermore that this loss of valour was even proverbial – as the saying went, 'the Milesians were stout-hearted (*alkimoi*) once' (schol. in Ar. *Pl.* 1002 = Demon *FGrHist* 327 F 16)[40] – nonetheless, neither Herodotus nor the proverb ought to obscure the fact that Ephorus was thinking along lines that were similar to Xenophon: it was self-discipline that made the citizens of Miletus, like those of Phlius, 'stout-hearted'.

Even closer to Xenophon in his thinking on the importance of self-control is Theopompus. He too can evaluate cities on the basis of the presence or absence of self-control. Indeed, in Theopompus we find a historian like Xenophon whose views are very much centred on the question of *enkrateia* and especially its opposite, lack of self-control or *akrasia*.[41] One sees this very clearly in *FGrHist* 115 F 40 on the Ardiaeans:

> every day they get drunk, hold parties and are very uncontrolled (*akratesteron*) when it comes to eating and drinking. For this reason the Celts, while they were at war with them, and after they learned of their lack of self-control (*akrasian*), told all their soldiers to prepare the most fabulous dinner possible in their tents and to put into the bread a certain poisonous herb capable of powerfully affecting the stomach and causing acute diarrhoea. When this happened some [of

the Ardiaeans] fell into the hands of the Celts and were killed, while others threw themselves into rivers, having lost control (*akratores*) of their stomachs.

For the Ardiaeans, like the Phliasians, self-control was not simply an issue of personal conduct, it was a matter of life and death: they were mastered by *akrasia*, and because of that they were killed. For Theopompus, as for Xenophon, all one really needs to know about a city, or more usually a person, is whether they have self-control; everything else they did is explained by the degree to which they possessed this virtue.[42]

This line of thinking appears (famously) in Theopompus' portraits of Philip of Macedon, and of these F 224 is perhaps the best example: after Philip had 'gained possession' (*enkrates*; ironic?) of a lot of money he became profligate, being the worst manager (*oikonomos*) in the world; he attracted to his company similarly reprobate persons; and even those who were not initially of the same temperament became corrupted through contact with Philip and his court. While this may seem to be no more than exaggerated and malicious gossip (indeed, cf. Polybius 8.11.1ff. = *FGrHist* 115 T 19 and F 27), there is nonetheless a point to it that is not sensationalist or frivolous – indeed, one that lies at the centre of Theopompus' historical vision: as Connor has put it, such a passage suggests that 'to Theopompus, Philip is the great paradigm, the engine of corruption, that draws evil to itself and destroys whatever good it finds'.[43] Philip's lack of *enkrateia* or his *akrasia*, combined with his undeniable success, serves to indict the age in which he lives as utterly evil: only in a corrupt age could a corrupt man to rise to such heights of power.[44] Surely this same idea lies behind Theopompus' treatment of the leaders of the Athenian democracy in the fifth and fourth centuries (F 85–100).[45] By drawing attention to the short-comings of her leaders, especially their greed (F 86, 90, 94), the greed of Athens as seen in her control over her empire is also alluded to and indicted. Interestingly, it is the fourth-century politicians in particular who are charged, like Philip, specifically with a lack of self-control – Callistratus (F 97) – and profligacy – Eubulus (F 100) – the architect of the Second Athenian Confederation, and Athens' ablest financial planner, respectively. Callistratus' own personal weakness, combined with his ability in public affairs, may mirror the cosmetic change in Athens' name for tribute ('contribution') which he in fact coined (F 98) – perhaps a graphic illustration of individual corruption standing for corruption on a larger scale.[46]

Be that as it may, just as for Xenophon, self-control for Theopompus was a virtue that encompassed all others; thus Philip's *akrasia* is manifested in his profligacy, a shortcoming that may seem insignificant but which in turn made him a bad administrator as well as a corrupt and corrupting leader – issues, it must be granted, of great historical importance.

It would be a mistake to dismiss Xenophon's and Theopompus' focus on self-control only as a narrowly moralizing procedure. While it cannot be denied that they do hold up Phlius and Philip as moral–didactic paradigms, the concept of *enkrateia* is also useful to them as an explanatory tool for their histories insofar as they employ character to account for events. But having said that, I should hasten to add that there are obvious differences between Xenophon's account of Phlius and Theopompus' treatment of Philip. The digression on Phlius is a self-contained passage, while evaluations of Philip were presumably found throughout the *Philippika*; furthermore, Theopompus is concerned with the actions and character of an individual, whereas Xenophon is telling the story of a community. Closer parallels for the use of an individual to represent larger truths about the world they live in will be found in Xenophon's portraits of the generals Mnasippus and Iphicrates, and the strongman of Thessaly, Jason of Pherae. Nonetheless, Theopompus' handling of the Ardiaeans shows that, like Xenophon, he was capable of employing the tools of moral evaluation in his accounts of cities as well as persons.

What can Xenophon's purpose have been in telling the story of Phlius? A possible antecedent for the digression, and one he must have known well, was Thucydides' characterizations of Athens and Sparta on the eve of the Peloponnesian War, which he has the Corinthians formulate at the conference at Sparta (1.70.2–9). However, even the briefest comparison of the two passages suggests that they are radically different. Thucydides' plan is evidently to offer useful characterizations of the major combatants of the war beforehand, so as to make the later course of the conflict understandable.[47] Conversely, the digression on Phlius concerns a place Xenophon wants us to think of as superficially or conventionally unimportant; furthermore, it comes late in the narrative, occupying a place where Xenophon might have chronicled the successive Theban invasions of Laconia.[48] Thus where Thucydides seems to offer an interpretive guide to the rest of his history, Xenophon departs from his main narrative near its conclusion in order to present a sketch of a city he himself has characterized as insignificant. The passage in Thucydides nonetheless presents a useful point of comparison. The speech of the Corinthians at Sparta, along with other passages in the history (e.g. the portraits of Pausanias and Themistocles), allows us to make sense of later actions; it is prospective in orientation. On the other hand, the Phlius digression seems to be retrospective, providing an important view of previous actions in the *Hellenica*, not future ones.

There are two reasons for thinking that the Phlius digression looks backward and not forward. In the first place it comes very late in the history. This may be intentional and not necessarily due to chronological demands; as I noted above (p. 134), Xenophon made a point of noticing the *enkrateia* of the Phliasians earlier and hence could have put in a digression there had he chosen to. Second, and more importantly, the apologetic tone of the introduction suggests that he expected or even welcomed a comparison to be made between Phlius' actions and those of the 'greater' cities.

If Xenophon wants us to look back at the events of the *Hellenica* from the vantage point of Phlius' gallant defensive actions in the 360s, what is it that he wants us to see? Perhaps that, like the Ten Thousand, the Phliasians had to struggle against great odds to win their salvation or *soteria* (7.2.9); that, again like the Cyreans in Asia during their most successful period, the Phliasians are for the most part unified (with the exception of the traitors who try to turn the city over to the enemy); and finally, that just as the Ten Thousand did not allow their goals to be subordinated to the short-term interests of individuals, so too the Phliasians by means of their self-control did not degenerate into criminal behaviour nor did they forfeit the long-term safety of their city because of the immediate pressures of shortage.

Phlius survived because she was unified and demonstrated self-control. The same could not be said about Athens. She lost the Peloponnesian War. Sparta too had been terribly humbled and would not survive the death blow dealt her at Mantinea. Perhaps the laudation of Phlius is an invitation to consider retrospectively why the great powers of Greece failed.

THE PARADIGMATIC COMMUNITY II: THE THIRTY AT ATHENS

While a retrospective glance helps to confirm or recapitulate important themes that have gone before, it cannot provide the sort of interpretive guide that a prospective passage can give, such as the

Corinthian speech at Sparta in Thucydides; one could also add Herodotus' treatment of Croesus at the beginning of his work. I will argue that Xenophon, too, provides us with a prospective passage at the beginning of his account that is meant to underscore the important themes found throughout the rest of the *Hellenica* – namely, the history of the Thirty at Athens.

Countless comparisons between Xenophon's account of the tyranny of the Thirty at Athens and the other narrative versions have been made.[49] I will only do that here when it bears on the issue I want to address: what did the recollection of the Thirty mean for people in general, and what did it mean for Xenophon in particular? Further, how does Xenophon's treatment function as a paradigm for the rest of the *Hellenica*?

Before considering Xenophon's history of the Thirty in detail, it is important to take a brief look at a few issues concerning the size of the account, its dating and placement in the overall structure of the *Hellenica*. Not counting the brief mention of their installation at 2.3.2–3, the Thirty's story extends (from 2.3.11 to 2.4.43) over twenty Oxford pages or more than a tenth of the entire history which covers almost fifty years; assuming that their rule extended from the summer of 404/3 to the summer of 403/2, no other year is covered in such detail in the *Hellenica*.[50] As for dating, it is widely believed that the entire second portion of the *Hellenica* begins with the account of the Thirty.[51] If this is true, then we are entitled to ask a subsidiary though enormously important question: why did Xenophon resume his history at this point once he had discharged his duty to 'fill out' the history of Thucydides (*anapleroi*, Marcellinus *Life of Thuc.* 45; see above, p. 9)? Theopompus, after all, ended his continuation of Thucydides with the battle of Cnidus of 394 (*FGrHist* 115 T 13) and began his *Philippika* with the year 360/59 (T 17), allowing for a considerable hiatus in the years he covered, even if he found ways to treat some of the episodes which fell in between the two works. Moreover, when Xenophon resumed work on his history, it was in all likelihood at least twenty-five years after he brought to a close the first section; he had waited a long time. He wanted to reexamine the events surrounding the Thirty at Athens; he did not have to.

Contemporary treatment of the Thirty

By the time Xenophon started writing his history again, sometime in the early 350s (see above, p. 14), treatment of the Thirty had tended to go in one of two directions. For some the oligarchic revolution and the subsequent restoration of the democracy were important, but as events that took place in a legendary past. This propensity to memorialize and simultaneously to obscure appears soon after the restoration. In 403/2, a year after Thrasybulus and the other men who came down from the hilltop fortress of Phyle won their battle over the oligarchs at Munychia, an inscription bearing an honourary decree, a list of their names and an epigram was put up next to the Council House on the Metroon (the depository for state records in the Agora). While only the first few letters of the epigram have survived, Aeschines records the entire poem (see Raubitschek (1941)): 'Because of their bravery the ancient people of Athens have bestowed crowns upon these men, who once upon a time checked for the first time those men who ruled the city unlawfully, putting their own lives at risk' (Aeschines 3.190).

One of the interesting features of this epigram is its temporal orientation; although the events it alludes to were very recent, they are referred to as happening in a remote past – 'once upon a time'. This is not an unusual perspective for epigrams to have; so-called 'inscriptional "once upon a time"' (*pote*) is used when a future audience is imagined, that is an audience for whom even an action that is recent can be viewed as a part of 'ancient history'.[52] Important also to note is the effect this type of language would have on the contemporary audience; to see the men from Phyle treated in the same way as, for instance, the heroes of the Persian Wars (note, e.g., the beginning of the epigram honouring the dead from Eurymedon: 'Those who once upon a time lost their shining youth beside the banks of the Eurymedon . . .', *GVI* 13), would have (one imagines) heroized them and put them into a hallowed past as far removed from the present as other significant episodes in Athenian history. It is useful to remember in this connection that for men like Isocrates, both the Trojan and the Persian Wars were *muthoi* and 'of equal historical value'.[53] One indication that the fame of the heroes of the democratic restoration was practically instantaneous comes from an odd source: according to Plato, Socrates in his speech of defence in 399, some four years after the events, spoke in a highly abbreviated fashion and with considerable familiarity about them in connection with his friend Chaerephon – 'you know Chaerephon! He was my friend from youth and a supporter of the democracy; he shared in this exile and *came back together with you*' (*Ap.* 21a).

In addition to the temporal distancing evident in the inscription, we should also note the simple sequence of events: the Thirty came to power; the exiled democrats seized Phyle in order to put a stop to the tyranny; the democrats moved down from Phyle, fought the tyrants and defeated them. This chronology became fixed for all later accounts of the period: to be sure, significant differences still emerged (see below, p. 147 and nn.74 and 76), but this basic outline remained in place. The precise time and extent of the Spartan interventions – both the installation of the regime and its removal – are (unsurprisingly) not mentioned, and this is precisely where the accounts of the Thirty differ most profoundly. This situation was not unusual. Already once before, the Athenians almost instantly memorialized and hallowed native sons who were the enemies of tyrants – Harmodius and Aristogeiton, the men thought to have removed the Pisistratids; and similarly they also used the legend of the 'tyrannicides' to obscure or at least play down Spartan involvement in freeing Athens of tyranny – and thus we see both Herodotus' and Thucydides' attempt to correct the popular tradition that the Pisistratid rule was destroyed by the assassination of Hipparchus (Hdt. 5.55–65, Thuc. 1.20.2, 6.54–59).[54]

In the largely oral traditions of families, the era embracing the Thirty and their defeat became a sort of magnet, attracting to it persons and events that properly belonged elsewhere. Thus in the pseudo-Demosthenic corpus we hear of the career of one Aristocrates, in a speech delivered around 341, in all probability by his great-great-nephew Epichares ([Dem.] 58.66–67): he claims that his ancestor 'destroyed [the fort at] Eetioneia into which Critias and his party were expecting to welcome the Spartans, he removed the wall put up against us and brought back the democracy, putting himself in not insignificant danger' (58.67). As has been expertly shown by R. Thomas, Epichares has conflated events related to the oligarchs of 411 with those of 404/3; moreover, he has credited his relative, who was actually dead by the time of the second oligarchic coup, with a democratic loyalty that he did not have.[55] Both from a desire to associate his ancestor with the restoration of the democracy and not the oligarchic supporters of the late fifth century, as well as a genuine confusion of events, the speaker of [Dem.] 58 has seriously erred. But the error was natural. The Thirty and the events subsequent to them formed something of a watershed in the popular imaginations of the Athenian people in the fourth century: according to the author of the Aristotelian *Constitution of the Athenians*, the restoration of the democracy was the last major change in the history of the Athenian state (41.2),[56] a point that he probably makes on his own authority.[57]

From the year immediately following the fall of the Thirty, then, right down to the period when Xenophon was writing the second part of the *Hellenica*, there seems to have been a tendency to treat the period in a quasi-legendary fashion, mixing it up with events from other years.[58] However, others had an interest in recording the events of 404/3 in detail. As we have just seen, the errors of [Dem.] 58 in remembering the Thirty were not entirely innocent. In point of fact, most accounts of the Thirty seem to have unspoken agendas that often involve defending the memory of someone, specifically Socrates and Theramenes. The apologist tradition for the former is widely known: because Critias and Charmides, both prominent members of the Thirty, were also friends of Socrates (as well as relatives of Plato), the effort was made by men like Plato, Xenophon and Antisthenes to prove that the philosopher had nothing to do with the coup, indeed that he opposed the oligarchs' violence (thus the famous story of Socrates' refusal to kill Leon of Salamis, Plato *Ap.* 32c–d; cf. Xenophon *Hell.* 2.3.39 and Andocides 1.94, who assumes the murder to be common knowledge). Xenophon goes to great lengths in the *Memorabilia* to show that Socrates was not responsible for the two great 'enemies of Athens', Critias and Alcibiades (*Mem.* 1.2.12–46; cf. Plato *Ap.* 33a where we are told that Socrates 'kept an eye on his students'). For his part, although an admirer of Sparta, like so many others similarly disposed, Antisthenes probably did not approve of the policies of the Thirty;[59] indeed, he wrote an *Alcibiades* in which he spoke of Alcibiades as 'unlawful' (*paranomon*, Giannantoni F 141) and 'uneducated' (*apaideutos*, Giannantoni F 198),[60] points that are central also to Xenophon's critique in the *Memorabilia* and which suggest that Antisthenes may have had a similar attitude to Critias and the Thirty. And related to the defence of the memory of Socrates may perhaps be the strange fact that in the otherwise detailed picture of the Thirty in the Aristotelian *Constitution of the Athenians*, the name of Critias has been left out, perhaps to protect the 'Platonic school'.[61] For some at least, it clearly meant a great deal to 'clear' the name of Socrates from the charge that he was ultimately responsible for the Thirty and so worthily punished with death after the restoration of the democracy.[62]

A similar tradition sought to exonerate the memory of Theramenes, one of the Thirty. Evidently as early as 403, the only time when Lysias could have delivered his famous speech *Or. 12* (*Against Eratosthenes* – another member of the Thirty), there was a fairly widespread effort to preserve (if true) or fabricate (if false) a picture of Theramenes as a moderate member of the Thirty who tried to curb their excesses from within (Lys. 12.62–78). In fact, if Lysias can be trusted, Theramenes' speech of defence before the Thirty was available to be consulted (Lys. 12.77); with the publication in 1968 of the so-called 'Theramenes Papyrus' there is further evidence to support this possibility. And even if the 'Theramenes Papyrus' is not directly from a pro-Theramenes source, the existence of such an apologetic tradition is supported by the invariably positive view we get of him in the major narrative sources for the period of the Thirty (Xenophon, the Aristotelian *Constitution of the Athenians*, Ephorus/Diodorus, Justin).[63]

In addition to the apologists of famous men, other contemporaries of Xenophon who wrote about the Thirty with as much if not more attention to detail, and probably with only a little less personal interest, were the local historians of Athens or Atthidographers. As historians who made it their business to write constitutional histories of their city, at least some prominent ones dealt with the Thirty: Androtion certainly provided an account of them (*FGrHist* 324 F 10–11),[64] as did Philochorus later (*FGrHist* 328 F 143). They were presumably interested in the oligarchy and democratic restoration as episodes in the constitutional evolution of Athens. More importantly, though, there may well have been some overlap with the apologists of Theramenes; Jacoby argued that while conservative in outlook Androtion would not have recommended the extreme oligarchy of the Thirty, and indeed may well have viewed Theramenes as one of the great Athenian politicians and hence the moderate oligarch he is so often presented as elsewhere.[65] One reason he probably criticized the programme of the Thirty was the opinion of them held by his teacher, Isocrates. In the *Areopagiticus* of 355, Isocrates contrasts the *demotikoi* or 'peoples' men' who were prepared to suffer anything rather than to betray Athens with the Thirty, who were quite willing 'to tear down the walls and submit [their city] to slavery'; he also notes in the same context that when 'the majority were in charge we [Athenians] set up garrisons in other peoples' citadels, whereas when the Thirty took over the enemy held ours' (64–65; cf. Lys. 12.63). This passage makes it clear that Isocrates at least, and probably also Androtion, viewed the oligarchy strictly in Athenian terms, considering their regime to be wrong because it led to the subordination of Athens to Sparta and the diminution of her power. Although this may seem to be a natural way for an Athenian to interpret the period of the Thirty, it is not the one Xenophon took, and that fact is very important.

If we consider Xenophon's account of the Thirty against the backdrop of other presentations of the same period, some interesting points emerge. As with largely oral family traditions as well as popular ideology connected with the men who defeated the tyrants, some levelling has taken place in Xenophon's version of events: as I will try to demonstrate below, there is some simplification of the motives of the principals involved in the story of the tyrants, making them into 'goodies and baddies',[66] with Critias seeming almost too evil and Theramenes too good to be believed. Additionally, as will be seen below, there is a strong Theramenean apologetic component to Xenophon's narrative; so much is suggested by the essentially positive treatment of him as a moderating force, a treatment which stands in sharp contrast with Xenophon's earlier presentation of him as an unscrupulous politician, especially in connection with the trial of the generals of Arginusae (1.7.4ff.).[67] The reason for this treatment of Theramenes may be that Xenophon may have been one of the knights who were on the offical citizen rolls drawn up by the Thirty,[68] and so may have wanted, like so many others (cf. Lys. 12.62 and 78),[69] to use Theramenes as an 'escape hatch', suggesting that not all those who were implicated in the regime of the tyrants were bent on destroying the city and its inhabitants.[70] Further, the picture we get of the almost maniacal Critias is consistent with Xenophon's attempts elsewhere to defend the memory of Socrates and so aligns his account with the Socratic apologists as well.

In other words, much that was written about the Thirty came from persons who had specific points they wished to make and axes to grind, and Xenophon was no exception. But having said that, it is important to see, by way of comparison, how he resisted major distortion. If the *Seventh Letter* of Plato is truly by Plato, it was written at about the time Xenophon was completing the *Hellenica*.[71] Towards the beginning of the epistle, Plato explains how the violence during the regime of the Thirty turned his own ambitions away from a political career and towards a life of philosophy. His description of the Thirty, while certainly more accurate than, e.g., [Dem.] 58.66–67, is written in very much the same spirit; the perspective is strangely vague, and for that reason elusive and disquieting:

once, when I was a young man, I suffered under the same delusion as many: I planned, as soon as I reached man's estate, to embark on a life of politics. But certain events in the affairs of the city turned out in the following way. For at that time, while the government was being criticized by many, a revolution occurred, and fifty-one men [!] were in charge of it, eleven in the city, ten in Piraeus – each of these groups looking after the marketplace and whatever else it was necessary to keep an eye on – and thirty men with absolute power over everything. Indeed, some of these men happened to be my relatives and friends, and they immediately invited me as into affairs that were naturally fitting to me. I not surprisingly made a mistake due to my youth; I believed that they would, by leading the city from an unjust manner of life to a proper way, set it in order, and accordingly I paid close attention to what they would do. Seeing in the event that the men in a short time made the previous government seem golden – in many ways, but especially when they sent an old friend of mine, Socrates, whom I would not dishonour by stating that he was the most just man of that time, in the company of others to a certain citizen to lead him away by force to his execution, in order that he be an accomplice in their affairs whether he liked it or not; he did not obey but sooner risked everything than be a party to their unholy deeds – seeing these things and certain other ones no less shocking, I grew disgusted and removed myself from the evils of those days. Not much later the Thirty fell and the entire regime of that period.

(Plato *Ep.* 7 324b–325a)

Here we have an account of the Thirty by a man who by his own admission was in some way connected to their rule and hence interested in distancing himself from their reputation, a man furthermore who was concerned to defend the memory of Socrates, and who is recollecting events over a period of about fifty years – a man, that is, with much the same view as Xenophon. But although similar in many respects to Xenophon, Plato's version of events is entirely unsatisfactory as a historical account. To be sure, he is not attempting to write history, and furthermore does hint that there are matters he is intentionally leaving out; nonetheless there are events that he passes over that cannot be explained away: most importantly he fails to tell us precisely how the Thirty got into power and that they met resistance both from within (Theramenes and the 'moderates') and without (Thrasybulus and the *demotikoi*). Plato, having mentioned the government in power before the regime of the Thirty, could have, indeed one would have thought should have, mentioned the heroes of Phyle and the other supporters of Thrasybulus who brought an end to the tyranny. Further, it would also have made sense to draw attention to the part played by men like Theramenes in curbing their excesses, insofar as such attention would have given further proof of the criminal nature of the Thirty. Most surprisingly, Plato does not mention that the Spartan Lysander helped to establish the regime, and that Spartan soldiers helped to enforce its rule. Xenophon, an admitted Spartan sympathizer, also omitted their role in setting up the Thirty (see below, p. 147), but did not fail to underscore their role in providing the inspiration for the rule of the Thirty, and this matters more than anything else: while we can hardly expect him to have written so brief a history of the tyrants as Plato does in the *Seventh Letter*, the epistle does suggest an alternative manner of presentation (the Spartans entirely absent) which the historian did not elect to follow.[72]

Xenophon's treatment of the Thirty

Xenophon's treatment of the Thirty (2.3.11–2.4.43) is perhaps one of the most illuminating sections of the *Hellenica*, signalling for us the most important themes and attitudes found throughout the history, and at the same time permitting us to view Xenophon's record against several other versions of the same events. As pointed out earlier, in the *Hellenica* no single period receives anything like the coverage the Thirty get. Furthermore, it is a very elaborate section, containing anecdotes, dramatic scenes of arrest and execution, combat and personal observation by Xenophon himself. Additionally, the circumstances of the composition of the episode are problematic and potentially very significant: the vividness of Xenophon's narrative plus the little we know about his life have led scholars to believe that he was at least present at much that he recounts, if not a participant (perhaps as a member of the three thousand citizens enrolled under the Thirty), thereby making the treatment an eyewitness one.[73] But complicating this view is the fact that Xenophon wrote up his account much later, perhaps as many as forty years. Finally, as I mentioned above, the history of the Thirty constitutes the inauguration of the second major portion of the *Hellenica*, perhaps marking the spot in the narrative where Xenophon felt he had to break from the vision of the past set for him by his predecessor Thucydides and strike out on his own. We get a picture seemingly derived on the one hand from eyewitness knowledge, one that can be corroborated by comparison with other accounts and related to sources we possess; on the other hand there is reminiscence, the omission or distortion of fact through deliberate choice or faulty memory and elaboration with the benefit of considerable hindsight.

How did Xenophon view the Thirty, and what does his understanding tell us about the *Hellenica* as a whole? Just as Phlius stands towards the end of the history as a retrospective paradigm of the good community that survives, the Thirty stand towards the beginning as a prospective paradigm of the bad community that fails.

In the first place, Xenophon's understanding of the role of Sparta in the Thirty's regime deserves special attention. Unlike some, notably Andocides and Plato (see above), he does give them a significant part to play: the harmost Callibius and his garrison support the actions of the tyrants; Lysander goes to Athens to help them after they had been forced to retreat to Eleusis; and King Pausanias first fights the democrats based in Piraeus and then intrigues with them to bring about a settlement of hostilities. However, unlike other sources (Lysias 12.71–76, Diodorus 14.3.5–7, [Arist.] *Ath.* 34.2), Xenophon does not say that the Thirty were imposed by the Spartans; rather, they are elected by the people of Athens to write down the laws (2.3.11). While his version of events does not rule out the other accounts,[74] Xenophon's silence regarding Sparta's involvement in the creation of the Thirty makes the rule of the Thirty, at least down to the intervention of Lysander, seem part of the internal history of Athenian politics. The Spartans are left out from the establishment of the Thirty not because they would in some way obscure the connection Xenophon wishes to make between them and other contemporary tyrannies (cf. 2.3.3),[75] but because he sees their rule as primarily relevant to the internal history of Athens. Just as outside forces (Chares and the Athenians) were important but not central to his account of the defence of Phlius, so with the Thirty Xenophon stresses that while the Spartans were important to their rule, the course of their regime – their conduct and especially their failure – was entirely of their own making.[76]

If the people of Phlius were characterized by Xenophon as models of self-restraint who because of that virtue managed to survive, the Thirty are the opposite: they lack self-restraint and are greedy, and because of this weakness embark on a course of action that leads to their own destruction. Deeply informing this understanding of the Thirty is what one may almost style a Socratic analysis, articulated for the most part by Theramenes: the Thirty lack self-knowledge, they do not know what is truly in their best interests and as a consequence seem never to cease from doing things that contribute directly to the failure of their regime.

Matters start out well enough for them. They first round up sycophants and others who had been 'burdens on the better sorts' of Athenians and take them away for execution. The Council gladly condemns them, and Xenophon tells us that those 'who knew that they themselves were not at all like such criminals' approved (2.3.12). The odd addition of this last group of people who are confident that they were not at all like the sycophants and other trouble makers raises the interesting possibility that there were individuals who would act like a sycophant without actually being one – a point worth remembering later.[77] Xenophon explains that the aim of the Thirty is 'to rule the city in the way they wish' (2.3.13), and when they send envoys to Sparta to ask for military support they say that it will be needed only until they remove 'the wicked' (*tous ponerous*) and establish their constitution. But having won over the support of the Spartan commander Callibius so that he approves all the things they wish to do, they turn not against the remaining *poneroi* and other worthless citizens; instead they arrest those who seem most likely to resist them and organize some kind of popular opposition (2.3.14; cf. Diod. 14.4.3). Xenophon prepares us for the change in plan, and this first clear example of the oligarchs' abuse of their position and resources prompts the first in a series of extremely important exchanges between 'the extremist' Critias and 'the moderate' Theramenes. Xenophon notes that while they were still friends Critias was 'determined to kill many' and that Theramenes objected. Critias' defence of his violence, the first justification of many, is most illuminating:

> there is no way for those wishing to claim more than their due (*pleonektein*) not to put out of the way those most capable of stopping them. And if, because we are thirty and not one, you think that we ought with any the less care to look after this

government just as if it were a tyranny (*turannidos*), you are a fool.

(2.3.16)[78]

Critias' choice of words here is significant. Since Xenophon tells us again that Critias was still on familiar terms with Theramenes (2.3.16), he may be understood as confiding in him; his frank admission that the policies of the Thirty were directed towards *pleonexia* – gaining possession or control of what was not rightfully theirs – although shocking, is not completely impossible. In the famous fragment of his satyr play *Sisyphus* (DK 88 B 25), Critias has a character assert that when law had driven the violence of primitive man into secrecy but had not stopped it, an especially clever person invented belief in the gods so that people were afraid to do, say or even contemplate any evil in private: what, according to Xenophon, Socrates believed completely (cf. *Mem.* 1.1.19: 'the gods know the things spoken and done and planned in silence'), Critias regards as invention.[79] Such a person, sensing no societal restraints on their conduct, might well advocate *pleonektein*.[80]

Equally interesting and revealing is Critias' second assertion: you, Theramenes, are a simple-minded fool not to recognize that, although we are a group and not a single individual, we need to pay as much attention to the upkeep of our rule as does a tyrant. One is reminded of Pericles and Cleon in Thucydides (2.63.2, 3.37.2), where they assume the same naive misapprehension of the nature of absolute power on the part of their audience and make the comparison between Athens' empire and tyranny. However, there is one important difference: Pericles' and Cleon's point is to make their listeners see their rule in a new light by applying to it a term that is in some sense at least technically misapplied or inappropriate and therefore unexpected, even if not unprecedented – it is in other words a simile. Critias, on the other hand, is not speaking in similes: 'tyranny' fits the regime of the Thirty and it is only the number of rulers that Critias believes will obscure this fact.[81]

By having Critias describe his ambitions with the word *pleonektein* and his understanding of the rule of the Thirty as a *turannis* Xenophon is demonstrating that Critias knew no self-control. Unbridled desires determine the tyrants' actions. And as Xenophon has Socrates say in the *Memorabilia* (4.6.12), tyranny is government 'of unwilling subjects and not according to law, *but rather however the ruler desires*'. Time and again Xenophon will draw notice to this solitary motivation of the tyrants.

149

Early on in his account, then, Xenophon draws our attention to the ambition and lack of restraint of the Thirty. He also highlights their miscalculation and failure. Critias justified the execution of potential adversaries on the grounds that the opposition would be removed. The violence has the opposite effect. As Xenophon tells us, 'while many were being killed, and killed unjustly, many were openly gathering together and wondering what the government was going to be' (2.3.17). Opposition was growing, not diminishing, as a result of the executions. At this point Theramenes again speaks out: unless a sufficient number of people are made participants in the government, it will not be possible for the oligarchy to continue (2.3.17). Xenophon reports that Critias and the rest of the Thirty then enrolled three thousand men to be citizens in the new *politeia*, motivated interestingly by fear, not of what Theramenes predicted, but of Theramenes himself, 'lest the citizens rush to his side' as a leader (2.3.18; cf. [Arist.] *Ath*. 36.1). The Thirty follow Theramenes' advice, but not for the reason he advocated – increasing the regime's base of support; rather, the tyrants want to forestall the increase of the opposition and in particular prevent the concentration of support for Theramenes. Theramenes is looking for ways to bring about stability, whereas the Thirty react in fear and distrust, generally behaving in a way that betrays an attitude that promises more instability.

Theramenes' response to the Thirty's enrollment of the three thousand is central to Xenophon's analysis of the oligarchy. Taking on again the role of critic and warner,

> Theramenes said that it seemed strange to him (*atopon*) that in the first place, wishing to make the best citizens their colleagues [the tyrants] made only three thousand their associates, as though this number guaranteed that they were good and honest men (*kalous kai agathous*), and that it was not possible that there be noble men outside this number nor wicked men within. 'Secondly,' he said, 'I see that we are doing two completely opposite things (*duo . . . enantiotata*) – we are making our rule both violent and weaker than those we rule (*biaian te ten archen kai hettona ton archomenon kataskeua-zomenous*)'.

(2.3.19)

In a sense countering Critias' charge that he was 'simple-minded', Theramenes puts his finger on the major contradiction in the

150

actions of Critias and the other members of the Thirty. Although they are seeking to secure their grip on Athens, their methods in fact jeopardize their authority. Theramenes' thinking seems to be as follows: the violence of the Thirty has alienated great numbers of people, and consequently he sees the need for increasing the participation in government; despite this glaring need, however, the tyrants set the number of associates in their regime at the low figure of three thousand. The similarity here between what Xenophon has Theramenes say and what the author of the *Constitution of the Athenians* attributes to him is worth noting:

> Theramenes again criticized them [the Thirty], first of all because, wishing to share the government with the better citizens, they gave it to three thousand only, as though excellence was confined to this number; and secondly because they were doing two completely opposite things (*duo ta enantiotata*), making their rule both violent and weaker than those they ruled (*biaion te ten archen kai ton archomenon hetto kataskeuazontes*).
>
> ([Arist.] *Ath.* 36.2)

The parallels of thought and word are sufficient proof that both Xenophon and the author of the *Constitution* were using the same source – probably an account or actual transcript of the speeches of Theramenes (see above, pp. 142–143).[82] It is tempting therefore to say that, insofar as the failure of the Thirty served as a model for Xenophon of the inherent self-destructiveness of despotic and autocratic rule (more on this below, pp. 161–163), Theramenes or the Theramenean apologetic tradition profoundly shaped his historical vision. While this may be partly true, we should not push the point too far. Elsewhere, Xenophon characterizes the Thirty in much the same way, except that the criticisms come not from Theramenes but Socrates.

In a chapter devoted to showing how Critias and Alcibiades were ill-suited to follow Socrates (*Mem.* 1.2.39) and that the philosopher was consequently not responsible for the injuries they did to Athens, Xenophon tells us the following story about Socrates. Noting that Critias was unable to control his lust for Euthydemus, Socrates remarked in a crowd that Critias was suffering a pig-like affliction, wanting to rub up against his friend just as swine do against rocks (*Mem.* 1.2.30). The observation not surprisingly offended Critias, and when the Thirty came to power he remembered the insult and made it illegal to teach the art of rhetoric – a ban Xenophon tells us was aimed at Socrates (*Mem.* 1.2.31). Then, later, when the Thirty were killing many worthy citizens and making others act as criminals, Socrates was reported to have made a second remark in connection with Critias:

> it seems odd to me (*thaumaston*) if a keeper of cattle who makes his animals fewer and worse should not admit that he is a bad keeper; and stranger still if the leader of a *polis* who makes the citizens less and worse should not be ashamed and not consider himself a poor leader of his city.
>
> (*Mem.* 1.2.32)

Although this anecdote shows obvious similarities with Theramenes' remarks at *Hellenica* 2.3.19 – the feigned shock of the speaker (*atopon, thaumaston*) and the focus on the illogicality of the leadership's actions – it is undoubtedly the work of Xenophon, dovetailing as it does closely with his notions of the responsibility of leadership and serving the specific purposes of his defence of Socrates at *Mem.* 1.2.[83] In all likelihood the words of Theramenes did not so much shape as conform to views that Xenophon had already formed.[84]

Again ignoring Theramenes' advice, the Thirty, far from looking for ways to increase their popularity and hence base of support, hold a review of the Athenians in the Agora and disarm them with the help of the three thousand. They feel that with the population defenceless they are in a position 'to do whatever they wish', and accordingly they 'kill many out of hatred and many for the sake of their money' (2.3.21). Their violence, however, reveals a weakness: growing dependence on the Spartan garrison. Xenophon reports that the Thirty, in order to pay for the soldiers, decide that each of them should arrest one of the resident aliens, kill him and confiscate his property (2.3.22). As Xenophon presents it, we have come full circle: Theramenes refuses to kill a metic and suggests that the Thirty have become even worse than the sycophants they killed early on in their regime, for they at least left the victims of their greed alive (2.3.22; cf. Diod. 14.4.5); as promised, we see that the sycophants were not the only ones to harm honest men. But once again the tyrants have miscalculated; Theramenes' opposition stands in the way of them 'doing whatever they wish', and the tyrants plot his destruction.

The stage is set for Critias' denunciation of Theramenes and Theramenes' speech of defence and his execution (2.3.24–56).

The author of the *Constitution of the Athenians* does not record the speeches; Ephorus/Diodorus give only the briefest summary: Critias denounced Theramenes for betraying the new government and Theramenes defended himself and won the sympathy of the Council (14.4.5). Only Xenophon, in a scene which takes up a disproportionate amount of space,[85] provides the speeches. And while there is much about the Thirty that is still to come, not least of which are the occupation of Phyle, the battle of Munychia, the arrival of Lysander and then Pausanias, and the reconciliation, this scene distills the major points of Xenophon's treatment of the Thirty and thus forms a case-study of the self-destructiveness of autocratic power.

It has recently been suggested that 'the theme of the whole debate from beginning to end is friendship and treachery'.[86] But this element is not the most important one. What it takes to safeguard one's authority, and similarly what erodes it, is the issue foremost in Xenophon's mind, and the question of loyalty and friendship is subsidiary to it. Thus at the beginning of his denunciation Critias makes a general comment about the nature of the rule of the Thirty:

> O men of the Council, if any one of you believes that more people are being put to death than the situation demands, let him consider that where constitutions change these kind of things happen everywhere. It is necessary that here most are hostile to those changing the government over to an oligarchy because the city is the most populous of all Greek cities and because the *demos* has been nurtured in freedom for a very long time.[87] We, knowing that democracy is a difficult government for the likes of men like you and us, and knowing that the *demos* would never be friendly towards the Spartans who saved us but rather that the best people would always be loyal to them, for these reasons, with the approval of the Spartans, we established this constitution.
>
> (2.3.24–25)

Critias tries to justify the violence he deems necessary to maintain a type of government more agreeable to 'the best' at Athens as well as to the authorities at Sparta (cf. 2.3.32). But true to form he does not recognize a fundamental inconsistency in his thought. While he concedes that the oligarchy at Athens is in a particularly precarious situation as the regime's potential enemies are both numerous and unaccustomed to being left out of government, he endorses a course of action that essentially narrows the tyrants' base of support rather than broadens it.

The inconsistency of Critias' argument is underscored at key points in his speech by outright self-contradiction as well as remarks that cannot but be viewed as ironic. Addressing the members of the Council Critias asks 'why on earth is it necessary to spare a man like this who is always manifestly interested in greed (*tou men pleonektein aei epimelomenos*) and at the same time gives no attention to goodness or his friends?' (2.3.33) In the defence of tyranny that he makes to Theramenes at the start of the regime, Critias noted that those eager for greed are compelled to put their adversaries 'out of the way' (2.3.16): what is a reasonable defence in his own eyes for himself is culpable in Theramenes'. Most strikingly, Critias asks in his peroration that the councilmen condemn Theramenes on the following grounds: 'if you are wise (*ean sophronete*), you will not spare this man but yourselves, since being free he would make many of your enemies conceive grand thoughts, whereas dead he would cut off all from their hopes, both those in the city and those abroad' (2.3.34). This passage is thick with irony. As events will prove, with Theramenes' voice of reason silenced, the oligarchy will encounter more, not fewer enemies. Indeed, it is especially in connection with these closing remarks of Critias, as well as throughout Theramenes' speech of defence, that one appreciates the impact of Xenophon's chronology of events (see above, p. 147). The subsequent occupation of Phyle shows precisely how far-sighted Theramenes was and how self-destructive Critias. Critias appeals to the Council to be 'wise' or 'prudent' (*sophron*). For Xenophon this is precisely the virtue that brings about self-restraint and moderation and the virtue most notably lacking in both Critias and Alcibiades (*Mem.* 1.2.17–23); like *enkrateia* – the virtue so central to Xenophon's understanding of the Phliasians – the allied concept of *sophrosune* was the 'foundation' of the other virtues (*Mem.* 4.3.1, cf. *Mem.* 1.5.4; see above, p. 134). The Thirty have in a sense shown themselves to be the opposite of the people of Phlius, for they have behaved as men motivated solely by the satisfaction of their own desires, and violent when they are prevented from getting what they want. The implication of Critias' closing remarks is that the Thirty need 'prudence', not the Council, and that their own lack of self-restraint leads them to their destruction.[88]

The speech of Theramenes is for the most part a critique of the self-destructiveness of the Thirty. Having countered Critias' specific accusations regarding his role in the Arginusae affair, he turns to his main point:

> I agree with Critias in the following matter, namely that if someone wishes to stop your rule and makes those who plot against you strong, it is right that he pay the stiffest penalty. But who is the one who does these things? I think you would best be able to decide if you pay careful attention to what each of us has done and what we do now.
>
> (2.3.37)

Theramenes then shows how the actions of the Thirty harmed the regime; how the arrest of good men (which he opposed) turned potential allies against the government; how the disarming of the people (which he also tried to prevent) weakened Athens; and finally how the banishments of men of note provided the exiled opposition with good leaders (2.3.38–42). He sums up his position in a telling retort to Critias' charge that he is a traitor:

> would the man who openly gives this advice appropriately be considered a loyalist or a traitor? Those who prevent making more adversaries, who show instead ways to obtain the most supporters, these do not make one's enemies stronger, Critias, but rather those who unjustly take away money and who kill those who do no wrong, these are the ones who make the opposition more numerous and who betray not only their friends but also themselves for the sake of the sordid love of gain (*aischrocherdeia*).
>
> (2.3.43)

The thrust of Xenophon's narrative finds its full expression here. Critias, and all others driven by greed, are the most dangerous enemies of the Thirty; their 'shameful desire for gain' has led them to make the government so loathed and so lacking in support that its ultimate failure seems assured.

Only Xenophon provides all of the details regarding the conclusion of Theramenes' trial. Both he and Diodorus (2.3.50, Diod. 14.4.5–6) report that Theramenes' speech was so well received by the members of the Council that they show by their applause that they were clearly on his side, and that Critias responded by a show of arms, having a group of men armed with weapons either stand at the railings of the council chamber (Xenophon) or around Theramenes himself (Diodorus). Xenophon and the author of the

Constitution of the the Athenians report specifically how the Thirty manage to put Theramenes to death despite this popular support. Both say that since a law prevented the Thirty from executing anyone on the register of the three thousand, Theramenes' name is struck from the list and he is condemned to death (2.3.51, [Arist.] *Ath.* 37.1). The major difference between the two is that the author of the *Constitution* constantly refers to 'the Thirty' and the Council doing these things, whereas in Xenophon it is Critias. The importance for Xenophon of Theramenes being removed from the list of the three thousand is significant. As Theramenes will make clear when he is dragged from the altar in the council chamber to his death (2.3.53; cf. Diod. 14.4.7), once the Thirty are permitted summarily to remove his name from the register, they will not stop there (2.3.53); that is to say, the Thirty are willing to break the laws they have themselves created – they rule by *anomia* or the breach of law. 'Lawlessness' is for Xenophon a self-destructive state of depravity, reducing men to the lives of wild beasts rather than human beings, a way of living where each man looks after his own interests and neglects the good of the community; such, indeed, was the condition Xenophon saw the Ten Thousand falling into after the abortive and unauthorized raid of Clearatus and the abuse of the people of Cerasus (*An.* 5.7.32–34; see above, pp. 82–83). Proof of the Thirty's lawlessness comes immediately after the condemnation of Theramenes: pulled from the altar where he sought refuge, he remarks that he knew that the shrine would not protect him but wanted to demonstrate how the tyrants were 'the most unjust towards men and the most impious towards the gods' (2.3.53; cf. Diod. 14.4.7). Indeed, lawbreaking is also an act of impiety in Xenophon's eyes, as I will show in connection with Sparta's activities after the King's Peace, when law- or oath-breaking accompanies impiety, most notoriously in the case of the seizure of the Cadmea (see below, p. 193).

Significant episodes, and sometimes ones Xenophon suspects will not be adequately treated by others, do not pass without comment. The death of Theramenes is no exception. Xenophon reports that when the executioner Satyrus threatened that he would suffer if he did not keep quiet, Theramenes replied that 'if I am silent will I not also suffer'; and we are told that when forced to take hemlock, he played *kottabos* with the dregs and said 'this to Critias the fair' (2.3.56). Xenophon believes that these sayings (*apophthegmata*) may be regarded as unworthy of notice (*ouk axiologa*) but includes them anyway as proof of Theramenes' wit and jocularity even at the point of death (2.3.56). What was Xenophon's point? He calls Theramenes' behaviour 'admirable' (*agaston*). But surely also the scene connects Theramenes to Socrates, who, according to Xenophon, met his death with the same type of gallows-humour (*Ap.* 27–28);[89] and just as Socrates' execution is meant to underscore the injustice of his sentence, so too Theramenes' death scene is meant to focus our attention on the injustice of the Thirty, and Critias in particular.[90]

With Theramenes dead, the Thirty believe that they may finally 'rule tyrannically without fear' (2.4.1), but then Xenophon reports Thrasybulus' occupation of Phyle and the beginning of concerted resistance against the regime (2.4.2). Matters go from bad to worse for the tyrants. An almost supernatural snow storm 'in especially fine weather' thwarts their first attempt to dislodge the democrats from Phyle (2.4.2; cf. Diod. 14.32.2), and their second is routed by a surprise counterattack (2.4.6). This failure prompts the tyrants to adopt a predictably even more self-destructive action: the fortification of the sanctuary at Eleusis and the murder of many of its residents – something that Xenophon himself notes 'was pleasing especially to those citizens for whom greed (again, *to pleonektein*) was their only concern' (2.4.10). The battle of Munychia follows. Thrasybulus' speech to his men before the battle and that afterwards by one Cleocritus, an Eleusinian herald, are particularly illuminating. When the democrats move down from Phyle and take up their position on heights in Piraeus, and the Thirty march out and prepare to attack them uphill, Thrasybulus notes that the tyrants have played into their hands; he claims that this situation, in addition to the snow storm, proves that the gods are on their side (2.4.14–15; cf *An.* 3.2.10, *Hell.* 3.4.11; cf. *Ages.* 1.11–12). Following the battle in which Critias himself is killed (2.4.19), Cleocritus addresses the partisans of the Thirty and appeals to them to stop serving the regime. Significantly, speaking in reference to the Peloponnesian War he reminds them of the dangers both they and the democrats showed for the sake of common safety (*koines soterias*; recall the hope of the Ten Thousand) and for the sake of freedom, and he beseeches them in the name of the Athenians' paternal and maternal gods, as well as by their kinship and marriage bonds, no longer to obey the Thirty 'who for *the sake of their own profit* have killed almost more Athenians in eight months than all the Spartans did in ten years of warfare' (2.4.21). The point is that whereas in the past all Athenians had worked for the common good, the Thirty are divisive, interested in their own gain and prodigiously destructive as a result. The view is similar to Theramenes': the Thirty constitute a narrow regime incapable of doing anything but making others their enemies as they search for profit and, in the end, they only succeed in destroying themselves.

The whole sad chapter of the Thirty comes to an end fairly quickly after Munychia. The three thousand depose the Thirty and set up a board of ten to run the city; the tyrants retreat to Eleusis. Lysander is called in to destroy the democrats in Piraeus, and Pausanias follows, ostensibly to help but in fact to prevent Lysander from scoring another personal success. Pausanias schemes with the men of Piraeus and eventually brokers a settlement (see above, p. 147).

Before leaving the Thirty behind, however, Xenophon offers a final analysis of their rule in the form of another address by Thrasybulus to 'the men of the city', that is the former supporters of the tyrants. It is a powerful indictment of the Thirty, focusing especially on their overestimation of themselves. Thus Thrasybulus begins with a terse piece of advice: 'know yourselves!' (2.4.40). The Delphic injunction is apt; as we have seen in Xenophon's account, time and again the oligarchs fail to see the self-destructive nature of their own policies. Further, the command may have a special force and relevance when connected to Critias in particular. It was of course Critias who urged the men of the Council to be 'prudent' in handing down their judgment against Theramenes. As we have seen, *sophrosune* commonly meant 'knowing one's own limitations' and acting with restraint and caution as a result: certainly Xenophon understood the Delphic command in this way (cf. *Cyr.* 7.2.20).[91] Given that *sophrosune* and self-knowledge were closely allied concepts, it is interesting that Critias seems to have devoted a fair amount of his literary output to defining the concept of moderation.[92] In Plato's *Charmides* he is made to say that knowing oneself and being prudent are really one and the same thing (164c–165a). Hence Thrasybulus' recommendation may be quite pointed: where Critias preached the virtues of moderation and self-control but acted in a fashion contrary to them, his followers must do otherwise.

Indeed, Thrasybulus' speech to the supporters of the tyranny is a rejection of all their claims to superiority and hence to legitimate rule of Athens. It is an exposure of their lack of self-knowledge. If they thought themselves more just, he asks, why was it that the *demos*, though poorer, harmed no one of them for the sake of money, whereas they, considerably richer, perpetrated many shameful acts for the sake of personal profit (2.4.40)? He dismisses any claim they may have to superior courage by pointing to the successes of the *demos* against them (2.4.41). As for superior intelligence, Thrasybulus notes that while they had all the advantages in the recent conflict (fortifications, weapons, money, help from Sparta), they were defeated by men who had none of these things (2.4.41). Finally, the backing of Sparta ought not to be grounds for the oligarchs forming ambitious plans since the Spartans abandoned them to the wrath of the people (2.4.41). On all counts, then, the partisans of the Thirty have shown themselves inferior to the *demos*.

What is the point of this long account of the Thirty? Krentz and Whitehead have argued that the oligarchs, especially the extremists led by Critias, were attempting to set up a government at Athens based on the Spartan constitution.[93] It is pointed out that the number of citizens under the regime was three thousand, a figure thought to approximate to the number of *homoioi* or full citizens at Sparta at this time; they further suggest that the expulsions from the city of those not on the list of three thousand may have corresponded to the creation of a class of *perioeci* or 'dwellers around' the city, and that the targeting of the metics was inspired by the periodic banishment of strangers from Laconia, the notorious *xenelasiae*. Finally, Krentz argues that the conflict between Critias and Theramenes regarding the size and function of the assembly of citizens under the revised constitution may have been the result of two different views of where supreme authority ultimately rested at Sparta: with the assembly and hence by analogy at Athens with the three thousand or an even larger number of citizens (Theramenes' position), or with the council of elders (*gerousia*) and ephors (Critias' position).[94] The probability that the tyrants were modelling their constitution of Athens along Spartan lines raises some very important points for our understanding of Xenophon's purpose in recording the events of the tyranny.

Out of all the historians it is only Xenophon who does not report the involvement of Sparta in the formation of the Thirty.[95] Furthermore, he may have completely obscured the Spartans' continuing role in supporting some of the more violent acts of the tyrants; Diodorus reports that the Spartans voted that all Athenian exiles should be returned from throughout Greece to the Thirty at Athens – an act that shocked all the Greeks (14.6.1–2). Indeed, as noted above, like many accounts going back to the Phyle inscription,

Xenophon's story tends to explain the regime as a function of the internal situation at Athens and not a result of Spartan intervention; the Spartan garrison led by Callibius is an instrument of the tyrants, not a form of Spartan control. But having said this, it is important to see that Xenophon does not attempt to conceal the Thirty's admiration for Sparta.[96] In two different places in the denunciation of Theramenes, he reports that Critias mentions Sparta in connection with the new *politeia* of Athens. First, Critias says that it was with their approval that they were setting up the government, implying some degree of influence over what the features of the constitution would be (2.3.25). And at the end of the speech, he defends the elimination of Theramenes on the grounds that at Sparta no ephor would be tolerated who instead of going along with the majority reproved the government and opposed what was being done. His justification for this position is most important: setting up the analogy with the ephorate at Sparta, he asserts, 'now without a doubt (*depou*) the best form of government is that of the Lacedaemonians' (2.3.34). Given what we know about Critias' writings, it is entirely possible that he said such a thing. But that being the case, the confidence with which Critias makes this observation[97] and the axiomatic truth he claims for it require some explanation.

If it is true that Xenophon characterizes the actions of the Thirty in general and of Critias in particular as violent, greedy and ultimately self-destructive, what can it mean for him to allow us to see such a connection between the most notorious member of the tyranny and Sparta? The suggestion has been made that Xenophon, insofar as he was probably a member of the oligarchy as one of the three thousand, may be trying to move the blame for the violence of the government away from himself and other 'moderates' and onto the shoulders of the Thirty.[98] But this does not explain the connection between the extremists and Sparta. Surely Xenophon could have left the Spartans completely out of the picture (as Andocides and Plato did) and still manage to defend his own part in the regime; the violence of the Thirty did not have to be explained by their devotion to Sparta, especially for a man who was well known for his sympathy for the Spartans.

It is useful at this point to return to the issue of the Thirty as a paradigm. In what sense are they an example? Of what and for whom? A comparison with the preface to Diodorus Book 14 is instructive; if Diodorus is a reliable guide to what Ephorus wrote, then this contemporary of Xenophon helps shed light on what he may be attempting. There the point is made that all men, but especially those who seek *hegemonia* or are in some other way possessors of noteworthy fortune, should avoid doing wrong, for the truth of history will find them out and make their wickedness known to all. Testifying to the evil memory such people earn, Ephorus offers 'clear paradigms (*emphane . . . paradeigmata*) for those who read (*anagnousi*) the following narrative' (14.1.1–3). The particular cases he has in mind are the Thirty at Athens, the Spartans during the period of their preeminence after the Peloponnesian War and Dionysius the tyrant of Syracuse (14.2.1–2). In a triadic *men / de / de* construction, the Thirty are characterized as men who because of their *pleonexia* cast their homeland into great suffering, while they themselves lost the power they sought and left behind a 'timeless censure' of their own deeds. The Spartans, on the other hand, having won control of Greece, are said to have lost it when they carried out 'unjust deeds' against their allies, proving that the preeminence of hegemons is secured by good will and justice, and lost by acts of injustice and the hatred of those they govern. Finally Dionysius, although the most fortunate of dynasts, is described as a man who was always plotted against while alive and so fearful that he had to wear a cuirass under his tunic; in death he is said to have left his life behind as an example for men to use in making their reproaches of others. Ephorus makes it very clear what these paradigms represent and for whom they are intended. They are examples of how tyranny or hegemony bring with them misfortune; in the cases of the Thirty and Sparta in particular, their power is said to be self-destructive. Further, they are case-histories for the readers of Ephorus' account, didactic and cautionary paradigms that they are presumably to take to heart in the conduct of their own lives. Noteworthy is the fact that Ephorus does not try to connect the Thirty with Sparta. Indeed, the inclusion of Dionysius in his list of examples suggests that he sees the three cases as falling into the same period of history but essentially as unconnected and distinct.

How does Xenophon compare with Ephorus? Clearly the point of his treatment of the Thirty is also to illustrate the self-destructiveness of their power. But can we say that the story is designed for the moral education of later readers? That is more difficult to say. Xenophon's inclusion of the picturesque details of Theramenes' death shows that he has future readers in mind, for he imagines some of them objecting to what he has written; but surely it would be odd to suggest that he is holding up Theramenes' death as an example to be followed. No, this is precisely where Xenophon is different from Ephorus. His account of the Thirty is, strictly speaking, not didactic but explanatory; it does not seek to educate but illuminate, and this is where the connection he permits us to see between the tyrants and Sparta comes in. The paradigm gives Xenophon the opportunity to set out not just his understanding of why the Thirty fell but also how any regime falls: starting out with considerable advantages (note Thrasybulus' final speech to the partisans of the Thirty), the tyrants alienate their potential allies by abusing them, thereby contributing to the growth of their opposition and ensuring their eventual downfall. Given that he wrote his account not only after the reconciliation at Athens but even later, after the collapse of Sparta as a leading power, he may be trying to lay out his structures of explanation in miniature for the much larger task of accounting for Sparta's demise; in this sense the Thirty may be a prospective paradigm. Xenophon was not the first historian to foreground by means of *exempla* what he thought were the important elements in the rise and decline of power towards the beginning of his history; Herodotus did the same thing with the story of Croesus and Thucydides with the Archaeology at the beginning of their works.

Seen in the context of what others were saying and writing in connection with the Thirty, the *Hellenica*'s account of them does not seem at all unusual. In Xenophon, the rise and fall of the tyrants is essentially constructed as a conflict between the 'good' moderate Theramenes and the 'evil' extremist Critias. This understanding obviously overlaps significantly with the popular view of the tyrants that tended to memorialize, oversimplify and even distort what was no doubt a complicated situation; further, Xenophon's version no doubt shares numerous points of contact with the tradition at Athens that attempted to defend the memory of Theramenes and thereby to make it possible for those who may have had some connection to the regime to claim that they, like he, were not responsible for the brutalities of the tyrants. Of course, in points of detail Xenophon agrees closely with the other accounts of the Thirty. And yet having said all this, the feeling that the Thirty are emblematic of a historical process that would shortly be repeated on a larger scale and over a longer period of time comes out most clearly in Xenophon. To be sure, something of the paradigmatic tendency is also to be seen in Ephorus/Diodorus, but there it is moral lessons we encounter, not patterns of action that explain history. When, more than three hundred years later, Dionysius of

Halicarnassus summarized the *Hellenica* as the book in which one reads about the fall of the Thirty and the rebuilding of Athens' walls (*Pomp.* 4.1), he may have been thinking of Xenophon's history strictly as a completion of Thucydides (cf. *Pomp.* 3.10), but he may also not have been far from the truth. Having read about the fall of the Thirty, having noticed in particular how Xenophon characterized their failure as brought about by the self-destructive forces of *pleonexia*, we are in a position to see why, as Xenophon understood it, Sparta failed too.

But before turning to the mechanics of Xenophon's explanation for the fall of Sparta, it is important first to consider how he explained history through the use of the individual and the paradigm.

6

THE PARADIGMATIC
INDIVIDUAL

Much attention has been given to Xenophon's interest in the ideal
field commander, especially since the important work of Breitenbach
(1950). Without wanting to challenge the validity or usefulness
of this approach, I would like to suggest that Xenophon's paradigmatic individuals serve, in addition to a moral-didactic purpose,
a historical one as well and function much like his paradigmatic
communities.[1]

Within the framework of the *Hellenica*, Leuctra and its aftermath
form the culmination of a process that had started with the return
of Agesilaus from Asia and the outbreak of the Corinthian War;
Xenophon did not turn a blind eye to the growing excesses of
Spartan foreign policy. In particular he sees in their illegal seizure of
the Theban citadel the seeds of disaster sown for Sparta. Leuctra and
what followed were in his mind the historical result of this act,
which itself was only the most outrageous in a series of wrongful
deeds. In Book 6 there are several anticipations of Sparta's defeat at
the battle of Leuctra; one of them is the failure of the Spartan leader
Mnasippus, made even more significant by being compared with
the signal success of the Athenian commander Iphicrates. The story
of Jason of Pherae brackets Leuctra and contains a penetrating
analysis of the perils of 'seeking after more', thus forming a sort of
commentary on the failure of Sparta.

THE PARADIGMATIC INDIVIDUAL I:
MNASIPPUS AND IPHICRATES

Immediately following the first Jason digression Xenophon details
the reasons for the peace of 375/4 between Athens and Sparta:
weary because of their own expenditures in maintaining a fleet and

guarding their lands, and anxious because of Thebes' expansion at their expense, the Athenians conclude a treaty with Sparta. Xenophon's account of this peace is far from satisfactory;[2] absent entirely from his record is the Persian king who probably played the decisive role in bringing about what was essentially a reissue of the Common Peace.[3] Even less satisfactory, however, is his treatment of the period following the peace. According to Xenophon, the peace is remarkably shortlived; hostilities break out almost immediately between Sparta and Athens when the Athenian Timotheus restores democratic exiles to Zacynthus, and Sparta responds by sending out an allied fleet to Corcyra with the Spartiate Mnasippus in command. Cawkwell has shown this chronology to be in error; it seems more likely that the peace was probably observed for two years.[4] In the account of the conflict in north-western Greece, Xenophon commits more chronological blunders. He reports that Mnasippus devastated the crops on the land of the Corcyraeans and blockaded them by sea, forcing them to send a delegation to Athens to ask for help. In another remarkable compression of time, Xenophon records no fewer than three Athenian generals sent to Corcyra: Ctesicles, who secretly lands on the island with 600 peltasts as reinforcements; Timotheus, who is charged with equipping a fleet, and who is removed from office by the Athenians for wasting time while encountering difficulties in manning his ships with levies drawn from the islands; and finally Iphicrates, who replaces Timotheus, raises a fleet and sails for Corcyra. Through all this time Mnasippus, the only Spartan commander reported by Xenophon to be operating in Corcyra (there appear to have been two others) runs into trouble with his own mercenary army, is attacked by the Corcyraeans while Iphicrates is still on his way and is killed, precipitating the rapid departure of Spartan troops from the island.[5]

What led Xenophon to come up with such a treatment of the events between the peace of 375/4 and that of 371?[6] In searching for reasons why he did not properly account for the origin and nature of the peace of 375/4, and why, in the subsequent campaigning around Corcyra, he seemed either to have wilfully compressed the events of three years into one, or was somehow unable to establish a correct chronology, it is of course possible to attribute the deficiencies either to his phil-Laconism or his lack of historical sense. But Bruns noted as long ago as 1889 that, if anywhere in the *Hellenica*, then in the description of Mnasippus' command one is compelled to set a limit on Xenophon's pro-Spartan bias, for it is not a flattering portrait.[7] Indeed, if the portrait of Mnasippus is set beside that of Iphicrates, a contrast between the actions of an incompetent general and a competent one becomes immediately evident. This observation gains considerable strength when Xenophon's own assessments of the two generals are considered, especially his evaluations of Iphicrates' efforts (6.2.32, 39).[8] However, the scholars who believe that Xenophon's interest in the Corcyra episode was limited to the deeds of the commanders involved do not really address the question whether Xenophon was unwilling or simply unable to deal with issues apart from his favourite topic (i.e. commanders). Krafft argued that his distortion of events was deliberate, that he set out to contrast the leadership of Mnasippus and Iphicrates at the price of providing an unsatisfactory account of the details and chronology of the campaign; he also claimed that any conclusions regarding the limits of Xenophon's phil-Laconism based on his negative appraisal of the Spartan commander and positive one of the Athenian are groundless, since his interests were solely in the paradigms of good and bad generalship.[9]

This argument credits Xenophon with a conscious decision to arrange his narrative in the way that he has – it is meaningful in some way, even if it is unsatisfactory from a modern historian's point of view. But the suggestion that the Mnasippus and Iphicrates portraits reflect only Xenophon's interest in the ideal commander does not seem to me a fair appraisal. The position of the Mnasippus and Iphicrates contrast must be taken into consideration; I find it hard to believe that Xenophon's decision to contrast these two officers just prior to his treatment of the peace of 371 was without purpose. Indeed, the Mnasippus/Iphicrates episode contributes to Xenophon's evolving picture of Spartan decline, for the events surrounding the Corcyra campaign, even those involving the Athenian fleet and Iphicrates, underscore the worsening condition of the Spartan army and Spartan interests generally.

The first thing to note about Mnasippus is the composition of his expedition: sixty ships drawn not only from Sparta but also from important allied cities on the isthmus and in the Peloponnese (6.2.3);[10] a Spartan contingent of soldiers; and finally 1,500 mercenaries (6.2.5). Mnasippus arrives at Corcyra and devastates the cultivated lands and buildings, which are described as especially fine. Indeed, the plunder is of such quality, Xenophon reports, that 'people were saying that his soldiers had come to such a stage of luxuriance that they would not drink wine unless it had a fragrant bouquet' (6.2.6).[11] Needless to say, such excess is in Xenophon's mind completely out of place in any army, particularly a Spartan one.[12] Mnasippus then encamps close enough to the city of Corcyra to cut off any sortie from it, and blockades the city from the sea with his ships stationed at points where they can get advance warning of the approach of vessels and where they can halt their advance, winter weather permitting (6.2.7).[13] All these procedures reduce the Corcyraeans to *aporia* ('helplessness'; 6.2.8). In response to their earnest request (6.2.9),[14] the Athenians send Ctesicles and 600 peltasts to the island, who manage to slip past the blockade and join the defenders. The Athenians also charge Timotheus with fitting out a fleet of sixty ships, but soon relieve him of his command because of what they perceive as dilatoriness; actually Timotheus' delay is due to his effort to recruit sailors for his ships from the islands, his reasoning being that it was 'no small matter without care to sail around [the Peloponnese] against a well-disciplined fleet' (6.2.12). Timotheus' caution introduces the suggestion that the Spartan forces are well trained, an expectation that is about to be proved wrong. Synchronized with Iphicrates' replacement of Timotheus is the return to the account of Mnasippus' seige: Xenophon tells us that it is so successful that many desert Corcyra, despite being warned they will be sold into slavery, and come over to the Spartan side anyway, forcing Mnasippus to drive them back to the city (6.2.16). Mnasippus came to believe that the city was 'all but his', and the implication is that because of this confidence he began to withhold pay from his own mercenaries – this despite the fact that he had plenty of cash on hand. The decision to withhold pay from his mercenaries is to prove a fatal blunder and, as Xenophon makes clear, an unnecessary one as well – whereas the Corcyraeans were in real *aporia* (6.2.8), Mnasippus is behaving as though he were.

As soon as the defenders of the city note that the enemy watches are less well kept and fewer in number (no doubt the result of dissatisfaction with Mnasippus' command), they launch a sortie (the very thing Mnasippus sought to avoid in his planning) and kill and capture some of the Spartan force (6.2.17). Mnasippus arms, gathers his own troops together (the Spartan detachment) and marches out; he also orders the officers of the mercenary contingent to marshal the soldiers. The scene which follows is instructive: when the officers respond by saying that it will be difficult to provide Mnasippus with obedient troops if they are not first given the necessary provisions (and, one imagines, pay), he strikes one with his baton and another with the butt of his spear (6.2.18–19). Thus his treatment of his enemy and his own officers have become the same – before, he was flogging deserters from Corcyra (the worst elements of the enemy, 6.2.15), and now it is his own troops, as though he cannot distinguish between them. The harsh treatment of the officers, coupled with the withholding of pay and necessities, have reduced the morale of the army, a situation Xenophon regards as least conducive to a successful battle (6.2.19). This judgment is immediately confirmed in the conflict that follows. Mnasippus and his own detachment of Spartans advance towards the enemy stationed by the gates of the city, turn them and pursue; the enemy retreat, but as they near the walls of the city, within the protection of the cemetery, they turn about (*anestrephonto*, 6.2.20) and fire a hail of missiles at the approaching Spartans while other defenders sally forth through posterns and fall upon the furthest end of the Spartan battle line. Deployed to their standard depth of eight men the Spartans, considering the end of their line weak, themselves attempt an about-turn (*anastrophe*) in order to place their best troops at the point of attack.[15] The enemy, thinking the Spartans in retreat, attack and put them to flight, isolating Mnasippus, who is eventually killed (6.2.21–23).

There are two important details to note about this series of events. In the first place, Mnasippus' cruelty to his own subordinates is shocking. Cloché observed some time ago that the scene may be emblematic of Sparta's growing brutality.[16] This may be going too far. But that Mnasippus is treating his own officers as no better than helots is disturbing and significant.[17] Further, as has been noted recently, the failure of the Spartans to effect the *anastrophe* towards the conclusion of the battle contributed substantially to their defeat,[18] and this is no doubt true. But comparison of the conduct of the *anastrophe* at *Hellenica* 6.2.21 with *Lac.* 11.7–8 demonstrates that something far worse had been exposed in the battle outside Corcyra than Spartan vulnerability. In the latter passage, Xenophon praises the flexibility and mobility of the Spartan phalanx. The ease with which the Spartans execute sudden reformations of their phalanx in confused moments is the unique mark of those educated in the *paideia* of Lycurgus, which is to say, the true Spartiate. Xenophon also details the advantages of the Spartan phalanx: when the Spartans are in marching order and the enemy appears in front of them, the platoon commanders are ordered to keep deploying to their left until a line is formed; if the enemy appears in the rear, each file breaks off from marching order in such a manner 'so that the best soldiers are always opposite the enemy' (11.8).[19] It was precisely with this in mind, to put the best troops opposite the threatening Corcyraeans, that the Spartans attempted the *anastrophe*. That they could not, and the Corcyraeans could, provides not only the immediate cause for the Spartan loss, but also suggests that the Spartans' storied discipline,[20] as it was manifested in precise tactical manoeuvres, was also lost. The Spartans in other words are perhaps not the soldiers they used to be; and if that is the case, what distinguishes them from other Greeks? Mnasippus' poor leadership is surely to blame, but the consequences of the loss seem much more far-reaching.[21]

Iphicrates, the Athenian admiral, stands in direct contrast with Mnasippus; since his mission is to defend Corcyra and defeat Mnasippus, since furthermore the Corcyraeans are able on their own (together with Mnasippus' blunders) to accomplish these goals, and since nonetheless Iphicrates' mission to Corcyra is described in careful detail, this conclusion seems secure.[22] Iphicrates' great achievement is stated at the outset of the description of his voyage to Corcyra: 'when Iphicrates began the navigation around [the Peloponnese], at the same time he sailed he made everything ready for a naval battle' (6.2.27): while managing to discharge his order to get to Corcyra quickly, he also trains his fleet to be battle-ready. He accomplishes this apparently impossible task by removing the big sails from his ships and forcing the men to row: 'making the trip by oar he made his men fit and his ships swift' (6.2.27); he also deploys the fleet into battle formation prior to landing for meals and makes a competition out of reaching the shore first, the winners being rewarded with more time to eat and rest and the losers with having to attend to the same needs in haste;[23] and as regards provisioning his men, if there is a following wind he either allows them all to eat and then continues on, or he permits some to eat and rest on board while others keep rowing (6.2.27, 29). It should be remembered that Mnasippus' force, initially well trained (if its opening success was any measure), was allowed to enjoy exceptionally fine plunder. Also, in contrast to Mnasippus' watches which grew weaker the more intolerable his command became, Iphicrates very cleverly uses the masts of his ships as watchtowers, allows no fires to be lit in camp, but rings his troops with fires so as to detect any advancing enemy. Iphicrates furthermore communicates to his men by signal when in hostile territory, ordering them suddenly to deploy in a line formation or at depth, 'so at the same time they sailed they trained and grew knowledgeable in all matters that relate to naval warfare while they made their way into waters they thought were held by the enemy' (6.2.30).[24] By such procedures Iphicrates makes record time in reaching Corcyra with a trained fleet. So impressed is Xenophon with Iphicrates' achievement that he writes:

> I know that all these things are practised and prepared for whenever men contemplate fighting a naval battle, but I praise this thing in particular: when it was necessary to come quickly to the place where Iphicrates knew he would fight the enemy, he found a way whereby his men were prepared for combat although they had to make a voyage, and a timely voyage was made despite the need for his men to train.
>
> (6.2.32)[25]

These words of praise have been anticipated in the description of the voyage;[26] although Xenophon is aware that all the procedures singled out in his account are not exceptional, to accomplish them *and* make speed is noteworthy. The apologetic tone, reminiscent of *Hellenica* 2.3.56 (Theramenes' gallows-humour) and 5.1.4 (the successful command of Teleutias), reminds us that the passage has programmatic significance. Just as in those places Xenophon's interest in the individual was the central focus of attention, so too here. Xenophon's assessment of Iphicrates gains in significance too when compared to what Ephorus seems to have said about the same voyage: according to Diodorus, Iphicrates arrived too late to aid Corcyra and he earns a rebuke from the historian because of his tardiness (15.47.7).

To paraphrase Breitenbach, the successful command of Iphicrates is brought into relief by the unsuccessful command of his opponent.[27] One last passage from the narrative of Iphicrates' campaign helps to bring this point home. After he arrives in Corcyra and learns that ships of Dionysius are on their way to help the now vanquished Spartans, Iphicrates sets up an ambush, stationing his vessels where they would not be seen by the enemy but where they could surprise and capture him (6.2.33). He orders twenty of his ship-commanders to be ready to follow him at his signal, warning that if someone fails to follow him he will pay the penalty (6.2.34).[28] When the signal is given that the enemy ships are approaching, Xenophon notes that the speed of the deployment of the ships was a sight to behold: 'for there was no one of those about to sail who did not run on board ship' (6.2.34). This detail is no doubt meant to contrast with Mnasippus' beating of his own officers. Whereas with Iphicrates the threat of discipline is never carried out because his troops are well trained and eager to obey, Mnasippus' act was merely the final demonstration of his poor leadership that rendered his force weak and ultimately unsuccessful. The contrast reminds us that the failure of Mnasippus on Corcyra was the failure of a Spartan commander who was overconfident, greedy and brutal; and that, in this instance at least, the Spartan forces, although initially successful, were eventually defeated by their own shortcomings and those of their commander as much as by their inferior opponent.

In only a few pages we will be treated to an overconfident Spartan assembly that insists upon leaving its army in Phocis against the terms of a new peace, an act that leads directly to their disaster at Leuctra. The account of Mnasippus and his army on Corcyra, by means of its distinctly Xenophontic concentration on generalship, provides a glimpse of things to come.

THE PARADIGMATIC INDIVIDUAL II: JASON OF PHERAE

The two digressions on Jason of Pherae[29] (6.1.2–19, 4.22–37) fit uncomfortably into the fabric of the *Hellenica*. In its otherwise spare narrative, lengthy excurses are rare;[30] Thessaly, where Jason is from, is not an area of Greece in which Xenophon is otherwise interested, and he invests the ruler with an importance not elsewhere attested.[31] Further, the presence of the digressions in Book 6 is intrusive, a part of the history that is clearly focused on the clash between Thebes and Sparta. And finally, the manner of Jason's presentation is very odd – he is described in a speech to the Spartans by one Polydamas of Pharsalus, who in turn quotes in direct speech a long conversation he had with the dynast in which the latter did most of the talking.[32] All these abnormalities need explanation.

Polydamas' report about Jason to the Spartans constitutes the first digression and is itself prefaced by a thumbnail sketch of Polydamas and his probity – no doubt assuring the audience of the accuracy of what he has to say.[33] Although ostensibly an appeal by Polydamas for Spartan aid in warding off Jason who is seeking the office of *tagos* (grand marshal) of Thessaly, fully half of his speech is taken up by a verbatim report of Jason's speech to him, urging Polydamas to join him as an ally. This indirect manner of reporting Jason's words has led to some interesting speculation;[34] of course in choosing to describe Jason's power by having a knowledgeable intermediary report to the Spartans, Xenophon is doing something similar to Herodotus and Thucydides, who both had concerned speakers describe in vain a real threat to the Spartans.[35]

The digression describes Jason's excellence as a military commander, very much in Socratic terms, a detail that has led several scholars to conclude that this excursus constitutes the clearest proof of Xenophon's interest in relating not just any events, but the deeds of great generals,[36] and therefore an early suggestion of the nascent genre of biography.[37] These explanations do not adequately explain the placement of the digression; why would Xenophon choose to inter-rupt his narrative, which has been building towards Leuctra since Book 4, to showcase a noteworthy general? There must be stronger links between the digression and the events of the narrative up to this point. Of course the history of the period shows that Jason started to play a more direct role in the affairs of Greece at the same time Sparta and Thebes came into conflict in Phocis, and so explains why we hear of Jason when we do in the *Hellenica*.[38] However, unlike the explanations that see the digression as an opportunity for Xenophon to express his views on the ideal field commander or the role of the individual in history, the chronological explanation does not satis-factorily explain precisely what is in the digression, and it does not at all explain the second excursus. Indeed, I think that it is with the second digression that a satisfactory explanation can be found.

In the aftermath of Leuctra, the Thebans send a herald to Athens to announce their victory and to ask for help in marching on Sparta; he is coolly received (6.4.20). Their mission to Jason proves more successful. Jason's response to their request for help is immediate, and his march south is so rapid that Xenophon draws our notice to it: 'well before any opposition could gather against him he everywhere appeared, making it clear that in all circumstances speed rather than force accomplishes whatever needs to be done' (6.4.21).[39] In his conference with the Thebans, he persuades them not to undertake the attack on Sparta for two reasons: first, they ought not to be involved in an enterprise that would either win them much more or would lose them all they had gained by their recent victory; and second, noting that it was in a state of *ananke* (necessity) that the Thebans were victorious, he urges them not to put the

172

Spartans in a similar situation and thereby give them extra incentive (6.4.22–23). He concludes his advice for the Thebans with the following observation: 'God, it seems, often delights in making the small great and the great small' (6.4.23), an observation Xenophon himself made while a commander of the Ten Thousand (*An.* 3.2.10; see above, p. 109). Xenophon next describes Jason giving advice to the defeated Spartans. Observing that all armies win and lose, he recommends that they regroup, regain their strength and then attempt to fight the Thebans again (6.4.24). In the meantime, they should sue for peace, for, as he explains, he wants to save them on account of the *philia* (friendship) his father had for them and for the sake of his own relationship of *proxenia* to them (6.4.24). But Jason is not actually motivated by *philia*; Xenophon cynically notes that his advice both to the Thebans and Spartans had a purpose other than creating peace: 'he was saying such things, but he was in fact trying to bring it about that they be at odds with one another and that they both become dependent on him' (6.4.25). The contrast between 'saying' and 'doing' is marked and suggests the future course of Jason's real policies.[40] Indeed, on his way back from the conference through Phocis, Jason devastates Hyampolis and tears down the walls of Heraclea, a strategic point on the north–south axis of Greece.[41] This last action, Xenophon explains, was undertaken,

> clearly not because he was afraid that with this city occupied invaders could make their way north against his own domain, but because he was intent on not allowing anyone to seize Heracleia and shut him out (situated as it was in a narrow pass), if he wanted to march to anywhere in Greece.
>
> (6.4.27)

Here at last the true motive for Jason's activities after Leuctra, including his peacemaking, is revealed – to prevent the Thebans from gaining complete supremacy of Greece by dealing Sparta a decisive blow at her heart, and to encourage the Spartans to regroup just enough of her resources so as to keep Theban expansion in check – all this so that he might march on Greece.[42]

At this point Xenophon underscores the extent of Jason's power in a carefully constructed triadic structure:[43]

> When he returned again to Thessaly, he was *great* because he was installed officially as *tagos* of the Thessalians and because he kept numerous mercenaries about him, both foot and

mounted, and these so well trained as to be the very best soldiers. He was *still greater* because of the many allies he had at that time and because of those who wanted to be his ally; and he was *the greatest man of his time* because he was taken lightly by no one.

(6.4.28)

Jason's preparations for the Pythian Games demonstrate his power; he orders great numbers of sacrificial animals from his client states and plans to preside over the games himself (6.4.29–30). Furthermore, he orders the Thessalians to muster at the time of the festival, ostensibly to make a 'gathering' for the god and for himself to conduct the games. Although he avoids confirming the charge, Xenophon also reports the following: 'regarding, however, the sacred monies, it is unclear even now if Jason had designs on them; it is said that when the people of Delphi asked the oracle what they should do if he seized the sacred wealth, the god answered that he would himself look after it' (6.4.30). Whether Jason really had designs on the sacred treasury is unclear, and there are reasons to suspect that he did not.[44] Nonetheless, Xenophon implies he might have;[45] he does not question that the people of Delphi were alarmed enough to consult the god about what should be done.[46] Moreover, his description of Jason's death offers positive confirmation that he believed that Jason desired control over Delphi's wealth:

> Being so great, and having such things in his mind, he held a review and examination of the Pheraean cavalry; while he was seated and replying to those who approached him with a specific need, he was cut down and slaughtered by seven young men who had approached him as though they had a quarrel among themselves.
>
> (6.4.31)[47]

Jason's death is in part due to his coveting the wealth of Delphi, for the sentence is clearly linked to the oracle immediately preceding.[48] But Jason's murder is also the *peripeteia* or downfall of a man who sought too much power. Indeed, it seems he is a victim of his very own maxim, that the gods can render 'the great small and the small great', especially when the former have plans that aim at everything and risk all. Interestingly, the reception of his murderers as heroes throughout Greece permits Xenophon to show that the Greeks feared he would become their tyrant (6.4.32).

As a coda to the story of Jason, Xenophon appends the bloody history of his family down to at least 358.[49] As soon as his brothers Polydorus and Polyphron take over the *tageia*, the latter kills the former and begins to change his rule into a tyranny (6.4.34), notably by putting to death the noteworthy citizens of Pharsalus, including Polydamas. Polyphron is in turn killed by Alexander, the son of Polydorus,[50] who also aims at tyranny and makes himself an enemy of Thebes and Athens (6.4.35). Finally, Alexander is murdered by conspirators who are encouraged by his own wife, and is replaced by Tisiphonus,[51] the ruler contemporary with Xenophon's writing of this portion of the *Hellenica* (6.4.37).

As Sordi noted some time ago, the two digressions on Jason concern his fall as well as his rise, and Xenophon's interest does not stop with Jason but continues with the troubles of his family after his death.[52] Even this most capable man is murdered and his family embroiled in a bloody feud. Sordi noticed that Xenophon was interested in Jason as an example of imperialism,[53] and more recently Higgins has argued that Jason was particularly disturbing for Xenophon precisely because he displayed all the qualities of the good Socratic general but was still a tyrant.[54]

But we can say more. The digressions on Jason bracket Leuctra and the beginning of the end for Sparta. This proximity to Leuctra suggests that the Jason-*logos* is not only another paradigm of the frailty of power and the ultimately self-destructive nature of tyranny, but is also meant to help us understand the significance of the battle in the broader context of the history. There may exist a meaningful similarity in the qualities Xenophon draws notice to in Jason and in Sparta and her king, Agesilaus; the Socratic virtues of Jason are also ones which Lycurgus tries to instil in the Spartan youth through his rigorous *paideia* in the *Constitution of the Spartans*,[55] and they also show up in the catalogue of Agesilaus' excellences in Xenophon's biography of him.[56] These points of contact may be due, however, to Xenophon's idealized view of all three – Jason, Sparta and Agesilaus. A closer parallel between Sparta and Jason might be that the dynast, while at the height of his powers, contemplated a religious crime which resulted in his demise, a scenario that might be seen as parallel to Sparta's seizure of the Cadmea, the citadel of Thebes, and her subsequent decline. All this suggests, I think, that Xenophon understood Jason's and Sparta's goals to be the same – domination. Indeed, the scene of Jason's death, beginning with the summary of his great stature, has much the same force as

Xenophon's assessment (5.3.27) of Sparta's powers before he passes comment on the crime that (in his mind) determined the outcome of Leuctra. In the conveniently brief compass of the story of Jason, detailed in the narrative around Leuctra, we are perhaps meant to see the same process of ascent, tyranny and decline which is spread over a much longer period for Sparta.

Through juxtaposition the Jason story invests Leuctra with this broader significance. The story of Jason, reproducing themes that are also present in the story of Sparta's decline, paratactically informs Leuctra and Sparta's fall. This method of using the story of an individual to harness themes that also unfold in the main narrative of a history was pioneered by Herodotus.[57] Its chief advantage is that a process of decline that takes place over years can be prefigured by the description of one man's life. Fornara knew of its importance for Herodotus:

> in the beginning of Herodotus' history (1.5.4) comes the initial statement of what is programmatic for the entire work. Greatness is ephemeral; 'human happiness is never stable'. A supreme example is shortly thereafter provided in the Solon–Croesus episode ... The immense importance he attached to this episode as indicative of the meaning of the work best explains why the Lydian *logos* was placed in the first position.[58]

So also with Jason near the end of the *Hellenica*.[59]

Part IV

XENOPHON, THE DIVINE AND THE CRIMES OF SPARTA

7

XENOPHON AND THE DIVINE

At *Hellenica* 5.4.1, prior to his account of the recapture of the Cadmea, Xenophon writes:

one could bring up many other instances, both Greek and barbarian, which show that the gods neglect neither impious persons nor those who do wicked deeds. Now I will take up the matter at hand. The Spartans, having sworn to let the cities [of Greece] be free, seized the acropolis at Thebes; by the very people alone whom they wronged they were punished, having themselves never been defeated in battle before. As for the Thebans who brought the Spartans into the citadel and who wanted to enslave their city to the Spartans so that they might be tyrants themselves, only seven of the exiles were needed to destroy their rule. I will now explain how this happened.

In this carefully constructed passage,[1] Xenophon traces a line of causation extending over ten years – from the seizure of the Cadmea in 382 to the Spartan defeat at Leuctra in 371. What is more, he is openly claiming that the battle, which signalled the beginning of Sparta's rapid decline, was in some sense the result of divine will. This passage has, for obvious reasons, scandalized some modern readers of the *Hellenica*,[2] who feel that no historian, let alone one working in the tradition of the sober Thucydides, could possibly be taken seriously after making what is tantamount to an admission of his reliance on the divine for explaining historical events. The Oxyrhynchus historian never spoke of the gods in this way. Even the flamboyant Theopompus seldom (if ever) had recourse to divine explanations for human events. Only in the turgid pages of writers like Ephorus and the Atthidographers can one find frequent mention of the divine, and even then it is of a rationalist and anti-quarian nature.[3] Xenophon and the divine, in particular the divine as historical agent, will form the subject of this chapter.

INTRODUCTION

Chapter 1 argued that it is where Xenophon's understanding of his age seems to break down, most notably in his analysis of the battle of Mantinea and its results, that one can see most clearly his reliance on the divine as an explanation for historical causation: if order and purpose, notions very important to Xenophon, could not be found in the human sphere according to human logic, they could perhaps be located in the world of the gods. This is not to say that Xenophon viewed the gods primarily as agents of disorder, but rather as the last place to situate order; Xenophon's attachment to the gods, it was suggested,[4] was the manifestation of a belief in the purposefulness of history even when history from a human perspective did not encourage such a conviction. And, although a position often advocated, Xenophon's reliance on the gods ought not to lead us to think that he abandoned his mission to document the history of Greece from the fall of Athens to the fall of Sparta *as he understood it*. At the risk of stating the obvious, Xenophon wrote the *Hellenica* in accordance with how he made sense of the events of his age; if he believed that the gods had a role in shaping history, this belief ought not to invalidate his account.[5] Why not?

Historical writing and belief in a powerful divine apparatus capable of 'changing' the course of human events do not seem to be compatible concepts. When a historian asserts that an event occurred in the a certain way because 'the god(s) made it so' it is often maintained that such an assertion invalidates the historical account as an accurate interpretation of the past. Xenophon is a case in point. He has often been criticized for relying on the divine to explain the shaping of human affairs, especially in his explanation for the fall of Sparta found at *Hell.* 5.4.1. As I have mentioned, Xenophon's readiness to see the gods at work in human events has even been held up as the surest indication that he failed to follow the precepts set down by Thucydides for the writing of history – a charge tantamount to saying that despite his best efforts Xenophon failed to be a historian at all. Yet Thucydides was an extremely unusual historian; much more widespread was a belief that the divine in some way guided human affairs. Consequently we must not measure Xenophon by the eccentric standard of Thucydides, but rather attempt to set him within a fuller context. We will then be in a position to see how his own view of history was like and unlike that of his contemporaries.

In support of this task it is appropriate at the outset to note that scholarship in Herodotean and Old Testament studies warn against taking the view of the divine in history uncritically as evidence for the lack of historical reasoning. When Felix Jacoby argued in his groundbreaking article (1913) that Herodotus' ability to apprehend human causality in history was irretrievably 'retarded' by his belief in the gods as historical agents, Friederich Focke responded quite reasonably that the argument could be made that it was precisely Herodotus' religious perspective which among other things allowed him to see a connection between apparently discrete events – a view that was reiterated by Charles Fornara.[6] John van Seters has made a similar defence of the 'Deuteronomic historian' of the Old Testament, suggesting that to disqualify his historical vision on the grounds that it has a theological orientation is simply to misunderstand him.[7] At the bottom of both defences is a very important principle: before evaluating the merits of these historical texts, an attempt should first be made to determine and understand their points of view, particularly with regard to the nature of the divine.

What I propose to do in the present chapter is to explore how a belief in the divine at work in human affairs may have helped Xenophon understand the history of his age. In the subsequent chapter I will take as the subject for my discussion Book 5 of the *Hellenica*, in which Xenophon's controversial observation on the gods as historical agents is found. I hope to show how this observation and other features of Book 5 that have been thought to typify the major shortcomings of the *Hellenica* are integral to an elaborate scheme of explanation that attempts to show how Sparta's rapid decline in the 370s and 360s was largely the result of its own tragic mistakes.

First, however, it is important to consider briefly Xenophon's religious views, especially as they are expressed in his philosophical works. Indeed, it should be noted that we are in an almost unique position when it comes to exploring Xenophon's religious views as they pertain to his understanding of history. Unlike the case of most other ancient historians, we do not have to reconstruct Xenophon's intellectual outlook from his historical works in order to determine how it influenced his historical writing (an obviously circular procedure). Xenophon expressed his views on matters of consequence for his understanding of history in his many non-historical works.[8] This is just as well, for as will become clear, Xenophon only rarely refers to the divine in the *Hellenica* itself, and he does so unsystematically.

XENOPHON'S RELIGIOUS VIEWS

Diogenes Laertius ends his brief biography of Xenophon as follows: 'he was pious, fond of sacrificing, capable at discerning sacred matters and extremely devoted to Socrates' (2.56). From this parting capsule summary of Xenophon's character we are left with two clear impressions: Xenophon was evidently a devout traditionalist in religious matters and at the same time found inspiration in the person of Socrates. These impressions accord well with the only glimpses Xenophon provides of his own religious life. In the *Anabasis* he tells two stories about himself, one from the time before he went to Asia and one from the period after this return. The first (*An.* 3.1.4–8) recounts Xenophon's visit to Delphi for guidance whether he should accept his friend Proxenus' invitation and join up with Cyrus' mercenaries. He consults Apollo on the advice of his friend Socrates, and it is Socrates who chastises the young Xenophon on his return for not asking the right question of the oracle: Xenophon did not ask the primary question 'should I go on the march with Cyrus?', but inquired instead 'to which god should I sacrifice in order to secure my safe return?', a question which assumes that it is proper for Xenophon to go.[9] It should be noted that Socrates is chiding Xenophon for following a regular Greek practice regarding divination, that is to ask a secondary question concerning a matter that one is already determined to take up;[10] this combination of traditional religious outlook (the appeal to the oracle) and revision (Socrates' rebuke) is central to Xenophon's religious attitude. In the second passage (*An.* 5.3.7–13) Xenophon has returned to Greece and is living in exile from his native Athens on an estate at Scillus near Olympia. In fulfilment of an obligation he was under to the goddess Artemis of Ephesus, Xenophon has built a miniature replica of the sanctuary to the goddess on his property near the Selinus river from money kept safe for him for many years by a Persian friend. We see Xenophon holding yearly festivals there and piously dedicating offerings. The passage closes with the transcript of an inscription Xenophon had put up warning the future holder of the property to dedicate a tenth of the yearly harvest;

otherwise, the inscription reads, 'he will be a concern for the goddess'. We learn in the same paragraph that Xenophon, in fulfilment of the same vow, made a dedication to Apollo at Delphi. On this dedication he had his own name inscribed as well as that of Proxenus; Xenophon's reason for including Proxenus is simple and powerful: 'for he was [Xenophon's] friend'.

These passages from the *Anabasis* support Diogenes' view. As is clear from the elaborate and extensive measures to which Xenophon went in the fulfilment of this obligation to Artemis, he was a man of rigorous traditional piety who took particular relish in his yearly offerings to the goddess. His trip to Delphi demonstrates his interest in discerning the will of the gods, and the same episode underscores his attachment to and respect for Socrates, qualities of friendship that are also suggested in Xenophon's loyalty to the memory of Proxenus.

It is very important to look in more detail at the centrality to Xenophon's character of traditional piety. Elsewhere in the *Anabasis*, when challenged to explain his frequent sacrifices to the gods,[11] Xenophon states: 'As you see, gentlemen, I sacrifice as often as I can both on your behalf and on mine, in order that I might happen to say, think or do those things which turn out to be best for you and most honourable for me' (*An.* 5.6.28). For Xenophon, sacrifice is essentially divinatory, important primarily for determining the will of the gods (see also *Hipparchicus* 1.1). The reason it is important to know the will of the gods is straightforward: as Cambyses makes clear to Cyrus in the *Cyropaedia* in a passage discussed more fully below (p. 226), human intelligence is fallible, the gods' is not – they know all things and are consequently the only reliable source for guidance regarding one's actions (*Cyr.* 1.6.46).

The consequences of this simple observation are of major importance for an understanding of Xenophon's thinking. The gods can help in all spheres of human activity, even thinking; they are, in other words, aware not only of human action and word but also thought. This point is made most forcefully in Xenophon's defence of Socrates' piety in Book 1 of the *Memorabilia*. At the end of the first chapter, he expresses astonishment that the jury which condemned Socrates to death for impiety forgot his devotion to his word. In particular Xenophon recalls Socrates' refusal to break his oath to serve as a member of the Council *kata nomous* – according to the laws of Athens – during the trial of the generals of Arginusae. Xenophon explains that Socrates was unwilling to break his bouleutic oath because he believed that the gods were concerned with humans not in the way that many believe they are. Most men believe that the gods know some things and do not know other things. Socrates on the other hand believed that the gods knew all things, the things spoken and done and planned in silence; that they were present everywhere and communicated to men concerning all human matters.

(*Mem.* 1.1.19)

Xenophon, in trying to defend Socrates' personal piety, is by his own admission suggesting that Socrates' views regarding the divine were uncommon:[12] while most hold that the gods are not omniscient, Socrates believed they were, in particular possessing a knowledge of the secret plans of men. What Xenophon seems to be saying is that the gods were aware not only of the outward signs of decision-making (deeds, words) but also the internal motivations that lead to these outward and hence perceptible manifestations. This view implies that it was not possible for Socrates to give in to outside pressure and join his colleagues in the Council in permitting the technically illegal trial, that the unanimity of opinion among the councillors would in a sense legitimize their decision – their judgment could be made to seem one which was 'according to the laws'. This position regarding the interpretation of law suggests that it is essentially human and therefore changeable. Socrates' refusal to break his oath speaks of a belief in the absolute sanctity of the oath and of the gods' total and absolute awareness of humans' adherence to them; even departures from the spirit of the oath were known to the divine. (This line of thinking is not unparalleled before Xenophon; see Hdt. 6.86.8, where the point is made that it is not good *even to contemplate* abandoning one's obligations. Cf. Hdt. 1.159.4.)

Two points can be drawn from the view of the divine expressed at *Mem.* 1.1.19. In the first place, it reveals Xenophon's profound commitment to the sanctity of the oath. Indeed, for Xenophon there was no greater act of impiety than the breaking of one's oath; it brought the wrath of the gods down on the oathbreaker's head. Both the *Anabasis* and the *Hellenica* characterize the Persian Tissaphernes as an oathbreaker who, by breaking his word with Greeks operating in his satrapy, actually does these adversaries a favour: he twice makes the gods his enemy and the allies of his own opponent (*An.* 3.2.10, *Hell.* 3.4.11).[13] More importantly, Xenophon's insistence on the thoroughgoing omniscience of the divine suggests that he was at heart an orthodox pietist who felt forced to make unimpeachable the traditional view of the divine. But in his defence of traditional piety he subtly changed it.[14]

At *Mem.* 1.1.19 Xenophon, through the reported opinions of Socrates, asserts that the divine is not only omniscient but also omnipresent; both these attributes suggest a sensitivity regarding what I will call the incomplete archaic view of the divine. In Homer Zeus can be distracted from the war by Hera (*Il.* 14.153ff.), Poseidon can be duped while he is away with the Ethiopians (*Od.* 1.19ff.), and even the all-seeing and all-hearing sun needs to be told that his cattle have been eaten (*Od.* 12.374ff.).[15] Related to this notion of the gods' restricted omniscience is the idea of divine spies (e.g. Hesiod *Op.* 122ff., Homer *Od.* 17.485–487) and of the gods themselves either concealing or disguising themselves and moving among men. So, Hesiod writes at *Op.* 249–250, 'for being near among men the gods take notice';[16] the idea that the gods have to be near humans in order to monitor them is common in archaic and classical poetry and precisely reveals the notion that the gods have an awareness that is spatially limited. The logical inconsistency of this archaic view (omnipotence and omniscience on the one hand, seeming physical and cognitive limitation on the other) came under increasing attack by the end of the fifth century, especially from the sophists. 'Optimistic rationalists', whose views were often echoed (which is not to say endorsed) in the plays of Euripides, countered the sophistic challenge and removed the inconsistencies of the archaic view;[17] the divine became truly omniscient, omnipotent and omnipresent. Xenophon was part of this response.

One of the consequences of Xenophon's attempt to defend traditional piety was his adherence to the proof of the existence of the divine from the apparent providential structure of the world and the human being, or the so-called argument from design. The argument tended to be made along the following lines: the human body was structured in such a way as to suggest careful and artful planning, and so too the universe; what is more, the universe seemed to be constructed so as to benefit especially human beings; these features of the world could not reasonably be explained by the workings of chance but rather must be the design of God. This line of reasoning was especially popular at the end of the fifth century and the beginning of the fourth. Indeed, some have tried to establish a direct link between Xenophon and a slightly earlier advocate of design in the cosmos and humans, Diogenes of Apollonia.[18] It is easier, however, to assume that Xenophon was dependent for his ideas on no one authority but was merely articulating concepts that were, if not mainstream, then not uncommon topics among learned circles of his day.[19] His thinking regarding the order of the universe and the privileged human place in it may well derive from an amalgam of a number of relatively common positions: an interest in physical philosophy, popular anthropological notions and a moral structure based on ends.[20]

MEMORABILIA 1.4 AND 4.3

Xenophon's arguments for divine providence are found chiefly in two chapters from the *Memorabilia* (1.4, 4.3). Plato's Socrates never makes such arguments; indeed, he eschews for the most part all discussions that do not concern human conduct, and especially those which are devoted to cosmological matters. In Plato's *Apology* (26d) Socrates sought to distance himself from the theories of men like Anaxagoras, a thinker whose ideas about the cosmic *nous* bear some interesting points of connection with Xenophon's divine *phronesis*. And even Xenophon preserves Socrates' hostility towards cosmological speculation: at *Mem.* 1.1.11 he notes that Socrates was dismissive of those who think about cosmological matters.[21] The views found at *Mem.* 1.4 and 4.3 which concern divine providence are so antithetical to the interests of the Socrates of *Mem* 1.1.11 and Plato that some have been led to speculate that these passages are wholly the work of Xenophon.[22] This position gains further support when it is seen that *Mem.* 1.4 and 4.3 correspond closely with views found in works of Xenophon in which Socrates does not appear, a correspondence that will emerge in the course of this discussion.

At *Mem.* 1.4 Xenophon recounts a conversation between Socrates and a certain Aristodemus 'the Small', an atheist who not only does not himself perform the acts of traditional piety (he does not sacrifice or make use of oracles), he even mocks those who do (*Mem.* 1.4.2).[23] Socrates tries to convince Aristodemus of the existence of the divine by drawing attention to the purposefulness in the design of the human being. The faculties of perception (*Mem.* 1.4.5–6), the mind (*Mem.* 1.4.8) and soul (*Mem.* 1.4.9), and special attributes both physical and spiritual (*Mem.* 1.4.11–14; cf. *Oec.* 7.18–31) suggest the work of a 'life-loving creator' (*demiourgos philozoios*, *Mem.* 1.4.7). So overwhelming is the evidence for thoughtfulness behind the construction of the human animal that the role of Chance in creating the human condition must be rejected (*Mem.* 1.4.4; cf. Plato *Laws* 889a).[24] Towards the end of the dialogue, Socrates tries to convince Aristodemus that not only do the gods exist, they are heedful of everyone, even him (*phrontizein, Mem.* 1.4.14). First Socrates suggests that when the divine communicates to Athens, to Greece or even to all human beings (*pasin anthropois, Mem.* 1.4.15), Aristodemus must of course be included. Socrates' second proof is more sophisticated. He notes that there is a universal belief in the gods' ability to help and hurt human beings; to deny that this supposed fact applies to a particular individual (something Aristodemus would say is true in his case) is to deny the ontological truth of the gods themselves, a point already granted once one accepts the universal belief in their ability to affect all humans (*Mem.* 1.4.16).

Socrates' third proof may be styled the anthropological: he argues that the most enduring and wisest human institutions ('cities and races', *poleis kai ethne*),[25] as well as the most mature and thoughtful period of human life (old age), are also the most pious (*Mem.* 1.4.16; cf. *Poroi* 3.10).[26] This observation is essentially conservative in outlook as well as novel. The notion that there is a connection between age, wisdom and piety goes back in historical writing at least to Herodotus (note especially what that historian has to say about the Egyptians);[27] it is conservative insofar as the oldest human institutions are thought to be the best and are cited in defence of traditional religion. The observation is at the same time new, because it assumes that the success of the oldest human institutions derives from their piety. This belief in turn implies that the divine operates through time and pays attention to the affairs of human beings, continually safeguarding the interests of those who are pious. What is more, the notion that the success of a person or community could continue unchecked by either the arbitrary or punitive vengeance of the gods is at odds with earlier notions regarding human prosperity as a source for *hubris* and consequently divine punishment.[28] The gods are not, as was traditionally believed, members of a class of 'super-friend' or 'super-enemy', aiding or harming with profound consequence the humans in whom they take an interest; the divine is not visible anthropomorphic beings, but instead an awesome, invisible force working for good throughout the universe and ordering everything at all times (*Mem.* 4.3.13).[29] Such a conception of the divine allows a historian such as Xenophon a belief that all history has a point. Presumably nothing happens without in some way being connected to the workings of this providential force. I will return to this issue in a moment.

The *Memorabilia* and other works of Xenophon make clear that the particular crimes the gods are most likely to punish, and in such a way as to affect the course of history, are in his estimation oath-breaking and disobedience to one's own laws. The example of Tissaphernes mentioned above (p. 173) is enough to illustrate Xenophon's interest in the first crime. As for the second, we learn from *Mem.* 4.3.16 that if a person is in doubt how to honour the gods, all he need do is obey the customs of his state. This line of thinking can be traced back again at least as far as Herodotus and his observation on the madness of Cambyses, son of Cyrus the Great (3.38).

Socrates concludes his discussion with Aristodemus with a series of provocative analogies: just as the human mind controls the body, so Thought, dwelling in all, controls all things (*ten en [toi] panti phronesin ta panta . . . tithesthai*); just as the human eye can travel a long way, so the divine eye can comprehend all things (no doubt a reference to the archaic notion of the 'eye of Zeus');[30] and as the human mind may think of more than one place at a time, so the divine mind can be heedful of all things (*Mem.* 1.4.17). Socrates urges Aristodemus to test the power of the divine mind in the same way he would humans: just as one finds out who is willing to do a good service by doing one first oneself, so if Aristodemus first serves the gods he will discover shortly how beneficial they can be in giving advice about matters unclear (*adela*) to humans. In the process, Aristodemus will learn that the gods hear and see everything, and that they are everywhere and notice everything (*Mem.* 1.4.18; cf. *Mem.* 1.1.19 above, p. 184).[31]

E.R. Dodds noted that this type of argument from design, proving the providential nature of the divine, 'issued ultimately in the stoic and Christian conception of history as providentially guided'.[32] Perhaps we can follow Dodds' lead and suggest that Xenophon's belief in the providence of the divine was not restricted to his philosophical writing but was carried over to the *Hellenica*, and thereby put him squarely in the historiographic tradition represented later by the Stoics and Christians. Indeed, judging from what he has to say about the most successful human institutions, it would seem that Xenophon believed the gods supervised the actions of mortals and rewarded those who remained pious; in a sense, then, the continued success of a community was a mark of its piety, and presumably if it met with a setback one could assume that it had lost the favour of the gods through impiety. This assumption is not hard to make if we remember that the gods in Xenophon's thinking scrutinize not only the actions and words of human beings but also their motivations, and that therefore it is easy to imagine them punishing immoral behaviour in such a way as to affect the course of history.

How precisely this punishment is carried out is a matter for speculation. It seems unlikely that Xenophon has in mind a type of direct physical intervention into the world of human beings. Rather, from what we know about his views on divine communication with mortals, the gods would simply not try to dissuade the humans in question from adopting a course of action that proves eventually to be self-destructive: without divine guidance, wicked mortals are allowed to entrust their well-being to the fickle control of Chance and in consequence ultimately fail. So much is implied by *Mem.* 1.4.18 and 1.1.19; so much is also suggested by Cambyses' advice to his son Cyrus from the *Cyropaedia* (see below, pp. 225–227). Two more passages from the *Anabasis* are illuminating in this regard. Xenophon, in contemplating whether to accept the Ten Thousand's offer of supreme command, knows that humans are ignorant of their future and so must ask for divine help (*An.* 6.1.21ff.). Wicked people, although they see, do not understand; although they hear, they do not remember (*An.* 3.1.27).[33] In a certain sense the wicked man in his ignorance is precisely the opposite of the gods who know all things.

What is it about Xenophon's views, particularly as they are expressed in *Mem.* 1.4, which may have had profound consequences for his historical vision? To begin to answer this question, we have to return to *Mem.* 1.4.16. Durability through time, both of institution and of human being, is for Xenophon proof of piety. What is more, it is tempting to see in this persistence through time also the reward that the divine bestows in return for piety. The importance this view of causation would have for a people for whom the world was a place governed by chance would have been considerable. Implicit in Xenophon's understanding of historical permanence as proof and reward for piety is that the institution or individual in question does not undergo significant change. Cities that remain stable, and furthermore those that are thought not only to encourage but even demand obedience to an unchanging code of conduct or law, are precisely the communities that are the most pious, longlived and successful.

Obviously, as suggested above, this view is conservative insofar as change is characterized as deterioration, not progress. But in at least one place, Xenophon expresses what appears at first glance to be a contrary understanding of the change over time. As has been seen, at *Hell.* 6.4.23 Jason of Pherae prophetically states before his own assassination that 'the divine often delights in making the small great and the great small'. Such a view of an omnipotent divine, a view which has many Greek and non-Greek parallels, implies that not all change is downward and destructive – as great powers decline, others rise up. Of all the communities in Xenophon, however, only the Ten Thousand of the *Anabasis* and the people of Phlius from the *Hellenica* illustrate the positive side of historical change, and of course the Ten Thousand also demonstrate decline as well as ascent. Athens and Sparta in the *Hellenica*, Sparta again in the *Constitution of the Lacedaemonians* and Persia in the *Cyropaedia* all illustrate the truth of the other, catastrophic side of the same historical process – the destruction of great human powers. Thebes, or (less likely) Athens of the time of the Second Athenian Confederation, may have served as cases of growth rather than decay, but for reasons that will emerge later in the next chapter, Xenophon chose not to characterize these cities as ascendant powers. Instead, his gaze is fixed on decline, principally the decline of Sparta. As suggested in Chapter 5, the opposite fortunes of Phlius and the Thirty of Athens suggest not the propensity of small communities to become great, but rather the advantage of small communities remaining small. In connection with this point, it is worth noting that in words similar to Jason's in the *Hellenica*, Xenophon, speaking as a character in the *Anabasis*, encourages his fellow Greeks with the thought that 'the gods are able quickly to make the great small and to save easily the small even in dire circumstances, whenever they wish' (3.2.10). No mention here of a rise to greatness for the beleaguered companions of Xenophon, only preservation and (perhaps) a return home.

This interest in durability and change, and in change chiefly as decline, was not unique to Xenophon. At about the same time Xenophon was completing the *Hellenica*, Plato was at work on the *Laws*. At the beginning of the third book, the anonymous Athenian turns the conversation to a consideration of the origin of government (676a). In language strikingly similar to *Hell.* 6.4.23, the

Athenian is convinced that in finding the cause of constitutional change one will also find the beginnings of government, given the fact that 'great states have emerged from lesser ones and powerful ones have become weaker, and that worse states have grown out of better ones and better ones from worse' (676c). Like Xenophon, Plato seems initially to perceive change as capable of bringing about improvement as well as deterioration. But as the discussion continues, it becomes clear that this is not so. Choosing the first so-called Dorian kingdoms as a starting point, the Athenian asks his interlocutors what led to the dissolution (*katalusis*) of two of the three, leaving only Sparta unchanged (683d–685a). For Plato, too, change is really decline.

Laws 3 not only provides a roughly contemporary parallel for Xenophon's view of change, it also suggests a very important point regarding the position of Sparta in the imagination of intellectuals in the mid-fourth century. Sparta was revered by men like Xenophon and Plato precisely because it was thought to have remained unchanged over time, a symbol of stability and order.[34] So, in the introduction to his biography of his friend Agesilaus, Xenophon could write: 'no other government [than the one at Sparta] has manifestly remained undisturbed, neither democracy, oligarchy, tyranny, or monarchy; it alone has continued always to be monarchy' (*Ages.* 1.4). While all the other states of Greece, including Xenophon's native Athens, had gone through significant changes of government, Sparta, it was thought, had remained the same and preeminent throughout its history.[35] Sparta's permanence was a given and its sucess proverbial, and both demanded explanation – at least Xenophon felt it did.[36] Consequently, when Sparta collapsed as a leading power in Greece in the 370s and 360s, there was not only a major political and military shift, and perhaps also a sense (for some) of personal loss, there was for men like Xenophon a corresponding intellectual shift – the perennial yardstick of political stability and moral probity, and the success that (to the Greek mind) these things bring, was gone.[37] This fact too demanded explanation.

Again, Plato's *Laws* offers a helpful line of approach. In his search for the cause of the change or (more properly) the destruction of government, the anonymous Athenian advances the notion that all forms of rule are destroyed by the rulers themselves – destruction of government is always self-destruction (683e). He traces the cause of this self-destruction to ignorance of what is good, of what to pray to the gods for; while humans tend to pray for everything to conform to their wishes, they ought to pray for wisdom, for they simply do not know what is best for themselves (687e). Too often, they think that great power leads to great happiness (686e). This ignorance of what is good is typical in states where the masses disobey their magistrates and their laws (689b). It is also similar to the perilous state of self-reliance outlined in Xenophon's treatment of the Thirty, as well as in the *Cyropaedia* (see above, pp. 154–156 and below, pp. 225–226).

Self-destruction, ignorance of the good, greed, disobedience – these are all themes that can also be found in Xenophon's account of the fall of Sparta. But in the most general sense, for Xenophon Sparta failed because Sparta changed. Given the city's excellence before, this change had to be for the worse. Indeed, it entailed the very problems Plato addresses in the voice of the Athenian. Xenophon brings all these themes together in the notorious four-teenth chapter of his treatise on the *Constitution of the Lacedaemonians*,[38] quoted here in full:

If someone should ask me whether also now the laws of Lycurgus still seem to me to remain undisturbed, this by Zeus I could not say with confidence. For I know that before, the Spartans used to prefer to live with one another at home with their modest means rather than be destroyed by being gover-nors in the cities [abroad] and by being bribed. And before, I know they were afraid of appearing to have gold; but now I know that there are some who even boast about possessing wealth. I know also that before, on account of this, there were expulsions of foreigners and it was forbidden to live abroad, in order that the citizens not become influenced by the easy living of outsiders. Now I know that the ones with the repu-tations for being the best have been diligent so that they never cease being governors overseas. There was a time when they used to make every effort to be worthy to lead; now they are much more concerned with ruling rather than being worthy of this distinction. For that reason the Greeks, who before used to come to the Spartans and ask them to lead them against those who seemed to be doing wrong, many of them are exhorting each other to prevent the Spartans from ruling again. It is not necessary to marvel at these shameful things attributed to them, for they are manifestly disobedient towards their god and the laws of Lycurgus.

By the litany of comparisons between 'then' and 'now', this passage hammers home its accent on change, and change for the worse. The chief targets: neglect of laws, greed, ambition, imperialism. The telling sentence is the last one: the shocking decline of the Spartans can be inferred from their lack of piety towards the divine and disobedience of their own laws. This is change indeed! Spartan *eusebeia*, Spartan *eunomia*, both previous hallmarks of Spartan society,[39] are no more.

Xenophon's solemn observation at *Hell.* 5.4.1 that the hitherto undefeated Spartans[40] were punished by the divine for impiety through defeat at the hands of the very people they had wronged serves as a useful guide to reading the *Hellenica*. It meant, in the first place, that he thought Sparta's demise was self-inflicted; if we find that he omits from his history the affairs of other states that are relevant to the fall of Sparta, we should not be surprised – Xenophon sees the process as essentially one internal to Spartan society.[41] The observation meant too that Xenophon saw that Sparta had changed, and had changed (necessarily) for the worse. In his eyes Sparta had become a place where the people did not know what was really good for them; a reckless people bent on supreme rule and consequently doomed to self-destruction: they were, in fact, a great deal like the Thirty. Here we can see most easily how the divine might prove a ready explanation for a man like Xenophon: a greedy, imperial power, neglecting its own laws and traditional regard for the divine, does not heed the warnings of the gods – as Cambyses and Xenophon knew (see above, p. 189). Relying on its own, human wisdom it embarks upon an enterprise that leads to its own destruction.

At a more general level, because Xenophon links the fall of Sparta to the gods' will at *Hell.* 5.4.1, he is also in a sense making a positive, optimistic declaration that even this catastrophe had a point, insofar as it had to be connected to a divine that works through time providentially. Without wanting to appear mechanical in making this point, and indeed allowing for Xenophon to have different conceptions of the divine at different times, I think that to forget entirely that he believed in a providential divine is both unrealistic and unacceptable. While Xenophon may have been able to see the working of providence in such a terrible event as the collapse of Sparta only retrospectively, to attribute it to the gods is, in the final analysis, a simple assertion of belief that the event was in some way meaningful. Charting the way Xenophon made sense – or perhaps tried to make sense – of Sparta's fall, discovering the way he explained the decline of Sparta to himself, will form the subject of the next chapter, in particular that book of the *Hellenica* which seems most emphatically shaped by his religious outlook – Book 5.

8

HELLENICA BOOK 5 AND THE CRIMES OF SPARTA

Before beginning my discussion of Book 5, I need to raise at the outset two important methodological problems relating to the study of the *Hellenica*. The first has to do with examining Book 5 as an isolable part of the history. Technically speaking, such an examination is based at best on a guess, and at worse on a fallacy. The book divisions of the *Hellenica*, like many other ancient histories, are not the original ones; it can be shown that what ancient readers knew as Book 3 is not our Book 3, and this discrepancy can be assumed for all the book divisions.[1] But having said that, there is a thematic integrity to the narrative leading up to and moving beyond Xenophon's denunciation of the Spartan seizure of the Theban acropolis, the Cadmea, at *Hell.* 5.4.1 that roughly corresponds with the Book 5 we know. I believe Xenophon composed this portion of the *Hellenica* as something of a unit and that is what matters most, even if the original boundaries of the book were marginally different.

The second problem is much more serious. Despite the ease, clarity and sometimes superficiality of his prose, Xenophon can be a subtle, even devious manipulator of his narrative.[2] Consequently, there is an ever-present danger to over-interpret him, finding especially in his silences ironic commentary on matters he does present: but it is difficult to see how omissions can be ironic. Although I will at times have to fall back on it, I will try to keep this kind of analysis to a minimum and confine myself to what he does say. But by the same token, it is important to take seriously the things Xenophon has to say; too often, it seems, his criticisms of Sparta have been discounted in the curt and (what I hope by now is clear) erroneous dismissal of Xenophon's reliance on the divine to explain Sparta's fall.

Book 5 of the *Hellenica* covers the years from 389 to 375, during which period three very important events happened: the ratification of the so-called King's Peace, bringing about the formal conclusion of the Corinthian War; the illegal seizure of the Cadmea by the Spartans; and finally, the foundation of the Second Athenian Confederation. Xenophon's handling of none of these moments has met with the approval of modern historians. Indeed, one of these events, the formation of Athens' new maritime alliance, is entirely omitted from the *Hellenica*. His treatment of the terms of the King's Peace, while providing the fullest text of the treaty we have, is still agonizingly brief and significant clauses of the agreement have to be conjectured. Perhaps only Xenophon's account of Phoebidas' capture of the Cadmea is coherent and credible, but comparison with other versions of the same event suggests that he has deliberately obfuscated Sparta's official role in instigating the seizure, especially the part played by King Agesilaus.

These omissions, and several others in the *Hellenica*, have been thought so monumental as to be 'scandalous' (see above, p. 179).[3] Along with his pro-Spartan and virulent anti-Theban bias and his general incompetence, these omissions have been found to be so great that, as a recent scholar has put it, 'all that can and should, I think, be salvaged from the case for Xenophon the thinker is a handful of banal moral platitudes which sort only too well with the kind of plain man's guide to Socratic thinking that he provides in the *Memorabilia*'.[4] Xenophon was not a great thinker, either historical or philosophical, and unrealistic efforts to rehabilitate his reputation by, for example, citing artistic reasons for his omissions are misguided. And while my study of Book 5 may at times resemble the work of Xenophon's apologists, I do not attempt to justify him as a great, or even good historian. I mean instead to study him as an interpreter, a voice of his age; a thoughtful if not brilliant man who tried to understand his times. Indeed, declaring Xenophon a bad historian ought not to relieve us of the duty of trying to figure out what he said and why he said it. His mediocrity can tell us much, indeed perhaps more, about what people thought about the momentous changes of their day; more, in all likelihood, than, say, the *Hellenica Oxyrhynchia*. Alternatively, while not the greatest historian of antiquity, Xenophon did bring an innovative set of concerns to bear on his historical writing. We may better appreciate the value of Xenophon's history if we examine Book 5 of the *Hellenica* in connection with another continous narrative of the same period, that of Ephorus as reflected in Diodorus. These historians have much in common; what distinguishes Xenophon from his slightly younger contemporary is revealing and often of a piece with what we might have expected based on his religious views outlined above.

Book 5 falls roughly into three parts: (i) 5.1, the events leading up to and including the King's Peace and its immediate aftermath; (ii) 5.2–5.3, the narrative of Sparta's ascendance in the wake of the Peace to just before Xenophon's denunciation at 5.4.1; (iii) 5.4, the denunciation of the Spartan seizure of the Cadmea to the account of Timotheus' victory over the Spartan admiral Nicholochus at Alyzia (the end of the book).

PART I: 5.1

This portion of Book 5 is devoted to Spartan naval operations, and in particular the activities of two admirals – Teleutias, half brother of Agesilaus, and Antalcidas. These events are not found in Diodorus: the last episode both Xenophon and Diodorus report before the ratification of the King's Peace is the death of Thrasybulus (*Hell.* 4.8.30, Diod. 14.99.4), the precise date for which is a matter of some dispute.[5] While this gap in Diodorus may have been original with Ephorus, it seems more likely that Diodorus has simply skipped over what Ephorus had to say and focused his attention instead on the affairs of Dionysius of Syracuse.[6] Xenophon has obviously compressed a great deal in the opening chapters, and chronological difficulties result.[7] Teleutias is reported to have sailed from 'the islands' where he was collecting revenue to the aid of Aegina which had been blockaded by the Athenians (5.1.2). Xenophon tells us that after driving off most of the Athenian force, Teleutias, already overdue for replacement, turns over his command of the fleet to one Hierax and leaves for Sparta. The scene of Teleutias' departure is remarkable:

> when he was going down to the sea, setting out for home, there was not one of his men who did not shake his hand; some crowned him, others placed ribbons on his head and the ones who came late nevertheless threw their wreaths into the water even as he departed and prayed that many good things befall him. I know that in these matters I do not recount any expenditure, risk or stratagem worthy of record. But, by Zeus, this seems to me to be worthwhile for a man to note: how Teleutias made his men so loyal.
>
> (5.1.3–4)

This passage has been taken to mark a shift away in Xenophon's thinking from an obligation to report the standard features of Thucydidean war monograph to an interest in recording the achievements of great leaders (see esp. Rahn (1971) 499–502). So much may have been guessed, given the short space Xenophon gives to the successful combat on Aegina which no doubt led in part to Teleutias' fame among his men. But of particular importance here is simply the way this passage spotlights Teleutias and prepares the reader for matters Xenophon will shortly relate, in which both Teleutias and the issue of leadership figure prominently.

After an interval during which we learn of Antalcidas' mission to Persia and the defeat of the Spartans under Gorgopas at Aegina, Teleutias again appears to restore the morale of the Spartan fleet after its recent setback. On his return he delivers a speech to his men that relates to the issue of the ideal commander possessing self-control (*enkrateia*) surpassing even that of his own men (see above, Chapter 6). But in concluding his speech, which is aimed primarily at allaying his men's fears about how they are to be provisioned, Teleutias makes a curious remark:

> for what is sweeter than not having to butter up any man, Greek or barbarian, for the sake of a wage, but being able to acquire provisions for oneself, and these in the manner which is best of all. For you know well that in war the abundance [which comes] from the enemy provides at the same time food and a good name among all men.
>
> (5.1.17)

These lines correspond closely to those of another Spartan much earlier in the *Hellenica* that I mentioned in connection with Agesilaus' departure from Asia (see above, pp. 117–118). At 1.6.7 Callicratidas, forced to wait for Cyrus to provide him pay for his men, exclaims 'the Greeks are the most wretched people, for they butter up barbarians for the sake of money', and adds that it is his intention to settle the differences between the Athenians and the Spartans.[8] The earlier passage demonstrates that Teleutias is here sounding a strong panhellenic note.[9] Indeed, lamenting the Greeks' dependence on Persian silver to fight other Greeks is a standard feature of panhellenic orations: Gorgias has such sentiments in his Funeral Oration (see above, pp. 53 and 117), as does Lysias in his *Olympicus* (delivered, significantly, at the ninety-eighth Olympiad in 388). While Teleutias' raid on the Piraeus (reminiscent of a raid planned by the Spartans in the early years of the Peloponnesian War; Thuc. 2.93.1) that soon follows his speech seems out of keeping with the spirit of these panhellenic remarks, Callicratidas was also engaged in hostile actions against fellow Greeks (again Athenians) when he made his own remarks. But Teleutias' speech and his raid and subsequent harassment of Athens in the Saronic Gulf do seem at odds with one another, and these details, combined with the fact that Callicratidas' words seem consistent with his character and behaviour while Teleutias' look more like an afterthought, suggest that Xenophon went to some lengths to characterize Teleutias as a panhellenist. Why? The answer is immediately forthcoming.

Directly following the report of Teleutias' raid on the Piraeus, we hear that Antalcidas had returned to the coast of Asia Minor, together with the satrap Tiribazus, bringing with him the terms of the King's Peace (5.1.25). Cawkwell has suggested that Teleutias' prominence in the preceding chapters is meant to show up Antalcidas as a Persian stooge, giving away the Greeks of Asia for Persian backing.[10] In particular, Teleutias' closing remarks are thought to be Xenophon's way of registering Spartan unease with the terms of the Peace.[11] It is unclear just how far one should push this contrast. That Xenophon chose to concentrate on Teleutias in the first place, and then less so Antalcidas and other Spartan commanders, seems a reasonable observation. Furthermore, while Xenophon is restricted in what he can say about Antalcidas (after all, he had to mention him, since he was the architect of the Peace which sometimes bears his name), he had considerable leeway in what he can say about Teleutias, and he elects to characterize him as a panhellenist. The conclusion we can perhaps draw from this is that Xenophon wanted to introduce a note of discord into his narrative of the preliminaries of the King's Peace, a suggestion that not everyone at Sparta favoured the Peace, and consequently to some at least the Peace was not a good idea.[12]

In the lead-up to the King's Peace, Xenophon details Antalcidas' activities in the Hellespont region; we are told that he is able eventually to accumulate a fleet of more than eighty ships and to prevent the Athenians from entering the Black Sea, crucial for their grain supply (5.1.28). Sparta, it seems, is in a good position. Indeed, the augmented Spartan fleet (which Xenophon tells us included Persian vessels) strikes fear into the Athenians who, along with the Argives, are characterized as ready for peace (5.1.29). Hence it comes as something of a surprise when we read that Sparta too was 'having difficulties in the war' (*chalepos epheron toi polemoi*, 5.1.29), especially in maintaining garrisons in hostile territory and keeping an eye on her allies, loyal and disloyal alike. It is hard to reconcile the diplomatic and military successes of Antalcidas summed up at 5.1.28 with the Spartans' eagerness for peace at 5.1.29. At this point we can conveniently reestablish a connection between Xenophon's narrative and that of Ephorus as found in Diodorus. At 14.110.2 we are told that the Spartans, 'being badly off (*kakopathountes*) in their war against the Greeks and their war against the Persians', despatched Antalcidas to the Persian court to negotiate a peace. From what we know about the reverses Sparta had suffered as recorded by (among others) Xenophon himself (e.g. Cnidus, 4.3.10–12), and the fact that Sparta had sought peace with Persia earlier in 392 (described imperfectly by Xenophon at 4.8.12ff.),[13] we must accept the picture of Spartan motivation that is given at *Hell.* 5.1.29, and which is corroborated by Diodorus. We must reject the one suggested at *Hell.* 5.1.28. Xenophon himself gives further reason to do this at 5.1.36 where he describes Sparta's fortunes during the Corinthian War and states that she did no better than her enemies. But again we must ask why there is a narrative discontinuity, indeed one which is separated by only a few lines in Xenophon's text. If there is a reasonable and consistent explanation for both Antalcidas' considerable success and the fatigue felt at Sparta (and it seems there must be), why does Xenophon not provide it?

The inconsistency in Xenophon's treatment of the prelude to the Peace permits us to see the treaty in two different ways: either it was essentially forced on the Spartans by necessity, or it was an initiative calculated to increase Spartan power and negotiated from a position of strength, at least relative to other Greek powers. In a sense, both were true: after Cnidus the Spartans knew that hostility against Persia was no longer in their interests (if indeed it ever was). Their earlier peace efforts of 392/1 suggest that they knew this full well, and so were in consequence almost bound to reach an arrangement with the Great King; alternatively, brokering a peace with the Persians that ostensibly affected all Greeks and that forbade at least their major rivals from creating or joining into alliances with other powers left Sparta as the hegemon *de facto*, if not *de iure*, of Greece. By accenting both Sparta's strength and the advantage to be gained by the Peace, as well as the necessity for negotiating it, Xenophon creates the possibility of characterizing the consequences of the

Peace, specifically Sparta's apparent disregard for the spirit of its leading idea and the troubles which resulted from this disregard, as the after-effects of something the Spartans thought would profit them.[14] In other words, the setbacks and disasters that Sparta experienced in the Greece shaped by the King's Peace could be represented as in a sense self-inflicted, the result ultimately of Spartan choice. And in fact the King's Peace is the most important benchmark of Spartan power in the *Hellenica*, allowing us to trace the trajectory of Sparta's fortunes: after the King's Peace they rise steadily, reaching (as Xenophon will tell us) their zenith immediately before the Thebans recapture their citadel in 382, when they level off and then begin a rapid decline first to Leuctra and then Mantinea.

After reporting the general conditions in Greece prior to the King's Peace, Xenophon writes:

> and so when Tiribazus ordered those to be present who were willing to abide by the peace which the King sent down, everyone quickly was in attendance. When they had gathered, Tiribazus showed them the seals of the King and then read the treaty. It was as follows: 'Artaxerxes the King believes it right that the cities in Asia be his and of the islands Clazomenae and Cyprus, and that the rest of the Greek cities, both small and large, be allowed to be autonomous, except Lemnos, Imbros and Scyros; these shall belong to the Athenians, as of old. Whichever [group] does not accept this peace, with these I will make war together with the signatories, on land and sea, with ships and money'.
>
> (5.1.30–31 = *SVA* 242)

With some minor exceptions, this is the only document Xenophon purports to quote in the *Hellenica*.[15] The note of uncertainty here is due to the fact that it is now widely believed that while Xenophon may have captured the gist of the treaty (or perhaps the preamble), the original document, or rather the Greek translation of it,[16] must have contained specific clauses.[17] Although we know from Isocrates that the Peace was inscribed on pillars and displayed in the precincts of shrines throughout Greece (*Pan.* 180, *Panath.* 107), regrettably Xenophon's is the fullest treatment we possess. Our incomplete knowledge of the Peace contrasts sharply with its notoriety in antiquity. Indeed, for Xenophon's contemporaries as well as later writers, the King's Peace is often brought up in connection with the condemnation of Sparta and the explanation for her decline.

This censure of Sparta takes one of two forms. One blames Sparta for abandoning the Greeks of Asia to the Persians in order to secure hegemony in mainland Greece. The other points to the guarantee of autonomy in the Peace and Sparta's subsequently frequent breaches of it, best represented by the seizure of the Cadmea. Isocrates and (perhaps) Ephorus present both views. Xenophon, like Theopompus, sees the Peace primarily as 'the treaty the Spartans broke', rather than 'the Spartan treaty that surrendered our Asian brethren'.[18] The reason Xenophon chose to portray the Peace in this way (and there is no reason he had to) will be explained below (pp. 207–221).

If we are to understand properly the place of the King's Peace in Xenophon's *Hellenica*, we have to come to grips with two problems; the stakes are high, for, as I hope to show, Book 5, and indeed much of the rest of the history, is structured around Sparta's behaviour seen in light of the Peace. The two problems that still trouble historians are, first, to whom did the Peace apply; and second, who swore to observe it, and was this group different from what we might call the membership of the Peace? The second set of questions has caused particular difficulties.

As Xenophon himself will later make clear, the King's Peace was formally the treaty that ended the Corinthian War. It applied to the combatants of that war, specifically Sparta on one side and the coalition of Athens, Thebes, Corinth and Argos on the other (the last two were, of course, thought of as one state prior to the Peace). The *hopoteroi* of Xenophon's text means literally 'whichever of two parties', not the more general 'whichever state', and consequently supports the view that the agreement was technically the settlement of a peace between two sides.[19] The status of the Great King is difficult to establish: a slightly later inscription refers to him as having sworn an oath to uphold the treaty (Tod 118), a scenario some scholars find improbable in the extreme and likely to be the product of Greek (specifically Athenian) imagination.[20] Be that as it may, the Peace clearly was aimed at the principal states of Greece. Xenophon's summaries of the conditions in Greece prior to and some years after the Peace, limited as they are to the chief combatants of the war (5.1.29,[21] 5.3.27), support this understanding, as does his description of the Greek embassies to Persia in 392 (4.8.12). Diodorus 14.110.4 provides a less precise (though not contradictory) list of those who accepted the Peace – Sparta, Athens, Thebes and 'certain others of the Greeks'.[22]

Xenophon tells us at 5.1.32 that when the ambassadors had heard the letter from the Great King, they each went back to their own cities to report the terms. Then, rather elliptically, he states that 'all the rest swore to abide by the agreement, and the Thebans thought it right to swear on behalf of all Boeotians' (5.1.32). We do not know where the oath-swearing took place, whether severally, each in their own city, or all together in one place. The fact that shortly after the swearing of the oaths Agesilaus was able to coerce the Thebans into swearing only for Thebes and not all of Boeotia (5.1.32–33) suggests that there was a congress at Sparta; note that the Athenian diplomat Callias refers later in the *Hellenica* (6.3.4) to two earlier meetings at Sparta involving peace negotiations. While it is perhaps unwise to build one uncertainty on top of another, our only real hope for understanding the negotiations that led to the King's Peace of 387/6 is to assume that they resembled the only slightly better documented ones of 392/1:[23] Tiribazus read the Great King's letter to the Greek ambassadors at Sardis; the ambassadors then returned to their cities to discuss the terms proposed (indeed, note should be taken of the Thebans at 5.1.32 when they insist that they were not instructed to do as Agesilaus bid them, and that they would have to return to Thebes to get the authorization to swear only in the name of Thebes); finally, empowered to negotiate, the ambassadors gathered again, this time at Sparta, where they finalized the terms and swore to uphold the agreement on behalf of their cities.[24]

While I think this reconstruction to be in the main correct, two further problems immediately present themselves. In the first place, this reconstruction clearly does not leave room for Persian involvement in the second stage of the process, the negotiations in Greece at the congress after the ambassadors have consulted with their home authorities. In all likelihood, the first document (the letter of the Great King) represented the parameters of what was negotiable and assumed that the details would be worked out in the second phase.[25] The perils of such a system may have been brought to light in the failed peace efforts of 392/1, when the Athenians apparently could not accede to the Great King's demand for control of the Greeks of Asia, a scruple they were later forced to overlook (cf. Diod. 14.110.4). The more serious problem raised by this reconstruction is that it is difficult to see at what stage in the process the participation could have been broadened from the belligerents of the Corinthian War to 'all the Greeks', or at least all those Greeks who wished to be members of the Peace.[26] If it is reasonable to infer that the ambassadors who heard the Great King's letter read by Tiribazus went home to report the terms to their respective governments (cf. 3.2.20,

3.4.26), and were then told what they could and could not agree to before the discussions and ratification at Sparta, how could those cities that did not send representatives to Sardis effectively and independently take part in the fine-tuning of the agreement? They were absent from the first meeting and so were not in a position to consent to the original letter of the Great King outlining his basic demands; what sort of meaningful decisions could the smaller states make before the second conference at Sparta, and then what sort of input could they expect to have at this the final stage of the negotiations?[27] That Thebes could even attempt to swear on behalf of Boeotia suggests that the other Boeotians were not in Sparta, or if they were, were silent until Agesilaus spoke up for them.

Yet as had been rightly pointed out, the King's Peace was concerned not just with the combatants of the Corinthian War but all Greeks.[28] The wording at 5.1.31 is unambiguous: all Greek states were encouraged, even threatened to join the peace. Indeed, by specifying that the Athenians, *despite the proposed agreement*, could still claim Lemnos, Imbros and Scyros, implies that in principle the guarantee of autonomy was assured all Greek states – as the letter of the Great King states, 'the rest of the Greek cities both small and large be permitted to remain autonomous'.[29] All the states of Greece may have been invited by the Spartans to come to their city and accept formally the new peace. But to my mind, while they may have been invited to swear to uphold the Peace, their swearing of the oaths was of little consequence. The real guarantors of the agreement were the same as the belligerents in the Corinthian War. The smaller states' acceptance of the peace, however, entitled them to its protections, and this would have been accomplished when they took the same oath which, when the larger powers swore, placed those cities under certain obligations. Indeed, this is precisely the main challenge in understanding the King's Peace: one has to recognize that it was in reality two agreements in one. It was a peace treaty aimed at the chief powers in Greece and at the same time a declaration of autonomy granted to all the cities of Greece, a declaration that was backed up by the same parties who formed the first group which heard the letter at Sardis. The official membership of the Peace, very likely recorded in a list appended to the final agreement, was considerably larger than the cities which fought in the Corinthian War. It probably included smaller states not directly concerned in the war, as well as those that had been allied to the chief powers, in particular those Boeotian cities that were in a position to swear for themselves after Agesilaus' intervention. It is difficult to establish the status of the states allied to Sparta; it may well be that some or all of the members of the Peloponnesian League did not swear the oath (see the discussion below, p. 207).

Of course, the great disadvantage to an agreement such as the one outlined above is that it leaves a significant grey area. What sort of protections are offered under the terms of the Peace to those states that do not formally accept it? Further, what are the responsibilities of the guarantors of the Peace when a non-member attacks another non-member? The answers to these questions are not at all clear. The members of the Peace, those who by their oath had formally accepted it at Sparta, were surely protected by it. But in theory even those states that had not taken the oaths were guaranteed their autonomy.[30] In practice, though, there was no doubt considerable leeway for aggressive powers to act against non-members in the interests of protecting real or alleged threats to the autonomy of either member or non-member states.

As a coda to his treatment of the ratification of the King's Peace, Xenophon attaches the all-important account of Agesilaus' run-in with the Thebans over the swearing of the oaths. When the Thebans try to swear on behalf of all Boeotia, Agesilaus refuses to accept their oath unless they swear 'that the cities be autonomous, both small and great', just as the letter of the Great King required (5.1.32). The ambassadors protest that they were not instructed to take the oath in the manner Agesilaus demands, and are rebuked and sent home to advise their government to swear in accordance with the letter of the Peace (5.1.32). Xenophon tells us that when, 'out of hatred against Thebes', Agesilaus marches out against Thebes and gets as far as Tegea, the Thebans give in and swear only for themselves (5.1.33). Likewise, the Corinthians and Argives are forced by Agesilaus to dissolve the formal union that made them into one state (5.1.34). While these passages do not take up much space in the *Hellenica*, they are very important. The Spartans, in particular Agesilaus, are portrayed as the upholders, the policemen of the new peace. The episode involving Agesilaus and the Theban ambassadors not only attests to Sparta's *de facto* hegemony as instigators and protectors of the Peace, but also helps to bring attention to the issue of the autonomy of smaller states and Sparta's interest in it – here to protect it. In his confrontation with the Thebans, Agesilaus makes real the provisions of the King's Peace, and specifically his words and his actions suggest that the autonomy of smaller states should be respected. The episode establishes a precedent against which later actions can be measured, notably Sparta's aggressions against her own allies.

Before picking up his account and continuing with the events after the King's Peace, Xenophon makes a significant intervention into his narrative. Coordinating the end of the Corinthian War with the end of the Peloponnesian War, he writes:

> thus it was the first peace for the Spartans and Athenians and their allies after the war which followed the destruction of the walls at Athens. Faring in the war rather evenly with their enemies the Spartans emerged from the so-called Peace of Antalcidas much more successful. For becoming the guardians (*prostatai*) of the peace sent down by the Great King and bringing about autonomy for the cities (*ten autonomian tais polesi prattontes*), they acquired Corinth as an ally and rendered the Boeotian cities autonomous from the Thebans (something they had long desired), and they brought an end to the Argives claiming Corinth as their own by declaring war on them if they did not leave Corinth.
>
> (5.1.35–36)

This passage fully supports Xenophon's characterization of the King's Peace as an instrument of advantage for the Spartans that was forced on them by circumstances rather than negotiated from a position of strength. What is more, the passage is also important because of the link Xenophon tries to establish between the Peloponnesian and Corinthian Wars. As I suggested above in Chapter 1, endings were very important to Xenophon, and the end of the Peloponnesian War especially so (recall 2.2.23; see above, p. 25). To characterize the King's Peace as the conclusion of the war *after* the Peloponnesian War seems awkward; Xenophon could, for instance, have styled the war 'the one that Thebes and Tithraustes instigated' (cf. 3.5.1ff.), or (if a more exact parallel is desired) 'the war that ended with Teleutias' raid on the Piraeus' (as Xenophon presents it). It must be admitted that neither of these provisional titles for what we call the Corinthian War has the same force as 'the war that concluded with their tearing down of the walls of Athens'; but then the later war did not have at its conclusion such a decisive and symbolic moment – except perhaps the surrender of the Greeks of Asia, and it is difficult to see Xenophon styling the war this way. But that he did not point out that the King's Peace also had the effect of thwarting Athens' new imperial interests as envisioned by

Thrasybulus should not be forgotten;[31] his gaze seems firmly on Sparta. Xenophon's connection of the endings of the Peloponnesian and Corinthian Wars is not accidental or simply a matter of convenience. The King's Peace may have seemed at the time to have been, at last, that end of hostilities which the close of the Peloponnesian War seemed to have promised. To invest this peace with such significance meant something very specific to Xenophon: in the *Hellenica* he seldom points to such moments of finality without also suggesting that their apparent decisiveness was, in the event, illusory. And here, in his treatment of the King's Peace as a diplomatic victory for Sparta, the notion of hegemony manages to find its way back into the narrative in spite of the attention placed on autonomy; and, of course, the two ideas are at odds with one another – there cannot be a hegemon and universal autonomy at the same time. This tension deeply informs Xenophon's account of Sparta as the 'guardians of the Peace' – the *prostatai tes eirenes*.

PART II: 5.2–5.3

In the winter of 385 or perhaps in the spring of 384, a little more than a year after the King's Peace had been ratified,[32] Xenophon tells us that the Spartans 'decided to punish those of their allies who had opposed them in the war and who were more favourable to the enemy than Lacedaemon, and to ensure that it was no longer possible for them to be distrusted' (5.2.1). The first place to be 'punished' by the Spartans is Mantinea. The reasons: sending grain to Argos when that city was attacked by Sparta; refusing to serve on a number of occasions in the Peloponnesian League army on the grounds of a sacred truce; and serving badly when they did participate in League actions (5.2.2).[33] The Spartans issue a demand that the Mantineans demolish their own walls, in keeping with their policy that League states should have no fortifications. When the Mantineans refuse, Sparta mobilizes for war.

Whether Sparta's decision to attack Mantinea was technically a breach of the King's Peace is impossible to tell.[34] In favour of the view that Sparta was not acting in contravention of the terms of the Peace is the possibility (perhaps likelihood) that all or some of the members of the Peloponnesian League did not swear the oath and so accept the Peace and the protection of its provisions; that Agesilaus forced the Thebans in effect to disband their network of alliances in Boeotia does not mean that Sparta voluntarily did likewise with respect to the

Peloponnese. Furthermore, we learn from Diodorus (15.5.5) that when the Mantineans asked the Athenians for help against Sparta they refused on the grounds that they did not wish 'to violate the common peace', suggesting that to have intervened would have brought Athens and Sparta back into conflict and that Mantinea was not or was not sufficiently protected by the autonomy clause; it may have been the case that maintaining peaceful relations between the former belligerents of the Corinthian War superseded the protection of a smaller state's autonomy. Finally, the point has been made that since Xenophon will attribute the fall of Sparta to her contravention of the King's Peace in the matter of the seizure of the Cadmea, if he had detected a breach before that episode, he would have drawn our attention to it.[35] At one level this is surely right: if the actions against Mantinea had been in outright violation of the King's Peace, Xenophon would have told us so. But at another level, we should not ignore those features of the account that suggest Xenophon's reservations regarding Sparta's campaign.

We learn from Xenophon that the Spartans had a great deal of difficulty finding a king to command the expedition against Mantinea: both Agesilaus and Agesipolis had personal reasons for wanting to be excused from serving on the campaign. Although Agesipolis accepts the command, Xenophon tells us that his father had friends among 'the champions of the people'; Agesilaus begs off by noting that Mantinea had often helped his father Archidamus in the war against the Messenians (5.2.3). It has been pointed out that Agesilaus' reasons for not accepting the command seem suspicious.[36] But whatever the real cause for Agesilaus' difficulty, the one he cites recalls the service Mantinea has rendered Sparta, and therefore constitutes something of an embarrassment on the eve of the assault on the city.

As for the actual progress of the attack, Xenophon tells us that after a protracted siege the Spartans dam the river that flows through Mantinea in order to flood the fortifications of the city (5.2.4–5; cf. Diod. 15.12.1–2); eventually the defences become compromised and the Mantineans are forced to capitulate and agree to demolish what is left of their walls. At this point Xenophon tells us 'the Spartans declared there would be no truce until they dispersed into their villages' (5.2.5). In other words, the Spartans make their punishment harsher and more intrusive into the affairs of Mantinea; while the destruction of walls could be construed as the infringement of a city's ability to defend herself, the destruction of the city herself and the movement of her population into villages constitutes perhaps the most radical intrusion into a state's autonomy – its physical elimination.

On precisely these two points, the reluctant leadership of the campaign and the escalation of the punishment of Mantinea, Xenophon differs from Diodorus. Diodorus makes no mention of the difficulty in finding a commander for the expedition, and he makes it clear that the Spartans demanded the so-called dioecism or break-up of Mantinea from the very start (15.5.4).[37] These differences, coupled with the fact that Xenophon makes no mention of any outside power becoming involved in the dispute, makes the enterprise look like a conflict that pitted Sparta against Mantinea alone,[38] that was undertaken with reluctance by the Spartan command, and that became more ambitious and oppressive as it proceeded. While Diodorus characterizes the action against Mantinea as a breach of the King's Peace (15.5.1) and Xenophon does not, and further that he actually seems to approve of the resettlement of the aristocracy near their lands and the removal of 'demagogues' (5.2.7),[39] we should remember that he could have omitted the episode entirely, or made it look a great deal less like a breach of the Peace. Indeed, we must remember that the aggression against Mantinea may not have been a technical violation of the Peace, if Mantinea did not swear the oath. But if that was so, why then has Xenophon made the whole episode look like one that involved the breaking of the spirit if not letter of the treaty? Why has he introduced the issue of the kings' reluctance? Why was the dioecism of the city made to seem a punitive modification of a less drastic initial plan? Why, finally, does Xenophon take no notice of other Greek involvement in this matter and focus so exclusively on Mantinea and Sparta?

Xenophon is establishing themes he will highlight throughout the rest of the book.[40] Although Mantinea may not be the clearest case of Sparta's new imperialism, it nonetheless contains elements that will resonate with other episodes that are less ambiguous. We notice problems of leadership; we also glimpse a kind of opportunism, a propensity perhaps to modify plans to maximize Sparta's advantage. Xenophon is introducing into his narrative patterns of action that will help account for episodes of greater significance later on – namely the seizure of the Cadmea.

If Xenophon's account of Mantinea leaves any doubt as to his purpose in Book 5, his treatment of Sparta's relations with Phlius should remove them.[41] Sparta's conflict with Phlius, an ally located some fifteen miles south-west of Corinth, is the subject of three long passages in Book 5 clustered around the Olynthus and Cadmea episodes (5.2.8–10, 5.3.10–17, 5.3.21–25). Each section registers an increase in Spartan hostility, especially after the formal breach of the King's Peace. Xenophon tells us that troubles begin at Phlius when certain of her exiles note the interest the Spartans have taken in examining the loyalty of their allies, especially how they acted in the Corinthian War. Seeing their opportunity, the exiles go to Sparta and explain that when they were in Phlius the city was a loyal Spartan ally, but after they were exiled, the city would not follow the Spartans nor allow them into their city. The ephors decide that the situation is worthy of attention (5.2.8–9). It is interesting to see how closely the account of Sparta's involvement in the affairs of Phlius corresponds to Diodorus' general description of how, following the Peace, the Spartans regain their hegemony by restoring their now exiled supporters to power in various Greek cities (15.5.2–3). Diodorus' account of this process, which barely mentions Sparta's actions against Phlius (15.19.3), certainly suggests that the cities were protected by the provisions of the Peace; Xenophon, on the other hand, nowhere states that Phlius was a member of the Peace. Again, as with the case of Mantinea, we must assume that the Peloponnesian League was left intact by the King's Peace,[42] perhaps thereby technically allowing the Spartans to meddle with the autonomy of Phlius. But again, if that was the case, then we must ask what Xenophon's purpose was in representing the humiliation of Phlius (again, events Diodorus does not really treat) as a violation of the spirit of the Peace. I will come back to this point in a moment.

In response to the Phliasian exiles' appeal, the Spartans send emissaries to Phlius to state that the exiles were their friends, and that they were exiled although they had done nothing wrong. Although the Spartans make it clear to the people of Phlius that they are requesting, not demanding a return of the exiles, the Phliasians understand the communication to be a threat. Fearing both the Spartans and their partisans still in Phlius, the Phliasians vote to recall the exiles and restore their property to them (5.2.9–10). So matters stood some time after the winter of 384. Two years later, in the summer of 381, approximately six months after the illegal seizure of the Cadmea, Xenophon tells us that after making a generous contribution to King Agesipolis' campaign against Olynthus, the Phliasians, believing that the Spartans would not allow both kings to be absent from the city at one time, refuse to honour any of the claims of the restored exiles and compel them to take any grievance they might have to the courts of Phlius herself. When the exiles and some of their supporters go to Sparta to complain, the Phliasians fine them (5.3.10–11). These actions provoke a quick response from the Spartans: the ephors order the mobilization of the army and Agesilaus takes command. Unlike the case of Mantinea, where private ties discouraged him from taking part in the campaign (or at least that was the reason he gave), on this occasion Agesilaus leads the expedition gladly because of personal bonds of friendship between himself and the Phliasians, bonds that are in part honoured because of the memory of his father (5.3.13).

On the march north, representatives come from Phlius to beg Agesilaus not to invade. When, finally, even bribery does not work, the Phliasians ask him what it would take for him not to attack: Agesilaus' response makes it clear that nothing less than surrendering their acropolis (presumably to a Spartan governor and garrison) will do. The Phliasians naturally refuse, and Agesilaus lays siege to the city (5.3.14–16). In a rare glimpse of internal dissension we are told that these actions met with widespread disapproval at Sparta:[43] as Xenophon reports, 'many Spartans were saying that for the sake of a few men they were antagonizing a city of more than 5,000' (5.3.16; cf. Theopompus *FGrHist* 115 F 321 and below, p. 230). The Phliasians manage to hold out longer than expected despite severe food shortages; in fact, Xenophon finds their resistance so noteworthy that he praises their 'self-control' (*enkrateia*; see above, p. 134) and singles out a certain Phliasian, Delphion, for his bravery and excellence in command (5.3.21–22). When, finally, the Phliasians are forced to surrender, they insist on turning their city over to 'the magistrates of the Spartans'. Agesilaus, angered (*orgistheis*) at what he regards as an insult, engineers it so that the people of Phlius have to surrender directly to him. He orders the formation of a provisional government that is to include fifty of the exiles and that has power of life and death over the citizens of Phlius, and he charges it to design a new constitution for the city (5.3.23–25).

It is worth taking another look at the exchange between the Phliasians and Agesilaus. When they ask Agesilaus what it would take for him not to invade, the king responds 'that which you did before and received no harm from us'; as Xenophon explains, 'this was the surrender of their acropolis' (5.3.15). The reference to an earlier handing over of the acropolis is to an episode related at *Hell.* 4.4.15, and a comparison between the two passages is instructive. In the late 390s, Iphicrates was active in the Corinthia and had wreaked considerable havoc there. The Phliasians, who had lost a number of men in an ambush he had set, became so alarmed they turned the control of their city, including the acropolis, over to the Spartans, even though at that time the city was governed by the democratic faction. In fact, before the arrival of Iphicrates the Phliasians would not permit the Spartans to enter their city (alluded to later by the Phliasian exiles), and they had exiled Spartan sympathizers. Xenophon tells us that the Spartans were so scrupulous in their management of Phlius that they never even brought up the subject of restoring the exiles, even though they were 'well minded towards them'. When the danger of Iphicrates passed, the Spartans turned the city back over to the people of Phlius and left. The central point of contrast is, of course, the role of personal attachments as opposed to the interests of the city. In the earlier episode, Xenophon lays great stress on the fact that although they had the opportunity, the Spartans did not abuse their authority and impose their wishes, specifically a government composed of their friends, on Phlius. In the later episode, Xenophon goes to great lengths to suggest the result of Agesilaus' own friendships and hatreds. The difficulty of finding a king to command in the campaign against Mantinea raised the issue of leadership and personal ties. In the Phlius campaign, the leadership of Agesilaus is the driving force: he accepts the command gladly because of his ties to the oligarchs in Phlius; he demands the surrender of the acropolis; the Spartans object that because of his friends they are alienating an entire city; finally, it is his anger that forces the Phliasians, a people Xenophon has characterized as heroic and ably led, to surrender to him. Unlike the final settlement at Mantinea where restraint was shown the opponents of Sparta (5.2.6), Agesilaus orders that a new constitution be drawn up and that, in the meantime, a provisional government be installed with the authority to put anyone to death. Although made up of fifty exiles and fifty from 'those from home', we know from earlier passages that there were a number of oligarchic supporters still in Phlius (5.2.9, 5.3.11, 5.3.17) and they were no doubt appointed.[44]

Agesilaus' settlement of Phlius, stark and brutal, is also Sparta's settlement, despite voices of opposition. Taken as a whole, the Phlius episode demonstrates how Sparta's policies, determined to a signifi-cant degree by the whims of individual commanders, could become nakedly hegemonic. The difference in Sparta's behaviour towards

Phlius before and after the King's Peace suggests a very important point: Sparta, though enjoying considerable success as a result of the Peace, was in Xenophon's eyes becoming an increasingly oppressive power.[45] The complete and radical destruction of autonomy at Mantinea and Phlius, while perhaps not forbidden by the Peace (if neither was an official member of the Peace), is presented in terms that point to grotesque violations of the spirit of the Peace.

Badian pointed out recently that Agesilaus' actions against Phlius cannot be construed as in any way 'based on or justified by' the King's Peace since the Spartans had decided formally to renounce the agreement with the seizure of the Cadmea and their subsequent decision to hold on to it.[46] This understanding of the Cadmea episode and Sparta's actions after it misrepresents the realities of the Spartans' decision making. While the illegal capture of Thebes' acropolis must have constituted a breach of the Peace, this action should not be construed as Sparta's formal declaration that they had abandoned the Peace. I find it hard to believe that any ancient power (or modern one for that matter) would willingly consider their own participation in a treaty at an end as a consequence of its own action. Rather, the opposite was usually the case: it was commonplace for one city to legitimize the initiation of hostilities against another by declaring that their enemy had broken a treaty between them. A case in point: although retrospectively the Spartans believed that they had broken the Thirty Years Peace with Athens (Thuc. 7.18.2), when they were contemplating action against Athens on the eve of the war they decided that in fact Athens was at fault (Thuc. 1.88). More normal was the situation described by Diodorus at 15.29.7: the Athenians voted that the Peace of Antalcidas had been broken by the raid of Sphodrias in 378; in other words, it is the injured party, not the injuring one, that declares a compact at an end. While states frequently acted in contravention of treaties, what good was it for them to admit publicly that they had done so and thereby lose whatever potential advantages they enjoyed under a given peace? A treaty could, for instance, guarantee that a rival state would not interfere in the dispute between a hegemon and a subordinate state; or it could lend legitimacy to an action directed against a neutral power in the name of protecting a member of the peace. Thus the Spartans could count on Athens (*pace* Diodorus) looking the other way when they set about 'punishing' their delinquent allies. Indeed, as Xenophon informs us (5.4.19), Athens severely punished the Athenian commanders who had helped the Theban exiles reclaim the Cadmea (death, exile) – an episode which suggests that as late as the winter of 379, months after the fall of Phlius, the Athenians, despite what the Spartans had done, still thought that maintaining the Peace with the Spartans was more important than holding them accountable for breaking it.[47] And if the Athenians wanted to believe that the Peace was still intact even after the Cadmea and Phlius, what good would it have done the Spartans to declare that they themselves had broken it? The action taken against Phlius reveals not that the Spartans had formally abandoned the Peace after the Cadmea and thus changed their foreign policy, but rather that they felt, before the Cadmea and after, that they enjoyed considerable latitude under its terms for taking action against other Greek states notionally protected by its provisions. The Phlius episode, framing the seizure of the Cadmea, shows that the more important event was actually part of a larger pattern.

As *Hell.* 5.4.1 makes clear, the central event of the history, the event that seems to help Xenophon trace a pattern of episodes that leads up to and away from a decisive moment, is the Spartans' illegal seizure of the Cadmea. But before turning to Xenophon's treatment of the episode, it is important to take note of the groundwork he lays for bringing into relief the themes that he thinks are typified by the crime. The Spartan campaign against Olynthus, beginning in 382, serves as the prologue to the seizure.

Xenophon tells us that about the time of the first conflict between Sparta and Phlius over the issue of the exiles (the autumn or winter of 383), ambassadors from two cities from north-east Greece, Acanthus and Apollonia, came to Sparta to appeal for help.[48] A certain Cleigenes from Acanthus makes a lengthy speech before the Spartans and (perhaps)[49] the Peloponnesian League members (5.2.12–19), in which he states that in their war with King Amyntas of Macedon the Olynthians have demanded the support of Apollonia and Acanthus. He characterizes Olynthus as the largest city in Thrace and complains that the Olynthians have compelled the cities of that region to join with them, forcing them 'to use the same laws and to be fellow citizens with them' (5.2.12). Asserting his city's wish to remain free, the Acanthian tells the Spartans that 'we want to observe our own ancestral laws and to be independent citizens' (5.2.14).[50] Towards the end of his appeal the ambassador suggests that, seeing that it was reasonable for the Spartans to ensure that Boeotia not become unified under one power (understand, of course, Thebes), it was even more in their interests not to ignore an even greater threat from the Olynthians – greater because of the massive resources at their disposal (5.2.16–17). And these resources, Cleigenes claims, are themselves the cause of increasing ambition at Olynthus: as he explains, 'for God, it seems, has made it that the ambitions of men grow along with their power' (5.2.18). Xenophon tells us that the Spartans, in their capacity as chief guarantor (*prostates*) of the Peace, were eager to check the growing power of the most powerful state of Chalcidice. They put the matter before 'their allies' and, it seems, the allies approved sending troops against Olynthus (5.2.20).

Scholars have noted that the missing words or rather missing document in the Acanthian appeal at Sparta is the King's Peace. Indeed, Cleigenes accuses the Olynthians of crimes whose wording falls precisely under the purview of the King's Peace:[51] it was abundantly clear that the Olynthians were seeking nothing less than the elimination of the autonomy of their neighbouring states. Yet, strangely, the Peace is not mentioned. Many have assumed that Xenophon has simply slipped – it would not be the first time.[52] However, I believe that this line of argument is highly problematic. With Badian, I believe that Cleigenes would have referred to Sparta's obligation under the terms of the King's Peace to defend Acanthus and Apollonia from Olynthus if in fact that obligation existed; it cannot, furthermore, be said that the possible relevance of the Peace has been overlooked here completely, since the ambassador makes an oblique reference to it when commenting on Sparta's dissolution of Thebes' Boeotian hegemony. It is easier to assume that Xenophon did not believe that Olynthus was a member of the Peace and so fell outside its provisions. It is useful (if also confusing) to add that Diodorus suggests that it was Sparta, not Olynthus, that was breaking the King's Peace in marching against Olynthus; so much is implied by his assertion that starting in 383 the Spartans began increasingly to transfer the hegemony of Greece into their own hands in contravention of the King's Peace, and his subsequent treatment of Sparta's operations in Thrace (15.19.1ff.). But, curiously, Diodorus makes no mention of Olynthus' aggressions against Acanthus; rather we are told that Olynthus is at war with Amyntas and that Sparta enters the picture by siding with Macedon, a not unusual procedure for a technically neutral power to enter into a conflict and gain power and a foothold as a result.[53] And herein lies the confusion: while Xenophon's narrative of Sparta's entry into the Thraceward theatre of action seems informed by the terms of the King's Peace, the Peace itself is not mentioned; Diodorus on the other hand mentions the Peace but then proceeds to recount a rather unexceptional string of events which seem to bear little relation to the Peace. Nonetheless, the scenario provided by Xenophon is the easier to understand: if Olynthus and Acanthus were not members of the Peace, or if Xenophon did not believe they were members of the Peace, then the nearness of Olynthus' actions to those of a violator of the King's Peace creates the impression that non-members of the Peace got better treatment at Sparta's hands than did nominal or (as we shall soon see at Thebes) even full members – so long as that treatment ultimately advanced Spartan interests. But even if the picture which Diodorus gives is correct, the Spartans in Xenophon's account still seem inconsistent at best when it comes to honouring the King's Peace: where their neighbours and allies are concerned they seem to be callous or wilfully ignorant of the spirit of the Peace; when distant states are threatened they become scrupulous enforcers. We are left wondering if Cleigenes' words regarding human ambition and imperialism were applied to the right city.

In the summer of 382, following the appeal of Acanthus, the Spartans send Phoebidas, a Spartiate and friend (possibly even a kinsman) of Agesilaus,[54] north against Olynthus.[55] He camps near Thebes and is encouraged by a conservative Theban polemarch, Leontiades, to seize the city's citadel. Phoebidas, whom Xenophon has characterized as a weak man not in possession of self-control (5.2.28), is persuaded to storm the Cadmea while the women of Thebes are celebrating the Thesmophoria (5.2.29).[56] Once the oligarchs are securely in power at Thebes, Leontiades immediately sets off for Sparta to try to consolidate his position. When he arrives at Sparta, Xenophon tells us he is coolly received: the ephors and the people (*to plethos*) are angry with Phoebidas because he did not follow orders (5.2.32). Agesilaus comes to Phoebidas' defence; he argues that the only question that should be considered is whether Phoebidas had helped or hurt Sparta. Agesilaus supports this position by insisting that there was an 'ancient law' (*archaion nomimon*) at Sparta that allowed field commanders to 'improvise' (*autoschediazein*) in the interests of the state (5.2.32). Leontiades then delivers a speech (5.2.33–34), and the Spartans are persuaded to retain control of the Theban citadel and to try and execute Leontiades' chief political rival, Ismenias (5.2.35–36). Although it is not stated, it seems fairly certain that Agesilaus succeeded in rescuing Phoebidas from punishment;[57] while Xenophon says nothing at all, others report that Phoebidas was fined.[58]

This passage contains a number of features that allow us to detect Xenophon's profound disapproval.[59] The illegal capture of the Cadmea was without doubt a breach of the King's Peace, an agreement that was protected by an oath; consequently the seizure was formally the breaking of an oath, and as was shown in the previous chapter (see above, pp. 184–185), Xenophon regarded few crimes as worse than this one. Second, Xenophon records the disapproval of the ephors and the people in response to Phoebidas' actions: they are angry with him because he was, in effect, insubordinate. Elsewhere in his corpus Xenophon points to the obedience (*peitharchia*) of the Spartans as noteworthy and expected of every citizen. In the *Hellenica*, just a few chapters earlier, the *peitharchia* of the Spartan troops is praised by Xenophon when they refused to abuse the departing Mantinean democrats (5.2.7). In the *Constitution of the Spartans*, he explains that *peitharchia* was central at Sparta:[60] Lycurgus made sure that the more powerful a person was at Sparta the more obedient he would be (8.2);[61] he established the ephorate because 'obedience is the greatest good in the city, army and home' (8.3); and Lycurgus himself is praised for having made obedience a religious obligation at Sparta (8.5). In other words, the seizure of the Cadmea entailed in Xenophon's mind the two worst crimes a human could commit – oath-breaking and disregard for one's own laws (see above, p. 188).

In light of the importance of obedience at Sparta, Agesilaus' response to the anger of the ephors and citizens is puzzling. What, one wonders, was this *archaion nomimon* (5.2.32) that permitted the Spartan commander to disobey orders? Powerful prohibitions should have stood in the way of Phoebidas' surprise attack: he was instructed to march against Olynthus, not seize the Theban citadel;[62] and, more generally, Sparta was bound under oath not to interfere with the internal affairs of other states. Modern historians have censured Xenophon here for suppressing what is preserved by other ancient authorities: both Diodorus (15.20.2) and Plutarch (*Ages.* 24.1) assert that Agesilaus had ordered Phoebidas to storm the Cadmea. Although no mention is made of this possibility in Xenophon, and Phoebidas is made out to be a poor commander (and hence someone who on his own could do something as foolish as he did),[63] Agesilaus' words ring hollow; whether he actually ordered the seizure or not, as Xenophon presents it, his defence of it is damning enough.[64] As Eduard Schwartz acutely noted, a better defence of 'interstate thievery' ('Räuberpolitik') could not be found than the phrase *archaion nomimon exeinai ta toiauta autoschediazein*.[65] Furthermore, Agesilaus' final plea to the Spartans is revealing and (I think) damaging: 'consider only if the action was good or bad for Sparta'. These are the words of naked imperialism, reminiscent of the query put to the Plataean survivors by their Spartan captors in Thucydides (3.52.4): 'having called them together [the Spartans] asked them only this, if they had in the present war rendered any good service to the Lacedaemonians and their allies'.[66] Agesilaus' words are also from the vocabulary of the expedient; gone, it seems, are considerations from justice which must ultimately underlie Sparta's famous *peitharchia*. In fact, Agesilaus' apparent disregard for the just, although his own conduct was always unimpeachable, illustrates the dichotomy between Sparta's internal *arete* and her external brutality. It is instructive to recall the words of the Athenian delegation at Melos in Thucydides:

> for the Spartans are exceedingly observant of moral excellence in matters regarding themselves and their native customs; as regards others, one could say many things about how they conduct themselves, but would summarize the point very clearly [by stating] that, most openly of all men whom we know, they reckon what is pleasant good, and what is advantageous just.
>
> (5.105.4)[67]

Agesilaus' attitude in the Phoebidas incident is precisely one wherein he equates justice with advantage (cf. Thuc. 3.56.3). That Xenophon should have Agesilaus speak the words of 5.2.32 is powerfully suggestive. Embodied in Agesilaus are all of the virtues of Sparta (cf. Xenophon *Ages.* 1.5), but also her fatal flaws – stubborn hostility, ambition and arrogance. Furthermore, Agesilaus' justification of Phoebidas' actions suggests that, in the field at least, the commander was supreme in deciding what was good for Sparta. But this was, especially to a pious man and one knowledgeable of Spartan ways, an arrogation of power that properly belonged to the government of Sparta, and ultimately to the gods.

At *Hell.* 5.2.35, we learn that the Spartans approve of the seizure of the Cadmea. We find out in the same sentence that Ismenias, an opponent of the Spartan sympathizers at Thebes, is to be put on trial. This trial ends with his condemnation and death (5.2.36). While this event may seem unexceptional, especially to those familiar with the normal course of *stasis* in Greek cities, the trial and execution of Ismenias is important when it is examined closely and set against the background of the other treatments of the Cadmea and its aftermath. In the first place, the circumstances of the trial are revealing: Ismenias is tried before the Spartans and their allies ('both the small and the great' – a bitter allusion to the King's Peace?), and what is more, the charges are patently ludicrous: 'siding with the barbarians, being an ally to Persia to no advantage for Greece, having been on the Great King's payroll, and being the most responsible, along with Androcleidas [another democratic leader], for the disturbance affecting the whole of Greece' (5.2.35). These charges, in addition to being grotesquely exaggerated, are in fact more accurately applied to Sparta under Agesilaus, not Thebes under Ismenias.[68] The sense of irony grows when one considers that in all the other accounts of the Cadmea episode, the place of Ismenias' trial is taken by the punishment of Phoebidas which is not mentioned in Xenophon (see above, n.58).

Following the execution of Ismenias Xenophon details the Spartan campaign against Olynthus commanded by Teleutias. Teleutias is cited with approval elsewhere in the *Hellenica*: indeed, Xenophon thought so highly of his ability to lead that he makes the memorable send-off Teleutias receives from his men one of the more important programmatic passages in the history (5.1.4; see above, p. 197). While the first phase of his campaign proceeds as well as his earlier accomplishments portended (5.2.37–43), the second phase turns out altogether differently. Angered (*aganaktesas*, 5.3.3) at the sally of Olynthian cavalry from their city, Teleutias unwisely sends his peltasts to meet them; when the Olynthians feign retreat, the Spartans pursue and are surprised by the enemy and slaughtered. Again angered (*orgistheis*, 5.3.5), Teleutias commits his entire force to the pursuit of the Olynthians. While the Spartans are drawing close to the city walls the Olynthians emerge from their positions in full force themselves and defeat the Spartan army; Teleutias falls. Significantly, just as Teleutias' successes had encourged Xenophon to draw the reader's attention to him as an ideal to be imitated, so in defeat he uses Teleutias as an example to avoid. After reporting Teleutias' death he observes,

> from disasters such as these I say that men especially learn how it is essential to punish not even slaves in anger (*orgei*). Now, often masters in their anger suffer more harm than they inflict;

but to launch an attack against an enemy in a state of anger and not with reason is the height of folly, for anger is careless of the future, whereas reason considers no less what harm may result than how to inflict harm on the enemy.

(5.3.7)

To be sure, Xenophon means just what he says here: the death of Teleutias is instructive for future commanders regarding the perils of engaging an enemy when blind with anger.[69] But this highly visible passage is also meaningful at a more general level, precisely because it comes so shortly after Xenophon's praise of the same man. The seizure of the Cadmea is situated between the two passages; no other 'editorial' remarks are to be found until Xenophon's condemnation of Sparta at 5.4.1. Perhaps Xenophon draws such notice to Teleutias because he somehow represents the city from which he comes: like Teleutias, the Spartans had recently committed themselves to a course of action that did not take sufficient account of the harm that would result to themselves from it, but rather they focused their attention on the harm they could inflict on others. Xenophon may be making a simpler point, however, and is just trying to connect brother to brother; it must be remembered that Agesilaus is steering Spartan policy at this point, and that he is, as his brother was before Olynthus, influenced by hatred and anger (primarily against Thebes: 5.1.33). It was after becoming angered that Agesilaus imposed harsh conditions on Phlius, an account that follows closely upon the story of Teleutias' death (5.3.24). The major difference between the two is that in Teleutias' case, only the welfare of an army is at stake, but with Agesilaus that of an entire state. With Teleutias, as with Mnasippus and Iphicrates, paradigmatic leadership is not only didactic, it is also historically explanatory.

Part II of Book 5 comes to an end with the accounts of the fall of Phlius and Olynthus. But immediately before the start of Part III and the denunciation of the Spartans' seizure of the Cadmea, Xenophon reviews the state of Spartan affairs in the winter of 380/79:

with matters having gone well for the Spartans – the Thebans and the rest of the Boeotians were completely under their power, the Corinthians had become most trustworthy, the Argives had been brought low because of the ineffectiveness of their monthly truce, the Athenians were deserted, and their own allies who had been ill-disposed towards them had been punished – their rule seemed (*edokei*) to have been established well and safely at last.

(5.3.27)

Given that the denunciation of Sparta and the story of decline towards Leuctra and Mantinea follows, the term 'seemed' is powerfully ironic. Indeed, Breitenbach and Cartledge have argued, quite reasonably, that Xenophon put this summation of Spartan success here to suggest a sort of tragic fall, a *peripeteia*.[70] In this connection, note that Diodorus' corresponding passage measuring the height of Spartan power (15.23.3–4), which reproduces in the same order the list of Sparta's enemies,[71] does not introduce the feeling of uncertainty that Xenophon's passage invites.

PART III: 5.4

Xenophon's condemnation of the seizure of the Cadmea comes not immediately following the story of the capture itself, nor after the decision of Sparta to maintain a garrison there, nor following the trial of Ismenias – all (one might think) suitable locations. The fact that the denunciation of Sparta comes immediately before the story of the liberation of Thebes suggests that the story is meant in some way to confirm it.

Before turning to the story of the liberation, it is useful to recall Xenophon's denunciation of Sparta at 5.4.1:

one could bring up many other instances, both Greek and barbarian, which show that the gods neglect neither impious persons nor those who do wicked deeds. Now I will take up the matter at hand. The Spartans, having sworn to let the cities [of Greece] be free, seized the acropolis at Thebes; by the very people alone whom they wronged they were punished, having themselves never been defeated in battle before. As for the Thebans who brought the Spartans into the citadel and who wanted to enslave their city to the Spartans so that they might be tyrants themselves, only seven of the exiles were needed to destroy their rule. I will now explain how this happened.

As discussed at the beginning of the last chapter (p. 179), the feature of this passage that has generated the most interest is Xenophon's appeal to the divine as a historical agent. But there is another, related problem that also deserves attention. The passage contains a paradoxical note suggesting the episode's uniqueness – the invincible Spartans vanquished for the first time by the very people they harmed. This colouring invites a very important question. Is Xenophon's condemnation in this passage specific to one isolable event or is it meant to comment on a pattern of behaviour? To put it another way, do the gods punish Sparta for the seizure of the Cadmea, or because the seizure is representative of a trend or tendency that needs to be checked? There seems to be support for both views.

On the one hand, Xenophon has been careful to record the subjugations of Mantinea and Phlius and the preparations against Olynthus: we have had a foretaste of Spartan aggression in contravention of at least the spirit of the King's Peace, and so are prepared for Phoebidas' capture of the Cadmea. Xenophon's chronicle of Spartan activities prior to and immediately following 382 makes the events of that year seem emblematic of a general outlook of imperialism. Insofar as the whole of Book 5 of the *Hellenica* has this effect, one could argue that the condemnation that Xenophon registers at 5.4.1 could reasonably be made to include those activities of Sparta that were but less dramatic and less important manifestations of the same ruthless and arrogant ambition evident in the capture of Thebes.

However, details in the passage suggest that one can also look at the censure of Sparta at 5.4.1 as bearing only on the seizure of the Cadmea. Xenophon lays great stress on the singular nature of Sparta's defeat at Leuctra and the expulsion of the pro-Spartan sympathizers by only seven men. It seems that Xenophon's thinking is as follows: since the Spartans were defeated at Leuctra by the very people whom they harmed (a Spartan defeat being something that had never happened before),[72] and since the puppet regime at Thebes was brought down by a mere seven men (something equally unusual), the gods must be thought the authors of such remarkable and indeed unprecedented events. Just as the capture's link with past events argues for seeing 5.4.1 as a condemnation of all Sparta's aggressions after the ratification of the King's Peace, so the link drawn forward between the seizure and the battle of Leuctra supports the notion that Xenophon understood Sparta's eclipse as the leading power in Greece as the result of this one act alone.

The seizure of the Cadmea: *aition* of Sparta's fall or an emblem of her flawed foreign policy? In a certain sense, it seems that we must understand the event in both ways. The crime, as Xenophon suggests, was of such magnitude that it earned the Spartans a place among the most notorious and impious of all mankind, both Greek and barbarian.[73] To Xenophon's way of thinking, furthermore, the seizure 'triggered' the battle of Leuctra more than ten years later. Understood in these terms, the event was unique. However, the episode was only the most outrageous in a series of acts that were in contravention of the very agreement the Spartans, and in particular Agesilaus, were so zealous to enforce. The Cadmea is both an isolated episode and illustrative of a pattern working through time. Polybius certainly understood the Cadmea episode as part of a general policy of aggression (4.27.4–7): he connected the seizure and Sparta's subsequent approval of the crime as illustrative of a flawed policy that was also in evidence in the treatment of Mantinea, especially the dioecism of that city. And it is this last notion, the capture as a representative of a series of related events, that I wish to explore further.

In order to appreciate more fully the significance of Xenophon's condemnation of Sparta at 5.4.1, it will be useful to take account of Ephorus and what he has to say about the Cadmea and the Spartans. If the preface to Diodorus Book 15 is in substance the work of Ephorus,[74] then a set of important similarities and one important difference emerge from a comparison of Xenophon's and Ephorus' characterization of 382 and the capture of the Cadmea. Like the implicit connection between the Cadmea episode and Sparta's aggressions prior to the capture which is suggested by Xenophon's account, Ephorus points to a tendency in Spartan policy to be harsh towards its allies or subjects;[75] while the Cadmea is not mentioned by name, Ephorus singles out the Thebans as the wronged group that exacts revenge on the Spartans for their earlier wrongdoing (15.1.5). Like Xenophon, Ephorus stresses that those who had never before been defeated were conquered by the very people they had harmed (15.1.4). And like Xenophon, Ephorus characterizes the defeat of Sparta at both Leuctra and Mantinea as unexpected (Leuctra *paradoxos*, Mantinea *anelpistos*, 15.1.2).[76] But, unlike Xenophon, Ephorus does not ascribe the process of punishment to the gods. Instead, he argues that the Spartans were overthrown by their own thoughtlessness or lack of good advice (*aboulia*, 15.1.3), and introduces the topic not as illustrative of the gods' role in human history but as yet another paradigm of immoral behaviour presented so as to give heart to the virtuous and to discourage the base (15.1.1). The same points are made at the beginning of Diodorus 14.1–2 where again the gods are absent.

This difference between Xenophon's and Ephorus' account of the fall of Sparta prompts an extremely important point: Xenophon may well have been alone among historians of the period in understanding the seizure of the Cadmea as an act punished by the gods.[77] Ephorus' interests in the divine were motivated primarily by a desire to rationalize myth and to enshrine *aitia* – that is to say an antiquarian tendency (thus *FGrHist* 70 F 15, 20, 54, 96) – although this was not always the case (so F 9).[78] When we cast around for other contemporaries or near contemporaries who would have characterized the seizure in the same way as Xenophon, we only run into figures to rule out. To judge from the fragments of Theopompus, he did not employ the gods as historical agents; rather, his interests in the sacred were, like Ephorus, primarily antiquarian.[79] Although we know that at least some of the Atthidographers discussed the Cadmea and its recapture in connection with Athens' offering refuge to the Theban exiles (i.e. Androtion *FGrHist* 324 F 50), they were primarily antiquarian in outlook as well, a fact that should not surprise us given their general interests in local *aitia* and local cult.[80] Followers of Thucydides can also be ruled out, but for a different reason, namely their adherence to the principle that the divine does not have a role in shaping human history;[81] the Oxyrhynchus historian does not mention the gods as historical agents in the fragments of his narrative that have come down to us, and if Philistus truly was 'an imitator of Thucydides' (e.g. Cicero *de Or.* 2.57 = *FGrHist* 556 T 17b), then he too could hardly be expected to have the gods in his historical writing. It would be interesting to know, however, what the source is for Diodorus' account of the 'divinely sent plague' and other misfortunes that beset the Carthaginians in 379/8 (15.24.2–3); if it was a writer contemporary with Xenophon, then we may well have a close parallel for the thinking behind *Hell.* 5.4.1.[82] But in any case, men like Xenophon represented the majority of Greeks when they saw the divine at work in history; Thucydides and those who closely followed him must have been in the minority on this point. Herodotus saw the divine as a historical agent and no doubt this view carried on through Xenophon to the majority of the later historians.[83] We should remember, too, in this connection that the Third Sacred War was being fought at the end of Xenophon's life, when this portion of the *Hellenica* was either being completed or had just been finished. It was a war ostensibly fought for religious reasons (Phocian sacrilege),[84] one in which Xenophon took a keen interest (cf. *Poroi* 5.9–10), and one that may well have been temporarily forestalled for a time out of respect for religious obligations, inasmuch as the Thebans may well have postponed their attack for a sacred procession sent by Athens to Delphi in the summer of 355.[85]

Xenophon's account of the Spartan seizure of the Cadmea, therefore, may have been unique in its reliance on the divine to explain the event's ultimate consequences. What should not be lost sight of, however, is that, as was pointed out above, *Hell.* 5.4.1 and Ephorus' account share the view that the fall of Sparta was unexpected. This point of contact, interestingly enough, sheds light on the very feature that distinguishes Xenophon's assessment – the presence of the divine.

How and why is this accent on the unexpected nature of Sparta's fall connected to the divine? A passage from Xenophon's *Cyropaedia* helps answer this question. At the very end of his long conversation with his son, the young Cyrus the Great, Cambyses says that the most important lesson to learn on the way towards being a successful ruler is to do nothing contrary to the instructions of the gods (*hiera* and *oionoi*, *Cyr.* 1.6.44). Cambyses explains that humans must make important decisions based on conjecture (*eikazontes*), since they do not know at all whence good things come. As proof of the fallibility of human reasoning and decision making, Cambyses offers a number of theoretical examples drawn from 'history' (*ton gignomenon*, 1.6.45). He begins,

> indeed, there have many men who seemed to be very wise; these men persuaded states to go to war, and these states were destroyed by the very people they were encouraged to attack. On the other hand, there are a number of examples of men who have helped both individuals and states, suffering the most terrible evils at the hands of those they so benefited. Many people, for whom it was possible to have friends and to treat their friends well and to be treated well in return, have wished to treat these as slaves rather than as friends, and by them they have been punished. And for many it was not enough for them to live well, but to be the masters of all, and because of these things they have lost even that which they had.
>
> (*Cyr.* 1.6.45)

All of Cambyses' examples regarding the futility of relying on human reason in decision making are paradoxes in the strict sense

– events that are unexpected or which turn out precisely the opposite from what was anticipated. This is precisely the structure of
thought so prominent in *Hell.* 5.4.1. Catastrophe and defeat occur
when humans depend on themselves alone for determining what
they should do. Also revealing in *Cyr.* 1.6.45 is the emphasis placed
on the self-destructiveness of human ambition and the punishment
that comes at the hands of those whom one has harmed. This
resonates powerfully with Xenophon's denunciation at *Hell.* 5.4.1.
What is more, the stress Cambyses lays on how some states can be
misled even by the wise, and as a consequence be destroyed, fits the
picture of Sparta led by Agesilaus. And finally, the observation that
those who strive after hegemony not only do not obtain what they
seek but even lose what they started with describes Sparta perfectly
in light of Leuctra and Mantinea.

Cambyses offers not only negative evidence regarding the inade-
quacy of human knowledge for decision making, he also presents a
case for why the gods should be heeded when important decisions
have to be made:

> thus human wisdom knows no better how to choose the best
> than if someone casting his lot should do that which the lot
> indicates. But the gods, my son, being eternal, know all things
> – the past, present and future – and when humans consult
> them and they are favourable, the gods show ahead of time
> what one must do and what one must not do. Nor is it
> surprising if they are not willing to advise everyone. For they
> do not have to look after those whom they do not wish to.
>
> (*Cyr.* 1.6.46)

The gods know all things because they are immortal; because they
are omniscient they can tell human beings what they need to do
regarding their future well-being, but only those whom they wish
to help (cf. *Ap.* 13, *Mem.* 1.1.9 and Plato *Ap.* 41d). Thus far
Xenophon's understanding of the divine seems straightforward.
Cambyses touches only briefly, however, on what one does to make
the gods willing to impart their knowledge of the future.

This question is answered again by Cambyses in the same
discussion with Cyrus. At the beginning of their conversation, in a
passage no doubt meant to dovetail with *Cyr.* 1.6.44ff.,[86] Cyrus
recalls an earlier lesson of his father to take care to remember the
gods at all times. Cambyses applauds his son and observes that since
Cyrus prays to the gods regularly 'you can expect to obtain what you

ask for because you are confident that you have never neglected them' (*oupopot' amelesas*, *Cyr.* 1.6.4). It is a matter of service and respect: if the gods are honoured or 'remembered' at all times, then they can be counted on to assist both individual and state in making correct decisions regarding the future. Should catastrophe strike, the individual or state must therefore be assumed to have been negligent in the service of the divine: either they do not revere and consult the gods at all, or they do but in other ways have shown their disregard for them. So much can be deduced from Cambyses' remarks at the beginning and end of his conversation with Cyrus.

Using Cambyses' lesson in personal piety as an interpretive guide we can perhaps extrapolate from *Hell.* 5.4.1 Xenophon's understanding of why the Spartans approved of the illegal seizure of the Cadmea, and so in his eyes set their state on a course of certain failure. The Spartans suffered the very sort of reversal that Cambyses spoke about; it seems reasonable to assume that they must have neglected their service to the divine, either by not consulting the gods or by acting in a way that made clear their disregard for them. The term found in all the passages discussed, *Hell.* 5.4.1, *Cyr.* 1.6.4 and 1.6.46, is service (the root *mel-* in Greek): humans must *care* for the divine at all times in order to secure their guidance, and the gods are *not unconcerned* when it comes to the wrongs men commit, but they pay attention to them. How precisely the Spartans showed their contempt for the gods can be gleaned from the Cadmea episode. The storming of the citadel in contravention of the terms of the King's Peace guaranteed by oath is clearly one source. But equally bad in Xenophon's eyes is the disobedience of Phoebidas, and, even more, the disobedience of all Sparta in not punishing him but, under the influence of Agesilaus, even finding a reason to legitimize what he had done. And while in Xenophon's mind the gods punished the Spartans for the seizure of the Cadmea, in his understanding of divine guidance and human ambition such a crime could only have been contemplated by the Spartans after they had embarked on a self-destructive course of action in which they paid no attention to the counsel of the gods. In a sense, then, it was not just a mistaken action for which Sparta was punished, but a mistaken set of actions.[87]

There is no more important section of the *Hellenica*, and no more problematic, than the narrative which follows the denunciation of Sparta for the illegal seizure of the Cadmea. We see two contradictory and apparently irreconcilable tendencies at work. In the first place,

Xenophon's pro-Spartan bias seems especially to be felt: most notoriously, the foundation of the Second Athenian Confederation has been omitted,[88] as well as the names of important Thebans who guided their city to its shortlived period of preeminence in Greece; furthermore, it is really the Thebans for the most part who are made to seem the instigators of Sparta's ill-advised activities, and they are the ones who are presented as brutal. But in this portion of the history there are also clear denunciations of Sparta that cannot and should not be explained away. Indeed, the central problem of Xenophon's historical writing is distilled in the chapters following *Hell.* 5.4.1: was he a critic or apologist of Sparta; a historian attuned to the forces that shaped the important events of his day, or an imprecise chronicler diverted by the actions of noteworthy individuals?

To answer these questions one needs to keep our eye focused on Xenophon's presentation of Agesilaus. As I suggested above, the best way to appreciate his understanding of what the Spartans' presence in Asia promised and what their withdrawal meant for themselves and for Greece is to examine closely the king's activities there. Similarly, Agesilaus' actions after the ratification of the Peace of Antalcidas, and especially his defence of Phoebidas' breach of that agreement, serve as an explanation for Sparta as a whole; to a lesser extent one could add Teleutias' signal career, before and after the Cadmea episode. Hence the events after *Hell.* 5.4.1 should be read as a sort of 'Agesiliaka' – affairs of the Greek world explained by the decisions and actions of one man, an approach not that different from one of the better modern treatments of this period of Greek history.[89]

The remaining part of Book 5, following Xenophon's censure of the Spartans at 5.4.1, breaks down into roughly three main sections: the liberation of Thebes; the unauthorized raid on the Piraeus of Athens by the Spartan Sphodrias and his scandalous acquittal at Sparta; and the Spartans' military operations in Boeotia against Thebes immediately following the liberation. While Agesilaus does not figure in all of these episodes, they do form a narrative unit that he dominates.

As I mentioned above, the defeat of the Spartans by the Thebans at Leuctra and the liberation of the Cadmea by only seven Theban exiles were cited by Xenophon at *Hell.* 5.4.1 as proof of the involvement of the divine in the punishment of Sparta. In other words, like the battle of Mantinea at the end of the history, they were events that disappointed or, better, confounded widely held expectations, namely that Sparta would never be defeated on the field of a major battle and Thebes would not be freed from Spartan control by only seven men. Again I think we are entitled to imagine that at the time Xenophon himself found these developments surprising.

The story of the liberation begins in a marked way: 'there was a certain Phillidas who was a secretary to the polemarchs in the party of Archias and he served them excellently in all respects, or so it seemed' (5.4.2). The introduction of Phillidas, who turns out to harbour a deep hatred of the puppet regime at Thebes and is one of the main architects of the conspiracy against it (Pelopidas is nowhere mentioned), is a story-teller's formula: fables begin with similar words; Plato employs the phrase to introduce passages he wants us to regard as *muthoi* or important tales; and, most importantly for our purposes, Herodotus frequently deploys the structure at the start of stories with significant symbolic and exemplary value.[90] And indeed, the account of the liberation is told very much as a story of vengeance against tyrants – inescapable, brutal but nevertheless just. Phillidas, in Athens on a suspiciously 'uncertain matter',[91] meets up with Melon, a Theban exile, and together they plot the murder of the polemarchs in Thebes. The plan is remarkably similar to one devised by the Macedonian prince (later king) Alexander more than a century before, as punishment for Persians who had insulted noble-women at his father's court, recounted by Herodotus:[92] Phillidas, who had for some time been promising to supply the polemarchs with the most respected and beautiful women of Thebes, said he was now prepared to bring them in to their chamber, an event Xenophon tells us the polemarchs were looking forward to because 'they were that sort of men' (5.4.4). Phillidas then got the polemarchs drunk, engineered the removal of all their attendants and brought in Melon and his men disguised as women; they sat down next to the magistrates and at a given signal killed them (5.4.5–6). At this point in his narrative, Xenophon tells us that there was another version of the story in which the assassins were dressed as revellers, not women (5.4.7; cf. Plutarch *Mor.* 596 D and *Pel.* 11.1–2), exhibiting a concern about alternative accounts found nowhere else in the *Hellenica* (though commonplace in Herodotus). Xenophon tells us that after the polemarchs who had been dining in their chambers had been killed, Phillidas himself went to the house of the ringleader of the regime, Leontiades, used the trust that was placed in him to gain entry and killed him in the presence of his wife who had been working at the loom (5.4.7). The prisons were then opened and a proclamation made that the tyrants had been killed (5.4.8–9). With the help of an Athenian contingent, the Thebans then surrounded their acropolis and beseiged the Spartan garrison stationed there, forcing them eventually to surrender. Despite assurances of personal safety, Xenophon tells us that many of the supporters of the polemarchs were killed (although a few were saved by the Athenians), and that even the children of the pro-Spartan faction were butchered (5.4.12).

Xenophon stresses the savagery and completeness of the revenge taken on the regime set up by the Spartans after the illegal seizure of the Cadmea. We are meant to be shocked by the murder of the children of the oligarchic faction; we are perhaps even to be somewhat troubled by the manner of Leontiades' death; but the polemarchs, as demonstrated by their interest in debauching free women, are clearly wicked men and deserve their punishment as tyrants. The Herodotean resonances are important. A recent commentator has broached the possibility that Xenophon is imitating Herodotus in his story of the liberation;[93] this is probably going too far. That he is trying to claim the authority of a historian telling a story with a moral, one that proves the inexorability of divine punishment, seems more likely. But whatever Xenophon's precise purpose may be, it is worth noting the story-teller quality of the narrative, because he will shortly assume a similar manner of presentation in connection with the acquittal of Sphodrias.

Xenophon informs us that the liberation of the Cadmea leads directly to a mobilization at Sparta for war against Thebes (5.4.13). As he had done before in the case of Mantinea (5.2.3), Agesilaus refuses the command of the expedition, this time on the grounds that he is too old; the real reason, Xenophon tells us, is that he feared that his fellow citizens would charge him with 'going to the help of tyrants' (5.4.13), something that we ought to recall actually happened when he was beseiging Phlius (5.3.16). This is a significant charge to make when it is remembered that, in Spartan propaganda at least, Sparta had the reputation for ousting tyrants, not establishing them (e.g. Hdt. 5.92.α; Thuc. 1.18.1).[94] The command falls accordingly to Agesilaus' colleague, Cleombrotus. The first Spartan campaign against Thebes, like almost all their subsequent military operations treated in this part of Book 5 with the exception of those commanded by Agesilaus, is an enormous failure: prevented by the Athenians from entering Boeotia by the standard route, Cleombrotus has to march through Plataea, Thespiae and Cynoscephalae; having encamped in Theban territory for a mere sixteen days, he retreats, leaving Sphodrias and a garrison behind at Thespiae, and marches back to the Peloponnese, causing his own soldiers to wonder whether Sparta was really at war with Thebes (5.4.14–16).[95] On their way back the Spartan forces get caught in a storm that kills several pack animals and strips some soldiers of their shields – an omen of things to come, namely Leuctra (5.4.17). Xenophon tells us that at Athens there was growing alarm at Sparta's aggression against Thebes, and that in order to remain neutral the Athenians actually condemned to death two generals who had helped Melon and his associates (5.4.19).

It is precisely at this point in his narrative, before the raid of Sphodrias and after Xenophon himself has given indications that Athens was in some sense more than unofficially involved in resisting the Spartan effort into Boeotia, that some believe he should have mentioned the formation of Athens' second maritime alliance, the so-called Second Athenian Confederation.[96] The problem of this silence must be addressed, for much of the recent dissatisfaction with Xenophon as a historian is traceable to his omissions of important facts, and this one is thought to be his worst. To say that he is simply not interested in discussing Athenian affairs at this juncture is unacceptable. Such an explanation assumes in the first place that the foundation of the League had nothing to do with Sparta, and second that Xenophon does not otherwise feature Athenians in this part of his narrative. The first assumption is patently wrong and the second one mistaken: Athenians are to be found throughout this part of the *Hellenica* reacting to the increasing attention shown by Sparta in Boeotia. One possible explanation for the silence, and one that I offer only as a provisional suggestion, is that if Xenophon wrote the *Hellenica* some time during and/or after the Social War (see below, p. 248), a war that pitted Athens against many of her allies from this same alliance and one that Athens lost, and further if he was writing for an Athenian audience, then he may have wanted to avoid mentioning the creation of a league the dissolution of which was so recent and so humiliating for Athens. Unlike Isocrates, in his attempt to indict all imperialist ventures as self-destructive, Xenophon may have thought that mentioning the Second Athenian Confederation was simply too much for an Athenian audience to bear. In the *Poroi*, published soon after the end of the Social War, while he clearly has the Second Athenian Confederation in mind, he nowhere refers directly to Athens having recently been at the head of a maritime alliance; rather, he talks around this subject (more on this below, p. 248). Likewise, in the remaining part of the *Hellenica* Xenophon does not mention Athens as the head of an alliance, and indeed he seems purposely to avoid mentioning the fact.[97]

But even if we cannot explain Xenophon's omission of the foundation, or more to the point, even if we believe that he omitted it because it did not reflect well on Sparta, this ought not to divert our attention away from what he does say about this crucial phase of Greek history. As we shall see, while Xenophon does represent the illegal raid of Sphrodrias on Piraeus as instigated by the Thebans, he also has Spartans give assurances to the outraged Athenians that the perpetrator of the crime would be punished. He is not – a miscarriage of justice that Xenophon himself says was the most unjust ever handed down at Sparta and which he finally places squarely on the shoulders of Agesilaus. The chief reason for his omission of the creation of the Second Athenian Confederation – pro-Spartan bias – seems contradicted by his evaluation of Sphodrias' raid.

As for the raid itself, Xenophon tells us that moved by fear that they would have to fight Sparta alone, the Thebans bribe Sphodrias to attack Attica (5.4.20). Marching out at night from Thespiae he heads towards Piraeus but gets only as far as Thria; he plunders the region and marches back. Inhabitants in the area flee to Athens and raise the alarm; the Athenians send out a force of cavalry and heavy infantry and prepare to defend their city. Only Xenophon tells us that a Spartan embassy happened to be in Athens at the precise time of Sphodrias' raid. This has been taken as proof that the Spartans were seeking diplomatically to halt the development of Athens' new league, already in existence, an argument that puts the raid after the formation of the confederation, not functioning as the event that precipitated it (the traditional view).[98] But be that as it may, the presence of the embassy permits Xenophon to make the point explicit that, like Phoebidas' seizure of the Cadmea some four years before, the raid was completely unauthorized: he says, in fact, that the Spartan ambassadors were as surprised as the Athenians; that had there really been an authorized attempt to invade Attica, they would have been fools to come to Athens and stay at the house of a man widely known as a Spartan guest-friend; and finally, that they were sure that, as proof of the illegal nature of the raid, the Spartan authorities would condemn Sphodrias to death. It is at this point that Xenophon tells us in an aside that when the ephors recalled Sphodrias he fled prosecution, and that despite the fact that he

232

avoided showing up for his trial (a sure admission of guilt) he was acquitted (5.4.24).[99] Many were scandalized; as Xenophon reports, 'this verdict seemed to many to be the most unjust ever handed down at Sparta'.[100]

Xenophon could have presumably ended his treatment of the entire episode at this point, but he does not. Instead, he goes out of his way to provide the reason for the unjust handling of the affair. The explanation is given in a long digression bracketed by introductory and concluding sentences that help to set off the story from the rest of the narrative – again, much in the manner of Herodotus. Furthermore, the story itself is introduced by the same story-teller formula that began the account of the liberation of Thebes: 'there was a son of Sphodrias, Cleonymus by name, who had just left his childhood behind, the most handsome and respected of his agemates' (5.4.25). Again, we are clearly being prepared for an episode of signal importance. The story itself is easy enough to follow: the son of Agesilaus, Archidamus, loved Cleonymus; Xenophon tells us that Cleonymus appealed to Archidamus to intercede with his father on behalf of Sphodrias, and this the prince does, but only after enduring considerable personal embarrassment and only after steeling himself to speak his mind to his father, the first time without success. It is a charming story, but a serious point runs throughout it. Xenophon tells us that Sphodrias' friends were at first afraid that Agesilaus would condemn him (5.4.25); further, that Agesilaus himself explained to his son after his first unsuccessful entreaty that he could not help but condemn a man who for the sake of money had so harmed Sparta (5.4.30); and finally, that Agesilaus eventually reversed this position and justified his decision on the grounds that Sparta actually needed such good men as Sphodrias (5.4.32). The obvious self-contradiction underscores the point that Sparta precisely did not need men like Sphodrias, men who endangered their city by their impulsive actions. This had been Phoebidas' problem, and his crime had similarly grievous consequences for Sparta; Teleutias too, although a better man than either Phoebidas or Sphodrias, died because of his recklessness, and later at Leuctra Cleombrotus will similarly fail because of impulsive decision making (6.4.5, 6.4.8). Clearly we are meant to see that Agesilaus has allowed his otherwise laudable respect for the personal obligations of friendship to undermine the interests of his state. Indeed, once before Agesilaus advocated (probably to Xenophon's chagrin) the subordination of all personal bonds of friendship to the advantage of the state (4.1.34; see above, p. 118); it would appear he had forgotten his argument. So much is subtly suggested at the end of the story. Xenophon reports that after the acquittal of his father, Cleonymus promised Archidamus that he would never regret their friendship, and that indeed Cleonymus did not ever bring shame on Archidamus but rather glory: both he and his father died fighting valiantly at Leuctra. This third advance notice of Leuctra (after 5.4.1 and the report of the omen during Cleombrotus' march from Boeotia) puts the two elements of the story side by side: personal bonds of friendship are preserved while the strength of the city is forever lost.

Cawkwell has argued in connection with 5.4.1 that the passage seems to be 'a curious dichotomy'; Xenophon condemns Sparta and yet does not place the blame for the actions that led to her demise on the man responsible, namely Agesilaus.[101] On the contrary, Xenophon shows us that it was precisely Agesilaus who was responsible for Sparta's troubles because of his inability or reluctance to place the advantage of the state ahead of the obligations of friendship. While he stops short of directly criticizing him, we cannot help but notice that the king ignores his own good sense regarding the Sphodrias affair. The Phoebidas and Sphodrias episodes are not 'side-shows' that are cynically included by Xenophon to show that he could criticize Sparta and Agesilaus, and so lend legitimacy to an otherwise uniformly pro-Spartan account. No; Forrest has wisely noted that Sphodrias was a 'would-be Phoebidas', and that the same pattern of 'brutality and aggressiveness' lay behind the actions of both men.[102] It is precisely Xenophon who lets us see this pattern emerge, and the common denominator in both cases is Agesilaus. His special pleading for both men is not hidden from us; rather, he puts the disastrous consequences of both men's actions, the hostility of Thebes and Athens towards Sparta, squarely at the feet of Agesilaus.

Immediately following his account of the acquittal of Sphodrias, Xenophon reports that when Sparta prepared a second invasion of Boeotia and again asked Agesilaus to command it, this time he does not beg off but rather declares that he refuses to do nothing that his city deems necessary (5.4.35). To dismiss the scene merely as an example of the king's 'wit' underplays its importance.[103] The king was similarly inconsistent during the campaigns against Mantinea and Phlius (see above, p. 211). Here we are meant, I think, to wonder what made Agesilaus change his mind. As Xenophon reports it, only Cleombrotus' failed expedition to Boeotia and the acquittal of Sphodrias come between Agesilaus' refusal and then acceptance of command. Perhaps Xenophon is suggesting that with his colleague's failure the door was open for Agesilaus to strengthen his grip on the direction of Spartan foreign policy, a control that his ability to secure Sphodrias' acquittal also suggests. Alternatively, it could be simply that once the nature of Sparta's presence in Boeotia was not so closely associated with her attempts to keep a friendly oligarchy in Thebes, Agesilaus felt that the risk of appearing a friend of tyrants was significantly lessened. Whatever the reason for the change, Agesilaus seems erratic and his decisions disturbingly labile.

Of all the military operations reported by Xenophon after the acquittal of Sphodrias, only those headed by Agesilaus succeed. After an initial setback on his first campaign against Thebes (5.4.39), he manages to devastate the land right up to the walls of the city (5.4.41). In his second campaign, he devastates much of the land east of Thebes (5.4.49). Both successes are due to the king's leadership. All the other Spartan commanders fare less well. Phoebidas, left by Agesilaus as governor of Thespiae, is defeated and killed after an initially successful repulse of Theban troops who had ventured into Thespian territory (5.4.42–46). Alcetas, helping to enforce the blockade of badly needed grain for Thebes, drops his guard and loses the acropolis of Oreus and with it the stranglehold on Thebes because of his affection for his boyfriend (5.4.56–57; cf. the similar failure of Thibron, 4.8.18–19). When Agesilaus cannot command a third invasion of Boeotia because of a debilitating leg injury, Cleombrotus conducts the campaign, no more successfully than his first (5.4.58–59). When a conference of allies is held at Sparta and complaints are made that the war against Thebes and Athens was being badly led, the Spartans send out Pollis and sixty warships to blockade Athens, an effort that also fails when Chabrias defeats the Spartan force in a naval battle (the battle of Naxos, 5.4.60–61).[104] Finally, we see the tables turned on Sparta at the very end of Book 5 with the Athenian Timotheus sent out to harry the Peloponnese so as to prevent the Spartans from sending an army to Boeotia, as well as the preliminaries to the conflict between Athens and Sparta at Corcyra (5.4.62–66; see above, p. 165). In a nutshell, then, we see a major difficulty emerge for Sparta, and simultaneously a very important point that Xenophon may be trying to make: Agesilaus himself succeeds on the field of battle, but almost all the other Spartan commanders who carry out their city's aggressive campaigns after the liberation of the Cadmea, a policy championed by Agesilaus, fail. Xenophon is interested in charting the success of the good commander, but he does not necessarily equate his success with the success of his *polis*. Indeed, as we see at the close of Book 5 of the *Hellenica*, the good commander can steer his state on a course that leads to disaster.

CONCLUSIONS

Xenophon pays close attention to the activities and character of individuals in his history. Indeed, this accent on the individual permits him to enter his narrative as a commentator; it helps him to mobilize the tools of moral evaluation as well as historical explanation. For Xenophon, the critique of states is a critique of individuals: thus Phoebidas and Sphodrias, Teleutias and Agesilaus are all in their way representative of growing Spartan ambition and its failure. Through them we can chart the progress of Sparta, her increasing power and aggressiveness, as well as her blunders. The Cadmea is one episode, albeit the most important one, in a series of episodes that mark the progress and decline of Sparta. The one feature that separates the capture of the Cadmea from other events is that Xenophon treats it both as an episode shaped by an individual or group of individuals, and as an episode for which an entire state is responsible: with the Cadmea alone is the connection between individual and state explicitly made.

A 'Socratic' historian, Xenophon fixed his gaze on the moral condition of individuals and states.[105] This is not to say that earlier historians lacked a moral view of human action (far from it), but rather that Xenophon's historical understanding was profoundly shaped by *his* (and I stress his) understanding of proper ethical conduct as defined and illustrated for him by Socrates. Underpinning this view of human conduct was Xenophon's belief in the power and authority of the divine – a divine that is providential, ordering the world and watching the activities of humans and rewarding them for their service. Given that in Xenophon's revised archaic understanding, the human condition is susceptible to great changes in fortune, and that in particular human achievement allows people to form an exaggerated sense of their own ability to predict the future, the reward of the divine (guidance regarding the future) is not a negligible item. Furthermore, the influence such a set of beliefs would have on a historian's vision of causality is obvious: a city's success and failure over time are accounted for in such a system of causation, with success when the state puts its trust in the divine for guidance and adheres to old ways in guiding its conduct, and failure when the city abandons its laws and neglects divine guidance and entrusts its affairs to ambitious and reckless men. Such a divine, Xenophon's divine, may perhaps be best characterized as 'the motor of history',[106] a force that does not so much shape history as drive it forward, setting the parameters of growth and decay. As such, Xenophon's view of the divine, while rarely seen in discrete events, certainly constitutes a general system of historical explanation.[107]

CONCLUSION

CONCLUSION

CONCLUSION

There are two issues I would like to take up in the conclusion of this book. First, taking a lead from Dover's suggestions as to the possible types of contemporary history that I quoted in the Introduction (p. 12), I would like to look at the necessarily speculative issue of what might be the 'considered design' of the *Hellenica* to which is 'subordinated' Xenophon's account of the events of his times. And second, and I believe even more importantly, in what ways do both the *Hellenica* and *Anabasis* bring us closer to understanding how Xenophon thought about the history of his age?

THE 'CONSIDERED DESIGN' OF THE *HELLENICA*

As I suggested in Chapter 1 no more important point could be made regarding the composition of the *Hellenica* than that much of it, from 2.3.10 to the end, was written up after the battle of Mantinea in 362, a battle that Xenophon and 'many others' (including Ephorus) thought would be decisive in determining the leadership of the Greek world, but in the event proved not to do so. The order Xenophon longed to see emerge from the bloody events of his lifetime was not forthcoming. But, with the evaluation of Mantinea in mind, are we to conclude that in the final analysis the *Hellenica* specifically discourages us from seeing any meaningfulness in the period of Greek history it chronicles? While I think we should never lose sight of the fact that at a very deep level Xenophon was in the end confounded by the outcome of his times, to argue that his history is in some sense meaningless is to take the pessimism of its final pages too far. The *Hellenica* is a pessimistic work, but it also has a positive point to make.

241

Above all, Xenophon's history attempts to prove the truth of what Sophocles has Agamemnon say with bitter irony in the *Ajax*: 'it is not an easy thing for a tyrant to be pious' (*Aj.* 1350). As I have tried to show, for Xenophon the quest for unlawful, absolute power over others is ultimately a self-destructive enterprise. An all-powerful and providential divine sees to it that the impiety and lawlessness of those who seek hegemony will be punished by their own folly. The story of the Thirty at Athens and Jason of Pherae, and especially the story of Sparta's rise and fall, bear out this simple truth. As Ischomachus, Xenophon's mouthpiece in the *Oeconomicus*, says, successful leadership is given to those who know how to rule over those who are willingly obedient; the despot rules over unwilling subjects and is bound to end up like Tantalus, tortured eternally in Hades (*Oec.* 21.11–12).

But to pursue this observation of Ischomachus further, where does this good form of leadership come from? It comes from education, excellent character and divine benefaction – that is, the gods grant successful authority to those who are 'truly perfected in *sophrosune*' or prudence (*Oec.* 21.12). This is a formula for success that I spoke about in the last two chapters: recognizing one's limits and acknowledging the power of the divine – in a word, piety – is a central component of successful leadership. Important also in Ischomachus' remarks is the emphasis he places on education (*paideia*, 21.11; cf. *Ap.* 21). To be sure, it is only one of three elements crucial to the art of being a good leader, and may mean no more here than being in some general sense 'cultivated';[1] nonetheless, the word usefully connects the concept of education to that of effective leadership, a connection I want to look at further in the context of the *Hellenica*.

Of course it is often remarked that central to much of Xenophon's corpus is a concern with defining good leadership and exploring ways that it can be learned.[2] Indeed, I have noted a number of places in the *Hellenica* where this tendency is clearly at work: the evaluations of Teleutias (see above, pp. 197 and 220) and of Mnasippus and Iphicrates (pp. 164–171) especially come to mind. I believe that, towards the end of the *Hellenica* in particular, Xenophon broadens the compass of this project, making the issue of learning good leadership applicable not only to individuals but to states, and specifically Athens and Sparta. This adjustment is especially in evidence in two sets of three speeches that help to frame Xenophon's account of the battle of Leuctra and its aftermath.

It has been remarked that the existence of two complementary sets of speeches is without parallel in the *Hellenica*.[3] It might further be added that this sheer concentration of directly quoted address is not found elsewhere in the history. Furthermore, in both sets of speeches Xenophon chose to have three voices represented although others are reported as being ambassadors on both occasions and presumably also spoke.[4] This fact helps to locate the two triads in a historiographic tradition;[5] in both Herodotus and Thucydides, one way of privileging episodes of great moment was by articulating them in carefully constructed sets of arguments that were to be viewed as single units.[6]

As for the context of the first set of speeches, Xenophon tells us that while Sparta and Athens were in conflict in the islands in the Adriatic, growing Theban aggression in Boeotia caused the Athenians great alarm: Plataea, Thespiae and Phocis were all feeling the brunt of Theban expansion. Xenophon reports that at this juncture (summer 371) Athens voted that peace should be made with Sparta and ambassadors were sent to Lacedaemon. Although Xenophon provides a list of eight or perhaps ten ambassadors,[7] as I mentioned above, only three are given speeches: Callias the son of Hipponicus, Autocles the son of Strombichides and Callistratus of Aphidna. Each of the three speakers is carefully introduced;[8] just as Thucydides was able to anticipate and so condition our reaction to Cleon's speech in the Mytilenean debate with an informative though brief portrait,[9] so too Xenophon colours his description of the speakers and thus prepares us for the speeches they give. Callias is a pompous and self-important man who pleads for peace between Athens and Sparta by retailing threadbare myth that links the two cities together through Athens' gift to Sparta of the art of agriculture (6.3.4–6).[10] It is a wooden speech that does not at all confront the issue of why Sparta and Athens should forget their grievances and ally. Autocles is much more formidable; he is described as an especially convincing speaker,[11] and the speech he gives is a scalding review of recent Spartan wrongdoing (6.3.7–9). He cites the hypocrisy of the Spartans who (he claims) often spoke of the 'autonomy of the cities' and yet were frequently the main reason for their lack of independence; he mentions the Spartans' preference for tyranny over lawful government; and most pointed of all his remarks, he notes that although they made themselves the champions of the King's Peace in opposition to Thebes, they broke this very agreement by seizing the Cadmea (6.3.9). Xenophon would himself fully agree with Autocles' criticism;[12] as I have tried to show, his treatment of the issues Autocles mentions runs along similar lines. Yet as he points out, Autocles' words bring only silence from the audience and the quiet satisfaction of 'those who hated the Spartans'; Xenophon was not one of these. Indeed, Autocles, while he is surely right, is not constructive; he does not lay the ground-work for peace; his are still the words of intransigent hostility and suspicion, even if they are justified.[13]

It is with Callistratus that we find Xenophon's voice,[14] and with him the all-important notion of cities learning to be good leaders. His words (6.3.10–17) are aimed at reconciliation, and as such they counter the speech of Autocles; but they are also direct and frank and do not, like Callias' opening remarks, smooth over the prob-lems impeding rapprochement or conceal the wrongs done by Sparta. In order to soften his criticism of Sparta he begins his speech by observing that both the Athenians and Spartans have erred. But having admitted this, he turns the notion of 'error', a concept he mentions no less than five times in the opening of his speech,[15] into something positive. Noting that 'everyone makes mistakes', he goes on to suggest that people who err are 'more reasonable' (*euporoteroi*) in their dealings with others – especially, he notes, 'if they have been punished for their errors as we [Athenians] have' (6.3.10). Pointing to how the Spartan seizure of the Cadmea backfired, inasmuch as the action was intended to prevent Thebes from gaining mastery over the cities of Boeotia and yet had precisely the opposite effect, he declares, 'and so I expect that we [Athenians and Spartans], having learned (*pepaideumenous*) that taking more than our due (*to pleonektein*) is an unprofitable enterprise (*akerdes*), now will be moderate in our friendship with one another' (6.3.11). After anticipating those who oppose the peace on the grounds that Athens is only trying to forestall another Persian brokered agreement that is solely to the advantage of Sparta (6.3.12), Callistratus wraps up his remarks with a proof of the advantage to be gained by both cities if they ally. He notes that all cities are favourable either to Athens or to Sparta, and further in every city there is a pro-Spartan and a pro-Athenian faction;[16] if, he reasons, the two cities could join forces before either were dealt an irreparable blow, then, with Athens' influence on the sea and Sparta's on land, they would both continue to remain strong, and would both in fact become greater than Athens had ever been in times past (6.3.12–17).

If the *Hellenica* has a 'considered design' or 'message', this speech of Callistratus is perhaps its clearest articulation. To be sure, criticism of Sparta is here – indeed, the seizure of the Cadmea is explicitly referred to. But a broader point is also being made. Imperial ambition, what Xenophon calls 'desiring more than is your due', is doomed to failure. However, this failure does not have to result in the permanent humiliation and ruin of a city. If it can learn that *to pleonektein* is *akerdes*,[17] then a new preeminence can be won. In the case of Athens and Sparta, an authority is imagined for them that is even greater than Athens had enjoyed in the fifth century at the head of its first maritime league (this is surely what Callistratus is alluding to at 6.3.17). This authority seems to be based on two things: the influence each city has among the communities of the Greek world, and the power each can wield, the one on land, the other on sea. But this authority cannot, it seems, be a coercive one because that would entail the problems associated with imperial 'greed' or *pleonexia*. The *Poroi*, a pamphlet written about the same time as the second portion of the *Hellenica*, provides some illumination. In it Xenophon encouraged the Athenians to appreciate the natural advantages their city enjoyed with respect to influence over the sea (*Poroi* 1.6–8). Further, he suggested that Athens could assume a position of leadership in the Greek world, not through force of arms, but rather by acting as a broker of peace between warring states (*Poroi* 5.8);[18] indeed, like Callistratus, Xenophon believes that those who think that war is more profitable (*kerdaleoteron*, *Poroi* 5.11) than peace are simply mistaken.[19] The world Callistratus imagines for both Sparta and Athens may be similar to what Xenophon has in mind. Both cities are to assume what he understands as natural leadership roles on land and sea, not through brute force, but on the basis of respect accorded them by the other Greek states. This is Xenophon's great hope.

There are two problems that complicate our acceptance of this vision. In the first place, the Spartans had not yet been fully 'punished' for their imperialist wrongs in quite the same way Athens had been when Callistratus made his speech. Sparta had suffered a strategic setback inasmuch as Thebes had regained control of Boeotia, but Athens had come perilously close to being destroyed at the end of the Peloponnesian War and had suffered Spartan occupation and the tyranny of the Thirty; the two situations are scarcely parallel, despite the efforts of Callistratus to make them seem so. Indeed, Xenophon recognizes that the Spartans had not yet 'learned their lesson', despite the compelling arguments of Callistratus' speech. He notes that when the time came for them to honour the new peace which came out of the conference at Sparta, they did not comply with the demobilization orders, but rather left their forces in Boeotia. They were warned against doing this by one of their own citizens, playing very much the part of the Herodotean 'tragic warner' (6.4.2).[20] But, as Xenophon notes, 'a divine force was leading them on' (6.4.3).[21] And of course, we know from *Hell.* 5.4.1 that Leuctra is the price the Spartans must pay for their seizure of the Cadmea, not simply the reemergence of Theban domination over Boeotia.

The second problem concerns Athens. From 357 to 355, roughly the period when Xenophon was completing the *Hellenica*, Athens was at war with many of the members of her second maritime alliance – the so-called Social War.[22] Well might we ask then, how convincing could Callistratus' remarks have been in light of the events that were in all likelihood contemporary with Xenophon's writing-up of the speech? What sort of influence in the cities and on the sea could a reader at this time credit to Athens? Where was the fruit of the hard lesson she had learned – a stable and moderate preeminence based on respect and influence, not coercion?

A possible solution to the problem of applying Callistratus' new vision of imperial power to both Sparta and Athens is suggested by the second set of speeches after Leuctra. The Athenians, alarmed by the first Theban invasion of the Peloponnese made possible by their victory at Leuctra, hold an assembly to consider what they should do. Just as years earlier, before the outbreak of the Peloponnesian War, Athenians 'happened to be' in Sparta and were thus able to make a timely address to the Spartans, so Spartans 'happen to be' in Athens at this time and make their appeal.[23] Xenophon does not report their speeches directly, but rather provides a summary of what they all said (6.5.33–35). Like Callias' speech in the first triad, their remarks are ineffective; in appealing for Athenian help, they refer to times past when Athens and Sparta helped each other during other crises – they mention in particular Spartan assistance in the expulsion of the Pisistratid tyranny, and the help Athens provided during the helot revolt (6.5.33). The examples are ill-chosen: the Spartans did help remove the sons of Pisistratus, but they later worked very hard to destroy the Athenian democracy and install another tyranny (first Isagoras – Hdt. 5.74.1, and then Hippias – Hdt. 5.91), not to mention their more recent imposition of the Thirty; the Athenians did send Cimon to assist in the quelling of the helots, but the Spartans rejected this help and in so doing precipitated a crisis at Athens that resulted in Cimon's ostracism (cf. Thuc. 1.102.2; Plut. *Cim.* 17.3).[24] Clearly, the Spartans' argument is poorly conceived and poorly made;[25] indeed, Xenophon tells us that the Athenians remained deeply suspicious of the Spartans' motives, noting that although they were friendly now, in times past, when they were strong, they were hostile to Athens (6.5.35). The Athenians were also concerned about the role Sparta was playing in settling a dispute between Tegea and Mantinea (6.5.36).

Like Autocles' speech at Sparta, the second address at Athens is blunt and straightforward; a Corinthian named Cliteles points out to the Athenians that whatever the particulars of the dispute between Tegea and Mantinea, one thing was certain: the Thebans had invaded his country and had laid waste to it. On these grounds alone, he argues, the Athenians are obliged to help stop Thebes (6.5.37). But, as with the shortcomings of Autocles' speech in the first group of speeches, the issue at stake is not as simple as Cliteles presents it. The Athenian fears regarding the plans of a Sparta restored to its old strength seem legitimate. This is where Procles comes in.

The statesman from Phlius argues that it is in the first place expedient for the Athenians to help the Spartans; with them defeated, nothing would prevent the Thebans from turning their attention to Athens in their quest for mastery over the whole of the Greek world (6.5.38–39). In order to obtain Athens' help, however, Procles knows that he must allay the Athenians' fears that a resurgent Sparta would become their enemy again (6.5.40). He assures them that if they help Sparta in her hour of need, there is every expectation that the city would feel bound to be their friend in the future; the Spartans are good men who live up to their obligations, and if they failed in this case to do so, they would incur the censure of the gods, as well as of the entire world – Greek and barbarian alike (6.5.41–43). As a representative from a city allied to Sparta, he promises the Athenians that the assistance of their old enemy would earn them the support of all those still loyal to Sparta (6.5.44–46). Borrowing a couple of favourite mythological stories the Athenians liked to bring up in orations praising their own city,[26] Procles declares that a rare opportunity had been given them to outdo their legendary ancestors and save the entire city of Sparta (6.5.46–47). Finally, he notes that insofar as the two cities have often been friends and often enemies, Athenian aid for Sparta would appear 'noble' (*gennaia*) because they chose to remember the good that had been done them, not the bad (6.5.48).

This last remark is crucial and helps with the interpretation of the entire episode. As Dover acutely observed in connection with what Procles says, the quality here of being 'noble' (*gennaios*) is in fact the opposite of being 'greedy' or devoted to *pleonexia*:[27] being 'noble' means not insisting on something that you might reasonably expect, whereas being 'greedy' means demanding something that is not rightfully yours. The Athenians are in a sense justified in not helping Sparta, but in generously coming to her aid they are doing more than is expected of them – they are being noble. Being noble earns one respect and loyalty, even from traditional enemies; further, it earns one authority and power based not on *pleonexia* at the expense of others, but on the good will of others.[28] This is Procles' point and is of a piece with Xenophon's understanding of the new form of leadership articulated in the comments of Callistratus and in the *Poroi* (see the example of Phlius too, p. 133).

But how does the second set of speeches, and Procles' in particular, help with the problems of applying this new picture of empire to the Sparta and Athens contemporary with the writing of the *Hellenica* in the early to mid-350s? In the first place, regarding Sparta, the second set of speeches takes account of the fact that the city had, as Athens at the end of the Peloponnesian War, been punished with a catastrophic defeat. The comments of Callistratus are germane to Sparta *following Leuctra*. Secondly, regarding Athens, in Procles' speech we see what can be gained through being noble and not following a course dictated by *pleonexia*. This would be especially relevant for an Athenian audience during or shortly after the Social War. Procles promises the eternal gratitude and respect of Sparta and her allies; perhaps Xenophon is saying that the Athenians should aim for the same kind of relationship with their former allies. It is true that the Second Athenian Confederation is all but erased from the historical record as preserved by the *Hellenica* (see above, p. 231); perhaps this was in deference to Athens; perhaps, too, Xenophon did not want to alienate his Athenian readers and so allow them to miss the lesson both Callistratus and Procles are trying to teach.[29]

The *Hellenica*, then, in the words of Callistratus and Procles, may have a considered design that struggles against the pessimism that is also to be found in its pages.[30] It may be that a new type of empire is being advocated, one based not on force, but on a reputation for fairness and generosity, and the respect and influence that come from such a reputation.[31] His hope for a lasting friendship between Athens and Sparta no doubt sprang from his belief that noble men and noble cities should not be in conflict with one another, for to be so resulted ultimately in disorder – *tarache*, in Xenophon's mind, that destructive force at the root of all failure. As Socrates once said to one of his acquaintances, 'it confuses you [literally: disorders your thinking, *tarattei*] that you often see men who both do good and keep away from shameful things, instead of being friends, fight with one another and treat each other more cruelly than men of no worth' (*Mem.* 2.6.17; see above, p. 34). Xenophon felt the same about good cities in conflict.

XENOPHON AND THE HISTORY OF HIS TIMES

I have felt it necessary to offer a possible candidate for the 'considered design' of the *Hellenica*, a 'message' that Xenophon may have been trying to communicate to his audience through his account of Greek affairs from 411 to 362. But this enterprise, while important to attempt, is necessarily speculative as well as narrow; it is even more important to consider briefly what Xenophon's history tells us about how he thought about his times, and perhaps how others, his contemporaries, thought about their times as well.

It is best to begin by appreciating the profound biographical component to Xenophon's thinking. Above all, when he thought about the past, he considered it in terms of individuals. Specifically, he thought about the past in terms of the good and bad that men had done. We catch a glimpse of this impulse at work in Xenophon when, at the end of his *Apology* of Socrates, he explains how he came to write of his beloved teacher: 'When I take note of the man's wisdom and nobility (*gennaioteta*), I cannot but remember him, and remembering him I cannot help but praise him' (*Ap.* 34). The process of memory begins for Xenophon when he calls to mind an individual's specific virtues, or, in other cases, their vices; this process then continues inevitably to an evaluation of the individual. The individual is important to him for two reasons. In the first place he can focus on their deeds for didactic purposes. He can point easily to a single person's accomplishments and encourage his readers either to emulate what he has done or avoid it. But the importance of the individual does not stop here. Second, and more importantly for the argument of this book, the individual is also emblematic of deep

forces at work in the history of the age. To Xenophon's way of thinking a man can draw into relief the strengths or weaknesses of the
society from which he comes, be it an army, navy, *polis* or even
region. An individual's personal excellence can show by way of
contrast the weakness or even depravity of the community to which
he belongs – Socrates and democratic Athens, or Theramenes and
the tyranny of the Thirty are good examples. Of course the
relationship between person and community can be one of simple
identification: Critias is a clear instance of this strategy. Naturally,
when the case is not so black and white, an individual can express
both the strengths and the shortcomings of his social unit; the
complexity of Agesilaus' character, made up as it is of great virtues as
well as real failings, not only mirrors Sparta, it actually stands in for
the entire city and explains its actions.

Xenophon's thinking turned easily to the paradigm as a mode
of explanation, but the paradigm was not always limited to the
exemplary individual. An entire community could also serve to illuminate important truths about the world he perceived. The survival
of the Ten Thousand in Asia Minor or the unlikely success of Phlius
in the face of great adversity come to mind as models for success in
Xenophon's mind, and the self-destructiveness of the Thirty as a
model for failure.

This interest in the paradigm was not unique to Xenophon. At
the risk of stating the obvious, Greek literature had been concerned
from its very earliest periods with treating individuals as models of
human conduct: the lesson about humanity that the *Iliad* attempts
to teach us is borne in large measure by its main character, Achilles.
And in historical writing, we would surely not want to deny the
central role that individuals play in the work of Herodotus and
Thucydides: the character and decisions of Xerxes on the one hand,
and Alcibiades on the other, go a long way towards explaining how
both of those historians understood episodes of vital importance in
their treatments of the past. But with these historians particularly
in mind, we do not I think sense the same reliance on the individual
as a mode of explanation that we find in Xenophon. Ultimately it
is the triumph of the Greek people that interests Herodotus, and the
defeat of Athens that interests Thucydides. While it would be a
mistake to say that Xenophon was not concerned to tell the story of
Spartan success and failure, it is hard to distinguish that story from
the story of Teleutias, or Phoebidas, or Agesilaus. Even when he has
made it his purpose to examine the affairs of a community, the

description of its actions becomes paradigmatic (e.g. Phlius) and, more often than not, its actions are made perceptible through the deeds of single men (e.g. the various 'heroes' of the Ten Thousand from the *Anabasis*, Critias and the Thirty). To put it another way, if we took away the individual or the paradigm from the narratives of Herodotus or Thucydides, we would still be able to see an over-arching structure of explanation and a coherent story, albeit with some noteworthy gaps;[32] if we did the same to the *Hellenica* of Xenophon, we would lose the very fabric of his account, leaving us with with fragments, some perhaps quite large, but all of them essentially unconnected and lacking coherence.

The paradigm is the building block of Xenophon's historical writing. It is, however, only a structure of explanation. The significant persons and communities of the *Anabasis* and *Hellenica* help to transmit ideas he formed about the world in which he lived. Clearly important to him was the attempt to understand why individuals and states succeed, and why they fail. The self-destructiveness of *pleonexia* or greed fascinated him (cf. Hdt. 7.16.α.2, 18.2; Thuc. 3.82.8). From his experiences with the Ten Thousand, at least as he recollected them later, Xenophon felt that short-term and ill-gotten gain netted only future difficulties. He felt, too, that when an individual or group subordinated the interests of the greater collectivity to their own desires, problems would result, not only for themselves, but also for the larger group to which they belonged. This understanding of greed, or desiring more than your due, underlies much of his thinking about the problems of tyranny and imperial power. Competing with this awareness, however, is a strong utopian tendency found throughout much of his work. For a couple of brief periods during his lifetime, during his military career in Asia Minor, he believed he witnessed ideal human society in action – the second phase of the Ten Thousand before their arrival at the Black Sea, and, to a lesser degree, the army of Agesilaus before its recall to Greece. Similarly, in a way few could attempt or imagine, Xenophon applied the lesson of the advantage of putting the interests of the community ahead of its individual members to the Greek world as a whole. To be sure, others spoke of panhellenism, but it was Xenophon who experienced one of its few genuine expressions (despite what men like Isocrates said), and it was Xenophon who knew better than most what it would take to achieve it.

But in a larger sense, Xenophon did not consistently privilege one of these ideas or modes of explanation over the rest. His historiographic legacy, the *Hellenica* and the *Anabasis* taken together, concerns the totality of his age as he understood it. There were other models available to him for the writing of history, but they were for the most part narrower in scope than what he finally achieved. There was the war monograph, a form pioneered by Thucydides and attempted by the likes of Theopompus (see *FGrHist* 115 T 13 and 14) and the author of the *Hellenica Oxyrhynchia*, as well as Xenophon himself;[33] but, as we have seen, Xenophon elected to go beyond the parameters suggested by one war alone. There was also the regional history, especially as it was beginning to be practised at Athens by the so-called Atthidographers; although significantly focused on the activities of Sparta, Xenophon's *Hellenica* takes in the whole of the Aegean world, from mainland Greece to Persia. Finally, there was the early experimentation of history centred on the affairs of one individual alone, such as we see with Theopompus' *Philippika*; to be sure this tendency, as I noted above, can be detected in Xenophon's work, and most especially in his biography of *Agesilaus*. The *Hellenica*, however, focuses on the deeds of many men. Only the universal history of Ephorus rivals, or even transcends, the temporal, geographical and thematic boundaries of Xenophon's work.

Xenophon was an historian who attempted to bring into one coherent order all the events he chronicled. Disparate episodes, the isolated actions of men and states, the varying fortunes of peoples everywhere were brought together into a single whole. This came naturally to him because he was a man devoted to the principle of order. He sought it everywhere – in the household, a chorus of dancers, an army of fighting men, a well-fitted warship (*Oec.* 8.2–9; see above, pp. 31–32). Disorder, consequently, was inimical to his nature. Hence the profound despair we detect in his description of the aftermath of Mantinea and the pessimism lurking in the final sections of his history. After that battle, in his darker moments, the ordering of the events of his lifetime – the project to which he devoted his final years – must have seemed a futile enterprise.

In one thing, though, he could take solace. He was a profoundly religious man. Indeed, he seemed to believe in a providential divine that ordered the world for the benefit of human beings. If the events of his day at times defied his ability to understand them, he could at least trust that there was some point to them, a purpose perhaps hidden from his eyes, but nonetheless fashioned by the will of the gods.

The ideas and structures of thought that we find in Xenophon's history did not emerge from a vacuum. Often, it seems, we moderns have felt dissatisfied with his historiographic contribution; we feel that in many ways he failed to give us a balanced and accurate account of Greek affairs, such as we imagine someone like an Oxyrhynchus historian would have provided if he survived to us intact. To put it more bluntly, he did not deliver the goods. But while our complaints may in certain ways be justified, we must at some point recognize that our concerns were not his concerns.[34] Concealed in our regrets about his shortcomings is the feeling that he wilfully rejected superior modes of understanding his world. And yet, as I have tried to show, he was not alone in his fascination with utopia and panhellenism; not alone in his belief in the inherent superiority of an idealized Sparta; not alone in seeing the profound influence single individuals could play in the events of their day; not alone in forming a view of the divine that seemed to be simultaneously a throw-back to archaic ways of thinking and yet at the same time strangely new. Xenophon's history is truly a history of his times inasmuch as it is deeply informed by how his contemporaries thought about their world. We cannot understand the *Hellenica* and *Anabasis* until we appreciate this simple fact.

After Xenophon's son Gryllus died in a skirmish before the battle of Mantinea, there was an outpouring of eulogies for him: Isocrates wrote one of them, and some time later, Aristotle actually named his first treatise on the art of rhetoric (now lost) the *Gryllus*.[35] Of course Xenophon passed over the death of his son in silence, something that should not surprise us from a man who chose not to mention his own actions when it would have been appropriate. Most famous of all the memorials for Gryllus was a painting in the Stoa of Zeus Eleutherios in the Agora of Athens, commissioned by the Athenian people. The second-century AD travel writer Pausanias tells us (1.3.4) that it was done by the artist Euphranor of Corinth, and depicted Gryllus at Mantinea in the ranks of the Athenians and Epaminondas among the Boeotians;[36] in fact elsewhere he reports that in the copy of the same painting at Mantinea, Gryllus was shown actually wounding the Theban general (8.11.6). It was not the only painting in the Stoa of Zeus. There was also a representation of Theseus, Democracy and the People.

Euphranor's painting echoes curiously with Xenophon's life and historiographic legacy. The artist was from the city where the historian may well have ended his days. The work itself was put up in a structure at Athens that was founded in honour of a cult of Zeus that was associated with the great panhellenic victory over the Persians at Plataea in 479; the building was also a common meeting place for Socrates and his friends.[37] The scene condensed a conflict of many soldiers into a meeting of two men, a meeting that never happened, although both principal figures did in fact die either shortly before or shortly after the battle. And while the facts were wrong, in spirit the painting celebrated Athenian help for Sparta in a time of need. If Xenophon ever saw the work, I think he would have understood the message it attempted to convey; for a number of reasons, he very probably would have appreciated the context in which it was placed; and even in the grief he no doubt felt, he would have in all likelihood been touched and honoured by the gesture of his native city.

NOTES

INTRODUCTION

1 All dates are BC unless otherwise stated.
2 See, e.g., Grayson (1975) esp. 31.
3 Notably Tuplin (1993).
4 See, e.g., Cicero *De Or.* 2.58, Dionysius of Halicarnassus *Pomp.* 4, Quintilian *Inst.* 10.1.75, Diogenes Laertius 2.48.
5 Thus in the authoritative *Cambridge History of Classical Literature*, Xenophon is found in two different sections, 'Historical Writing of the Fourth Century and in the Hellenistic Period' (Connor (1985)) and 'Plato and the Socratic Work of Xenophon' (Sandbach (1985)).
6 See, e.g., Bury (1909) 151: 'in history as in philosophy [Xenophon] was a dilettante; he was as far from understanding the methods of Thucydides as he was from apprehending the ideas of Socrates'. Cf. Cawkwell (1973) 64: 'all that can and should, I think, be salvaged from the case for Xenophon the thinker is a handful of banal moral platitudes which sort only too well with the kind of plain man's guide to Socratic thinking that he provides in the *Memorabilia*'.
7 Momigliano (1990) 113.
8 Bloch (1953) esp. 43–45.
9 See Marcellinus *Life of Thucydides* 45, Diogenes Laertius 2.57 and Dionysius of Halicarnassus *Pomp.* 4; note Dover's words of caution concerning the testimonia (1945–1981) 5 439; cf. Krüger (1836) 263–264.
10 The structural features most often cited for supporting the view that the first section of the *Hellenica* was intended to complete Thucydides' history are the presence of time-markers in this portion of Xenophon's history, a precision regarding numbers (esp. of ships), and a preference for what is thought to be Thucydidean mannerisms not found elsewhere in Xenophon. The bibliography on this issue, both pro and con, is vast and I do not intend to repeat the arguments here. Of particular importance are Baden (1966), Breitenbach (1967) 1671–1680, Delebecque (1957) 43–47, Hatzfeld (1930), Henry (1967) 54–88, Lotze (1962 and 1974), MacLaren (1934a), Raubitschek (1972) and, most recently, Gray (1991).

11 See esp. Dover's criticisms (1945–1981) 5 437–444. Cf. Krentz (1989) 5–6. The ancient testimonia are in reality not very convincing; the features alleged to be Thucydidean can be found elsewhere in the *Hellenica*; and the first part of the history can be seen to contain distinctly un-Thucydidean features. There is the added difficulty of determining how long Thucydides may have lived. The traditional view places the first part of the *Hellenica* early in Xenophon's career, and yet recent epigraphical research has raised the possibility that Thucydides may have been at work on his history until the mid-390s: see Pouilloux and Salviat (1983 and 1985). Note that serious reservations have been made regarding the epigraphical argument: Cartledge (1984) and cf. Hornblower (1987) 151–152.

12 Wiseman (1979) 143–153; Gabba (1981) esp. 50.

13 Cf., e.g., Novick (1988), esp. 21–46.

14 See Jacoby (1949) 301 n.38. *Hell.* 3.1.2 would have served well as the prooemium to the *Anabasis*; see below, p. 101.

15 E.g. *Hell.* 2.3.56, 4.8.1, 5.1.4, 5.4.1, 6.2.32, 7.2.1; cf. Rahn (1971).

16 Cf. Jacoby (1949) 82 and Hornblower (1981) 25.

17 See, e.g., Lesky (1966) 83 and n.2.

18 Cf., e.g., Higgins (1977) 103.

19 Dover (1945–1981) 5 384.

20 Bloch (1953) 44.

21 Cf. Connor (1984) 233–235. Note also the cautions of de Romilly (1963) 107 and 344–347.

22 The position is defined first by Niebuhr (1828) 466–467; contrast, however, de Sanctis (1931) 228–229 and Andrewes (1982) 18, who feel that the battle of Notion is told from a Spartan perspective.

23 Müller (1856) 6–8.

24 Nitsche (1871) and Grosser (1873); cf. Roquette (1884) 57.

25 Dittenberger (1881); see, however, Dillery (1989) Appendix 1.

26 Hartman (1887) 36ff. and Schwartz (1889) 184–185; cf. Baden (1966) 47–48 and Henry (1967).

27 Hatzfeld (1930) 120–126 noted that *IG* 5 1565 (= Tod 120) showed that the exiled Spartan king Pausanias outlived his son and successor Agesipolis, who died in 381 (*Hell.* 5.3.19). At 3.5.25 we are notified of Pausanias' own death. Hence it was concluded that some portion at least of Book 3 of the *Hellenica* had to have been composed at the earliest in 381, although it treats events from 401 to 395. Hatzfeld was thereby able to argue that those who sensed that 5.1.36 would have marked a clear division in Xenophon's mind because of the apparently conclusive nature of the King's Peace, and that as a result he would have completed what he had written of his history shortly thereafter, had to revise their thinking.

28 Gray (1991) esp. 206 and 211.

29 Cf. Hatzfeld (1930) 225–226 and MacLaren (1934a) 262.

30 See, e.g., Tuplin (1993) 11.

31 Cf. Hatzfeld (1930) 220–221, and MacLaren (1934a) 138; see Dillery (1989) Appendix 1.

NOTES

32 For the reasoning behind the date of Xenophon's work on 3.5.25, see above, n.27. As for the dating of 6.4.37, Xenophon reports that the Thessalian king Tisiphonus had been in power during the writing of that section of the *Hellenica*; Diodorus Siculus places his accession in 357/6 (16.14.1) and implies his removal in 353 (16.35.1): cf., e.g., Underhill (1900) xiv, Breitenbach (1967) 1691 and Cawkwell (1979) 334 n. But even these passages are limited in their applicability; we do not know how much of the text Xenophon was working on at those moments; in the most extreme case, he may only have inserted the chronological notices into already written text at a later point. For a helpful description of this problem, see de Romilly (1963) 7 on Thucydides: 'If, finally, we can fix a *terminus ante quem* or a *terminus post quem* for any particular passage, we shall not be very far advanced, for we shall still have to decide how long this particular passage is: the reference could be valid for a group of words, for a sentence, for a paragraph, or for a whole book.'

33 Note Dover's sober analysis of the differences between the 'continuation' and the rest of the *Hellenica*, (1945–1981) 5 444: '[The differences] suggest on the one hand that Xenophon regarded the continuation not so much as the supplementation of a great literary work in fidelity to the spirit of the original author as the completion of the story of a war of which what he regarded as the most authoritative account was unfortunately left unfinished; on the other hand, the tincture (positive and negative) of Thucydidean usage present in the continuation suggests that at the time he wrote the continuation his own language was more strongly influenced by Thucydides' than it later became.'

34 Bruns (1896) 33–45, Breitenbach (1950) and Rahn (1971).

35 Cf. Grayson (1975) 34–35. The passages in question are *Cyr.* 8.8 and *Lac.* 14; Grayson adds *An.* 7.8 (see below, p. 91). There is a considerable debate regarding the authenticity of the passages from the *Cyr.* and *Lac.* Both works describe sympathetically the social and political structures of Persia and Sparta respectively. But *Cyr.* 8.8 and *Lac.* 14 both assert that those institutions, laws and customs are no longer observed, and that both Persia and Sparta have become corrupt because of luxury and greed (see esp. *Cyr.* 8.8.18 and *Lac.* 14.3; consult Lewis (1977) 149–150). Since such condemnation is not at all anticipated in either text (the ἔτι καὶ νῦν formula found sparingly throughout the *Cyr.* does not, *pace* Delebecque (1957) 405–406 and Jaeger (1943) 326 n.56, prepare us for the 'present day' evaluation at 8.8 because, as Hirsch (1985) 93 points out, they are used to assert that certain norms are still kept up, contrary to the claim of 8.8), some scholars have been tempted to deny the authenticity of *Cyr.* 8.8: so e.g., Schenkl (1861) 540–557, Roquette (1884) 90, Holden (1890) 196 and recently Hirsch (1985) 91–97. Others have wanted to move *Lac.* 14 to the end of that treatise after §15 on the institution of the kingship: thus, Ollier (1934 and 1933) 377ff., Luccioni (1947) 171, Delebecque (1957) 194–195 and Breitenbach (1967) 1751 – note Chrimes (1948) 8 and (1949) 490 moves §14 to the beginning of the *Lac.*, but she denies that Xenophon was the author of the work. The authenticity of *Cyr.* 8.8 has

been upheld by Eichler (1880) and, more recently, Breitenbach (1967) 1741–1742, Higgins (1977) 57 and n.70, Meulder (1989) and Gera (1993) 299–300; the traditional position of *Lac.* 14 has been defended by Momigliano (1936) 170–173 = (1966) 341–345, who argues that §15 closely answers §14, and much more daringly, that because §15 does not concern νόμοι (laws) but συνθῆκαι (agreements) the kingship is exempt from the criticism of §14 by position and terminology – all in an effort to protect his friend King Agesilaus. I find the most compelling argument for the authenticity of both passages to be their mutual similarity (cf. Naumann (1876) 52–53, Jaeger (1944) 326 n.56, Momigliano (1936), Due (1989) 16–22 and Tatum (1989) 217–220); whether originally part of each work, or inserted later into earlier strata of composition by Xenophon himself, both *Cyr.* 8.8 and *Lac.* 14 are palinodes datable to the same time as the latter portion of the *Hellenica*; cf. Cartledge (1987) 57, although he does not consider *Cyr.* 8.8.

36 Cf. Momigliano (1935) 195.
37 Cf. Dillery (1993) with the bibliography found there.

1 XENOPHON, HISTORY AND ORDER: THE BATTLE OF MANTINEA

1 Cf. Badian (1991) 40 and n.31; contrast de Romilly (1992) 11.
2 The standard treatments of the peace of 362/1 are Taeger (1930), Accame (1941) 168–177 and Ryder (1965) 140–144. For a translation of Tod 145, see Harding (1985) 78 no. 57.
3 Cartledge (1987) 314–330.
4 See Introduction above, pp. 13–15.
5 Xenophon comes at the beginning of a very long tradition in Greek historiography of turning one's work over to future historians; see esp. Ammianus 31.16.9, and cf. Fornara (1983) 33 and n.55, and Matthews (1989) 455 and n.5. It is interesting to note that Ammianus may have been making an essentially negative point at the conclusion of his history as well.
6 οὐδεὶς ἦν ὅστις οὐκ ᾤετο: note the strength of the negation.
7 On Ephorus as a source for Diodorus 15, see Volquardsen (1868) 48, Schwartz (1903) 681 and Jacoby (1923–1958) 2 C 33. Recently Sacks (1990) has attacked the view that Diodorus is a reliable guide to Ephorus' work; he argues that programmatic statements found in Diodorus may be Diodorus' own words, including his evaluation of Mantinea. While I find his views provocative, I cannot agree with them. One problem I see is precisely in relation to Diodorus' comments on Mantinea. It has traditionally been argued that Ephorus was in some way indebted to Isocrates for his views on the battle, hence making parallels between the orator and Diodorus probable areas where the later historian is closely following the earlier one. When Sacks states (42–43) that Isocrates' evaluation of the Athenian and Spartan hegemonies do not resemble those found in Diodorus,

and thereby do not suggest an intermediary (namely Ephorus), I have reservations. At 43 n.82 he concedes that Isocrates in *de Pace* 99–115 comes close to Diodorus' views. This seems special pleading; in fact, the sentiments expressed are almost identical. See below, p. 129 and n.20.

8 Cf. Momigliano (1935) 195.
9 See esp. Momigliano (1977) 165 and cf. Pohlenz (1937) 174 and Gould (1989) 77.
10 Fornara (1971) 12.
11 Gould (1989) 78.
12 Gomme (1945–1981) 2 15 and Hornblower (1991) 250 ad Thuc. 2.12.3.
13 Cf. Schwartz (1929) 206–216.
14 See, however, Flory (1993) esp. 122–123.
15 Cf. Walbank (1957) 43 ad loc. Signficantly Polybius connects Thucydides' κίνησις with Xenophon's ταραχή, 3.4.12; cf. Walbank (1972) 30 with n.152 and 99.
16 Parke (1977) 54–55; Barron (1988) 620; Burkert (1992) 260.
17 Thomas (1989) 225. It is interesting to compare how Thucydides collapses the Persian wars into four battles; see Immerwahr (1960) 279.
18 Cf. Raubitschek (1953) 37.
19 Cf. Demont (1990) 283–285.
20 Nilsson (1967) 787.
21 Cf. Hamilton (1991) 30–32.
22 For a recent treatment of the amnesty see Loening (1987).
23 De Sanctis (1932/1951) 144–146. For a criticism of this argument see Henry (1967) 171–172.
24 Joël (1893–1901) 1 113. See also Chapter 7, pp. 183–185.
25 On the interpolations, see Lotze (1962 and 1974).
26 See Shipley (1987) 131–133.
27 Cf. Krentz (1989) 191–192.
28 The suggestion that Xenophon saw in false ends a 'continuum' of hegemonic war was made by Henry (1967) 52 and Grayson (1975) 34 (the term 'continuum' is his). Cf. Hatzfeld (1930) 124.
29 Cf. Rahn (1971) 508.
30 Cf. Löwith (1949) 5 and White (1978) 96–98.
31 Rahn (1971) 508 and n.18.
32 Cf. the title of the recent biography of the American Civil War general William Tecumseh Sherman, Marszalek (1993): *Sherman: A Soldier's Passion for Order.*
33 Cf. de Romilly (1967) 169 on ταραχή as a predictor of military success in Thucydides.
34 Cf. *An.* 3.4.19.
35 There is a problem with the precise date in Xenophon; cf. Diod. 14.91.3 and Cawkwell (1979) 212–213 n.
36 See Buckler (1980) and Tuplin (1987b).
37 A celebrated passage: see Polybius 10.20.6, Athenaeus 10.421B; see below, p. 87 n.68.
38 Usher (1969) 94.

39 See, e.g., *Cyr.* 2.1.29–30, *An.* 3.2.8–10, *Lac.* 4.5, 12.5–7. Cf. Hornblower (1981) 188–189, 205–206.

40 Cf. Parker (1989) 162.

41 Luccioni (1947) 38 n.46; cf. Powell (1989) 180.

42 Cf. Epyaxa's thrill at beholding the order of the Ten Thousand, *An.* 1.2.18.

43 There is an abundance of passages which suggest the close relation in Xenophon between the chorus and the army: see, e.g., *Cyr.* 3.3.70, *An.* 6.1.5–13; cf. Onasander *Strat.* 10.3. The connection was not unusual in ancient Greece at all periods: see Wheeler (1982) 223, with n.1 for bibliography. Note, however, that there was also a view that saw dance and war as opposed: *Il.* 15.508; *Od.* 8.248.

44 See Breitenbach (1967) 1853.

45 Cf. Diller (1956) 53–54. This interest in order as demonstrated in the activities of soldiers seems to be common to nostalgic generals; General W.T. Sherman was very fond of marching, Marszalek (1993) 19.

46 Note that Plato recognized that the art of running a city and the art of warfare were part of the same skill, *Prt.* 322b.

47 Joël (1893–1901) 2 1085. Cf. Soph. *Ant.* 672–676.

48 For a discussion of these passages as disruptions of the human order, see Kitto (1966) 272–273.

49 Walbank (1951).

50 See, e.g., Diodorus/Ephorus 15.40.1; Isocrates *de Pace* 25, 132–133 (= *Ant.* 66); Demosthenes 14.5, 18.18.

51 See Dodds (1959) 158–159 ad 508a.

52 Cole (1990) 107–120.

53 Süss (1910) 90; Bona (1974) 6 and n.3.

54 Whitehead (1990) 28–29.

55 See Dodds (1951) 51 n.3.

56 E.g. Isocrates *Pan.* 48, *Areop.* 30.

57 For Jason's greatness, see esp. 6.4.28: μέγας . . . μείζων . . . μέγιστος.

58 For a discussion of the role of τύχή in Hellenistic historiography, see Walbank (1972) 60–62.

59 Cf. Higgins (1977) 104.

60 Cf. Grayson (1975) 34 for a clear statement of Xenophon's pessimism; cf. Momigliano (1935) 195.

2 XENOPHON, UTOPIA AND PANHELLENISM

1 Bonner (1910).

2 All citations in this chapter and the next, unless otherwise indicated, are to Xenophon's *Anabasis*.

3 The term 'panhellene' is found in Hesiod *Op.* 528; Strabo (8.6.6 p. 370) reports that both Hesiod (= fr. 130 Merkelbach–West) and Archilochus (= fr. 120 West) used the term to mean 'all Greeks'. West (1978) 292 ad *Op.* 527–528 is more cautious, suggesting that the term meant '*the* Greeks'. See also Aristophanes *Pax* 302. Cf. Nagy (1990) chs 2 and 3.

NOTES

4 See, e.g., the remarks of Baldry following the presentation of Reverdin (1962) 109.
5 See, e.g., Ferguson (1975) 9–15, 18.
6 Cf. Richardson (1992) 225. See also the terms of the Peace of Nicias (Thuc. 5.18.2).
7 Cf. Perlman (1976) 1–2 n.1, and Walbank (1951) 52–54.
8 Cf. Seager and Tuplin (1980) 152 and nn.121–123.
9 Dodds (1973) 13.
10 Cf. Austin and Vidal-Naquet (1977) 131–132.
11 It is disputed whether Thurii was truly panhellenic in conception: see Brunt (1967), esp. 90 n.15, and de Ste. Croix (1972) 381 Appendix 34.
12 Cf. Reverdin (1962).
13 See Hall (1989) 149; cf. Trüdinger (1918) 133–146.
14 Cf. F 158, and see the discussions of Fornara (1983) 110–112 and Giangrande (1976) 20.
15 Note Scheller (1911) 77.
16 Cf. Bertelli (1976) 196. Theopompus' focus on the two critics may be related to the shield of Achilles (*Il.* 18.490 ff.)
17 Note, e.g., Herodotus' account of Libya (4.168–196), where there are found among others pacifists (174) and people who harvest the fruit of the land (183); interestingly, as in Theopompus' account, there is also an exceedingly wretched race and all we know about them is that they continually curse the sun (184.1–2).
18 See esp. Brown (1949) 61 and 65.
19 Cf. Brown (1955) 58 and Trüdinger (1918) 138–140. For the term 'ethnographic utopia' cf. Jacoby (1923–1958) 3 a 29.
20 See Fränkel (1938).
21 So, e.g., Lane Fox (1986) 114.
22 See Lana (1951) and Shrimpton (1977) 128–129 and n.13; contrast Shrimpton (1991) 143–144.
23 Cf. Brown (1949) 74.
24 Cf. Romm (1992) 67.
25 See Shrimpton (1977) 129, von Fritz (1941) 779, Dusanic (1977) 35 n.62. Bruce (1970) 78 considers the story 'a didactic myth in the Platonic style'; others have argued that Theopompus' utopia parodies Plato's Atlantis myth.
26 The Persian debate: see, e.g., Waters (1985) 36–37 and 78–79 with n.9, and Gould (1989) 15. On the possibility of influence from the older sophists, see Kerferd (1981) 150.
27 Kerferd (1981) 140–142.
28 Diogenes Laertius 9.8.50 cites Heraclides Ponticus as the source for the claim.
29 The evidence is admittedly not of the first rank: Hesychius and Photius s.v. Ἱπποδάμου νέμησις; cf. Burns (1976) and Giangrande (1976) 17.
30 Note that a direct connection between Hippodamus and Euhemerus has been argued: von Pöhlmann (1912) 2 380–382, and cf. Brown (1946) 264.
31 Kerferd (1981) 154.

32 So 'Iambulus' tells us that the people dwelling on the Blessed Island do not marry but hold even their women as common property (Diod. 2.58.1); note also that the Panchaeans of Euhemerus hand their agricultural produce over to common storage (Diod. 5.45.3–5).

33 Cf. Kerferd (1981) 140.

34 For what follows see esp. Strasburger (1954) 230–231.

35 See in general Redfield (1975), esp. 123–124 and Scully (1990) ch. 8.

36 It seems fairly certain that Xenophon was at least familiar with the Funeral Oration of Pericles as it is found in Thucydides (based on the nearness of *Mem.* 3.5.4 to Thuc. 2.39.2), and probably the other two speeches as well. Cf. Dillery (1993) 3 n.11.

37 See Ferguson (1975) 27 and in general Loraux (1986), esp. 173. Gomme (1945–1981) 2 177, sees a strong contrast between the Funeral Oration and the last speech of Pericles (2.60–64), between lofty idealism and stark realism, with the Plague in between as an explanation for the change in tone. De Romilly (1963) 130–132 sees no fundamental contradiction but essentially the same arguments for empire.

38 For the problems of relying on 2.65 as a basis for an understanding of Thucydides' view of the war, see Rusten (1989) 212–213 ad 2.65.11–13.

39 See in general Carter (1986).

40 See Hornblower (1987) 123–126 with n.67. The passages he cites in connection with Thuc. 2.60.2 are Sophocles *Ant.* 187ff., Euripides *Erechtheus* fr. 360 lines 19–21, Plato *Cri.* 51a, Xenophon *Mem.* 3.7.9, as well as Plato *R.* 519e. Of course in the *Crito* Socrates is arguing for a course of action which prevailing codes of conduct would not endorse, thus Crito's position. Similarly Glaucus in the *Memorabilia* is being urged by Socrates to take part in affairs of the state, something he is not naturally inclined to do. Creon's position in the *Antigone* is admittedly complicated, but at the very least it seems to be intended to be viewed as an extreme one, if not downright peculiar: see Nussbaum (1986) 59 and Connor (1971) 52, and cf. Blundell (1989) 118. Judging from the summary provided by Lycurgus (*Against Leocritus* 98), the situation of the *Erechtheus* of Euripides pits familial bond against civic responsibility and is, I think, therefore *de facto* unusual (cf. *Antigone*); for a contrary conclusion on both Thucydides and Euripides, see de Romilly (1963) 136 and n.1.

41 Cf. Farrar (1988) 258–259 and 161–162.

42 Cf. Hussey (1985), esp. 119–122, and see also Farrar (1988), esp. 274–275.

43 Hornblower (1987) 178 makes it very clear that Thucydides had an organic view of the state. I cannot agree, however, with his arbitrary and unnecessary division between an organic Thucydidean view as opposed to an external (perhaps 'fashionable') totalitarian view as found in 2.60.2 (179 and n.86). The view Hornblower styles 'totalitarian' and hence not truly Thucydidean is fully consistent with organic views as represented by the medical writing of the period. It was known at a fairly early date that the body was susceptible to infection and

mortification: recall Herodotus' account of Atossa's affliction, as well as the mortal injury to Miltiades (Hdt. 3.133.1; 6.136.3); cf. Soph. *Ph.* 573 and *Mem.* 1.2.54. As early as Alcmaeon of Croton, excision was known (see Lloyd (1979) 156 and n.159), admittedly for investigation and not cure. Certainly the notion that it was important to purge material (typically humour) from the body in order to preserve balance also suggests that there was a recognition that constituents of the body could damage the whole and should be removed or moderated. Hence the mutual 'failure' argument Hornblower presents is not convincing. For humoral theory see Lloyd (1979) 147–150.

44 On the connection between Thucydides and medical writing see, e.g., Cochrane (1929), Lichtenthaeler (1965) and most recently Swain (1994); for the Corcyrean revolution in particular see Cochrane (1929) 132–134 and Lichtenthaeler (1965) 115.

45 I borrow the phrase from Hussey (1985) 120.

46 Cf. Dover (1974) 177.

47 Cf. Momigliano (1960) 101 n.33.

48 See de Romilly (1972) 199–200.

49 See esp. de Ste. Croix (1972) 16.

50 Hussey (1985) 122.

51 See, e.g., West (1977), esp. 313.

52 Dodds (1973) 100–101.

53 Wilcken (1967/1931) 18–19.

54 Cf. Hall (1989) 215–216.

55 See Dodds (1973) 100–101.

56 West (1977) 312. Note that I am assuming Lysias is the author of both speeches. Admittedly, this may not be the case; cf. Dover (1968).

57 Lehmann (1980) 71.

58 See Whitehead (1990) 29: 'the need for *homonoia* could fairly be said to be implicit throughout the treatise'.

59 See, e.g. Mühl (1917), esp. 11; more recently see Perlman (1976) 25, and cf. de Romilly (1958) 98: 'concord, of course, is [Isocrates'] one great idea. He celebrates its virtues in nearly all of his works, either thinking of concord within the city or of concord between cities, this being, naturally, the most important thing.' The scholarship on Isocrates, *homonoia* and panhellenism is vast. For useful bibliographies see Dobesch (1968) 242–247 and Funke (1980) 172–178.

60 The foundation for this view would seem to be the notion that a friend is 'another self', someone who shares with one the same preferences and dislikes: see. esp. Aristotle *EN* 1166a and 1171a; cf. Blundell (1989) 47 and n.109.

61 So, e.g., Kessler (1911), esp. 1 and 27; cf. the more moderate views of de Romilly (1992) esp. 8–9.

62 In what follows I am most indebted to Perlman (1957, 1969 and 1976). See also Mathieu (1925) 69–75, Wilcken (1929) 313, Momigliano (1934) 183–199, Walbank (1951) 43 and 49–51, Baynes (1955) 153–159, Ryder (1965) 99 and Bringmann (1965) 23–25. As Hamilton has noted recently (1992) 43 n.58, more still needs to be done to refine our views of Isocrates' 'panhellenism'.

63 In general see Finley (1983) 61.
64 The attack on Sparta comes especially at *Pan.* 110–128; his defence of Athens' actions against Melos and Scione in the Peloponnesian War (*Pan.* 100–102; cf. *Panath.* 53 and 62–64) is notoriously unsatisfactory. Cf. Xenophon *Hell.* 2.23
65 See esp. Perlman (1976) 25–29 and cf. Walbank (1951) 43.
66 Cf. Perlman (1976) 27.
67 Perlman (1969) 371–372.
68 Perlman (1957) 311.
69 Cf. esp. Perlman (1976/1977) 248–249.
70 See above all Baynes (1955) 154–155, and cf. van Soesbergen (1982/1983). On the widespread fear of mercenaries at this time, see Aeneas Tacticus 10.7 and Whitehead (1990) ad loc.
71 Parke (1933) 29 and Cawkwell (1972) 26.
72 Seager and Tuplin (1980), esp. 145–146.
73 Note in this connection Wilamowitz's (1893) 2 380–386 characterization of the *Panegyricus* as propaganda for the Second Athenian Confederation.
74 Runciman (1990).

3 XENOPHON'S *ANABASIS*: PANHELLENISM AND THE IDEAL COMMUNITY

1 After, that is, the loss of Xenophon's estate at Scillus: see, e.g., Körte (1922) 16, Cawkwell (1972) 15–16, and most recently Stoneman (1992) xii. Cf. van Soesbergen (1982/1983) 137 and Wylie (1992a) 131–133.
2 See Cawkwell (1972) 17–18 and Westlake (1987).
3 Cf. Saïd (1978) 177.
4 Cf. Brunt (1983/1989) 1 538–539 nn.8–9.
5 Momigliano (1979), esp. 145–146.
6 Cf. esp. Saïd (1978) 20–21; on the term 'autoethnography' see Pratt (1992) 7.
7 A popular view: see, e.g., Wilamowitz (1893) 2 13, Körte (1922), Morr (1926/1927), Luccioni (1947) 44 and recently Dandamaev (1989) 284.
8 Cawkell (1972) 28; contrast, e.g., Masqueray (1930) 1 67 n.1 ad 1.5.9, and Davies (1978) 156.
9 Cf. Cawkwell (1972) 23–24.
10 Note Jacoby (1923–1958) 2 B 357 ad loc.
11 Most notably Dürrbach (1893); see also Mesk (1922/1923) and Erbse (1966).
12 See, e.g., Cawkwell (1972) 18.
13 See Breitenbach (1967) 1575–1576, Rahn (1981), Cartledge (1987) 60 and Tuplin (1987a).
14 Cf. Fornara (1983) 176.
15 Due (1989) 30–31 with n.3.
16 Nussbaum (1967) esp. 147–152 divides up the chronicle of the Ten Thousand into roughly four phases. Marinovic (1988) 192–194 notes

that it is true that the Ten Thousand adopt a familiar social organization, but also observes that there are important differences between the Ten Thousand and a *polis*; cf. Dalby (1992) 16–17. Moreover Dalby adds (17) that the *polis* everyone thinks of in connection with the Ten Thousand is Athens, and that given that there were only very few Athenians involved this is a dangerous comparison to make. As I will make clear below (p. 92), I find only one phase of the Ten Thousand similar to a city.

17 Parke (1933) 27 and Roy (1967) 287 and 292.

18 Cf. Parke (1933) 31.

19 Cf. Roy (1967) 292.

20 Some have detected an echo of Andromache's famous words to Hector at *Il.* 6.429–430: see Kühner (1852) and Pretor (1881) ad loc. Leaf (1900–1902) 1 ad *Il.* 6.429 notes that Andromache's words were often imitated. Note too that Plutarch *Mor.* 240 F preserves a saying of a Spartan woman which has similarities with Clearchus' statement.

21 Parke (1933) 30 compares Clearchus to an unscrupulous 'leader of the people' such as Theramenes (contrast Pearson (1962) 152–153), and there is no doubt that he is being deceptive. However, his words would not be persuasive unless they were plausible, and this suggests that his dependence on his soldiers for his authority was obvious to all.

22 On the growing tendency in the fourth century for the officer to be incorporated into the fighting unit, see Smith (1990) 153–154.

23 Roy (1967) 292–293 with n.25.

24 Cf. Roy (1967) 292–293.

25 Dalby (1992) 16.

26 Cf. Griffith (1935) 265–266 and Pritchett (1971) 6.

27 Cf. Perlman (1976/1977) 259–260.

28 Griffith (1935) 266.

29 On the problems associated with the wagon-train, see Roy (1967) 311 n.93.

30 Perlman (1976/1977) 263.

31 Hirsch (1985) 24–25.

32 Persian gifts of land and even cities to Greeks were not uncommon: see Briant (1985) 58–59.

33 Technically the word becomes a κληδών or chance utterance that has prophetic force: cf. *Od.* 17.541.

34 It is interesting to recall that Xenophon first appears in the *Anabasis* when he reports to Cyrus on the eve of Cunaxa that the password for the day is 'Zeus Soter and Victory' (1.8.16).

35 For an exhaustive treatment of the field of meaning for *soter/soteria* in Classical Greek, see Foerster (1971).

36 Cf. Kirk (1990) 114 ad loc.

37 See Roy (1968) 38–39 and Dalby (1992) 22, and cf. Christensen and Hansen (1989) 206 n.28.

38 Momigliano (1993) 34 and 40–41; cf. Stuart (1928/1967) 36–37.

39 Momigliano (1993) 57, and cf. Fornara (1983) 179–180.

40 Cf. Bruns (1896) 137–144.

41 Momigliano (1993) 49; cf. Collard (1975) 2 445 ad *Supp.* 857–917.

42 Cf. Lossau (1990) 49.

43 It should be noted that Aristarchus athetized these lines in part precisely because he felt that status did not affect the ability of a dreamer to receive a dream from the divine (scholia to the *Iliad* (Erbse) 1191–1192 ad *Il.* 2.82). However, as Leaf notes (1900–1902) 1 ad *Il.* 2.82, the passage seems to reflect a belief in the 'innate right' of supreme commanders to be the only ones to have communications from heaven: cf. Dodds (1951) 125 n.35, citing Artemidorus 4 prooemium (Pack 239).

44 Cf. Rinner (1978), who suggests other parallels between *Iliad* 2 and *Anabasis* 3.1–2, most intriguingly the presence of the anti-heroes Thersites and Apollonides: cf. Dalby (1992) 21.

45 Callinus 1.1 (West) μέχρις τέο κατάκεισθε; note also the similarity between Xenophon's κατακείμεθα ὥσπερ ἐξὸν ἡσυχίαν ἄγειν and Callinus 1.3–4, ἐν εἰρήνῃ δὲ δοκεῖτε/ἧσθαι. Cf. also Archil. 128 and Tyrtaeus 11 (West). Bowie (1990) 223 has argued that the context of the first line of Callinus is in all likelihood the *symposion*, not the battlefield or the assembly; this may be so, and the first use of κατάκεισθαι for 'lie idle' may indeed be here at *An.* 3.1.13. However, the subject of the poem, even if set at a *symposion*, is still a call to action. Cf. *Il.* 240ff. and Latacz (1977). See also *Mem.* 1.2.58.

46 Cf. Nilsson (1967) 789. Note Agamemnon's meeting *Il.* 2.53.

47 See Dillery and Gagos (1992) 179 and n.18. Cf. Callinus 1 (West) 20–21.

48 Cf. Roy (1968) 41–42.

49 I assume Eurylochus is an officer or in some position of authority, for he is given special duties (7.1.32). I do not see why we have to conclude that he was promoted; cf. Roy (1967) 300 n.61.

50 This is standard military parlance, of course; see, for instance, Charles Carleton Coffin's description of the Union defence of Little Round Top at the battle of Gettysburg during the American Civil War: 'The fight was fierce. The rebels greatly outnumbered Chamberlain, but he had the advantage of position. He was on the crest of the hill, and at every lull in the strife his men piled the loose stones into a rude breastwork . . .' (Coffin (1881) 286). The shorthand of commander standing in for his unit is clear and seems to be reserved for moments of great drama.

51 It is appropriate here perhaps to cite Aymard (1953), esp. 143, who discusses how the affairs of state in the Hellenistic period become increasingly described by military language and also become associated with important individuals, namely the kings; cf. the influence of powerful men 'on the tone' of Hieronymus' history, Hornblower (1981) 130.

52 See Barber (1935) 151 and n.2 on the placement of Ephorus' biography of Cimon, and cf. Blamire (1989) 7.

53 Cf. Fornara (1983) 108 and Connor (1963) 112–113.

54 Cf. Dalby (1992) 17. On the structure of authority in the *Iliad*, see, e.g., Donlan (1979), Van Wees (1986), Scully (1990) ch. 7 and cf. Thalmann (1988) 3 n.7. In general see Finley (1965).

55 Cf. Christensen and Hansen (1989) 206 n.28.

56 Contrast Roy (1967) 317–318 and van Soesbergen (1982/1983) 134–135.

57 Cf. Griffith (1935) 3.

58 Cf. Cawkwell (1972) 280 n.8.

59 The Pontic cities were always worried about incursions from the hinterland: see, e.g., Pippidi (1963) and Davies (1984) 313.

60 Cf. Hall (1989) 126 and Shaw (1982/1983) 13–19; on the Mossynoeci in particular as representative of the barbarous confusion of public and private and therefore as 'un-Greek', see esp. Pembroke (1967) 17 and n.62 and in general cf. Hartog (1988).

61 Cf. Hall (1989) 164–165.

62 ἐπὶ τούτοις ἐθύετο; cf. 3.5.18 and LSJ s.v. ἐπί B III 2.

63 Cf. Parke (1933) 35 and Burstein (1976) 40.

64 See esp. Malkin (1987) 102–104. Cf. Wood (1964) 55: 'if the ultimate of rational communities is the well-organized and well-commanded army, its form most nearly resembling the polity is the encampment'.

65 Cf. Austin and Vidal-Naquet (1977) 152 and nos 108 and 130, and van Soesbergen (1982/1983).

66 See Aymard (1953), and cf. Vidal-Naquet (1965) 137 on the growing influence of military thinking towards problem solving of all sorts. Cf. Arrian *An.* 4.1.4.

67 Cf. Pritchett (1974) 219–220.

68 Indeed, the term 'workshop of war' (πολέμου ἐργαστήριον) had an almost immediate celebrity; according to Athenaeus 10.421 B, Mnesimachus, a poet of Middle Comedy active in the middle of the fourth century, used the term to describe Philip's parties. Walbank (1967) 220 ad 10.20.7 believes the phrase was proverbial.

69 Cf. van Soesbergen (1982/1983) 141 and Dalby (1992) 18–19 and n.21.

70 See Jameson (1988) 88, and note Hutchinson (1987) 182, who observes that '[utopianism's] method is implicitly comparative, not comparative between two existent contexts but between one in some sense existent and another that is an imaginary displacement away from the first'. Cf. White (1973) 47.

71 The items that are especially noteworthy in this regard: *abundant springs* (6.4.4) ≈ Dionysius Scytobrachion (Diod. 3.68.5), Iambulus (Diod. 2.57.3), Euhemerus (Diod. 5.43.1, 44.3); *blessed with beautiful trees* (6.4.4–5) ≈ Euhemerus (Diod. 5.43.1), Iambulus (Diod. 2.59.3); *abundance of fruit from the earth, including grape-vines* (6.4.6) ≈ Dionysius Scytobrachion (Diod. 3.68.4), Iambulus (Diod. 2.57.2, 59.3), Euhemerus (Diod. 5.43.3). Cf. Brown (1955) 60. Also note Arrian *Peripl. M. Eux.* (Roos) 12.5: ὁ δὲ Κάλπης λιμὴν ὁποῖόν τι χωρίον ἐστὶν καὶ ὁποῖος ὅρμος, καὶ ὅτι πηγὴ ἐναὐτῷ ψυχροῦ καὶ καθαροῦ ὕδατος, καὶ ὅτι ὗλαι πρὸς τῇ θαλάσσῃ ξύλων ναυπηγησίμων, καὶ αὗται ἔνθηροι, ταῦτα Ξενοφῶντι τῷ πρεσβυτέρῳ λέλεκται. Arrian was in all likelihood quoting this passage from memory, for Xenophon nowhere calls the woods 'full of wild beasts'; cf. Müller (1855) 382. It should be noted that the utopian focus on variety of trees as well as the abundance of good water is widespread: cf. Ibn Khaldûn on the fantastic city of Iram in Rosenthal (1967) 17.

NOTES

72 We see the same kind of wishful undertone to Odysseus' description of the island of the Cyclops, *Od.* 9.116–151: soil, harbour, springs, trees. Is it significant that Theopompus also mentions Port Calpe, *FGrHist* 115 F 15?

73 Cf. Grayson (1975) 34; note Higgins (1977) 93, with whose more charitable attitude towards Xenophon I am often in sympathy. But I cannot believe that Xenophon was deceiving himself or thought his description of his actions would produce a negative effect.

74 Cf. Mossé (1963).

75 Cf. esp. Sophocles *OT* 56–57; also Aeschylus *Pers.* 349. In general see the very helpful observations of Kearns (1990) 324–327.

76 See Connor (1971) 110 n.34.

77 This way of looking at the life of a community through the life of its leaders is examined by Sahlins (1985) 35–54 in connection with Fijian history in a section called 'Heroic History'. Cf. Scully (1990) ch. 8.

78 Dalby (1992).

79 Cf. Vernant (1990) 53 and n.46, citing Mossé (1968).

80 Marinovic (1988) 194; cf. Schmitt-Pantel (1990).

81 For an important discussion of the Greeks and intellectual 'transcendence' see Humphreys (1978) 209–241, esp. 240–241.

82 Pohlenz (1937) 8 n.2 and Immerwahr (1960) 264 n.7; cf. Jacoby (1909) 89.

83 See also, e.g., Aristophanes *Av.* 37. The phrase had quite a long life: cf., e.g., Dexippus *FGrHist* 100 F 3 and Potter (1990) 79–80. The language in the imperial period was evidently so common that Lucian *Hist. Conscr.* 31 could spoof it; see Jones (1986) 62–63.

84 See Cawkwell (1972) 162 n.9. The sixth-century Milesian poet Phocylides anticipates much of Xenophon's thinking regarding the true worth of cities, importantly also in connection with Nineveh: πόλις ἐν σκοπέλῳ κατὰ κόσμον οἰκεῦσα σμικρὴ κρέσσων Νίνου ἀφραινούσης (Diehl³ 1 no. 4.) Note that Xenophon's contemporary Ctesias (*FGrHist* 688 F 1 ap. Diod. 2.3.2–4) devotes considerable space to the founding of Nineveh. Cf. Hdt. 1.178.1.

85 Cf. Geysels (1974) esp. 33.

86 Münscher (1920) 124–126, Stadter (1967 and 1980) esp. 31, and Jones (1986) 62; cf. *FGrHist* 156 T 1–2.

87 I find strong echoes between Arrian *An.* 3.1.5 and Xenophon *An.* 5.6.15–16: καλὸν αὐτῷ ἐδόκει εἶναι ≈ καὶ ἔδοξεν αὐτῷ ὁ χῶρος κάλλιστος, καὶ γενέσθαι ἂν αὐτῷ ἐδόκει μεγάλη ≈ καὶ γενέσθαι ἂν εὐδαίμονα τὴν πόλιν, καὶ ἐπὶ τούτοις ἐθύετο = καὶ ἐπὶ τούτοις ἐθύετο. Regarding the last set of correspondences, it should be noted that the precise collocation of the four words is found nowhere else in Greek literature. Note also that Arrian elsewhere noticed and reproduced quite closely Xenophon's other utopian vision at Port Calpe, *Peripl. M. Eux.* 12.5 (Roos, see above, n.71).

88 An enormous question: see Bosworth (1980) 264–265 ad 3.1.5 and the bibliography cited there.

89 Similarly General W.T. Sherman often returned to West Point during his lifetime; it was a symbol to him of the excellence and even security

that military life provided him: see Marszalek (1993) 28.

90 Cf. Tarn (1927) 449.

91 Cf. Gitti (1954) 24. Of course, this was not the first instance of aggressive and strategic colonization: see e.g. Gomme (1945–1981) 1 367–368.

4 THE LEGACY OF THE TEN THOUSAND? XENOPHON'S VISION AND THE SPARTANS IN ASIA

1 See especially the camp at Ephesus at 3.4.11, pp. 86 and 113. (All references in this chapter are to the *Hellenica* unless otherwise stated.)

2 At 3.5.1 Tithraustes fears that Agesilaus will attack the Great King himself.

3 The sacrifice at Aulis betokens great ambitions (3.4.3); Agesilaus, shortly before his recall, planned to detach large portions of the Persian empire (4.1.41); he vows to return to Asia and lead the Greeks again (4.2.4).

4 Since, as Cawkwell has noted (1979) 196 n., the invasion of Laconia could not have been considered possible at this time, Timolaus' proposal at 4.2.11–12 must be meant to contrast directly with Agesilaus' noble plans.

5 Cf. Cartledge (1987) 59.

6 There are a few noteworthy dissenters: Beloch (1922) 1 35 and Lewis (1977) 144 think Spartan panhellenism genuine; Andrewes (1978) 102 doubts the possibility of a coherent imperialist policy at Sparta owing to her social structure. But for the majority opinion, see Parke (1930) 37–79, Taeger (1930) 7–8, Ollier (1933) 416, de Ste. Croix (1972) 159, Cawkwell (1976a) 67, Perlman (1976) 18 and Cartledge (1987) 195–196.

7 Cawkwell (1979) 193 n.

8 Although see Rühl (1913) 173: 'Xenophon ist ein *bewusster* Geschichtsfälscher.'

9 Henry (1967) 201, in his attack upon it, has neatly summed up this approach: 'it is not that he fabricates history outright . . . his method consists rather in distortion, suppression, and exaggeration; in minimizing or omitting the achievements of those who represent ideals contrary to his own and in exaggerating the importance of events that suit his own moral and political interests'.

10 The question of the authorship of the *Hellenica Oxyrhynchia* opened with the publication in 1908 of the London fragments by Grenfell and Hunt (1908) no. 842, and has not been closed. The major candidates are Theopompus (*FGrHist* 115), Cratippus (*FGrHist* 64), Daimachus (*FGrHist* 65) and an author whose name is lost to us. The bibliography on the issue is immense; overviews are available in Bloch (1940) 303–341, Griffith (1954) 160–162, Bartoletti (1959) xvii–xxv, Bruce (1967) 22–27, Breitenbach (1970) 410–423, Koenen (1976) 65–66 and McKechnie and Kern (1988) 7–14. In the most

recent edition of the historian, Chambers (1993) xxv comes down in favour of Cratippus.

11 De Sanctis (1932/1951) 153.

12 Breitenbach (1967) 1680.

13 Indeed, we learn from Diodorus (14.12.2–7) that he abused his power at Byzantium, setting himself up as a tyrant and fighting forces sent out from Sparta to remove him.

14 Cf. Judeich (1892) 42 and Cartledge (1987) 191.

15 The astonishing attribution of the authorship of the account should be noted. Plutarch, *Mor.* 345e, felt that Xenophon attributed the *Anabasis* to the mysterious Themistogenes 'in order that he seem more trustworthy, mentioning himself as though another person'. Misch (1949) 104 and Delebecque (1957) 17 and 205–206, have made much the same argument. The only authority to preserve the name of the historian Themistogenes is the Suda, and its entry, vague as it is, betrays someone's attempt at generating plausibility; see MacLaren (1934b) 241.

16 In the *Anabasis*, Xenophon does mention the nauarch Pythagoras (*An.* 1.4.2, who may be Samius) who assists Cyrus with thirty-five Peloponnesian ships in his siege of Miletus, and that Syennesis is distracted by the approach of Tamos with an unspecified number of Peloponnesian ships (*An.* 1.2.21). Note, however, that the Spartans tried very hard to keep their participation in Cyrus' revolt clandestine; see Cartledge (1987) 320 on the contingent under the command of Chirisophus.

17 See Perlman (1964) 77 and de Ste. Croix (1972) 159.

18 Contrast Diodorus 14.35.2, where the planned reduction of Ionia is the result of Artaxerxes' initiative.

19 Note again 2.2.23 on the reaction to the destruction of the Long Walls at Athens by Lysander: νομίζοντες ἐκείνην τὴν ἡμέραν τῇ Ἑλλάδι ἄρχειν τῆς ἐλευθερίας.

20 Seager and Tuplin (1980) 144 with n.37.

21 According to Macan (1895) ad 5.49.2 Spartan προστασία had been recognized since the middle of the sixth century; see also Thucydides 1.69.

22 Thucydides 8.18, 37, 58; also, perhaps, in the controversial Treaty of Boiotios: see Lewis (1977) 124–125, and contrast Tuplin (1987c).

23 The sending away of one's enemies on hazardous duty in the hope that they be destroyed seems not to have been uncommon. See Herodotus 3.44 and Thucydides 3.75.2.

24 Cf. Cartledge (1987) 191.

25 Estimates put the number of survivors at about half strength: Beloch (1922) 1 34 puts the number at 6,000, as does Hatzfeld (1936/1939) 1 164. More recently Cartledge (1987) 355 has proposed 5,000.

26 On the families of these two men and their relations with each other, see Lewis (1977) 54 n.29.

27 The designation of Caria, Tissaphernes' headquarters and private residence (3.2.12), as a prime target for Spartan action is another strategic feature common to the campaigns.

28 Cf. Tuplin (1993) 48.
29 The words which describe the officer are deliberately vague: ὁ τῶν Κυρείων προεστηκώς. Breitenbach (1967) 1574, among others, has argued that the officer is Xenophon himself. If true, this concealing of himself is not typical of ancient historians. Thucydides repeatedly asserts his authorship at the close of each year (2.70.4 etc.), and where he is involved directly in the events of the narrative, he does not withhold his name (4.104.4, 105.1, 106.3). Xenophon does not include his name at the outset of his work, since it has no proem (cf. Hdt. 1.1 and Thuc. 1.1), and suppresses his name here, at 3.1.2 and perhaps at 3.4.20. Nor does he mention the death of his son at the battle of Mantinea. For another view of Thibron, see Krentz (1987).
30 Note Parke (1933) 44.
31 Delebecque(1957) 134 and Westlake (1966–1967) 254. This view is supported by Thibron's activities later in the *Hellenica*, 4.8.17–19.
32 Judeich (1892) 44–45 n.3.
33 Cf. Cloché (1944) 24.
34 It is important at this point to contrast Xenophon's account of Thibron's campaign with Diodorus'. Before connecting up with Xenophon and the remnants of the Ten Thousand, Thibron attacks Magnesia, ἧς ἦρχε Τισσαφέρνης (14.36.2). He tries to storm Tralles and fails, returns to Magnesia, moves the city to a neighbouring hill and invades enemy land (14.36.3). After they join with Xenophon, we learn only that they 'fight the Persians' (14.37.4). Diodorus explains Thibron's recall as brought about by Sparta's dissatisfaction with his prosecution of the war (14.38.2). This does not match up well with Xenophon's version. Thibron does not wage a cold war, but rather is very aggressive, and all this before joining with Xenophon. He seems to attack only enemy lands. The discrepancy between Diodorus and Xenophon is probably due to the fact that the Oxyrhynchus historian preserved an account different from Xenophon.
35 Wheeler (1988) 34–35 has shown that μηχανητικός and Σίσυφος are terms of positive evaluation for Xenophon; he cites (29) Xenophon's words at *Cyr.* 1.6.38 and at *Mem.* 3.1.6 in support. Σίσυφος for Ephorus, on the other hand, had very different connotations in connection with Dercylidas' character; see *FGrHist* 70 F 71 = Athenaeus 11.101 p. 500 C (accepting, with Jacoby, Reiske's emendation of Σκύφος, based on *Hell.* 3.1.8), where we read that Dercylidas was a far from typical Spartan: 'he was not at all Laconian in habit nor simple in character, rather he was wicked and bestial; for this reason the Spartans called him "Sisyphus"'.
36 For a good explanation of the Persian strategy see *Ages.* 7.7.
37 Recall Alcibiades' advice to Tissaphernes at Thucydides 8.46, misleading though it may have been (Thuc. 8.47.1).
38 The clue ἐπὶ Λυσάνδρου ναυαρχοῦντος (3.1.9) suggests either 407 or 405; see Underhill (1900) ad loc. and Hatzfeld (1936/1939) 1 163 (n. to 114).
39 Dercylidas and Pharnabazus worked in cooperation in the Hellespont in 411; see Thucydides 8.61–62.

40 Lewis (1977) 140 has taken the appeal of the Asiatic Greeks as a sign of their dissatisfaction with Dercylidas' prosecution of the campaign.

41 See Herodotus 1.143.2, 4.142.1 and 6.12, and Thucydides 5.9.1 and 6.77.1 for the proverbial cowardice of the Ionians.

42 Cf. Andrewes (1945–1981) 5 459, who suggests that Xenophon criticizes Dercylidas for not keeping his troops in battle-ready formation.

43 Cf. Seager and Tuplin (1980) 144.

44 See Tuplin (1993) 50–51.

45 Cf. Glotz (1936) 44 and Westlake (1986) 416.

46 I do not deal with the accession story of Agesilaus. With its suggestions of impropriety, Lysander's machinations, associations with past accession disputes at Sparta (cf. Hdt. on Dorieus and Demaratus) and mention of the 'lame kingship', the entire passage sounds an ominous chord. To this sense of foreboding can be added the intriguing story of Cinadon and the potential revolt of Sparta's underclasses. Cf. Tuplin (1993) 52–53 and Dillery (1989) 53–58.

47 Cf. Forrest (1968) 123 and Lewis (1977) 141.

48 Cf. de Ste. Croix (1972) 162 n.192; for a different view, see Cawkwell (1976a) 68.

49 3.4.5 = *Ages*. 1.10; cf. Plutarch *Ages*. 9.1 and Polyaenus 2.1.8.

50 Cf. Seager and Tuplin (1980) 144.

51 Cf. Lewis (1977) 141–142 n.45.

52 It should be pointed out that Dercylidas is also pious: he holds an important sacrifice to Athena on the acropolis of Scepsis immediately before turning the city over to its inhabitants, 3.1.21.

53 See above, n.10.

54 The possibility that the two authors represent two different battles was broached early on by Grenfell and Hunt (1908) 217, only to be rejected. It has not won wide acceptance; see, however, Cawkwell (1968), an important review of Bruce (1967). Cf. also Hamilton (1979) 203.

55 See, e.g., Cawkwell (1979) 406: 'Unless the whole of the *Hellenica Oxyrhynchia* is here wildest fantasy, Xenophon has misled us very greatly . . . only those who believe that Xenophon was "a really well-informed and truthful reporter" will shrink from the awful truth that here at least he has seriously failed us, a case of *inextricabilis error*.' De Voto (1988) attempts to combine the accounts of Xenophon and P; without subscribing to his conclusions, I am much indebted to his work. Cf. Tuplin (1993) 12.

56 For Ephorus' dependence on P, see Jacoby (1923–1958) 2 C 6, Breitenbach (1970) 423, Rice (1975) 95, Andrewes (1982) 15, Gray (1987) 73. On the similarity of P and Diodorus in this passage, see Grenfell and Hunt (1908) 117–118 and 214–217, Busolt (1908) 256–257, Meyer (1909) 14–15, Dugas (1910) 60–62, Lins (1914) 22, Kaupert (1926) 265 and n.1.

57 Diodorus 14.80.1: Ἀγησίλαος . . . ἀντείχετο τῆς παρὰ τὸν Σίπυλον παρωρείας. This manoeuvre is evidently for protection against Persian cavalry; cf. 3.1.5.

58 Unfortunately the papyrus is extremely fragmentary at the point where Tissaphernes' dispositions are given, making certain knowledge of the numbers of troops involved impossible. All that can be said with any confidence is that the number of infantry was probably larger than that of the cavalry, and that the figures for both groups were given after the nouns πεζούς and ἱππεῖς. As it stands, the papyrus has]κισχιλίους κα[ὶ] μυ[ρίους ... c.20 ... ο]ὐκ ἐλάττους. Diodorus has for the same units the following figures: Τισσαφέρνης δὲ μυρίους μὲν ἱππεῖς πεντακισμυρίους δὲ πεζούς ἀθροίσας. Wilamowitz supplements the papyrus πεζούς μὲν πεντα]κισχιλίους κα[ὶ] μυ[ρίους ἔχων ἱππέας δὲ μυρίων ο]ὐκ ἐλάττους, and he correspondingly emends Diodorus to πεντακισ⟨χιλίους καὶ⟩ μυρίους. There are two difficulties: first, whereas the normal order in Diodorus for figures of combined infantry and cavalry is first the number of foot then the number of horse, in P the order is not formulaic; and second, in large numbers Diodorus almost always has the multiple of 10,000 first and then the multiple of 1,000 (thirty-three instances of 10,000 number followed by 1,000, one instance the other way around (36.8.1)). Furthermore, Diodorus has a tendency to increase numbers of all kinds, thereby bringing Wilamowitz's emendation of Diodorus' πεντακισμυρίους into question (note Diod. 11.21.1, 14.22.7, 16.67.2 and 17.87.2 for expeditionary forces numbering 50,000 infantry). That Tissaphernes' army was very large is suggested by Pausanias 3.9.6: γενομένης δὲ πρὸς Τισσαφέρνην σατράπην τῶν περὶ Ἰωνίαν μάχης ἐν Ἑρμου πεδίῳ τήν τε ἵππον τῶν Περσῶν ἐνίκησεν ὁ Ἀγησίλαος καὶ τὸ πεζὸν τότε πλεῖστον ἀθροισθὲν μετά γε τὸν Ξέρξου ... στρατόν. What can be said with safety is that P has Tissaphernes personally command two sizeable detachments, one each of infantry and cavalry; see Busolt (1908) 257.

59 Bruce notes (1967) 81–82 that the river could be either the Pactolus or the Hermus.

60 In contrast to Diodorus 14.80.3, where Agesilaus gives the command to come out of the ambush.

61 Diodorus 14.80.4 puts the figure at 6,000. Bruce (1967) 83–84 notes: 'It is easy to imagine how a copyist's error could have converted 600 to 6,000, since Diodorus is clearly dependent upon P, albeit through the work of Ephorus. It is also a possibility, however, that Ephorus (or Diodorus) increased the number intentionally, since in view of the size of the Persian force – 60,000 men in all according to Diodorus – 6,000 may have appeared a more realistic, or more exciting, number of dead. In this connection we may note that while there is no trace of a hard-fought battle in P, Diodorus refers to a καρτερὰ μάχη, and this, as Jacoby observed (1923–1958 2 C 12), is an Ephoran phrase.' It should be remembered that Diodorus/Ephorus consistently have higher figures than Thucydides; contrast the numbers given for the Phoenician fleet, Thucydides 8.87.3 (147), and Diodorus 13.36.5, 37.4, 38.4, 41.4, 42.4, 46.6 (300). Whether or not there was a hard-fought battle near Sardis, the consequences of the engagement in P were significant, for Agesilaus was enabled to march on the outskirts of Sardis (12.1).

NOTES

62 Earlier, 3.4.12, Tissaphernes thought that Agesilaus was going to march on Caria, but Agesilaus marched on Phrygia instead. Grenfell and Hunt (1908) 217 thought that Xenophon could not be right in this detail insofar as it would have been unlikely that Tissaphernes would have made the same mistake twice. It is important for Xenophon to show that deception is Tissaphernes' own downfall, hence the concentration of attention on ψεῦδω at 3.4.6 and 3.4.21, and ἀπάτη at 3.4.12 and 3.4.21.

63 Early in the debate one of the major areas of contention was whether Xenophon was on the expedition. This was a problem because Xenophon describes the reassignment of Xenocles and some other (καὶ ἄλλον) to the command of the horse, and Herripidas to the command of the Cyreans. Xenophon had probably been in command of the Cyreans up to this point (see 3.2.7). Some argue that he might be the mysterious 'other' person in charge of the cavalry. Whatever the case, it is not important here whether Xenophon was along or not.

64 See, most recently, De Voto (1988) and Wylie (1992b); cf. Busolt (1908) 259.

65 Busolt (1908) 259; Kaupert (1926) 266.

66 Busolt (1908) 259–260. One major source of contention has been P's fairly detailed itinerary of the march and Xenophon's rather vague description. But what has not been noted is that P's version is the normal route and the one known even to people who had not travelled it (for example Herodotus, see Ramsay (1890) 30 and 60), and Xenophon's is the unusual; see Macan (1895) 250 ad 5.90. Another detail which has been suspected in P is the strategem of Agesilaus involving Xenocles; note esp. Walker (1921) 128: 'the ambush in particular, which figures again in the autumn campaign of Agesilaus, looks like a conventional touch'; similarly Gray (1979) 195–196.

67 *An.* 3.4.19: ἔνθα δὲ οἱ Ἕλληνες ἔγνωσαν πλαίσιον ἰσόπλευρον ὅτι πονηρὰ τάξις εἴη πολεμίων ἑπομένων. Busolt (1908) 262 notes that the Greeks would not have employed the square in precisely the same circumstances again, let alone Xenophon in particular (if he was along, which seems unlikely). Lins (1914) 21 n.1 concurs. See also Kaupert (1926) 267. However, it should be noted in favour of P that because a mistake is made once does not rule out its being made again; indeed, note 6.5.18–19, where Agesilaus, in circumstances similar to the march in the Caustrian plain, makes a similar error.

68 Note that even Bury (1909) 158, a severe critic of Xenophon when compared with P, admits Xenophon's superior knowledge of warfare.

69 It is not important, again, whether Xenophon was present on the march, for he would have had access to first-hand reports of such an important battle. Henry (1967) 202–203 makes much the same type of argument for the opportunities Xenophon missed in describing the defence of Sparta after Mantinea, assuming of course that Xenophon wanted to praise Agesilaus.

70 E.g. Busolt (1908) 263.

NOTES

71 E.g. Grenfell and Hunt (1908) 117, Meyer (1909/1966) 13–15, Rühl (1913) 193, Dugas (1910) 64. Both Meyer (146) and Dugas (92) believe that P's detail comes from a good source, either a day book or camp journal. Bruce accepts this suggestion (1967) 7 and 155.

72 Grenfell and Hunt (1908) 123, Meyer (1909) 13, Dugas (1910) 71 and Nellen (1972) 53. But Henry's caution (1967) 204–205 in citing prejudice as the cause for distortion in Xenophon should be kept in mind.

73 Rühl (1913) 193.

74 Cf. Bengtson (1977) 264 n.1; Breitenbach (1970) 393–395 is also cautious.

75 Cf. the judgment of Sekunda (1988) 175, relying on Xenophon.

76 Dugas (1910) 71 does not consider Busolt's arguments on this point but simply asserts that Xenophon presents a bigger battle. Anderson's criticisms of Nellen, (1974) 49 n. 74, are similar.

77 Cf. 6.4.14.

78 Gray (1979) 198 n. 2 refuting Anderson (1974) 49 n.74.

79 Gray (1979) 188–191.

80 Cf. Grenfell and Hunt (1908) 117 and 214–215. See now Wylie (1992b) esp. 125.

81 For a close analysis of the rhetorical features of this passage, see Bigalke (1933) 8, who considers it an 'unverhüllt epideiktische Stück'. Note especially how Xenophon relies on the adjective μεστός, first referring to the gymnasia teeming with training men, then the marketplace bristling with the instruments of war and finally the camp itself full of good hopes (ἐλπίδες ἀγαθαί). For a similar passage from the *Anabasis*, see *An.* 4.8.27–28, where the Ten Thousand took time out from their march to hold athletic contests in the Persian hinterland.

82 Cf. Usher (1969) 94: 'Xenophon is using his own reminiscences of Agesilaus to propagate his own views on the ideal aims and occupations of man.' See also Wood (1964) 55, Rahn (1971) 499 and n.7 and Powell (1989) 180.

83 Cartledge (1987) 214.

84 Note Grenfell and Hunt (1908) 123: 'the brilliant and showy but ultimately fruitless triumphs of Agesilaus'.

85 Scharr (1919) 58–62; for a similar observation, see Hatzfeld (1936/1939) 1 140 n.2 and Cawkwell (1979) 17.

86 Cf. Scharr (1919) 62.

87 For what follows, cf. Tuplin (1993) 59.

88 Regarding the point at which *Agesilaus* diverges from the *Hellenica* after the battle of Sardis, Opitz (1913) 42 queries whether Xenophon got his information for this passage from P. Opitz rests most of his argument on the similarity of P καὶ τὴν γῆν ἅπασαν ἐπόρθησεν and *Agesilaus* καὶ ἐπόρθει τὰ περὶ τὸ ἄστυ. But this is the sort of activity one can expect after a successful battle near a city, and these are the words one uses. Moreover, if Xenophon had seen P's account, would he not have added the detail about the return of the dead and the

setting up of a trophy? Finally, even if he saw P, Xenophon added Agesilaus' challenge and the vengeance on the Persians.

89 Cf. Luccioni (1947) 195–196 and Delebecque (1957) 465. The two outrages, compelling the Greeks to προσκυνεῖν and claiming honours due to the gods, are closely related; see *An.* 3.2.13 where it seems προσκυνεῖν was a possible form of worship of the gods, but not at all suitable for the honouring of men. Cf. also Isocrates *Pan.* 151.

90 See Cartledge (1987) 65–66 for the argument on the earlier date of the *Agesilaus*. If *Hellenica* 3–7 was composed after the biography (published after Agesilaus' death in 360), then the latter portion of the history had to be composed quickly, seeing that Xenophon probably did not live to the end of the 350s.

91 The *Agesilaus* is commonly regarded as pure encomium. But Hirsch (1985) 51 has argued that the *Agesilaus* is primarily apologetic. He reconstructs (52–53) the major accusations against the king from Plutarch's *Agesilaus* (that Agesilaus let his hatred of Thebes compromise Sparta's interests, e.g. 27.5–6) and Diodorus 15.19.4 (that he surrendered control of Asia to the Persians). On the subject of Xenophon's *Agesilaus* as *apologia*, see Delebecque (1957) 462–470 and Breitenbach (1967) 1702.

92 On the different purposes of the *Hellenica* and the *Agesilaus*, cf. Momigliano's important remarks (1993) 50.

93 Note Breitenbach (1967) 1703 and especially his remarks in (1950) 110: 'Im Enkomion auf Agesilaos hingegen hat Xenophon die Farben des Panhellenismus in stärkstem Maße angewendet.'

94 *Ages.* 1.6: ἐξηγγέλθη βασιλεὺς ὁ Περσῶν ἀθροίζων καὶ ναυτικὸν καὶ πεζὸν πολὺ στράτευμα ὡς ἐπὶ τοὺς Ἕλληνας; cf. 3.4.1: Ἡρώδας τις Συρακόσιος ... ἐξήγγειλε τοῖς Λακεδαιμονίοις ὡς βασιλέως καὶ Τισσαφέρνους τὸν στόλον τοῦτον παρασκευαζομένων· ὅποι δὲ οὐδὲν ἔφη εἰδέναι. In actual fact, the fleet was being assembled for action in the Aegean, and was the one which Conon commanded at Cnidus.

95 Contrast Cawkwell (1976a) 66–67 and Cartledge (1987) 212.

96 Cf. Nilsson (1967) 786–787.

97 Compare Plutarch *Ages.* 16.6 and *Mor.* 211F.

98 On the significance of this passage see de Romilly (1963) 178, Ollier (1933) 415, Gomme (1945–1981) 3 458 and Ronnet (1981).

99 Cf. Macan (1895) ad Hdt. 4.142.1 who notes Herodotus' use 'of making the intelligent foreigner a mouthpiece for home truths'. Here too a foreigner prompts Agesilaus to explain Greek customs; however, Agesilaus' response is not typical of Greek practice. This scene from the *Hellenica* was plagiarized, according to Porphyry, by Theopompus (*FGrHist* 115 T 21 = Porph. ap. Euseb., *Praep. Ev.* 465c).

100 Cf. de Ste. Croix (1972) 160 who cites Xenophon *Ages.* 1.17–19, 2.21–22 and 11.12 in support of his point. For a detailed discussion of φιλία in Xenophon's thought, see Joël (1893–1901) 2.2 1030–1053. It is interesting in this context to note Theopompus' observation (*FGrHist* 115 F 321) on the greatness of Agesilaus 'won more by his excellence than his leadership'—a comment perhaps on

his propensity to put friendship before the good of his country: see below, p. 211.

101 See especially *Ages.* 1.36 and 7.1, cf. Soph. *Ant.* 184–190.

102 *An.* 5.3.5 is testimony enough of Xenophon's own views on ξενία, when years after the adventures of the Ten Thousand he made good a vow to make a dedication for Proxenus at Delphi for the simple reason that 'he had been his friend (ξένος γὰρ ἦν αὐτοῦ)'. We know too that Xenophon was exiled from Athens (*An.* 7.7.57), most likely because of his service with the Spartans (see Diogenes Laertius 2.51, ἐπὶ Λακωνισμῷ φυγὴν ὑπ᾽ Ἀθηναίων κατεγνώσθη), if not for his time in Asia, then certainly after the battle of Coronea where he fought on the Spartan side against the Athenians. Further it should also be remembered that Xenophon benefited personally from his friendship with the Spartans, and probably Agesilaus in particular, for he was given the estate at Scillus for his efforts (*An.* 5.3.7). On these matters, see Breitenbach (1967) 1575 and Cartledge (1987) 60–61.

103 Scharr (1919) 63.

104 Cf. Delebecque (1957) 462–470, Momigliano (1993) 51 and Hirsch (1985) 49.

5 INTRODUCTION TO THE PARADIGM: PHLIUS, THE THIRTY AND THE MODEL COMMUNITY

1 Cf. Breitenbach (1950) 17–22 and 47–60, and Rahn (1971) 498–502.

2 Alcock (1991) 431 and n.21.

3 See Breitenbach (1950) 22, and cf. Immerwahr (1960).

4 Immerwahr (1960) 284 and n.71: he also notes the case of Ambracia (3.113.6).

5 See Jacoby (1923–1958) 2 B 397 ad loc.

6 On the date and authorship, see Usener and Radermacher (1904–1929) 2 xxii–xxvi.

7 Cf. Scheller (1911) 75 and Fornara (1983) 109. Note Thuc. uses παράδειγμα not infrequently (e.g. 5.90, 95).

8 Gomme (1945–1981) 1 149 ad loc.

9 Gomme (1945–1981) 1 150 ad loc.

10 Scheller (1911) 77 and Fornara (1983) 108–109; cf. Barber (1935) 78 and Avenarius (1956) 161.

11 So, Ullman (1942) 28; the notion of 'tragic history' is a hotly debated one: see, e.g., Walbank (1955 and 1960), North (1956), Brink (1960) and Gray (1987b); cf. Murray (1972) 211 with n.2.

12 Walbank (1967) 41 ad loc.

13 Cf. Scheller (1911) 49.

14 Jacoby believes the context for T 23 belongs in one of Ephorus' proems. This does not seem likely to me for the reasons discussed below in the text.

15 On the problem of what κατὰ γένος means, see Drews (1963), Walbank (1972) 100 and n.15 and Fornara (1983) 43.

16 Cf. Barber (1935) 72.
17 See Sacks (1990) 9–22, esp. 10–13 and nn.8–9.
18 Laqueur (1911) esp. 203–204; cf. Andrewes (1985) 190.
19 See Barber (1935) 70 and n.1, citing Laqueur. Cf. Krentz (1982) 139–140 and n.15.
20 Sacks (1990) 43 n.82 concedes that there are close parallels between Diodorus and Isocrates. Nonetheless, he implies that Diodorus' understanding of the fall of empires is in some way fundamentally different. That Diodorus should apply this type of language to other, non-Ephoran sections of his history is not decisive: it is the structure of the preface which is the point at issue. When Diodorus felt the need to use the language of moral evaluation, he relied on a specific set of words; this fact does not affect the issue of when Diodorus elected to use such language. The traditional position that the prefaces of Ephorus provided the inspiration and the substance of the prefaces of Diodorus remains largely intact. Cf. Stylianou (1991) 391.
21 Cf. Andrewes (1985) esp. 190 on Myronides and the battle of Oenophyta.
22 See Grenfell and Hunt (1919) 99 and 107, and esp. Hornblower (1981) 28 and 227.
23 Cf. Fornara (1983) 108.
24 Cf. de Ste. Croix (1981) 608 n.49.
25 Cf. Beloch (1922) 1 180 n.1.
26 For the most recent discussion of the date, see Gehrke (1985) 370–372.
27 Cf. Gehrke (1985) 130–131.
28 Hunter (1927) 227 treats this episode as a first-rate example of a night assault on a city with scaling ladders. Whitehead notes (1990) 196 ad 10.32.12 and 198 ad 10.36.1 that both the firing of the attempted breach of the wall as well as the use of scaling ladders are points which Aeneas discusses.
29 It is instructive to compare also *Hell.* 7.1.32 where Xenophon comments on the same phenomenon of 'mirth-in-tears' at Sparta after news of a victory by Archidamus: 'thus tears are a common thing both to joy and to sorrow'.
30 LSJ assumes a direct allusion, s.v. εἰμί III.
31 Pollux *Onomasticon* 2.64; cf. Gautier (1911) 154, Rhys Roberts (1902) 288 and Underhill (1900) ad loc.
32 Cf. Cawkwell (1979) 370 n.: 'his purpose [for the excursus] is made plain at 7.2.16 and 3.1'.
33 The term can also mean for Xenophon simply 'of noble birth'; cf. *Lac.* 1.8.
34 Cf. Gautier (1911) 167 s.v. ἄλκιμος. Although the word is found ten times in Herodotus and once in Plato – where significantly it is used to introduce the Myth of Er – it is not found in, e.g., Thucydides, Isocrates, Lysias or Demosthenes.
35 See Fränkel (1975) 163 n.11 and 337–339 with n.5; see also in general Scully (1990) esp. 110. Note Aeschylus' epigram, ἀλκὴν . . . εὐδόκιμον (*GVI* 43.3).

278

36 See Dover (1974) 126; note, however, that many of the passages cited there are from Xenophon.

37 See esp. Walsh (1963) 4–16; also Maier (1913) 66 and 324–325, Jaeger (1943) 54, Breitenbach (1950) 62–70, North (1966) 125–132, Nickel (1979) 27–28, Due (1989) 170–181 and most recently Gera (1993) 26–27 and 66–67.

38 See Gigon (1953) 149–150 and Breitenbach (1967) 1793. Giannantoni (1990) 246 notes that Xenophon's views may be derived from Antisthenes on freedom, slavery and *autarkeia* or self-sufficiency: see Giannantoni on Antisthenes F 82–83 and Rankin (1986) 111–114; cf. Joël (1893–1901) 2 46–47 and 561–628, and Maier (1913) 325. In this context it is important to remember that Xenophon tells Prodicus' story of the temptation of Heracles at *Mem.* 2.1.21–34, and Antisthenes wrote about the teachability of virtue in his *Heracles*. Cf. *Ap.* 16–18.

39 Cf. Walsh (1963) 15–16 n.20. Note also Higgins (1977) 25: ἐγκράτεια has for Xenophon a 'civic dimension'.

40 Jacoby (1923–1958) 3 b 1 213 ad loc. even thinks that Ephorus may have been the source for Demon.

41 Cf. Connor (1967) 144–145 and Shrimpton (1991) 136.

42 For the terms of Theopompus' understanding of moral shortcoming, see Pédech (1989) 226–227.

43 Connor (1967) 146; cf. Shrimpton (1991) 165–167. Compare *Mem.* 1.2.20.

44 Cf. Tacitus *Annales* 3.65.2: 'ceterum tempora illa adeo infecta et adulatione sordida fuere, ut non modo primores civitatis, quibus claritudo sua obsequiis protegenda erat, sed omnes consulares, magna pars eorum qui praetura functi multique etiam pedarii senatores certatim exsurgerent foedaque et nimia censerent.' See Syme (1958) 2 545, 562.

45 Cf. Pédech (1989) 221–222.

46 Cf. Connor (1968) 19–76, esp. 64–67; and cf. Meiggs (1972) 130 and n.4 and Shrimpton (1991) 70.

47 See, e.g., Brunt (1993) 179 and cf. 162 n.24.

48 Cf. Breitenbach (1950) 141.

49 Cf. Rhodes' useful survey of the sources (1981) 416–419.

50 Rhodes (1981) 462–464 ad *Ath.* 39.1.

51 This is the prevailing opinion; see, however, Gray (1991): in general, consult the Introduction, p. 14.

52 See Raubitschek (1941) 294–295 and n.29, and esp. Young (1983) 35–40; cf. Lateiner (1989) 40 and see, e.g., Aesch. *A.* 577.

53 Wiseman (1979) 147.

54 For the Athenian tradition of the tyrannicides, see Taylor (1981) and Thomas (1989) 238–282.

55 Thomas (1989) 132–138; cf. Ober (1989) 265. On confusion and levelling, see Thomas (1992) 108–113.

56 Cf. Finley (1983) 102.

57 Rhodes (1981) 482, 10 and 29.

58 For an excellent discussion of the inaccuracies of recent history present in speeches in the fourth century, see Harding (1987).

59 See Rankin (1986) 6–7.
60 Cf. Momigliano (1993) 47.
61 Rhodes (1981) 421.
62 It is widely believed that Socrates' associations with Critias and Charmides led to his trial and execution: see, e.g., Finley (1960) 62–63 and Irwin (1992) 60.
63 Merkelbach and Youtie (1968). There is a considerable bibliography on it and the Theramenean tradition: for the most recent discussion, see Engels (1993).
64 Cf. Harding (1994) 106–108.
65 Jacoby (1923–1958) 3 b 1 96–97 with 3 b 2 91–93 n.86; see also Pearson (1942) 84.
66 Cf. Ostwald (1986) 483.
67 Noticed by Andrewes (1974) 114–115.
68 On the possibility that Xenophon was a member of the three thousand, see Schwartz (1889) 165 = (1956) 141, Cloché (1915) viii–ix and Lenschau (1937) 2355.
69 Cf. Murphy (1989) 48–49.
70 Cf. Krentz (1987).
71 The *Seventh Letter* is often believed to be by Plato, but it may perhaps be the work of a knowledgeable imitator; see, e.g., Dodds (1959) 25 and n.3 and Momigliano (1993) 60–62; cf. Irwin (1992) 83 n.40.
72 It should be noted in this context that Andocides too left the Spartans out of his account of the Thirty (3.10–12): cf. Missiou (1992) 65–66 and n.20.
73 Cf. Ostwald (1986) 481 and the bibliography he cites in n.87. See also above, n.68.
74 Ostwald (1986) 477 and n.69.
75 Cf. Higgins (1977) 103.
76 Cf. [Arist.] *Ath.* 33.2 for an internal explanation of the fall of the 400 (no mention of the forces at Samos). I do not wish to enter into a discussion here of the differences and relative merits of Xenophon and the other accounts of the tyranny. It is enough for me to endorse Ostwald's view (1986) 481, that whether accurate or not, the disputed points of Xenophon's chronology of events – especially the sequence of the request by the Thirty for Spartan aid followed by the execution of Theramenes and then the occupation of Phyle by Thrasybulus – make 'Theramenes' opposition to the Thirty ... principled and born of resentment of their violent, arbitrary methods'.
77 Cf. Christ (1992) 343–346.
78 I have used in part Underhill's translation of this difficult passage (1900) ad loc.
79 Cf. Davies (1978) 189.
80 Cf. Tuplin (1993) 43.
81 Cf. Tuplin (1985) 368–369.
82 Rhodes (1981) 421. I doubt that all or even most of the words Xenophon gives to Theramenes and Critias were actually the precise ones they used, especially in the case of the latter where there obviously was not a tradition preserving his addresses: for a different view see

Usher (1968); against Usher see Gray (1989) appendix. The speeches were probably a mixture of recollection, transcript (real or more likely fabricated) and outright invention. On Theramenes as an advocate of broader franchise, cf. Thuc. 8.89.2.

83 Cf. Breitenbach (1967) 1787.
84 Cf. Gray (1989) 97 and n.6.
85 Cf. Krentz (1982) 145 and Gray (1989) 94.
86 Gray (1989) 96.
87 There is a strange resonance between Critias' description of the πολυανθρωπία of Athens, nurtured by freedom, and Herodotus' famous statement at 5.78: Ἀθηναῖοι μέν νυν ηὔξηντο· δηλοῖ δὲ οὐ κατ' ἓν μοῦνον ἀλλὰ πανταχῇ ἡ ἰσηγορίη ὡς ἐστὶ χρῆμα σπουδαῖον, εἰ καὶ Ἀθηναῖοι τυραννευόμενοι μὲν οὐδαμῶν τῶν σφέας περιοικεόντων ἦσαν τὰ πολέμια ἀμείνους, ἀπαλλαχθέντες δὲ τυράννων μακρῷ πρῶτοι ἐγένοντο. δηλοῖ ὧν ταῦτα ὅτι κατεχόμενοι μὲν ἐθελοκάκεον ὡς δεσπότῃ ἐργαζόμενοι, ἐλευθερωθέντων δὲ αὐτὸς ἕκαστος ἑωυτῷ προεθυμέετο κατεργάζεσθαι. Cf. also Thuc. 8.68.4.
88 There may be a further irony: see below, p. 158.
89 Cf. Higgins (1977) 12 and Gera (1993) 130.
90 The death of Theramenes raises two interesting problems. The first is the toast to Critias. At *DK* 88 B 6 Critias shows a detailed knowledge of Spartan drinking customs which he contrasts with Athenian ones:

καὶ τόδ' ἔθος Σπάρτῃ μελέτημά τε κείμενόν ἐστι
πίνειν τὴν αὐτὴν οἰνοφόρον κύλικα,
μηδ' ἀποδωρεῖσθαι προπόσεις ὀνομαστὶ λέγοντα
μηδ' ἐπὶ δεξιτερὰν χεῖρα κύκλῳ θιάσου

. . .

ἄγγεα Λυδὴ χεὶρ εὗρ' Ἀσιατογενής
καὶ προπόσεις ὀρέγειν ἐπὶ δεξιὰ καὶ προκαλεῖσθαι
ἐξονομακλήδην ᾧ προπιεῖν ἐθέλει.

I wonder if Theramenes' playing κότταβος with the dregs of his hemlock and calling Critias by name (the latter apparently an Athenian custom, see line 8 in poem above, ἐξονομακλήδην) at 2.3.56 was meant to enrage the Laconophile. Usher (1979) has noted this. However, his conclusion that Xenophon could not have invented the episode because of his pro-Spartan sympathies, and hence that it really happened, misses the point. Whether Theramenes really spoke these words or not, Xenophon is casting Theramenes as the opponent of Critias and his violent policies, and his own Spartan leanings must be kept separate from Critias' peculiar brand of phil-Laconism. As to the authenticity of the remark, I think Xenophon would have had less access to information about this event – it took place in prison – than about Theramenes' speech (although Usher himself (1968) 133 doubts that any of Theramenes' speeches were transmitted). My objection to that point is that something must have constituted the Theramenes pamphlet. In addition to meaning 'Here's to the symposiastic authority!',

Theramenes' remark might also suggest that in calling Critias καλός, he is insinuating that Critias is his pathic lover; for a general discussion of καλός and its associations with homosexuality, see Dover (1978) 111–124.

Secondly, and more importantly, why has Xenophon left Socrates out of his account of the Thirty? Diodorus reports that Socrates tried to rescue Theramenes when he sought refuge at the altar (Diod. 14.5.1–2). Xenophon himself mentions Leon of Salamis, another appropriate place to bring Socrates in; cf. Cawkwell (1979) 118 n. In addition, Xenophon does not mention the trial and death of Socrates in the *Hellenica*. These are troubling matters to which I have no answers. See, e.g., Connor (1985) 460.

91 Cf. Dover (1974) 269 and Gera (1993) 273.
92 North (1966) 95–96; cf. Rawson (1969) 30–32. Note, too, that σώφρων could have an oligarchic taint: cf., e.g., Thuc. 8.53.3.
93 Krentz (1982) and Whitehead (1982/1983).
94 Cf. Cawkwell (1979) 113 n., Krentz (1982) 63–68, Whitehead (1982/1983) and Ostwald (1986) 484–485 and n.101.
95 I am excluding Andocides and Plato inasmuch as they are not historical writers.
96 Cf. Tuplin (1993) 45.
97 Cf. Rawson (1969) 30.
98 See, e.g., Krentz (1987).

6 THE PARADIGMATIC INDIVIDUAL

1 For a defence of ancient biography as a fundamentally historical enterprise, cf. Gentili and Cerri (1988) esp. ch. 3.
2 For the peace, see esp. Jacoby (1923–1958) 3 b 1 522–526 (on Philochorus F 151), Cawkwell (1963) and Ryder (1965) 58–63 and 124–126. For other ancient *testimonia* on the peace see Diodorus 15.38.1–4, Philochorus *FGrHist* 328 F 151, Cornelius Nepos *Timotheus* 2.2.
3 Diodorus, who notes that Artaxerxes brought about a peace in Greece so that he could acquire mercenaries for his war against the Egyptians (15.38.1), is now widely believed: see Jacoby's commentary to Philochorus (1923–1958) 3 b 1 522, Ryder (1965) 124 and Cartledge (1987) 378.
4 Cawkwell (1963) 88 and n.39. Beloch (1922) 2 235f. noted the illogical nature of Xenophon's account and made Mnasippus nauarch for 373/2, thereby bringing Xenophon's chronology into line with the one suggested by Philochorus *FGrHist* 328 F 151.
5 Diodorus' account for the events of Corcyra is preferred, although far from satisfactory; see Cawkwell (1963) 85–88. The principal difficulty is the order of events; it is unlikely that Sparta would have attacked a member of the Second Athenian League so quickly. Furthermore, if Timotheus was sent out in response to Mnasippus' attack, his delay is inherently unlikely.

6 So, e.g., Cawkwell (1979) 308–309. See Sordi (1950–1951) 324 for a defence of Xenophon on the grounds that the peace really was short-lived, an argument vitiated by the absence of discussion of Philochorus.

7 See Bruns (1896) 44.

8 Schwartz (1889) 180 = (1956) 158; see also Breitenbach (1950) 78 n.120 and Westlake (1966–1967) 254.

9 Krafft (1967) 142–144.

10 It was Sparta's regular practice to enlist naval support from traditional maritime powers within the Peloponnesian League; see, e.g., Thuc. 2.80.3 and the list of naval allies at Thuc. 2.9.3.

11 As Gautier notes (1911) 169 ἀνθοσμίας is a comic expression. It is particularly associated with the very best wine and hence no doubt luxury – see, e.g., Aristophanes *Frogs* 1150 and Dover (1993) ad loc.

12 See Lycurgus' provisions for controlling the diet of the Spartan army, *Lac.* 2.5.

13 We learn later (6.2.38) that the Corcyraeans have about ninety ships, and we know from 6.2.3 that the Spartans have sixty. I do not see how sixty ships in bad weather can keep ninety trapped in a harbour. Isocrates *Phil.*109 reports that Corcyra possessed eighty ships. On the size of the Corcyraean fleet in the fifth century, see Herodotus 7.168 (sixty vessels at the time of the Persian Wars) and Thucydides 1.25.4 (120 ships at the outbreak of the Peloponnesian War).

14 Vorrenhagen (1926) 84, Underhill (1900) ad loc., Hatzfeld (1936–1939) 2 225 n. to p. 124 and Breitenbach (1950) 127–128 argue that the plea of the Corcyraeans in the *Hellenica* bears a remarkable similarity to their speech at Thucydides 1.33 and 36.

15 See Buckler (1980) 84 on the use of the term here and at 6.5.18.

16 Cloché (1944) 33–34 suggests that the episode is intended to be an emblem of Spartan brutality.

17 Cf. Cartledge (1987) 324, who notes that Mnasippus was 'perhaps over-conditioned by the *agoge* or [was] thinking he was dealing with Helots'. Some comment on Sparta seems to lie behind the passage.

18 Cartledge (1987) 324.

19 This manoeuvre was successfully executed at the first battle of Mantinea, Thuc. 5.73.2. A similar tactic may have been employed on a smaller scale at Thermopylae, Herodotus 7.211.3.

20 On the identification of the Spartans by their supreme discipline in the field, see Rawson (1969) 7, Moore (1975) 115 on *Lac.* 11.7–10 and Cartledge (1987) 324; and note Xenophon *Ages.* 6.4. For an ancient discussion of the ἀναστροφή, see Asclepiodotus 10.1 and 10.3.

21 The aftermath at Corcyra (6.2.25) presents an interesting parallel with 1.1.23; in both cases the secretary to the nauarch (ἐπιστολεύς, 1.1.23; ἐπιστολιαφόρος, 6.2.25) has to take over for the fallen leader; see Pritchett (1974) 46.

22 See Breitenbach (1950) 80 and Krafft (1967) 137.

23 Cf. Agesilaus' competitions at Ephesus, 3.4.16 = *Ages.* 1.25.

24 Iphicrates was evidently famous for his mock battles; see Polyaenus 3.9.32 and Pritchett (1974) 220. Compare Dionysius of Phocaea and his attempt at training the Ionian rebels' fleet (Hdt. 6.12).

25 This is a rough translation; the passage is corrupt in certain points.

26 Note the resemblance of the passage to 6.2.27, πάντα ... εἰς ναυμαχίαν, and more fully to 6.2.30, πάντα ... εἰς ναυμαχίαν καὶ ἠσκηκότες καὶ ἐπιστάμενοι εἰς τὴν ⟨ὑπὸ⟩ τῶν πολεμίων, ὡς ᾤοντο, κατεχομένην θάλατταν ἀφικοῦντο.

27 Breitenbach (1950) 80.

28 The language is similar here to Herodotus 8.106.3: ὑπήγαγον ἐς χεῖρας τὰς ἐμάς, ὥστε σε μὴ μέμψεσθαι τὴν ἀπ' ἐμέο τοι ἐσομένην δίκην.

29 For the family of Jason of Pherae and the chronology of his reign (390–370), see Beloch (1922) 2 80–84.

30 Cf. Bandaret (1919) 41 and Sordi (1950–1951) 329. For the discussion that follows, cf. Tuplin (1993) 117–121.

31 Diodorus discusses him at 15.30.3, 54.5, 57.2, 60.1–2 and 5. He was of some importance to Isocrates' search for a panhellenic commander; see *Archidamus* 119, as well as his letter *To the Children of Jason* 1, where he mentions to the children of Jason his friendship for him. For a discussion of Isocrates' view of Jason, see Mathieu (1925) 100–101.

32 Cf. Vorrenhagen (1926) 81 and Westlake (1966–1967) 253.

33 See Bruns (1896) 44 and Usher (1969) 95.

34 Vorrenhagen (1926) 81 argued that Xenophon sensed he was violating the principles of Thucydides and tried to cover his tracks by having a character in his history indulge his interest in biography. Cawkwell (1979) 302 n. writes, 'Xenophon presents the affairs of Thessaly through the mouth of Polydamas of Pharsalus, perhaps because that is how he knew of them.'

35 Herodotus has Aristagoras describe Persian power to Cleomenes before the Ionian revolt, 5.49–51; Thucydides has Archidamus describe the Athenian national character to the Spartan assembly, 1.80–85.

36 Note especially Breitenbach (1950) 60 on the 'Socratic' virtues of the ideal field commander: 'ein Musterbeispiel dafür ist Iason von Pherai'. Cf. Krafft (1967) 107–108, who notes that Jason has the Socratic ideals of ἄσκησις (6.1.6), φιλοπονία (6.1.6), ἐγκράτεια (6.1.16), ἀγρυπνία (6.1.15) and φιλανθρωπία (6.1.6, 16).

37 See Bruns (1896) 35–45 and esp. Fornara (1983) 34.

38 See Beloch (1922) 2 80–84, for the standard chronology of Jason; caution is required in Beloch's treatment at (1927) 2 236–238, for he believes that Jason's reported conference with Polydamas, and King Cleombrotus' invasion of Phocis reported at 6.1.1, are antedated from 371 and are doublets. For arguments against this view, see Hatzfeld (1936) 447–448 and Gray (1980) 311–312. If Diodorus is to be believed (15.30.3), Jason actually started to interfere in Greek matters in Euboea in 377.

39 Diodorus (15.54.5) mentions that Jason was with the Thebans before Leuctra. Beloch (1922) 1 166 and 2 237 discusses the passages from Xenophon and notes that Jason was an ally of Thebes before Leuctra (see 6.1.10), but he does not mention the Diodorus passage.

40 As Parry showed (1957) 47–57, the antithesis between speech = deceit and act = reality appears early in Greek literature and is widespread; the

antithesis at 6.4.25 would be for Parry a representative of the 'β' type, 'where a clear synonym of [either λόγος or ἔργον] appears' (63). He notes, however, that this antithesis was not regularly observed by fourth-century writers (58).

41 Hyampolis stood in the valley that joined Locris to Phocis and Boeotia; note Thuc. 3.92.6, and cf. Parke (1930) 38–39 and Andrewes (1978) 95–99. For Jason's strategy, see Cartledge (1987) 380.

42 The similarity of Jason's strategy to Philip's, both in keeping the Greek states warring with each other, and in securing the geographic entry points to Greece from the north, has led some scholars to argue for the portrait of Jason to be of Philip 'in disguise' (e.g., Usher (1969) 95), and others to come close to saying the same thing, e.g. Sordi (1950–1951) 332, Hatzfeld (1936–1939) 2.116 n.1, Mathieu (1925) 100 and Cartledge (1987) 308.

43 Xenophon likes this pattern; cf. 6.2.9 and 6.5.47. For a discussion of the structure in Xenophon, see Schacht (1890) 20.

44 Westlake (1935) 99 notes that to have threatened Delphi in such a way would 'at a blow have estranged all the Greek powers, whose friendship he had so assiduously courted'.

45 See Bouché-Leclercq (1880) 178, Parke and Wormell (1956) 211 and Cawkwell (1978) 65.

46 Note the similarity between 6.4.30 and Herodotus 8.36.1: οἱ δὲ Δελφοὶ πυνθανόμενοι ταῦτα [Xerxes' interest in the treasures of the shrine] ἐς πᾶσαν ἀρρωδίην ἀπίκατο, ἐν δείματι δὲ μεγάλῳ κατεστεῶτες ἐμαντεύοντο περὶ <u>τῶν ἱρῶν χρημάτων</u> εἴτε σφέα κατὰ γῆς κατορύξωσι εἴτε ἐκκομίσωσι ἐς ἄλλην χώρην. ὁ δὲ θεός σφεας οὐκ ἔα κινέειν, φὰς <u>αὐτὸς ἱκανὸς εἶναι τῶν ἑωυτοῦ προκατῆσθαι</u>. Underhill (1900) ad 6.4.30, Hatzfeld (1936–1939) 2 146 n.2 and Parke and Wormell (1956) 211 have noted the similarity. Nachtergael (1977) 155 with n.131 adds Aelian fr. 52 (Hercher (BT) 2 209) to 6.4.30: ὁ δὲ Ἰάσων ὁ Θετταλὸς ἐπὶ τοῖς ἀναθήμασιν ἐν Δελφοῖς ἐφλέγετο. ὁ δὲ θεὸς λέγει ἐκείνους μὴ πολυπραγμονεῖν· αὐτῷ γὰρ εἶναι διὰ φροντίδος. All these passages suggest that the oracle responded similarly to external threat.

47 Cf. the murder of Tarquinius Priscus, described in Livy 1.40.5; Ogilvie (1965) 161 ad loc. argues that the story of Jason's death, as well as that of Clearchus (Justin 16.5.15), were well enough known in the third century AD to form the source for the account of the assassination of Tarquinius.

48 Bouché-Leclercq (1880) 178 and Cawkwell (1978) 65 argue that for Xenophon, Jason's assassination is the result of his plan to seize the property of Delphi.

49 See Westlake (1935) 126 on the rapid decline of Pherae as a power.

50 We know this from Plutarch *Pel.* 29.

51 A famous episode: see Diodorus 16.14.1; Cicero, *de Div.* 1.24.53, *de Inv.* 2.144; Plutarch, *Pel.* 35.4–12; Val. Max. 9.13.3.

52 Sordi (1950–1951) 329–332.

53 Sordi (1950–1951) 332.

54 Higgins (1977) 110.

55 *Lac.* 2.3 for ἄσκησις; 2.5, 4.7, 5.8 for φιλοπονία; and 2.7 for ἀγρυπνία.

56 *Ages.* 1.35 = *Hell.* 3.4.16 for ἄσκησις; 1.22 for φιλανθρωπία; 4.3, 5.1, 10.2 for ἐγκράτεια; and 5.3 and 9.3 for φιλοπονία.

57 See, e.g., Immerwahr (1966) 153–154, 306–307 (on Croesus anticipating Xerxes), and especially 148: 'history becomes intelligible only when individual happenings are viewed together as parts of an orderly process. Thus the work of Herodotus mirrors reality not only in the individual λόγος, *but fundamentally also in the perception of the relations between single* λόγοι' (my emphasis).

58 Fornara (1971) 77: note I have combined his n.6 with the relevant passage from the text. See also Immerwahr (1966) 76: 'This is the pattern of the rise and fall of rulers, which is basic for the *logoi* dealing with Croesus, Cyrus, and Darius. This pattern in turn is based on the idea of a reversal of fortune, which is so basic to Herodotus' philosophy of history that he sometimes seems to report on the complete life story of an individual merely to give emphasis to change of fortune.' Cf. Immerwahr (1956) 254–255.

59 Useful comparisons could be made between Jason and, e.g., Lysander, Iphicrates and Euphron; see, e.g., Higgins (1977) 110. Jason's portrait is, however, the most detailed. The *Hieron* of Xenophon is obviously relevant.

7 XENOPHON AND THE DIVINE

1 πολλὰ μὲν οὖν ἄν τις ἔχοι καὶ ἄλλα λέγειν καὶ Ἑλληνικὰ καὶ βαρβαρικά, ὡς θεοὶ οὔτε τῶν ἀσεβούντω οὔτε τῶν ἀνόσια ποιούντων ἀμελοῦσι· νῦν γε μὴν λέξω τὰ προκείμενα. Λακεδαιμόνιοί τε γὰρ οἱ ὁμόσαντες αὐτονόμους ἐάσειν τὰς πόλεις τὴν ἐν Θήβαις ἀκρόπολιν κατασχόντες ὑπ' αὐτῶν μόνων τῶν ἀδικηθέντων ἐκολάσθησαν πρῶτον οὐδ' ὑφ' ἑνὸς τῶν πώποτε ἀνθρώπων κρατηθέντες, τούς τε τῶν πολιτῶν εἰσαγαγόντας εἰς τὴν ἀκρόπολιν αὐτοὺς καὶ βουληθέντας Λακεδαιμονίοις δουλεύειν τὴν πόλιν, ὥστε αὐτοὶ τυραννεῖν, τὴν τούτων ἀρχὴν ἕπτα μόνον τῶν φυγόντων ἤρκεσαν καταλῦσαι. ὡς δὲ τοῦτ' ἐγένετο διηγήσομαι. The asyndeton of the sentence Λακεδαιμόνιοι ... καταλῦσαι is remarkable. Note also the marked alliteration in the phrases ἀσεβούντων/ἀνοσια/ἀμελοῦσι and κατασχόντες/ἐκολάσθησαν/κρατηθέντες.

2 For recent reactions to Xenophon's belief in the divine as historical agent see especially Cawkwell (1979) 45, Cartledge (1987) 65; cf. Luccioni (1953) 137.

3 For further discussion of Xenophon's contemporaries and their attitudes toward religion, see below, pp. 224–225 and nn.77–85.

4 See above, pp. 36–38.

5 Cf. the illuminating remarks of Momigliano (1977) 165.

6 Jacoby (1913) 479; Focke (1927) 57; Fornara (1971) 77–78. Note that Gould (1989) ch. 4 has reasonably cautioned that Herodotus had an

overdetermined system of causation; that discrete instances of divine intervention should be distinguished from beliefs about causation generally; and that Herodotus' most important tool for explaining why things happen is the notion of reciprocal action. Such an understanding of Herodotus, while technically at odds with the views I have mentioned, is still usefully comparable with the picture of Xenophon I am advocating.

7 Van Seters (1983) especially 360–361. Note especially his perceptive comments on 52: 'But the themes of divine providence, of retribution and salvation, and the use of the past as a mirror for present and future events in order to deal with the problem of change appear to be basic concerns addressed by both [the Hebrew and Greek] historiographic traditions and constitute a major motivation for their existence.'

8 Cf. Higgins (1977) 102.

9 See Bruit Zaidman and Schmitt Pantel (1992) 124–125. Cf. Diogenes Laertius 2.49–50 and Cicero *Div.* 1.54.122.

10 Fontenrose (1978) 43. Note that Socrates uses oracular language in his reproof of Xenophon; on the frequency of λῷον in sacred language, see Gautier (1911) 194–195.

11 Nilsson (1967) 788 notes the incredible number of sacrifices reported by Xenophon in the *Anabasis.* Cf. Riedinger (1991) 249.

12 Mikalson (1983) 38.

13 See *An.* 2.5.7; cf. Dover (1974) 249–250 and note Joël (1893–1901) 1 102: 'die wichtigste Erscheinungsform der ἀσέβεια ist für Xenophon der Eidbruch'.

14 On Xenophon as a reformer of traditional attitudes towards the divine, see especially Dodds (1973) 7; see also Solmsen (1942) 51 and Festugière (1949) 91.

15 See West (1988) 217 ad *Od.* 4.379–381. Cf. *Od.* 11.573–574.

16 ἐγγὺς γὰρ ἐν ἀνθρώποισιν ἐόντες/ἀθάνατοι φράζονται. On the gods as hidden observers, note also *Od.* 10.574, where the gods are described as moving so quickly that humans cannot perceive them. Cf. Euripides *Ba.* 392–394.

17 I borrow the term 'optimistic rationalist' from Mastronarde (1986) 202. On Euripides and the crisis of belief in the last quarter of the fifth century, see Reinhardt (1957) and Dodds (1973) 78–91. See above, n.9, and Jaeger (1947) 165–171 and 176–179 (243 n.59 on the prayer of Hecuba in Euripides' *Suppliants*). On Xenophon's relationship to the sophists, see, e.g., Nestle (1940) and Classen (1984). On the variety of religious attitudes in late fifth-century Athens, see Burkert (1992) 267.

18 Theiler (1924) 14–54; see also Jaeger (1947) chs 9 and 10.

19 Cf. Sandbach (1985) 480.

20 I borrow this list from Gigon (1953) as condensed by Laks (1983) 257. On Xenophon as illustrative of a general intellectual climate, see, e.g., Solmsen (1942) 58 n.17, Laks (1983) 250–257 and Gulley (1968) 189.

21 Kerferd (1981) 39. Cf. *Mem.* 4.7.6, where Xenophon also describes Socrates' disdain for cosmological thinkers, especially Anaxagoras.

22 Irwin (1974) 410; see now especially Vlastos (1991) 161–162 with n.26. Note, however, the cautions of Morrison (1987) 16.

23 Nilsson (1969) 77 believes that Aristodemus is representative of what was widespread 'unbelief . . . among the educated'.

24 See Festugière (1949) 79. On the passage from the *Laws* see Lloyd (1987) 47–49 and nn.161 and 163.

25 Gigon (1953) 141 noted that Xenophon's mention here of both cities and races is meant, like his reference to 'all men' warned by gods, to embrace all human beings, both Greek (whose major population division is the city) and barbarian (whose major division is the tribe).

26 See Gauthier (1976) ad loc.

27 Egyptian piety, Herodotus 2.37.1; Egyptian antiquity, Herodotus 2.2 and 2.142. Cf. also Plato *Ti.* 22b, Aristotle *Pol.* 1329b and Diodorus 1.101.

28 Cf. Aeschylus *A.* 750–756, and note Dover (1974) 254.

29 Cf. Riedinger (1991) 251. On Xenophon and the shift from the anthropomorphic divine to the invisible *demiourgos*, see Solmsen (1942) 51.

30 See, e.g., Hesiod *Op.* 267. The connection between *Mem.* 1.4.17 and Hesiod was noted by Gigon (1953) 118. Cf. Homer *Il.* 15.80–83.

31 Cf. Rankin (1986) 98.

32 Dodds (1973) 7–8; on the possible connection between the Socrates of Xenophon and Zeno the Stoic regarding the design of the human and nature, especially in connection with *Mem.* 1.4.8, see, e.g., Schofield (1980) 303. It is interesting to note that Lincke in 1906 argued that Socrates' proof of the divine from the argument from design was a later, stoic addition; cf. Morrison (1987) 16. For a careful general description of a 'stoic historian', with interesting resonances with Xenophon, see Colish (1985) 290–292 who cites Verbeke (1964).

33 Evidently a proverbial expression; see Aeschylus *Pr.* 447–448, *A.* 1623 and Demosthenes 25.89. Cf. Plato *Ap.* 23a on the worthlessness of human wisdom.

34 See, e.g., Thuc. 1.18.1, and cf. Ferguson (1975) 29. Cf. the Greeks' admiration for the stability of Egypt and its customs, e.g. Hecataeus of Abdera *FGrHist* 264 F 25 = Diod. 1.69.2–4 with Murray (1970) 150.

35 This was, of course, not true, but all part of the 'Spartan mirage': see Ollier (1933) and esp. Andrewes (1938).

36 *Lac.* 1.1.

37 Cf. Tigerstedt (1965) 112: 'Leuctra and Mantinea made an indelible impression on contemporary opinion. For friend and foe alike, those who envied her and those who admired [Sparta], it was a world which had vanished.'

38 The bibliography on the authenticity of *Lac.* 14 is enormous. See above, pp. 15–16 and n.35.

39 See, e.g., Andrewes (1938), Rawson (1969) 14, Goodman and Holladay (1986) 152–160 and Parker (1989) 161–162. Cf. Demaratus' famous words, Hdt. 7.104.4–5.

40 This is, of course, an exaggeration; see below, p. 222 and n.72.

41 I am aware of Cartledge's difficulty with this kind of analysis (1987) 62. In reply, I would point out that omission in the *Hellenica* is not the result of an artistic sense of continuity; I am trying to suggest that it is

rather the result of the way Xenophon's mind worked. For a different explanation of Sparta's fall, see Cawkwell (1983).

8 *HELLENICA* BOOK 5 AND THE CRIMES OF SPARTA

1 Büchsenschütz (1859) 518 and n.20, Persson (1915) 89–90, Münscher (1920) 165–166 n.6 and Hatzfeld (1930) 124, who observe that Harpocration s.v. Θέογνις (*Hell.* 2.3.2) reports this name occurring in Book 2 (ἐν β' 'Ελληνικῶν), and πενέσται (*Hell.* 2.3.36) in Book 3 (ἐν γ' 'Ελληνικῶν); see also Dover, Andrewes and Gomme (1945–1981) 5 438.

2 See Norden (1909) 101–103, Cawkwell (1979) 33–35 and especially Henry (1967) 191: 'his unaffected manner is too often deceptive and easily leads us to conclude that because it is simple it is also transparent or because it is candid it is uncontrived'.

3 Cawkwell (1973) 57; cf. Connor (1985) 460 and Cartledge (1987) 62.

4 Cawkwell (1973) 64; cf. p. 7 and n.6, and n.88 below.

5 Cawkwell (1976b).

6 Cf. Volquardsen (1868) 72–80 and Westlake (1986) 406.

7 Cawkwell (1979) 245 n.

8 Cawkwell (1979) 79 n. and 249–250 n., Cartledge (1987) 195. For a general comparison between both the Callicratidas and Teleutias scenes, see Henry (1967) 60–61 n.132. For a recent study of Callicratidas, see Ronnet (1981).

9 Breitenbach (1967) 113 n.30. See also de Romilly (1963) 178, Ollier (1933) 415 and Gomme, Andrewes and Dover (1945–1981) 3 458.

10 See, e.g., Cawkwell (1979) 250 n.

11 De Ste. Croix (1972) 161–162.

12 Cf. Tuplin (1993) 83.

13 For recent discussions of this attempted peace, see Hamilton (1979) 233–259, Jehne (1991) and Badian (1991) 26–34, and see below, n.23.

14 Cf. the astute though tendentious reasoning of an early student of the Peace, Aelius Aristides, *Pan.* 172, who skilfully suggests that Sparta was forced to make peace with Persia (and thereby admit her inferiority to Athens), for to imagine them as traitors to the Greeks (that is voluntary advocates of the Peace) is unimaginable.

15 Note also Hippocrates' desperate letter to Sparta after the death of Mindarus at Cyzicus, 1.1.23.

16 Badian (1987/1993) 41–42 argues that the text as Xenophon has it is in accord with Achaemenid imperial formulae; he also asserts, however, that the phrase 'the great and the small' (the order in the Greek is the other way around) is a Spartan formula, (1991) 35–36. Can the document be both? See Perlman (1976) 9.

17 The most important contributions towards determining the possible terms of the King's Peace have been made by Cawkwell, especially (1973) 52–56 and (1981). For recent attempts to modify his views, see Clark (1990) and Badian (1991).

NOTES

18 For the first view, which concentrates on the peace as an abandon-
ment of the Asian Greeks, see Isocrates *Pan.* 180, Demosthenes 15.29
and 23.140, Diodorus 14.110.4, Plutarch *Art.* 21.2 and *Ages.* 23.1,
Aelius Aristides 13.172; this view often connects the King's Peace
with the Peace of Callias. For the second view, stressing Sparta's
subsequent disregard for the autonomy of Greek states, see again
Isocrates *Pan.* 126 and Diodorus 15.1.3 and 15.20.2, as well as
Theopompus *FGrHist* 115 F 103.7 (on which see Shrimpton (1977)
128) and Polybius 4.27.4–7. Could the fact that both views are
present in Diodorus reflect Isocrates' influence on Ephorus? There
seems little doubt that Diodorus and Polybius share a similar source,
in all likelihood Ephorus; but as Walbank suggests (1957) 476 and
(1972) 79 n.72, Polybius may be using a source used by Ephorus,
namely Callisthenes. If that is true, then Isocrates' authority for
Ephorus on this matter would seem questioned. Note that
Callisthenes started his history with the King's Peace, *FGrHist* 124 F
27a = Diodorus 14.117.8.
19 Lewis (1977) 147; cf. Andrewes (1945–1981) 4 55 and Badian
(1991) 37 and n.25.
20 Notably Badian (1991) 37–39. Another inscription, the so-called
Charter of the Second Athenian Confederation or the Decree of
Aristoteles (Tod 123), may also contain a reference to the Great King
swearing an oath to uphold the Peace, but the restoration is widely
doubted.
21 Thebes has been left out of this list.
22 Note that Ἑλλήνων in the text of Diodorus is Dindorf's correction
of ἄλλων.
23 I am indebted to Cawkwell (1981) 69–71 for this reconstruction.
The texts relating to the peace negotiations of 392/1 are Xenophon
Hell. 4.8.12–15, Philochorus *FGrHist* 328 F 149 and Andocides *Or.*
3. A main problem I see with this peace is determining precisely when
the Athenians expressed their refusal to give up the Greeks of Asia to
the Great King, and how this refusal relates to the formal break-off
of negotiations. Presumably the order of events would have been
something as follows: the Persians indicate their wishes first (that is
the surrender of the Asiatic Greeks); the Athenians hear this and then
break off negotiations at Sardis. Consequently it is safe to assume that
the Athenian ambassadors knew that the Athenians were unwilling to
surrender their Ionian brothers. But we know that the ambassadors
later get into trouble with the Athenians after they agree to the Great
King's demands at Sparta. Perhaps the first demand at Sardis was
never communicated to the Athenian people, and only later when the
ambassadors tried to convince them to ratify the peace after the
Sparta conference did this concession to the Great King come out
into the open. Cf. Thuc. 5.18.1.
24 Cf. Andrewes, Dover and Gomme (1945–1981) 5 165 on
αὐτοκράτορας.
25 Cf. Cawkwell (1973) 52.
26 See Badian (1991) 39.

27 Badian (1991) 40.
28 Cawkwell (1981) 79; cf. Badian (1991) 41.
29 The precise meaning of the Greek word αὐτονομία is difficult to establish; see Gomme (1945–1981) 1 384–385, Bickerman (1958), Ostwald (1982) and Sealey (1993) 241–244. Bickerman argued (336–337) that ἐλευθερία refers to the sovereignty of a state *jure naturali* or φύσει, and hence is not found to describe the acts of states; αὐτονομία, on the other hand, which exists *jure gentium* or νόμῳ, is descriptive of the acts of a state and hence used to refer to the relations between states. Ostwald refined Bickerman's argument by suggesting that the origin of the term αὐτονομία is to be found not in the relations of Greek cities in Asia Minor to external powers there, but in the relations of members of the Delian League. But whatever its precise meaning, it is clear that the term applied to a sovereign state's ability to govern itself by a constitution of its own choosing. Cf. Brunt (1993) 12.
30 Badian (1991) 42–43.
31 Cawkwell (1979) 256 n.
32 See Harding (1985) 44 no. 30 n.1. Note Diodorus on the short interval of time between the ratification of the Peace and the first breach (15.5.3).
33 Cartledge (1987) 258–259.
34 Cawkwell (1981) 70, 77–78.
35 Badian (1991) 44 n.39.
36 Cawkwell (1979) 258 n.
37 Badian (1991) 45 believes that the dioecism would not have happened if the Mantineans had agreed to demolish their walls.
38 As mentioned above, according to Diodorus (15.5.5) Mantinea appealed to Athens for help. We learn from Pausanias (9.13.1) and Plutarch (*Pel.* 4) that Thebes sent help to the Spartans; cf. Cartledge (1987) 259.
39 See Finley (1983) 42–43 and Cartledge (1987) 259.
40 Cf. Tuplin (1993) 87–90.
41 Cf. Tuplin (1993) 90–93.
42 Cf. Badian (1991) 44.
43 See Smith (1953–1954) 279–280.
44 Cartledge (1987) 265–266.
45 Cf. Perlman (1964) 75, who selects Sparta's relations with Phlius before and after the King's Peace to document a fundamental change in Spartan policy.
46 Badian (1991) 46.
47 Cf. Badian (1991) 47 n.44.
48 For what follows, cf. Tuplin (1993) 93–96.
49 For the problems in identifying precisely who was in the audience when Cleigenes spoke, see de Ste. Croix (1972) 341.
50 The term Xenophon uses for 'independent citizens' here is αὐτοπολῖται, a correction by Valesius of αὐτοὶ πολῖται. The word is a *hapax legomenon*: see Gautier (1911) s.v.
51 See especially Cawkwell (1981) 79 and Badian (1991) 44.

52 See, e.g., de Ste. Croix (1972) 341 and Cartledge (1987) 270.
53 Cf. Badian (1991) 44: 'Sparta was entitled to declare war on Olynthus, just as any Greek city had always been entitled to declare war on any other, unless there were oaths between them preventing it.'
54 Cartledge (1987) 147–148.
55 For Sparta's treatment of Thebes and what this might represent for Xenophon, cf. Tuplin (1993) 96–100.
56 Xenophon elsewhere views with horror attacks made during religious events: see *Hell.* 4.4.3. The celebration of the Thesmophoria in particular seems to have been a difficult and anxious time for Greek cities; cf. Hdt. 6.16.
57 De Ste. Croix (1972) 135.
58 Diodorus 15.20.2, Polybius 4.27.4, Plutarch *Mor.* 576a, *Ages.* 23.11, *Pel.* 6.1.
59 For a different view, see Hamilton (1991) 139–149.
60 See Finley (1968) 155.
61 Note the extraordinary passage at Xenophon *Ages.* 1.36.
62 Cf. the nearly parallel case of Clearchus, who is ordered to return to the Isthmus after being sent out to Thrace, and who refuses to comply and is condemned to death (*An.* 2.6.4); note also Clearchus' tyranny at Byzantium and the Spartans' attempt to stop it, Diodorus 14.12.4–7.
63 Cawkwell (1979) 266 n.
64 Cf. Cartledge's excellent discussion (1987) 296–297.
65 Schwartz (1889) 171 n.1 = (1956) 147 n.3. Cf. Scharr (1919) 58 and von Fritz (1968) 565.
66 Cf. Tigerstedt (1965) 172.
67 De Ste. Croix (1972) 17–18 notes that this attitude was not unusual in the Greek world.
68 Henry (1967) 163.
69 Cf. Xenophon's evaluation of Clearchus, *An.* 2.6.9.
70 Breitenbach (1967) 1684; cf. Cartledge (1987) 298.
71 Diodorus' list does not mention disloyal allies.
72 This is, of course, an exaggeration; and while Xenophon may perhaps be excused for neglecting earlier Spartan defeats, he himself recorded the Spartan disasters at Haliartus (3.5.17ff.) and Lechaeum (4.5.10ff.); indeed, for the latter defeat he states that failure on the battlefield was 'not usual' for the Spartans, which is not to say 'unheard of'. It should be noted too that Xenophon also records a number of significant naval setbacks prior to 371, chief among them Cnidus (4.3.10ff.).
73 The phrase Ἑλληνικὰ καὶ βαρβαρικά recalls the proems of Herodotus and Thucydides: τὰ μὲν Ἕλλησι, τὰ δὲ βαρβάροισι ἀποδεχθέντα, ἀκλεᾶ γένηται, τά τε ἄλλα καὶ δι' ἣν αἰτίην ἐπολέμησαν ἀλλήλοισι (Hdt. 1.Proem); cf. κίνησις γὰρ αὕτη μεγίστη δὴ τοῖς Ἕλλησιν ἐγένετο καὶ μέρει τινὶ τῶν βαρβάρων, ὡς δὲ εἰπεῖν καὶ ἐπὶ πλεῖστον ἀνθρώπων (Thuc. 1.1.2). Cf. Plato *R.* 423a. These passages set out for the reader the major theme of each work and the

collocations Ἕλλησι . . . βαρβάροισι and τοῖς Ἕλλησιν . . . μέρει τινὶ τῶν βαρβάρων describe not only the participants in the respective conflicts, they also give universal scope to the events about to be treated: the whole world is the show-place of the Persian and Peloponnesian Wars. But, unlike his great predecessors, Xenophon uses the collocation to give universal importance to what is essentially an exemplary action; the Cadmea episode is representative of Sparta's foreign policy from the time of the King's Peace. Cf. Dietzfelbinger (1992) 141.

74 See above, p. 20 and n.7.

75 Barber (1935) 100.

76 Ephorus did not treat the two battles together, unless he brought up both in a single preface; cf. Barber (1935) 71. Unprecedented Spartan disaster, cf. Thuc. 5.14.3.

77 For what follows, cf. Momigliano (1990) 44.

78 On Ephorus and the rationalizing of myth see Barber (1935) 144–148.

79 See Connor (1968) 123 with n.18 and Lane Fox (1986) 114; cf. von Fritz (1941) 786. Shrimpton (1991) 133 suggests that Theopompus' interests in the divine were primarily antiquarian. Note the wording of Theon of Smyrna *Prog.* 2 = *FGrHist* 115 F 74a, referring to the story of Silenus (F 75; see above, pp. 45–46): 'there are fine examples of the recounting (διηγήσεως) of mythical stories . . . [e.g.] the story of Silenus found in the eighth book of Theopompus' *Philippika*'. Curiously, Theopompus does provide an extensive report of omens that preceded the fall of Dionysius, F 331.

80 See esp. Jacoby (1949) 141 and Pearson (1942) 20.

81 To be fair, it should be pointed out that Thucydides did disapprove of the breaking of oaths, and perhaps for religious reasons: see de Ste. Croix (1972) 20. But cf. Hornblower (1992).

82 It is difficult to determine Diodorus' source here, or even if he had an outside source: cf. Volquardsen (1868) 83, Schwartz (1903) 682, Jacoby (1923–1958) 3 b 500–502 with 3 b (*Noten*) 300 n.37 and Pearson (1987) 189 with n.108.

83 On the important role played by Herodotus in the development of Hellenistic historiography, see Murray (1972).

84 As Sacks notes (1990) 36–37 n.56, there is a disproportionate number of references to the divine in Book 16 of Diodorus, explained primarily by the fact that they are found in connection with the Phocian sack of Delphi. Again, if there is an external source here, and if it was contemporary with Xenophon, we would have another useful parallel.

85 See Parke (1939) 82. One may also want to add Athenian hostility towards Megara because of perceived impiety in 350/49: see Brunt (1993) 14, de Ste. Croix (1972) 254 and Connor (1962).

86 Due (1989) 93 and Tatum (1989) 86. Cf. Plato *Euthphr.* 13a on the θεραπεία of the gods.

87 Cf. modern historians' reactions, e.g. de Ste. Croix (1972) 162: 'after the King's Peace Sparta, her fortunes at the highest level they had ever

reached, showed herself at her most aggressive, and her policy, under Agesilaus' leadership, was consistent. The crowning folly was the occupation of the Cadmeia of Thebes and, when that city was liberated at the end of 379, the unrelenting pressure which Sparta exercised upon Thebes, under the influence of Agesilaus, right down to 371, when the battle of Leuctra marked the beginning of Sparta's great decline.'

88 Thus Cawkwell's observation on the omission of the foundation of the Second Athenian Confederation (1973) 57: 'the silences of Xenophon have ceased merely to amaze; they have become a scandal'.

89 Cartledge (1987).

90 On the traditional nature of this phrase, see Gray (1981) 331. That the phrase is typical of the start of traditional tales, see Aly (1928) 258. Note also some examples from the *Aesopica*: ἄνθρωπός τις ἦν πένης, ὃς καὶ ξύλων γόμον ἐπὶ τῶν νώτων ἐβάσταζε (Perry (1952) 529 no. 2); ἦν τις ἀνὴρ . . . (Perry 493). Cf. Aesch. *A.* 577. Aly (1929) 74 notes that Plato is also aware of the formula; see *Phaedrus* 237b, ἦν οὕτω δὴ παῖς . . . τούτῳ δ' ἦσαν. To this may also be added *Gorgias* 523a, ἦν οὖν νόμος ὅδε, and *Protagoras* 320c, ἦν γάρ ποτε χρόνος, both passages occurring in contexts where a story (μῦθος) is clearly being told: see Dodds (1959) 376 at 523a1 and Taylor (1976) 76 at 320c2–4, respectively. For Herodotean examples, see 3.4.1 and 1.6.1.

91 The very vagueness of the phrase raises suspicion; the reader knows that whatever the business is for which Phillidas came to Athens, it will only be the pretext for a more meaningful event which contributes directly to the story-line. Herodotus provides two interesting parallels. At 8.106.1 Hermotimus happens to go to Mysia on 'some matter' (καταβὰς κατὰ δή τι πρῆγμα) precisely when the man who castrated him as a youth also happens to be there, and he takes his revenge; at 9.89.3 Artabazus, in order to avoid the suspicion of the Thessalians, explains that he is leaving Greece in such a hurry 'having been sent out on some business' (πεμφθεὶς κατὰ τι πρῆγμα), not because the Persians have been beaten.

92 See Burkert (1979) 75 who connects the Herodotus and Xenophon passages in his discussion of the transformation of the 'virgin scapegoat' motif.

93 Gray (1989) 73. For discussions of Xenophon's relation to Herodotus, see, e.g. Keller (1910/1911), Riemann (1967) 20–27 and Brown (1990).

94 See Hooker (1989) 128.

95 Cleombrotus was suspected of being pro-Theban partly because of his two dilatory campaigns against them, 5.4.15 and 5.4.59; Smith (1953/1954) 280–285 argued that Cleombrotus led a group at Sparta in opposition to Agesilaus' anti-Theban faction – the same group that supported his brother Agesipolis and their father, Pausanias – see Hatzfeld (1936–1939) 2 138 n.5 and de Ste. Croix (1972) 134 and 140. Cawkwell (1976a) 79 moderates this view, arguing that Cleombrotus did not blindly support Thebes but rather was more a supporter of 'diplomacy and alliance', and cites Polybius 9.23.7 effectively. See also Breitenbach (1950) 117.

96 Most notably Cawkwell, esp. (1973) and (1979) 285 n. Cf. Connor
     (1985) 460. For the raid of Sphodrias, see Marshall (1905) 12–13,
     Accame (1941) 23–30, Cargill (1981) 57–59 and Kallet-Marx (1985).
97 Cf. Cawkwell (1979) 285 n.
98 See Cawkwell (1973); for a recent treatment of the issues involved in
     the vexed dating of the formation of the Second Athenian
     Confederation relative to the raid of Sphodrias, see Clark (1990). Cf.
     also Kallet-Marx (1985).
99 Cf. de Ste. Croix (1972) 134.
100 Bandaret (1919) 33 believes that this statement, with its negative
     colouring, represents a change in Xenophon's source on the episode,
     implying that on the whole we see Agesilaus in a positive light. I cannot
     agree; indeed, such a division of the narrative into units of source mate-
     rial reflects more what is convenient for the modern scholar than what
     may have been true for Xenophon's materials and method.
101 Cawkwell (1979) 279 n.
102 Forrest (1968) 127. For a different view of the failure of Sparta, see
     Cawkwell (1983).
103 Cawkwell (1979) 289 n.; he cites Agesilaus' refusal of command
     against Mantinea, but not the more relevant refusal at 5.4.13.
104 There is a serious omission here of the attempted peace of 375; see
     Cawkwell (1979) 297 n. and above, p. 165 and n.2.
105 Cf. Fornara (1983) 106 and Higgins (1977) 102.
106 I borrow the phrase from Sordi (1950–1951) 336–339.
107 Cf. Gould's remarks regarding causation in Herodotus (1989) 80:
     'to understand Herodotus' thinking about divinity we need to
     distinguish between supernatural explanations of specific events
     which befall specific individuals, and a general theory of historical
     causation'. Xenophon's divine would fit the latter, not the former
     description.

CONCLUSION

1 Cf. Breitenbach (1967) 1870.
2 Note esp. Breitenbach (1950).
3 Dalfen (1976) 60; see also Buckler (1982) 182–183.
4 See 6.3.2 and 6.5.33.
5 Of course, organization of speeches in groups of three goes back at least
    to Homer (the Embassy to Achilles in *Il.* 9).
6 For Herodotus I am thinking particularly of the debate of the Persian
    conspirators at 3.80–82 and the Persian council before the invasion of
    Greece, 7.8–11; for Thucydides, the debate between Nicias and
    Alcibiades before the Sicilian expedition, 6.3–26: cf. Aly (1929)
    102–103. It should also be noted that in the *Anabasis* Xenophon, at the
    crucial assembly after the murder of the generals, has three speakers,
    3.2.2–32. Note Vorrenhagen (1926) 97: 'quod vero tres orationes non
    seiungendas Xenophon hoc Hellenicorum loco una inseruit, in memo-
    riam nostram redigunt cum Thucydidem tum Herodotum'.

NOTES

7 Mosley (1962) 41–46 and more generally (1973) 43–47 argues in favour of the list of ambassadors as printed by all editors. Tuplin (1977) 51–56 argues that Leonclavius' emendation is wrong, and that the only ambassador honoured with a patronym was Callias, increasing the number to ten. Whitehead (1988) 146 restores the patronym to Autocles.
8 See Vorrenhagen (1926) 96–97.
9 Cf. in general Pearson (1947).
10 Further the speech is self-congratulatory, in keeping with Xenophon's warning that Callias enjoyed praising himself. Callias makes a great deal out of his family's ties with Sparta, and furthermore, the myth he tells concerns the mysteries of Demeter; as an Eleusinian official himself, this makes the foundation myth of the cult he supervises the basis for peace between Athens and Sparta! Cf. Isocrates *Pan.* 28.
11 Autocles is described as μάλα δοκῶν ἐπιστρεφὴς εἶναι ῥήτωρ (6.3.7). The important word here is ἐπιστρεφής; translated as 'accomplished' or even 'attentive', the context demands a meaning closer to δεινὸς λέγειν with its associations not only of ability but also awesome persuasive power. Cf. Breitenbach (1950) 29–30, who compares this introduction to those of Pericles at Thuc. 1.139.4 and Theramenes at Thuc. 8.68.4.
12 Cf. Luccioni (1947) 188, and contrast Dalfen (1976) 70.
13 See esp. Vorrenhagen (1926) 91 on Autocles: 'orator enim importunissimus videtur esse . . . re vera orator videtur ἐπιστρεφής, ut ait Xenophon (6.3.7). Sed ad animos Lacedaemoniorum conciliandos Autoclis verba sane apta non sunt.'
14 Cf. Vorrenhagen (1926) 97.
15 Cf. Vorrenhagen (1926) 95.
16 Compare Isocrates *Pan.* 16.
17 The word 'to learn' is used only twice in the *Hellenica*; here at 6.3.11, and at 5.3.7–the analysis of the failure and death of Agesilaus' brother, Teleutias: see above, pp. 219–220.
18 Cf. Gauthier (1976) 208 ad loc., and Dillery (1993) 6.
19 Cf. Dillery (1993) 10.
20 The man is Prothous and his identity is something of a mystery. He was perhaps an ephor or a member of the Gerousia. He is found only here and at Plutarch *Ages.* 28. Poralla (1913/1985) 169 thinks him an ephor; de Ste. Croix (1972) 129 n.104 finds no grounds for this view. Cartledge (1987) 307–308 suggests that he was one of the Gerousia or one of the Pythioi. Vorrenhagen (1926) 99 notes sensibly that the indefinite is not present in the introduction to him, indicating that he was probably a known figure. Forrest (1968) 130 and Cawkwell (1976a) 56 are non-committal. He should be compared with Herodotus' Solon (1.32), Croesus (1.207, 3.36), Artabanus (7.10, 7.46–49), Demaratus (7.102, 104) and Artemisia (7.68), to name a few. For discussions of the Herodotean 'tragic warner' see Bischoff (1932), Lattimore (1939) and Immerwahr (1966) 73–78.
21 Cf. Riedinger (1991) 251.
22 Cf. Marshall (1905) 109–115 and Cargill (1981) 161–188.

23 Compare 6.5.33 with Thucydides 1.72.1.
24 Cf. Hignett (1952) 197.
25 Dalfen (1976) 64. Cf., however, Ar. *Lys.* 1141–1156.
26 See Loraux (1986) 69 and 83. Cf. Hdt. 9.27; Isocrates *Pan.* 54–70, *Panath.* 168ff., 193ff.; Plato *Mx.* 239; [Lysias] 2.3; [Dem.] 60.8.
27 Dover (1974) 193–194.
28 Cf. de Romilly (1958).
29 I do not discuss the joint hegemony of Sparta and Athens that Procles advocates later in his second speech (7.1.2–11). Obviously it has much in common with what Callistratus argues earlier.
30 Cf. Tuplin (1993) 117.
31 Cf. Schwartz (1889) and Hornblower (1987) 153.
32 I am thinking of passages such as Solon's mention of Tellus, and Cleobis and Biton in Herodotus, and the portraits of Pausanias and Themistocles in Thucydides. Alcibiades approaches in Thucydides the role the individual plays in Xenophon.
33 Cf. Fornara (1983) 33.
34 Briant (1987) 29 has summed up the problem nicely in connection with Xenophon's and Isocrates' attitudes towards the Persian empire.
35 See Diogenes Laertius 2.55 and 5.22.
36 Cf. Wycherley (1957) 27 no. 30 and Camp (1986) 105–107.
37 For this information, see Camp (1986) 106–107.

BIBLIOGRAPHY

Accame, S. (1941) *La lega ateniese del sec. IV a.c.*, Rome: Signorelli.
Alcock, S.E. (1991) 'Urban Survey and the *Polis* Phlius', *Hesperia* 60: 421–463.
Aly, W. (1928) 'Märchen', *RE* 27: 254–281.
Aly, W. (1929) *Formprobleme der frühen griechischen Prosa*, Philologus suppl. 21.3.
Anderson, J.K. (1974) 'The Battle of Sardis in 395 BC', *CSCA* 7: 27–53.
Andrewes, A. (1938) 'Eunomia', *CQ* 32: 89–102.
Andrewes, A. (1967) 'The Government of Classical Sparta', in E. Badian (ed.) *Ancient Society and Institutions* (*Fest.* Ehrenberg), New York: Barnes & Noble: 1–20.
Andrewes, A. (1974) 'The Arginousai Trial', *Phoenix* 28: 112–122.
Andrewes, A. (1978) 'Spartan Imperialism?', in P.D.A. Garnsey and C.R. Whittaker (eds) *Imperialism in the Ancient World*, Cambridge: Cambridge University Press: 91–102 and 301–306.
Andrewes, A. (1982) 'Notion and Kyzikos: The Sources Compared', *JHS* 102: 15–25.
Andrewes, A. (1985) 'Diodoros and Ephoros: One Source of Misunderstanding', in J.W. Eadie and J. Ober (eds) *The Craft of the Ancient Historian: Essays in Honor of Chester G. Starr*, Lanham: University Press of America: 189–197.
Andrewes, A., K.J. Dover and A.W. Gomme (1945–1981) *A Historical Commentary on Thucydides* 1–5, only the last two multiple authorship, Oxford: Oxford University Press.
Austin, M.M. and P. Vidal-Naquet (1977) *Economic and Social History of Ancient Greece*, Berkeley and Los Angeles: University of California Press.
Avenarius, G. (1956) *Lukians Schrift zur Geschichtsschreibung*, Meisenheim/Glan: Anton Hain.
Aymard, A. (1953) 'Esprit militaire et administration hellénistique', *REA* 55: 132–145.
Baden, H. (1966) *Untersuchungen zur Einheit der Hellenika Xenophons*, diss. Hamburg.
Badian, E. (1987/1993) 'The Peace of Callias', *JHS* 107: 1–39 = *From Plataea to Potidaea: Studies in the History and Historiography of the*

Pentecontaetia, Baltimore: Johns Hopkins University Press: 1–72. I cite from the latter.

Badian, E. (1991) 'The King's Peace', in M. Flower and M. Toher (eds) *Georgica: Greek Studies in Honour of George Cawkwell*, BICS suppl. 58: 25–48.

Bandaret, A. (1919) *Untersuchungen zu Xenophons Hellenika*, Leipzig/Berlin: B.G. Teubner.

Barber, G.L. (1935) *The Historian Ephorus*, Cambridge: Cambridge University Press.

Barron, J.P. (1988) 'The Liberation of Greece', *CAH* 4 2nd edn: 592–622.

Bartoletti, V. (1959) *Hellenica Oxyrhynchia*, Leipzig: Bibliotheca Teubneriana.

Baynes, N.H. (1955) 'Isocrates', in R.A. Humphreys and A.D. Momigliano (eds) *Byzantine Studies and Other Essays*, London: The Athlone Press: 144–167.

Beloch, K.J. (1922) *Griechische Geschichte* 3.1–2, Berlin and Leipzig: Walter de Gruyter.

Bengtson, H. (1975) *Die Staatsverträge des Altertums* 2, Munich: C.H. Beck.

Bengtson, H. (1977) *Griechische Geschichte*, Munich: C.H. Beck.

Bertelli, L. (1976) 'Il modello della società rurale nell'utopia greca', *Il Pensiero Politico* 9: 183–208.

Bickerman, E.J. (1958) 'Autonomia: Sur un passage de Thucydide (1.144.2)', *RIDA* (ser. 3) 5: 313–344.

Bigalke, J. (1933) *Der Einfluß der Rhetorik auf Xenophons Stil*, diss. Greifswald.

Bischoff, H. (1932) *Der Warner bei Herodot*, diss. Marburg.

Blamire, A. (1989) *Plutarch: Life of Kimon*, BICS suppl. 56.

Bloch, H. (1940) 'Studies in Historical Literature of the Fourth Century BC I: The *Hellenica Oxyrhynchia* and its Authorship', in *Athenian Studies* (*Fest.* W.S. Ferguson) = *HSCP* suppl. 1: 303–341.

Bloch, M. (1953) *The Historian's Craft*, trans. P. Putnam, New York: Vintage Books.

Blundell, M.W. (1989) *Helping Friends and Hurting Enemies: A Study in Sophocles and Greek Ethics*, Cambridge: Cambridge University Press.

Bona, G. (1974) 'ΛΟΓΟΣ e ΑΛΗΘΕΙΑ nell' *Encomio de Elena* di Gorgia', *RFIC* 102: 5–33.

Bonner, R.J. (1910) 'The name "Ten Thousand"', *CP* 5: 97–99.

Bosworth, A.B. (1980) *A Historical Commentary on Arrian's History of Alexander* vol. 1, Oxford: Oxford University Press.

Bouché-Leclercq, A. (1880) *Histoire de la divination dans l'antiquité* vol. 3, Paris: E. Leroux.

Bowie, E. (1990) 'Miles *Ludens*? The Problem of Martial Exhortation in Early Greek Elegy', in O. Murray (ed.) *Sympotica: A Symposium on the Symposion*, Oxford: Oxford University Press: 221–229.

Breitenbach, H.R. (1950) *Historiographische Anschauungsformen Xenophons*, diss. Basel.

Breitenbach, H.R. (1967) 'Xenophon', *RE* 9A part 2: 1569–2052.

Breitenbach, H.R. (1970) 'Hellenika Oxyrhynchia', *RE* suppl. 12: 383–426.

Briant, P. (1985) 'Dons de terres et de villes: L'Asie Mineure dans le contexte Achéménide', *REA* 87: 53–72.

Briant, P. (1987) 'Pouvoir central et polycentrisme cultural dans l'empire Achemenide', in H. Sancisi-Weerdenburg (ed.) *Achaemenid History* vol. 1, Leiden: Nederlands Instituut voor het Nabije Oosten: 1–31.

Bringmann, K. (1965) *Studien zu den politischen Ideen des Isokrates*, Hypomnemata 14, Göttingen: Vandenhoeck & Ruprecht.

Brink, C.O. (1960) 'Tragic History and Aristotle's School', *PCPS* 6: 14–19.

Brown, T.S. (1946) 'Euhemerus and the Historians', *HTR* 39: 259–274.

Brown, T.S. (1949) *Onesicritus: A Study in Hellenistic Historiography*, University of California Publications in History 39, Berkeley and Los Angeles: University of California Press.

Brown, T.S. (1990) 'Echoes from Herodotus in Xenophon's *Hellenica*', *Ancient World* 21: 97–101.

Brown, W.S. (1955) 'Some Hellenistic Utopias', *CW* 48: 57–62.

Bruce, I.A.F. (1967) *An Historical Commentary on the Hellenica Oxyrhynchia*, Cambridge: Cambridge University Press.

Bruce, I.A.F. (1970) 'Theopompus and Classical Greek Historiography', *History and Theory* 9: 86–109.

Bruit Zaidman, L. and P. Schmitt Pantel (1992) *Religion in the Ancient Greek City*, trans. P. Cartledge, Cambridge: Cambridge University Press.

Bruns, I. (1896) *Das literarische Porträt der Griechen im fünften und vierten Jahrhundert vor Christi Geburt*, Berlin: Wilhelm Hertz.

Brunt, P.A. (1967) 'Athenian Settlements Abroad in the Fifth Century B.C.', in E. Badian (ed.) *Ancient Society and Institutions: Studies Presented to Victor Ehrenberg*, New York: Barnes & Noble: 71–92.

Brunt, P.A. (1980) 'On Historical Fragments and Epitomes', *CQ* 30: 477–494.

Brunt, P.A. (1983/1989) *Arrian*, 2 vols, London: William Heinemann.

Brunt, P.A. (1993) *Studies in Greek History and Thought*, Oxford: Oxford University Press.

Büchsenschütz, B. (1859) 'Xenophons griechische Geschichte', *Philologus* 14: 508–549.

Buckler, J. (1980) 'Plutarch on Leuktra', *SO* 55: 75–93.

Buckler, J. (1982) 'Xenophon's Speeches and the Theban Hegemony', *Athenaeum* 60: 180–204.

Burkert, W. (1979) *Structure and History in Greek Mythology and Ritual*, Berkeley and Los Angeles: University of California Press.

Burkert, W. (1992) 'Athenian Cults and Festivals', *CAH* 5 2nd edn: 245–267.

Burns, A. (1976) 'Hippodamus and the Planned City', *Historia* 25: 414–428.

Burstein, S.M. (1976) *Outpost of Hellenism: The Emergence of Heraclea on the Black Sea*, University of California Publications in Classical Studies 14, Berkeley and Los Angeles: University of California Press.

Bury, J.B. (1909) *The Ancient Greek Historians*, London: Macmillan & Co.

Busolt, G. (1908) 'Der neue Historiker und Xenophon', *Hermes* 43: 255–285.

Camp, J.M. (1986) *The Athenian Agora*, London: Thames & Hudson.

Cargill, J. (1981) *The Second Athenian League*, Berkeley: University of California Press.

Carter, L. (1986) *The Quiet Athenian*, Oxford: Oxford University Press.

Cartledge, P. (1984) 'A New Lease of Life for Lichas Son of Arkesilas?', *LCM* 9: 98–102.

Cartledge, P. (1987) *Agesilaos and the Crisis of Sparta*, Baltimore: Johns Hopkins University Press.

Cawkwell, G. (1963) 'Notes on the Peace of 375/4', *Historia* 12: 84–95.

Cawkwell, G. (1968) Review of Bruce (1967), *CR* 18: 288–290.

Cawkwell, G. (1972) Introduction and notes to *Xenophon: The Persian Expedition*, translation of the *Anabasis* by R. Warner, Harmondsworth: Penguin Books.

Cawkwell, G. (1973) 'The Foundation of the Second Athenian Confederacy', *CQ* 23: 47– 60.

Cawkwell, G. (1976a) 'Agesilaos and Sparta', *CQ* 26: 62–84.

Cawkwell, G. (1976b) 'The Imperialism of Thrasybulus', *CQ* 26: 270–277.

Cawkwell, G. (1978) *Philip of Macedon*, London and Boston: Faber & Faber.

Cawkwell, G. (1979) Introduction and notes to *Xenophon: A History of my Times*, translation of the *Hellenica* by R. Warner, Harmondsworth: Penguin Books.

Cawkwell, G. (1981) 'The King's Peace', *CQ* 31: 69–83.

Cawkwell, G. (1983) 'The Decline of Sparta', *CQ* 33: 385–400.

Chambers, M. (1993) *Hellenica Oxyrhynchia*, Stuttgart and Leipzig: Bibliotheca Teubneriana.

Chrimes, K.M.T. (1948) *The Date and Authorship of the Res Publica Lacedaemoniorum Ascribed to Xenophon*, Manchester: Manchester University Press.

Chrimes, K.M.T. (1949) *Ancient Sparta*, Manchester: Manchester University Press.

Christ, M.R. (1992) 'Ostracism, Sycophancy, and Deception of the Demos: [Arist.] *Ath. Pol.* 43.5', *CQ* 42: 336–346.

Christensen, J. and M.H. Hansen (1989) 'What is *Syllogos* at Thukydides 2.22.1?', in M.H. Hansen (ed.) *The Athenian Ecclesia* 2, Copenhagen: Museum Tusculum Press: 195–209.

Clark, M. (1990) 'The Date of *IG* II^2 1604', *ABSA* 85: 47–67.

Classen, C.J. (1984) 'Xenophons Darstellung der Sophistik und der Sophisten', *Hermes* 112: 154–167.

Cloché, P. (1915) *La Restauration démocratique à Athenes*, Paris: E. Leroux.

Cloché, P. (1944) 'Les "Helléniques" de Xénophon (livres iii–vii) et Lacédémone', *REA* 46: 12–46.

Cochrane, C.N. (1929) *Thucydides and the Science of History*, London: Oxford University Press.

Coffin, C.C. (1881) *The Boys of '61; or, Four Years of Fighting, Personal Observation with the Army and Navy*, Boston: Estes & Lauriat.

Cole, T. (1990) *Democritus and the Sources of Greek Anthropology*, Atlanta: Scholars Press.

Colin, G. (1933) *Xénophon historien d'après le livre II des Helléniques*, Paris: Les Belles Lettres.

301

Colish, M.L. (1985) *The Stoic Tradition from Antiquity to the Early Middle Ages* vol. 1, Leiden: E.J. Brill.

Collard, C. (1975) *Euripides: Supplices*, Groningen: Bouma's Boekhuis b.v.

Connor, W.R. (1962) 'Charinus' Megarean Decree', *AJP* 83: 225–246.

Connor, W.R. (1963) 'Theopompus' Treatment of Cimon', *GRBS* 4: 107–114.

Connor, W.R. (1967) 'History without Heroes: Theopompus' Treatment of Philip of Macedon', *GRBS* 8: 133–154.

Connor, W.R. (1968) *Theopompus and Fifth-Century Athens*, Cambridge, Mass.: Harvard University Press.

Connor, W.R. (1971) *The New Politicians of Fifth-Century Athens*, Princeton: Princeton University Press.

Connor, W.R. (1984) *Thucydides*, Princeton: Princeton University Press.

Connor, W.R. (1985) 'Historical Writing in the Fourth Century and in the Hellenistic Period', in P.E. Easterling and B.M.W. Knox (eds) *The Cambridge History of Classical Literature*, 1 *Greek Literature*, Cambridge: Cambridge University Press: 458–471.

Dalby, A. (1992) 'Greeks Abroad: Social Organisation and Food among the Ten Thousand', *JHS* 112: 16–30.

Dalfen, J. (1976) 'Xenophon als analytiker und politischer Rede: Zu *Hellenica* 6.3.4–17 und 6.5.33–48', *Grazer Beiträge* 5: 59–84.

Dandamaev, M.A. (1989) *A Political History of the Achaemenid Empire*, trans. W.J. Vogelsang, Leiden: E.J. Brill.

Davies, J.K. (1978) *Democracy and Classical Greece*, Stanford, Stanford University Press.

Davies, J.K. (1984) 'Cultural, Social and Economic Features of the Hellenistic World', *CAH* 7.1 2nd edn: 257–320.

Delebecque, E. (1957) *Essai sur la vie Xénophon*, Paris: C. Klincksieck.

Demont, P. (1990) *La Cité grecque archaïque et classique et l'idéal de tranquillité*, Paris: Les Belles Lettres.

De Voto, J.G. (1988) 'Agesilaos and Tissaphernes near Sardis in 395 BC', *Hermes* 116: 41–53.

Dietzfelbinger, R. (1992) 'Religiöse Kategorien in Xenophons Geschichtsverständnis', *WJA* 18: 133–145.

Diller, H. (1956) 'Der vorphilosophische Gebrauch von ΚΟΣΜΟΣ und ΚΟΣΜΕΙΝ', in *Festschrift Bruno Snell*, 47–60, Munich: C.H. Beck.

Dillery, J. (1989) *Xenophon's Historical Perspectives*, diss. Univ. of Michigan.

Dillery, J. (1993) 'Xenophon's *Poroi* and Athenian Imperialism', *Historia* 42: 1–11.

Dillery, J. and T. Gagos (1992) 'P. Mich. Inv. 4922: Xenophon and an Unknown Christian Text with an Appendix of All Xenophon Papyri', *ZPE* 93: 171–190 with pl. vi.

Dittenberger, W. (1881) 'Sprachliche Kriterien für die Chronologie der platonischen Dialoge', *Hermes* 16: 321–345.

Dobesch, G. (1968) *Die panhellenische Gedanke im 4. Jh. v. Chr. und der 'Philippos' des Isokrates*, Vienna: Österreichisches Archäologisches Institut.

Dodds, E.R. (1951) *The Greeks and the Irrational*, Berkeley and Los Angeles: University of California Press.

Dodds, E.R. (1959) *Plato: Gorgias*, Oxford: Oxford University Press.

Dodds, E.R. (1973) *The Ancient Concept of Progress and Other Essays on Greek Literature and Belief*, Oxford: Oxford University Press.

Donlan, W. (1979) 'The Structure of Authority in the *Iliad*', *Arethusa* 12: 51–70.

Dover, K.J. (1974) *Greek Popular Morality in the Time of Plato and Aristotle*, Oxford: Basil Blackwell.

Dover, K.J. (1978) *Greek Homosexuality*, Cambridge, Mass.: Harvard University Press.

Dover, K.J. (1993) *Aristophanes: Frogs*, Oxford: Oxford University Press.

Dover, K.J., A. Andrewes and A.W. Gomme (1945–1981) *A Historical Commentary on Thucydides* 1–5, only the last two multiple authorship, Oxford: Oxford University Press.

Drews, R. (1963) 'Ephorus and History Written κατὰ γένος', *AJP* 84: 244–255.

Due, B. (1989) *The Cyropaedia: Xenophon's Aims and Methods*, Aarhus: Aarhus University Press.

Dugas, C. (1910) 'La Campagne d'Agésilas en Asie Mineure', *BCH* 34: 58–95.

Dürrbach, F. (1893) 'L'Apologie de Xénophon dans l'*Anabase*', *REG* 6: 343–386.

Dusanic, S. (1977) 'On Theopompus' *Philippica* VI–VIII', *Aevum*: 27–36.

Eichler, G. (1880) *De Cyropaediae capite extremo*, diss. Leipzig.

Engels, J. (1993) 'Der Michigan-Papyrus über Theramenes und die Ausbildung des "Theramenes-Mythos"', *ZPE* 99: 125–155.

Erbse, H. (1966) 'Xenophons *Anabasis*', *Gymnasium* 73: 485–505.

Farrar, C. (1988) *The Origins of Democratic Thinking: The Invention of Politics in Classical Athens*, Cambridge: Cambridge University Press.

Ferguson, J. (1975) *Utopias of the Classical World*, Ithaca: Cornell University Press.

Festugière, A.-J. (1949) *Le Dieu cosmique* 2, Paris: Librarie Lecoffre.

Finley, M.I. (1960) *Aspects of Antiquity*, New York: Viking Press.

Finley, M.I. (1965) *The World of Odysseus*, New York: Viking Press.

Finley, M.I. (1968) 'Sparta', in J.-P. Vernant (ed.) *Problèmes de la guerre en Grèce ancienne*, 143–160, Paris: Mouton & Co.

Finley, M.I. (1983) *Politics in the Ancient World*, Cambridge: Cambridge University Press.

Flory, S. (1993) 'The Death of Thucydides and the Motif of "Land on Sea"', in R.M. Rosen and J. Farrell (eds) *Nomodeiktes: Greek Studies in Honor of Martin Ostwald*, Ann Arbor: University of Michigan Press: 113–123.

Focke, F. (1927) *Herodot als Historiker*, Tübinger Beiträge zur Altertumswissenschaft 1, Tübingen: W. Kohlhammer. (Portions reprinted in Marg (1962) 35–39).

Foerster, W. (1971) 'σῴζω, σωτηρία, σωτήρ, σωτήριος', in G. Kittel and G. Friedrich (eds) *Theological Dictionary of the New Testament* 7, trans. G.W. Bromiley, Grand Rapids: W.B. Eerdmans: 965–969.

Fontenrose, J. (1978) *The Delphic Oracle*, Berkeley: University of California Press.

Fornara, C.W. (1971) *Herodotus: An Interpretative Essay*, Oxford: Oxford University Press.

Fornara, C.W. (1983) *The Nature of History in Ancient Greece and Rome*, Berkeley and Los Angeles: University of California Press.

Forrest, W.G. (1968) *A History of Sparta 950-152 BC*, New York: W.W. Norton.

Fränkel, H. (1938) 'A Thought Pattern in Heraclitus', *AJP* 59: 309–337.

Fränkel, H. (1975) *Early Greek Poetry and Philosophy*, trans. M. Hadas and J. Willis, Oxford: Basil Blackwell.

Fritz, K. von (1941), 'The Historian Theopompus: His Political Convictions and his Concept of Historiography', *AHR* 46: 765–787.

Fritz, K. von (1968) Review of Henry (1967), *Gnomon* 40: 556–568.

Funke, P. (1980) *Homónoia und Arché*, Historia Einzelschriften 37, Wiesbaden: Franz Steiner Verlag.

Gabba, E. (1981) 'True History and False History in Classical Antiquity', *JRS* 71: 50–62.

Gauthier, P. (1976) *Une Commentaire historique des Poroi de Xénophon*, Geneva and Paris: Libraire Droz.

Gautier, L. (1911) *La Langue de Xénophon*, diss. Geneva.

Gehrke, H.-J. (1985) *Stasis: Untersuchungen zu den inneren Kriegen in den griechischen Staaten des 5. und 4. Jahrhunderts v. Chr.*, Vestigia Beiträge 35, Munich: C.H. Beck.

Gentili, B. and G. Cerri (1988) *History and Biography in Ancient Thought*, trans. D. Murray and L. Murray, Amsterdam: J.C. Gieben.

Gera, D.L. (1993) *Xenophon's Cyropaedia*, Oxford: Oxford University Press.

Geysels, L. (1974) 'Πόλις οἰκουμένη dans l'*Anabase* de Xénophon', *Les Etudes Classiques* 42: 29–38.

Giangrande, L. (1976) 'Les Utopies hellénistiques', *Cahiers des études anciennes* 5: 17–33.

Giannantoni, G. (1990) *Socratis et Socraticorum reliquiae* 4, Naples: Bibliopolis.

Gigon, O. (1953) *Kommentar zum ersten Buch von Xenophons Memorabilien*, Schweizerische Beiträge zur Altertumswissenschaft 1, Basel: Friedrich Reinhardt.

Gitti, A. (1954) 'La colonia ateniese in Adriatico del 325/4 A.C.', *PP* 34: 16–24.

Glotz, G. (1936) *Histoire Grecque* 3, Paris: Presses Universitaires de France.

Gomme, A.W. (1937) *Essays in Greek History and Literature*, Oxford: Basil Blackwell.

Gomme, A.W., A. Andrewes and K.J. Dover (1945–1981) *A Historical Commentary on Thucydides* 1–5, only the last two multiple authorship, Oxford: Oxford University Press.

Goodman, M.D. and A.J. Holladay (1986) 'Religious Scruples in Ancient Warfare', *CQ* 36: 151–171.

Gould, J. (1989) *Herodotus*, New York: St Martin's Press.

Gray, V. (1979) 'The Different Approaches to the Battle of Sardis in 395 BC', *CSCA* 12: 183–200.

Gray, V. (1980) '375–371 BC: A Case Study in the Reliability of Diodorus Siculus and Xenophon', *CQ* 30: 306–326.

Gray, V. (1981) 'Dialogue in Xenophon's *Hellenica*', *CQ* 31: 321–334.

Gray, V. (1987a) 'The Value of Diodorus Siculus for the Years 411–386 BC', *Hermes* 115: 72–89.

Gray, V. (1987b) 'Mimesis in Greek Historical Theory', *AJP* 108: 467–486.

Gray, V. (1989) *The Character of Xenophon's Hellenica*, Baltimore: Johns Hopkins University Press.

Gray, V. (1991) 'Continuous History and Xenophon, *Hellenica* 1–2.3.10', *AJP* 112: 201–228.

Grayson, C.H. (1975) 'Did Xenophon Intend to Write History?', in B. Levick (ed.) *The Ancient Historian and his Materials* (in honour of C.E. Stevens), Westmead: Gregg International: 31–43.

Grenfell, B.P. and A. Hunt (1908) *The Oxyrhynchus Papyri* Part 5, London: Egypt Exploration Fund.

Grenfell, B.P. and A. Hunt (1919) *The Oxyrhynchus Papyri* Part 13, London: Egypt Exploration Fund.

Griffith, G.T. (1935) *The Mercenaries of the Hellenistic World*, Cambridge: Cambridge University Press.

Griffith, G.T. (1954) 'The Greek Historians', in G.T. Griffith (ed.) *Fifty Years of Classical Scholarship*, Oxford: Basil Blackwell, 160–162.

Grosser, R. (1873) *Zur Charakteristik der Epitome von Xenophons Hellenika*, Progr. Barmen.

Gulley, N. (1968) *The Philosophy of Socrates*, London: Macmillan.

Habicht, C. (1961) 'Falsche Urkunden zur Geschichte Athens im Zeitalter der Perserkriege', *Hermes* 89: 1–35.

Hall, E. (1989) *Inventing the Barbarian: Greek Self-Definition through Tragedy*, Oxford: Oxford University Press.

Hamilton, C.D. (1979) *Sparta's Bitter Victories: Politics and Diplomacy in the Corinthian War*, Ithaca: Cornell University Press.

Hamilton, C.D. (1991) *Agesilaus and the Failure of Spartan Hegemony*, Ithaca and London: Cornell University Press.

Hamilton, C.D. (1992) 'Lysander, Agesilaus, Spartan Imperialism and the Greeks of Asia Minor', *AW* 23: 35–50.

Harding, P. (1985) *From the End of the Peloponnesian War to the Battle of Ipsus*, Translated Documents of Greece and Rome vol. 2, Cambridge: Cambridge University Press.

Harding, P. (1987) 'Rhetoric and Politics in Fourth-Century Athens', *Phoenix*: 25–39.

Harding, P. (1994) *Androtion and the Atthis*, Oxford: Oxford University Press.

Hartman, J.J. (1887) *Analecta Xenophontea*, Leiden: S.C. Doesburgh.

Hartog, F. (1988) *The Mirror of Herodotus*, trans. J. Lloyd, Berkeley and Los Angeles: University of California Press.

Hatzfeld, J. (1930) 'Notes sur la composition des Helléniques', *RPh* 4: 113–117, 209–226.

Hatzfeld, J. (1936) 'Jason de Phères a-t-il été l'allié d'Athènes?', *REA* 36: 441–461.

Hatzfeld, J. (1936–1939) *Xénophon: Helléniques* 2 vols, Paris: Les Belles Lettres.

Henry, W.P. (1967) *Greek Historical Writing: A Historiographical Essay Based on Xenophon's Hellenica*, Chicago: Argonaut.

Higgins, W.E. (1977) *Xenophon the Athenian*, Albany: State University of New York Press.

Hignett, C. (1952) *A History of the Athenian Constitution*, Oxford: Oxford University Press.

Hirsch, S.W. (1985) *The Friendship of the Barbarians: Xenophon and the Persian Empire*, Hanover and London: University Press of New England.

Holden, H.A. (1890) *The Cyropaedeia of Xenophon* 2, Cambridge: Cambridge University Press.

Hooker, J.T. (1989) 'Spartan Propaganda', in A. Powell (ed.) *Classical Sparta: Techniques Behind her Success*, London: Routledge: 122–141.

Hornblower, J. (1981) *Hieronymus of Cardia*, Oxford: Oxford University Press.

Hornblower, S. (1987) *Thucydides*, Baltimore: Johns Hopkins University Press.

Hornblower, S. (1991) *A Commentary on Thucydides* 1, Oxford: Oxford University Press.

Hornblower, S. (1992) 'The Religious Dimension to the Peloponnesian War, or, What Thucydides Does not Tell Us', *HSCP* 94: 169–197.

Humphreys, S. (1978) *Anthropology and the Greeks*, London: Routledge & Kegan Paul.

Hunter, L.W. (1927) *Aeneas on Siegecraft*, Oxford: Oxford University Press.

Hussey, E. (1985) 'Thucydidean History and Democritean Theory', in P.A. Cartledge and F.D. Harvey (eds) *Crux: Essays in Greek History Presented to G.E.M. de Ste. Croix on his 75th Birthday*, London: Duckworth: 118–138.

Hutchinson, S. (1987) 'Mapping Utopias', *Modern Philology* 85: 170–185.

Immerwahr, H. (1956) 'Aspects of Historical Causation in Herodotus', *TAPA* 87: 241–280.

Immerwahr, H. (1960) '*Ergon:* History as Monument in Herodotus and Thucydides', *AJP* 81: 261–290.

Immerwahr, H. (1966) *Form and Thought in Herodotus*, Cleveland: American Philological Association.

Irwin, T.H. (1974) Review of L. Strauss (1972), *Philosophical Review* 83: 409–413.

Irwin, T.H. (1992) 'Plato: The Intellectual Background', in R. Kraut (ed.) *The Cambridge Companion to Plato*, New York: Cambridge University Press: 51–89.

Jacoby, F. (1909) 'Über die Entwicklung der griechischen Historiographie und den Plan einer neuen Sammlung der griechischen Historiker-fragmente', *Klio* 9: 80–123.

Jacoby, F. (1913) 'Herodotos', *RE* suppl. 2: 205–520. (Portions reprinted in Marg (1962) 27–34.)

Jacoby, F. (1923–1958) *Die Fragmente der griechischen Historiker*, Leiden: E.J. Brill.

Jacoby, F. (1949) *Atthis: The Local Chronicles of Ancient Athens*, Oxford: Oxford University Press.

Jaeger, W. (1944) *Paideia: The Ideals of Greek Culture* 3, trans. G. Highet, New York: Oxford University Press.

BIBLIOGRAPHY

Jaeger, W. (1947) *The Theology of the Early Greek Philosophers*, Oxford: Oxford University Press.

Jameson, F. (1988) 'Of Islands and Trenches: Neutralization and the Production of Utopian Discourse', in *The Ideologies of Theory: Essays 1971–1989* 2, *Syntax of History*, Minneapolis: University of Minnesota Press: 75–101.

Jehne, M. (1991) 'Die Friedensverhandlungen von Sparta 392/1 v. Chr. und das Problem der kleinasiatischen Griechen', *Chiron* 21: 265–276.

Joël, K. (1893–1901) *Der echte und der Xenophontische Sokrates*, 2 vols, Berlin: R. Gaertners.

Johnstone, S. (1994) 'Virtuous Toil, Vicious Work: Xenophon on Aristocratic Style', *CP* 89: 219–240.

Jones, C.P. (1986) *Culture and Society in Lucian*, Cambridge, Mass. and London: Harvard University Press.

Judeich, W. (1892) *Kleinasiatische Studien*, Marburg: N.G. Elwertsche.

Kallet-Marx, R.M. (1985) 'Athens, Thebes, and the Foundation of the Second Athenian League', *CA* 4: 127–151.

Kaupert, W. (1926) 'Sardes 395 v. Chr.', in J. Kromayer (ed.) *Antike Schlachtfelder: Bausteine zu einer antiken Kriegsgeschichte* 4, Berlin: Weidmann: 261–289.

Kearns, E. (1990) 'Saving the City', in O. Murray and S. Price (eds) *The Greek City From Homer to Alexander*, Oxford: Oxford University Press: 323–344.

Keller, W.J. (1910–1911) 'Xenophon's Acquaintance with the History of Herodotus', *CJ* 6: 252–259.

Kerferd, G.B. (1981) *The Sophistic Movement*, Cambridge: Cambridge University Press.

Kessler, J. (1911) *Isokrates und die panhellenische Idee*, Studien zur Geschichte und Kultur des Altertums 3, Paderborn: Ferdinand Schöningh.

Kirk, G.S. (1990) *The Iliad: A Commentary* 2, Cambridge: Cambridge University Press.

Kitto, H.D.F. (1966) *Poiesis: Structure and Thought*, Berkeley and Los Angeles: University of California Press.

Koenen, L. (1976) 'Fieldwork of the International Photography Archive in Cairo', *Studia Papyrologica* 15: 39–79.

Körte, A. (1922) 'Die Tendenz von Xenophons *Anabasis*', *Neue Jahrbücher für das klassische Altertum und für Pädagogik* 49: 15–24.

Krafft, P. (1967) 'Vier Beispiele des Xenophontischen in Xenophons *Hellenika*', *RhM* 110: 103–150.

Krentz, P. (1982) *The Thirty at Athens*, Ithaca and London: Cornell University Press.

Krentz, P. (1987) 'Thibron and the Thirty', *AW* 15: 75–79.

Krentz, P. (1989) *Xenophon Hellenika I–II.3.10*, Warminster: Aris & Phillips.

Krüger, K.W. (1836) 'Prüfung der Niebuhrschen Ansicht über Xenophons *Hellenika*', in *Historisch philologische Studien* 1, Berlin: Rucker: 244–264.

Kühner, R. (1852) *Xenophontis de Cyri Minoris expeditione libri septem*, Gotha: Bernh. Hennings.

Laks, A. (1983) *Diogène d'Apollonie*, Lille: Presses Universitaires de Lille.

Lana, I. (1951) 'L'Utopia di Teopompo', *Paideia* 6: 3–22.

Lane Fox, R. (1986), 'Theopompus of Chios and the Greek World, 411–322 BC', in J. Boardman and C.E. Vaphopoulou-Richardson (eds) *Chios: A Conference at the Homereion in Chios 1984*, Oxford: Oxford University Press: 105–120.

Laqueur, R. (1911) 'Ephoros', *Hermes* 46: 161–206 and 321–354.

Latacz, J. (1977) *Kampfparänese, Kampfdarstellung und Kampfwirklichkeit in der Ilias, bei Kallinos und Tyrtaios*, Zetemata 66, Munich: C.H. Beck.

Lateiner, D. (1989) *The Historical Method of Herodotus*, Toronto: University of Toronto Press.

Lattimore, R. (1939) 'The Wise Adviser in Herodotus', *CP* 34: 24–35.

Leaf, W. (1900–1902) *Iliad*, 2 vols, London: Clark.

Lehmann, G.A. (1980) 'Krise und innere Bedrohung der hellenischen Polis bei Aeneas Tacticus', in W. Eck, H. Galsterer and H. Wolff (eds) *Studien zur antiken Sozialgeschichte: Festschrift F. Vittinghoff*, Kölner Historische Abhandlungen 28, Cologne: Böhlau Verlag: 71–86.

Lenschau, T. (1937) 'Οἱ τριάκοντα', *RE* 6 A 2: 2355–2377.

Lesky, A. (1966) *A History of Greek Literature*, trans. J. Willis and C. de Heer, New York: Thomas Y. Crowell Co.

Lewis, D.M. (1977) *Sparta and Persia*, Leiden: E.J. Brill.

Lichtenthaeler, C. (1965) *Thucydide et Hippocrate*, Geneva: Librairie Droz.

Lincke, K. (1906) 'Xenophon und die Stoa', *Neue Jahrbücher für das klassische Altertum* 17: 673–691.

Lins, H. (1914) *Kritische Betrachtung der Feldzüge des Agesilaos ein Kleinasien*, diss. Halle.

Lloyd, G.E.R. (1979) *Magic, Reason and Experience: Studies in the Origins and Development of Greek Science*, Cambridge: Cambridge University Press.

Lloyd, G.E.R. (1987) *The Revolutions of Wisdom*, Berkeley: University of California Press.

Loening, T.C. (1987) *The Reconciliation Agreement of 403/2 BC in Athens*, Hermes Einzelschriften 53, Wiesbaden: Franz Steiner.

Loraux, N. (1986) *The Invention of Athens: The Funeral Oration in the Classical City*, trans. A. Sheridan, Cambridge, Mass. and London: Harvard University Press.

Lossau, M. (1990) 'Xenophons *Odyssee*', *Antike und Abendland* 36: 47–52.

Lotze, D. (1962) 'Die chronologischen Interpolationen in Xenophons *Hellenika*', *Philologus* 106: 1–13.

Lotze, D. (1974) 'War Xenophon selbst der Interpolator seiner *Hellenika* I–II?', *Philologus* 118: 215–217.'

Löwith, K. (1949) *Meaning in History*, Chicago: University of Chicago Press.

Luccioni, J. (1947) *Les Idées politiques et sociales de Xénophon*, Paris: Ophrys.

Luccioni, J. (1953) *Xénophon et le Socratisme*, Paris: Presses Universitaires de France.

Macan, R.W. (1895) *Herodotus: The Fourth, Fifth, and Sixth Books* 1, London: Macmillan & Co.

McKechnie, P.R. and S.J. Kern (1988) *Hellenica Oxyrhynchia*, Warminster: Aris & Phillips.

MacLaren, M. (1934a) 'On the Composition of Xenophon's *Hellenica*', *AJP* 55: 121–139, 249–262.

MacLaren, M. (1934b) 'Xenophon and Themistogenes', *TAPA* 65: 240–247.

Maier, H. (1913) *Sokrates: Sein Werk und seine geschichtliche Stellung*, Tübingen: J.C.B. Mohr.

Malkin, I. (1987) *Religion and Colonization in Ancient Greece*, Leiden: E.J. Brill.

Marg, W. (1962) *Herodot: Eine Auswahl aus der neueren Forschung*, Munich: C.H. Beck.

Marinovic, L.P. (1988) *Le Mercenariat grec et la crise de la polis*, Annales Littéraires de l'Université de Besançon 372, trans. Y. Garlan, Paris: Les Belles Lettres.

Marshall, F.H. (1905) *The Second Athenian Confederacy*, Cambridge: Cambridge University Press.

Marszalek, J.F. (1993) *Sherman: A Soldier's Passion for Order*, New York: Random House.

Masqueray, P. (1930–1931) *Xénophon Anabase*, 2 vols, Paris: Les Belles Lettres.

Mastronarde, D.J. (1986) 'The Optimistic Rationalist in Euripides', in M. Cropp, E. Fantham and S.E. Scully (eds) *Greek Tragedy and its Legacy* (in honour of D.J. Conacher), Calgary: University of Calgary Press: 201–211.

Mathieu, G. (1925) *Les Idées politiques d'Isocrate*, Paris: Les Belles Lettres.

Matthews, J. (1989) *The Roman Empire of Ammianus*, Baltimore: Johns Hopkins University Press.

Meiggs, R. (1972) *The Athenian Empire*, Oxford: Oxford University Press.

Merkelbach, R. and H.C. Youtie (1968) 'Ein Michigan-Papyrus über Theramenes', *ZPE* 2: 161–169.

Mesk, J. (1922–1923) 'Die Tendenz der Xenophontischen Anabasis', *WS* 43: 136–146.

Meulder, M. (1989) 'La Date et la cohérence de la *République des Lacédémoniens* de Xenophon', *L'Antiquité Classique* 58: 71–87.

Meyer, E. (1909/1966) *Theopomps Hellenika*, Hildesheim: Georg Olms.

Mikalson, J.D. (1983) *Athenian Popular Religion*, Chapel Hill: University of North Carolina Press.

Misch, G. (1949) *Geschichte der Autobiographie* 1.1, Bern: A. Francke.

Missiou, A. (1992) *The Subversive Oratory of Andokides: Politics, Ideology and Decision-Making in Democratic Athens*, Cambridge: Cambridge University Press.

Momigliano, A. (1934) *Filippo il Macedone: Saggio sulla storia greca del IV secolo A.C.*, Florence: Felice Le Monnier.

Momigliano, A. (1935) 'La storia di Eforo e le Elleniche di Teopompo', *RFIC* 63: 180–204.

Momigliano, A. (1936/1966) 'Per l'unità logica dell *Lakedaimonion Politeia* di Senofonte', *RFIC* 14: 170–173 = *Terzo contributo alla storia degli studi classici e del mondo antico* 1, Rome: Edizioni di Storia e Letteratura: 341–345.

Momigliano, A. (1942/1960) 'Camillus and Concord', *CQ* 36: 111–120 = *Secondo contributo alla storia degli studi classici*, Roma: Edizioni di Storia e Letteratura: 89–104.

Momigliano, A. (1977) 'Tradition and the Classical Historian', in *Essays in Ancient and Modern Historiography*, Middletown: Wesleyan University Press: 161–177.

Momigliano, A. (1979) 'Persian Empire and Greek Freedom', in A. Ryan (ed.) *The Idea of Freedom: Essays in Honour of Isaiah Berlin*, Oxford: Oxford University Press: 139–151.

Momigliano, A. (1990) *The Classical Foundations of Modern Historiography*, Berkeley: University of California Press.

Momigliano, A. (1993) *The Development of Greek Biography*, Cambridge, Mass.: Harvard University Press.

Moore, J.M. (1975) *Aristotle and Xenophon on Democracy and Oligarchy*, Berkeley: University of California Press.

Morr, J. (1926–1927) 'Xenophon und der Gedanke eines all-griechischen Eroberungszuges gegen Persien', *WS* 45: 186–201.

Morrison, D. (1987) 'On Professor Vlastos' Xenophon', *Ancient Philosophy* 7: 9–22.

Mosley, D.J. (1962) 'The Athenian Embassy to Sparta in 371 BC', *PCPS* 8: 41–46.

Mosley, D.J. (1973) *Envoys and Diplomacy in Ancient Greece*, Historia Einzelschriften 22, Wiesbaden: Franz Steiner.

Mossé, C. (1963) 'Armée et cité grecque', *REA* 65: 290–297.

Mossé, C. (1968) 'Le Rôle politique des armées dans le monde grec à l'époque classique', in J.-P. Vernant (ed.) *Problèmes de la guerre en Grèce ancienne*, Paris: Mouton & Co.: 221–229.

Mühl, M. (1917) *Die politischen Ideen des Isokrates und die Geschichtsschreibung*, diss. Würzburg.

Müller, C. (1855) *Geographi graeci minores* 1, Paris: A.F. Didot.

Müller, E.H.O. (1856) *De Xenophontis Historiae Graecae parte priori*, diss. Leipzig.

Münscher, K. (1920) *Xenophon in der griechisch-römischen Literatur*, Philologus suppl. 13.2, Leipzig: Dieterich'sche Verlagsbuchhandlung.

Murphy, T. (1989) 'The Vilification of Eratosthenes and Theramenes in Lysias 12', *AJP* 110: 40–49.

Murray, G. (1946) 'Theopompus, or the Cynic as Historian', in *Greek Studies*, Oxford: Oxford University Press: 149–170.

Murray, O. (1970) 'Hecataeus of Abdera and Pharaonic Kingship', *JEA* 56: 141–171.

Murray, O. (1972) 'Herodotus and Hellenistic Culture', *CQ* 22: 200–213.

Nachtergael, G. (1977) *Les Galates en Grèce et les Sôtéria des Delphes*, Académie royale de Belgique, Memoires de la classe des lettres 63.1, Brussels: Palais des Academies.

Nagy, G. (1990) *Pindar's Homer*, Baltimore: Johns Hopkins University Press.

Naumann, E. (1876) *De Xenophontis libro qui* Λακεδαιμονίων Πολιτεία *inscribitur*, diss. Berlin.

Nellen, D. (1972) 'Zur Darstellung der Schlacht bei Sardes in den Quellen', *Ancient Society* 3: 45–54.

Nestle, W. (1940) 'Xenophon und die Sophistik', *Philologus* 94: 31–50.

Nickel, R. (1979) *Xenophon*, Darmstadt: Wissenschaftliche Buchgesellschaft.

Niebuhr, B.G. (1828/1827) 'Über Xenophons *Hellenika*', in *Kleine historische und philologische Schriften* 1: 465–482 = *RhM* 1 (1827) 169ff.; I cite from the former.

Nilsson, M.P. (1967) *Geschichte der griechische Religion* 1, Munich: C.H. Beck.

Nilsson, M.P. (1969) *Greek Piety*, New York: W.W. Norton.

Nitsche, W. (1871) *Über die Abfassung von Xenophons Hellenika*, diss. Berlin.

Norden, E. (1909) *Die antike Kunstprosa* 1, Berlin: B.G. Teubner.

North, H. (1956) 'Rhetoric and Historiography', *Quarterly Journal of Speech* 42: 234–242.

North, H. (1966) *Sophrosyne: Self-Knowledge and Self-Restraint in Greek Literature*, Ithaca: Cornell University Press.

Novick, P. (1988) *That Noble Dream: The 'Objectivity Question' and the American Historical Profession*, Cambridge: Cambridge University Press.

Nussbaum, G.B. (1967) *The Ten Thousand: A Study in Social Organisation and Action in Xenophon's Anabasis*, Leiden: E.J. Brill.

Nussbaum, M.C. (1986) *The Fragility of Goodness: Luck and Ethics in Greek Tragedy and Philosophy*, Cambridge: Cambridge University Press.

Ober, J. (1989) *Mass and Elite in Democratic Athens*, Princeton: Princeton University Press.

Ogilvie, R.M. (1965) *A Commentary on Livy Books 1-5*, Oxford: Oxford University Press.

Ollier, F. (1933) *Le Mirage spartiate*, Paris: E. de Boccard.

Ollier, F. (1934) *La République des Lacédémones*, Lyons: A. Rey.

Opitz, A. (1913) *Quaestiones Xenophonteae de Hellenicorum atque Agesilai necessitudine*, Breslauer philologische Abhandlungen 46, Vratislava: Wil. Koebner.

Ostwald, M. (1982) *Autonomia: Its Genesis and Early History*, APA Monographs 11, Chico, CA: Scholars Press.

Ostwald, M. (1986) *From Popular Sovereignty to the Sovereignty of Law*, Berkeley and Los Angeles: University of California Press.

Parke, H.W. (1930) 'The Development of the Second Spartan Empire', *JHS* 50: 37–79.

Parke, H.W. (1933) *Greek Mercenary Soldiers*, Oxford: Oxford University Press.

Parke, H.W. (1939) 'The Pythais of 355 BC and the Third Sacred War', *JHS* 59: 80–83.

Parke, H.W. (1977) *Festivals of the Athenians*, Ithaca: Cornell University Press.

Parke, H.W. and D.E.W. Wormell (1956) *The Delphic Oracle* 1, Oxford: Basil Blackwell.

Parker, R. (1989) 'Spartan Religion', in A. Powell (ed.) *Classical Sparta: Techniques Behind her Success*, London: Routledge: 142–172.

Parry, A. (1957) *Logos and Ergon in Thucydides*, diss. Harvard; repr. 1981, New York: Arno Press.

Pearson, L. (1942) *The Local Historians of Attica*, Chico, CA: Scholars Press.

Pearson, L. (1943) 'Lost Greek Historians Judged by Their Fragments', *G & R* 12: 43–56.

Pearson, L. (1947) 'Thucydides as Reporter and Critic', *TAPA* 78: 37–60.

Pearson, L. (1962) *Popular Ethics in Ancient Greece*, Stanford: Stanford University Press.

Pearson, L. (1987) *The Greek Historians of the West: Timaeus and his Predecessors*, Atlanta: American Philological Association.

Pédech, P. (1989) *Trois historiens méconnus: Théopompe, Duris, Phylarque*, Paris: Les Belles Lettres.

Pembroke, S. (1967) 'Women in Charge: The Function of Alternatives in Early Greek Tradition and the Ancient Idea of Matriarchy', *Journal of the Warburg and Courtauld Institutes* 30: 1–35.

Perlman, S. (1957) 'Isocrates' "Philippus": A Reinterpretation', *Historia* 6: 306–317.

Perlman, S. (1964) 'The Causes and Outbreak of the Corinthian War', *CQ* 14: 64–81.

Perlman, S. (1969) 'Isocrates' "Philippus" and Panhellenism', *Historia* 18: 370–374.

Perlman, S. (1976) 'Panhellenism, the Polis and Imperialism', *Historia* 25: 1–30.

Perlman, S. (1976–1977) 'The Ten Thousand: A Chapter in the Military, Social and Economic History of the Fourth Century', *Rivista storica dell' Antichita* 6/7: 241–284.

Perry, B.E. (1952) *Aesopica* 1, Urbana: University of Illinois Press.

Persson, A.W. (1915) *Zur Textgeschichte Xenophons*, Lunds Universitets Årrskrift 10.2, Lund: C.W.K. Gleerup.

Pippidi, D.M. (1963) 'Note sur l'organisation militaire d'Istros à l'époque hellénistique', *Klio* 41: 158–167.

Pohlenz, M. (1937) *Herodot der erste Geschichtschreiber des Abendlandes*, Neue Wege zur Antike 7–8, Leipzig and Berlin: Teubner.

Pöhlmann, R. von (1912) *Geschichte der sozialen Frage und des Sozialismus in der antiken Welt*, 2 vols, Munich: C.H. Beck.

Poralla, P. (1913/1985) *Prosopographie der Lakedaimonier bis auf die Zeit Alexanders des Grossen*, Chicago: Ares.

Potter, D.S. (1990) *Prophecy and History in the Crisis of the Roman Empire: A Historical Commentary on the Thirteenth Sibylline Oracle*, Oxford: Oxford University Press.

Pouilloux, J. and F. Salviat (1983) 'Lichas, Lacédémonien, Archonte à Thasos et le livre VIII de Thucydide', *CRAI*: 376–403.

Pouilloux, J. and F. Salviat (1985) 'Thucydide après l'exil, et la composition de son histoire', *RPh* 59: 13–20.

Powell, A. (1989) 'Mendacity and Sparta's Use of the Visual', in A. Powell (ed.) *Classical Sparta: Techniques Behind her Success*, London: Routledge: 173–192.

Pratt, M.L. (1992) *Imperial Eyes: Travel Writing and Transculturation*, London and New York: Routledge.

Pretor, A. (1881) *The Anabasis of Xenophon*, 2 vols, Cambridge: Cambridge University Press.

Pritchett, W.K. (1971) *Ancient Greek Military Practices* Part 1, University of California Publications in Classical Studies 7, Berkeley: University of California Press.

Pritchett, W.K. (1974) *The Greek State at War* Part 2, Berkeley and Los Angeles: University of California Press.

Rahn, P.J. (1971) 'Xenophon's Developing Historiography', *TAPA* 102: 497–508.

Rahn, P.J. (1981) 'The Date of Xenophon's Exile', in G.S. Shrimpton and D.J. McCargar (eds) *Classical Contributions: Studies in Honour of Malcolm Francis McGregor*, Locust Valley: J.J. Augustin.

Ramsay, W.M. (1890) *The Historical Geography of Asia Minor*, Royal Geographical Society, Supplementary Papers 4, London.

Rankin, H.D. (1986) *Antisthenes Sokratikos*, Amsterdam: Adolf M. Hakkert.

Raubitschek, A.E. (1941) 'The Heroes of Phyle', *Hesperia* 10: 284–295.

Raubitschek, A.E. (1953) Review of Breitenbach (1950), *CP* 48: 36–37.

Raubitschek, A.E. (1972) 'Die sogenannten Interpolationen in den ersten beiden Büchern von Xenophons *Griechische Geschichte*', *Vestigia* 17: 315–325.

Rawson, E. (1969) *The Spartan Tradition in European Thought*, Oxford: Oxford University Press.

Redfield, J.M. (1975) *Nature and Culture in the Iliad: The Tragedy of Hector*, Chicago and London: University of Chicago Press.

Reinhardt, K. (1957) 'Die Sinneskrise bei Euripides', *Eranos Jahrbuch* 26: 279–313.

Reverdin, O. (1962) 'Crise spirituelle et évasion', *Grecs et Barbares*, Entretiens sur l'Antiquité classique 8: 85–120.

Rhodes, P.J. (1981) *A Commentary on the Aristotelian* Athenaion Politeia, Oxford: Oxford University Press.

Rhys Roberts, W. (1902) *Demetrius on Style*, Cambridge: Cambridge University Press.

Rice, D.G. (1975) 'Xenophon, Diodorus and the Year 379/378 BC: Reconstruction and reappraisal', *YCS* 24: 95–130.

Richardson, N.L. (1992) 'Panhellenic Cults and Panhellenic Poets', *CAH* 5 2nd edn: 223–244.

Riedinger, J.-C. (1991) *Etude sur les Helléniques: Xenophon et l'histoire*, Paris: Les Belles Lettres.

Riemann, K.-A. (1967) *Das herodoteische Geschichtswerk in der Antike*, diss. Munich.

Rinner, W. (1978) 'Zur Darstellungsweise bei Xenophon, *Anabasis* III 1–2', *Philologus* 122: 144–149.

Romilly, J. de (1958) '*Eunoia* in Isocrates, or the Political Importance of Creating Good Will', *JHS* 78: 92–101.

Romilly, J. de (1963) *Thucydides and Athenian Imperialism*, trans. P. Thody, Oxford: Basil Blackwell.

Romilly, J. de (1967) *Histoire et raison chez Thucydide*, Paris: Les Belles Lettres.

Romilly, J. de (1972) 'Vocabulaire et propaganda ou les premiers emplois du mot ὁμόνοια', in A. Ernout (ed.) *Mélanges de linguistique et de philologie grecques offerts à Pierre Chantraine*, Paris: Klincksieck: 199–209.

Romilly, J. de (1992) 'Isocrates and Europe', *G & R* 39: 2–13.

Romm, J.S. (1992) *The Edges of the Earth in Ancient Thought: Geography, Exploration and Fiction*, Princeton: Princeton University Press.

Ronnet, G. (1981) 'La Figure de Callicratidas et la composition des *Helléniques*', *RhP* 55: 111–121.

Roquette, A. (1884) *De Xenophontis vita*, diss. Königsberg.

Rosenthal, F. (1967) trans. *Ibn Khaldûn: The Muqaddimah*, Princeton: Princeton University Press.

Roy, J. (1967) 'The Mercenaries of Cyrus', *Historia* 16: 287–323.

Roy, J. (1968) 'Xenophon's Evidence for the *Anabasis*', *Athenaeum* 46: 37–46.

Rühl, F. (1913) 'Randglossen zu den *Hellenika* von Oxyrhynchos', *RhM* 68: 161–201.

Runciman, W.G. (1990) 'Doomed to Extinction: The *Polis* as an Evolutionary Dead-End', in O. Murray and S. Price (eds) *The Greek City From Homer to Alexander*, Oxford: Oxford University Press: 347–367.

Rusten, J.S. (1989) *Thucydides: The Peloponnesian War Book II*, Cambridge: Cambridge University Press.

Ryder, T. (1965) *Koine Eirene*, London: Oxford University Press.

Sacks, K.S. (1990) *Diodorus Siculus and the First Century*, Princeton: Princeton University Press.

Sahlins, M. (1985) *Islands of History*, Chicago and London: University of Chicago Press.

Saïd, E.W. (1978) *Orientalism*, New York: Random House.

Ste. Croix, G.E.M. de (1972) *The Origins of the Peloponnesian War*, London: Duckworth.

Ste. Croix, G.E.M. de (1981) *The Class Struggle in the Ancient Greek World*, Ithaca: Cornell University Press.

Sanctis, G. de (1931) 'La battaglia di Notion', *RFIC* 59: 222–229.

Sanctis, G. de (1932/1951) 'La genesi dell' Elleniche de Senofonte', *Annali Scuola Normale Superiore di Pisa* (ser. 2) 1: 15–36 = *Studi de storia della storiografia greca*, Florence: La Nuova Italia: 127–161. I cite from the latter.

Sandbach, F.H. (1985) 'Plato and the Socratic Work of Xenophon', in P.E. Easterling and B.M.W. Knox (eds) *The Cambridge History of Classical Literature* 1 *Greek Literature*, Cambridge: Cambridge University Press: 478–497.

Schacht, H. (1890) *De Xenophontis studiis rhetoricis*, diss. Berlin.

Scharr, E. (1919) *Xenophons Staats- und Gesellschaftsideal und seine Zeit*, Halle: Max Niemeyer.

Scheller, P. (1911) *De hellenistica historiae conscribendae arte*, diss. Leipzig.

Schenkl, K. (1861) 'Über die Echtheit des Epilogs der Xenophontischen *Kyropädie*', *Neue Jahrbücher für classische Philologie* 83: 540–557.

Schmitt-Pantel, P. (1990) 'Collective Activities and the Political in the Greek City', trans. L. Nixon, in O. Murray and S. Price (eds) *The Greek City From Homer to Alexander*, Oxford: Oxford University Press: 199–213.

Schofield, M. (1980) 'Preconception, Argument, and God', in M. Schofield, M. Burnyeat and J. Barnes (eds) *Doubt and Dogmatism: Studies in Hellenistic Epistemology*, Oxford: Oxford University Press: 283–308.

Schwartz, E. (1889/1956) 'Quellenuntersuchungen zur griechischen Geschichte', *RhM* 44: 161–193 = *Gesammelte Schriften* 2: 136–174, Berlin: de Gruyter.

Schwartz, E. (1903) 'Diodorus', *RE* 5: 663–704.

Schwartz, E. (1929/1960) *Das Geschichtswerk des Thukydides*, Hildesheim: Georg Olms.

Scully, S. (1990) *Homer and the Sacred City*, Ithaca: Cornell University Press.

Seager, R. and C.J. Tuplin (1980) 'The Freedom of the Greeks of Asia Minor: On the Origins of a Concept and the Creation of a Slogan', *JHS* 100: 141–157.

Sealey, R. (1993) *Demosthenes and his Time*, New York: Oxford University Press.

Sekunda, N.V. (1988) 'Persian Settlement in Hellespontine Phrygia', in A. Kuhrt and H. Sancisi-Weerdenburg (eds), *Achaemenid History* 3, Leiden: Nederlands Instituut voor het Nabije Oosten: 175–196.

Seters, J. van (1983) *In Search of History: Historiography in the Ancient World and the Origins of Biblical History*, New Haven and London: Yale University Press.

Shaw, B. (1982–1983) ' "Eaters of Flesh, Drinkers of Milk": The Ancient Mediterranean Ideology of the Pastoral Nomad', *Ancient Society* 13/14: 5–31.

Shipley, G. (1987) *A History of Samos 800–188 BC*, Oxford: Oxford University Press.

Shrimpton, G.S. (1977) 'Theopompus' Treatment of Philip in the *Philippica*', *Phoenix* 31: 123–144.

Shrimpton, G.S. (1991) *Theopompus the Historian*, Montreal and Kingston: McGill–Queen's University Press.

Smith, F.W. (1990) 'The Fighting Unit: An Essay in Structural Military History', *L'Antiquité Classique* 59: 149–165.

Smith, R.E. (1953–1954) 'The Opposition to Agesilaus' Foreign Policy 394–371 BC', *Historia* 2: 274–288.

Soesbergen, P.G. van (1982–1983) 'Colonisation as a Solution to Social-Economic Problems in Fourth-Century Greece', *Ancient Society* 13/14: 131–145.

Solmsen, F. (1942) *Plato's Theology*, Ithaca: Cornell University Press.

Sordi, M. (1950–1951) 'I Caraterri dell' opera storiografica di Senofonte nelle Elleniche', *Athenaeum* 28: 1–53, 29: 273–348.

Stadter, P.A. (1967) 'Flavius Arrianus: The New Xenophon', *GRBS* 8: 155–161.

Stadter, P.A. (1980) *Arrian of Nicomedia*, Chapel Hill: University of North Carolina Press.

Stoneman, R. (1992) Introduction and notes to *Xenophon: The Education of Cyrus*, translation of the *Cyropaedia* by H.G. Dakyns, London: J.M. Dent & Sons.

Strasburger, H. (1954) 'Der Einzelne und die Gemeinschaft im Denken der Griechen', *Historische Zeitschrift* 177: 227–248.

Strauss, L. (1972), *Xenophon's Socrates*, Ithaca and London: Cornell University Press.

Stuart, D.R. (1928/1967) *Epochs of Greek and Roman Biography*, New York: Biblo & Tannen.

Stylianou, P.J. (1991) Review of Sacks (1991), *BMCR* 2: 388–395.

Süss, W. (1910) *Ethos: Studien zur älteren griechischen Rhetorik*, Leipzig and Berlin: Teubner.

Swain, S. (1994) 'Man and Medicine in Thucydides', *Arethusa* 27: 303–327.

Syme, R. (1958) *Tacitus* 2, Oxford: Oxford University Press.

Taeger, F. (1930) *Der Friede von 362/1*, Tübinger Beiträge zur Altertumswissenschaft 11, Stuttgart: Kohlhammer.

Tarn, W.W. (1927) 'Greece: 355 to 321 BC', *CAH* 6: 438–459.

Tatum, J. (1989) *Xenophon's Imperial Fiction*, Princeton: Princeton University Press.

Taylor, C.C.W. (1976) *Plato: Protagoras*, Oxford: Oxford University Press.

Taylor, M.W. (1981) *The Tyrant Slayers: The Heroic Image in Fifth Century BC Athenian Art and Politics*, New York: Arno Press.

Thalmann, W.G. (1988) 'Thersites: Comedy, Scapegoats, and Heroic Ideology in the *Iliad*', *TAPA* 118: 1–28.

Theiler, W. (1924) *Zur Geschichte der teleologischen Naturbetrachtung bis auf Aristoteles*, diss. Zurich.

Thomas, R. (1989) *Oral Tradition and Written Record in Classical Athens*, Cambridge: Cambridge University Press.

Thomas, R. (1992) *Literacy and Orality in Ancient Greece*, Cambridge: Cambridge University Press.

Tigerstedt, E.N. (1965) *The Legend of Sparta in Classical Antiquity* 1, Stockholm Studies in History of Literature 9, Stockholm: Almqvist & Wiksell.

Tod, M. (1948) *Greek Historical Inscriptions* 2, Oxford: Oxford University Press.

Trüdinger, K. (1918) *Studien zur Geschichte der griechisch-römischen Ethnographie*, diss. Basel.

Tuplin, C.J. (1977) 'The Athenian Embassy to Sparta, 372/1', *LCM* 2: 51–56.

Tuplin, C.J. (1985) 'Imperial Tyranny: Some Reflections on a Classical Greek Political Metaphor', in P.A. Cartledge and F.D. Harvey (eds) *Crux: Essays in Greek History Presented to G.E.M. de Ste. Croix on his 75th Birthday*, London: Duckworth: 348–375.

Tuplin, C.J. (1987a) 'Xenophon's Exile Again', in M. Whitby, P. Hardie and M. Whitby (eds) *Homo Viator: Classical Essays for John Bramble*, Bristol: Bristol Classical Press: 59–68.

Tuplin, C.J. (1987b) 'The Leuctra Campaign: Some Outstanding Problems', *Klio* 69: 72–107.

Tuplin, C.J. (1987c) 'The Treaty of Boiotios', in H. Sancisi-Weerdenburg and A. Kuhrt (eds) *Achaemenid History* 2, Leiden: Nederlands Instituut voor het Nabije Oosten: 133–153.

Tuplin, C.J. (1993) *The Failings of Empire: A Reading of Xenophon Hellenica 2.3.11–7.5.27*, Historia Einzelschriften 76, Stuttgart: Franz Steiner Verlag.

Ullman, B.L. (1942) 'History and Tragedy', *TAPA* 73: 25–53.

Underhill, G.E. (1900) *A Commentary on the* Hellenica *of Xenophon*, Oxford: Oxford University Press.

Usener, H. and L. Radermacher (1904–1929) *Dionysius Halicarnaseus opuscula* 2, Stuttgart: Bibliotheca Teubneriana.

Usher, S. (1968) 'Xenophon, Critias and Theramenes', *JHS* 88: 128–135.

Usher, S. (1969) *The Historians of Greece and Rome*, London: Hamish Hamilton.

Usher, S. (1979) 'This to the Fair Critias', *Eranos* 77: 39–42

Verbeke, G. (1964) 'Les Stoïciens et le progrès de l'histoire', *La Revue philosophique de Louvain* 62: 5–38.

Vernant, J.-P. (1990) *Myth and Society in Ancient Greece*, trans. J. Lloyd, New York: Zone Books.

Vidal-Naquet, P. (1965) 'Economie et société dans la Grèce ancienne: L'œuvre de Moses I. Finley', *Archives Européennes de Sociologie* 6: 111–148.

Vlastos, G. (1991) *Socrates: Ironist and Moral Philosopher*, Ithaca: Cornell University Press.

Volquardsen, C.A. (1868) *Untersuchungen über die Quellen der griechischen und sicilischen Geschichten bei Diodor Buch XI bis XVI*, diss. Kiel.

Vorrenhagen, E. (1926) *De orationibus quae sunt in Xenophontis Hellenicis*, diss. Elberfeld.

Walbank, F.W. (1951) 'The Problem of Greek Nationality', *Phoenix* 5: 41–60.

Walbank, F.W. (1955) 'Tragic History: A Reconsideration', *BICS* 2: 4–14.

Walbank, F.W. (1957) *A Historical Commentary on Polybius* 1, Oxford: Oxford University Press.

Walbank, F.W. (1960) 'History and Tragedy', *Historia* 9: 216–234.

Walbank, F.W. (1967) *A Historical Commentary on Polybius* 2, Oxford: Oxford University Press.

Walbank, F.W. (1972) *Polybius*, Berkeley and Los Angeles: University of California Press.

Walker, E.M. (1921) 'The Oxyrhynchus Historian', in J.U. Powell and E.A. Barber (eds) *New Chapters in the History of Greek Literature*, Oxford: Oxford University Press: 124–133.

Walsh, J.J. (1963) *Aristotle's Conception of Moral Weakness*, New York and London: Columbia University Press.

Waters, K.H. (1985) *Herodotus the Historian: His Problems, Methods and Originality*, Norman: University of Oklahoma Press.

Wees, H. van (1986) 'Leaders of Men? Military Organisation in the *Iliad*', *CQ* 36: 285–303.

West, M.L. (1978) *Hesiod: Works and Days*, Oxford: Oxford University Press.

West, S. (1988) *A Commentary on Homer's Odyssey* 1, with contributions by A. Heubeck and J.B. Hainsworth, Oxford: Oxford University Press.

West, W.C. (1977) 'Hellenic Homonoia and the New Decree from Plataea', *GRBS* 18: 307–319.

Westlake, H.D. (1935) *Thessaly in the Fourth Century BC*, London: Methuen.

Westlake, H.D. (1966–1967) 'Individuals in Xenophon's *Hellenica*', *Bulletin of the John Rylands Library* 49: 246–269.

Westlake, H.D. (1986) 'Spartan Intervention in Asia, 400–397 BC', *Historia* 35: 405–426.

Westlake, H.D. (1987) 'Diodorus and the Expedition of Cyrus', *Phoenix* 41: 241–254.

Wheeler, E.L. (1982) '*Hoplomachia* and Greek Dances in Arms', *GRBS* 23: 223–233.

Wheeler, E.L. (1988) *Stratagem and the Vocabulary of Military Trickery*, Mnemosyne suppl. 108.

White, H. (1973) *Metahistory*, Baltimore and London: Johns Hopkins University Press.

White, H. (1978) *Tropics of Discourse: Essays in Cultural Criticism*, Baltimore: Johns Hopkins University Press.

Whitehead, D. (1982–1983) 'Sparta and the Thirty Tyrants', *Ancient Society* 13/14: 105–130.

Whitehead, D. (1988) 'Athenians in Xenophon', *LCM* 13 (1988) 145–147.

Whitehead, D. (1990) *Aeineias the Tactician: How to Survive a Siege*, Oxford: Oxford University Press.

Wilamowitz, U. von (1893) *Aristoteles und Athen*, 2 vols., Berlin: Weidman.

Wilcken, U. (1929) 'Philipp II. von Makedonien und die panhellenische Idee', *Sitzungsberichte der preussischen Akademie der Wissenschaften* 18: 291–318.

Wilcken, U. (1967/1931) *Alexander the Great*, trans. G.C. Richards, New York and London: W.W. Norton & Co.

Wiseman, T.P. (1979) *Clio's Cosmetics*, Leicester: Rowman & Littlefield.

Wood, N. (1964) 'Xenophon's Theory of Leadership', *CM* 25: 33–66.

Wycherley, R.E. (1957) *The Athenian Agora* 3 *Literary and Epigraphical Testimonia*, Princeton: American School of Classical Studies at Athens.

Wylie, G. (1992a) 'Cunaxa and Xenophon', *L'Antiquité Classique* 61: 119–134.

Wylie, G. (1992b) 'Agesilaus and the Battle of Sardis', *Klio* 74: 118–130.

Young, D.C. (1983) 'Pindar *Pythians* 2 and 3: Inscriptional ποτέ and the "Poetic Epistle"', *HSCP* 87: 31–48.

INDEX OF PASSAGES

319

GENERAL INDEX

249–253; and false beginnings
and ends 23; 'Greek Affairs', 4';
and hellenistic historiography
127; lacking conclusion 11;
lacking preface 10–11; and
'motor' of history 237; narrative
of meaningful 166; and
Oxyrhynchus historian compared 109–113; and pessimism
35–38, 241; second part of and
King's Peace 14; as Spartan
history 15, 207; triadic speeches
of 16, 242–249; unique 11
'Hellenism' 83; see also 'Greekness'
hellenistic age and military
thinking 86
hellenistic historiography 37, 46,
127; mimetic 128
Heraclea (Black Sea) 79
Heraclea (Greece) 173
Heraclitus, on apes and humans
47
Herodotus 10; on Alexander I and
Persians 229; and beginnings 21;
on Cambyses 188; on Cleobis
and Biton 126; on Croesus 126,
138, 176; and Deuteronomic
historian 181; and divine as
historical agent 181, 224; on
Egyptians 187; and ergon 30; on
Greece 35; and liberation of
Cadmea 230; on Libyan tribes
83; and the 'other' 45; on
Pactyes 133; and Persian debate
48; and Pheretime of Cyrene;
on small and large states 124;
on Tellus 126; and Thersander
of Thebes 61; on tyrannicides
141; on Xerxes 250
Hesiod 36; and archaic view of
divine 185; and Golden Age 43;
and Zeus 37
Hipparchus 141
Hippias of Elis 53
Hippias, son of Pisistratus 246
Hippodamus of Miletus 48–49
histories, contemporary with
Xenophon fragmentary 123; and
practical value 127

history, purposeful 180, 188
Homer and archaic view of divine
185
homonoia 36, 52, 54–58, 132
housebuilding and order 32
household as model 252
hubris 187
Hyampolis 173
Hyperboreans 46

Iambulus 46, 52
Imbros 204
individual, categorically same as
state 52
'inhabited' 95–97
'inscriptional pote' 140
institutions oldest 187
intelligence human fallible 183,
188, 225, 236
Iphicrates 29, 164, 165, 242;
contrasted with Mnasippus
169–171; and Phlius 212; and
Spartan decline 166; and
Teleutias 220; trains fleet and
fulfils duty 169
Isagoras 246
Ischomachus 242
Ismenias 216, 218–219, 221
Isocrates 43, 231; and date of
Panegyricus 54; demesman of
Xenophon 54; and eunoia 57;
on Gryllus 253; on homonoia
54–58; influence on Androtion
143; and King's Peace 56, 201;
and mimetic historiography 128;
on muthoi as history 140; and
panhellenism 54–58, 94;
partisan of Athens 56–57; and
Philip 57; 'preacher of unification', 55; simplification of views
of 55; on Ten Thousand 57, 90,
94

Jacoby, F. 143, 181
Jason of Pherae 37, 164, 171, 190;
ambitions of 173; coda to story
of 175; and Croesus story in
Herodotus 176; his death 174;
and Delphi 174; on divine 173;

fall at height of power 174; his family 175; and Greece 173; and Leuctra 172; as paradigm for imperialism 175; as paradigm for Sparta 175; placement of digression on 172; his power 173; punished 242; and Socratic virtues 175; substance of digression on 172; as threat to Sparta 172; as tyrant 174

Joël, K. 33

Justin on Theramenes 143

karteria 134; *see also enkrateia*

katabasis 42

katalusis 191

King's Peace 3, 17, 130, 196–197, 213, 228; a bilateral agreement 202; Boeotians and 203; breached by Sparta 202, 207–208, 217, 243–244; characterizations of 202; and conclusion of Corinthian War 202–203; guarantors of 204; members of 205; and Phlius 210; preliminaries to 199–200; publication of 201; and Sparta 201, 206; states protected by 214; terms of 201; two agreements 204; uncertainties of 205; where sworn 203; who swore to it 202; to whom did it apply 202; *see also* Cadmea Corinthian War oathbreaking Phoebidas

klausigelos and Phlius 132

kottabos and Theramenes' death 156

Krafft, P. 166

Krentz, P. 159

Laqueur's Thesis 129; *see also* Ephorus; Diodorus

lawbreaking 156, 188, 192, 217–218

League of Corinth 55

Lechaeum 29

Lemnos 204

Leon of Salamis and Socrates 142, 281 n.90

Leontiades 216; his death 230

Leuctra, battle of 4, 7, 15, 29, 59, 123, 164, 171, 175, 179, 201, 231, 246; aftermath of 172–173

local history 252; *see also* Atthidographers

Long Walls, destruction of at end of Peloponnesian War 22, 25–26

Lotus eaters, Ten Thousand as 62, 87

Lucian 10; and utopia 43

Lycon 88

Lycophron of Thessaly 25

Lycurgus and Spartan *paideia* 168

Lysander 25, 107, 146, 158; and Agesilaus 272 n.46; fall from power 104

Lysias: his Funeral Oration 54; his Olympic Oration 54, 198; on Theramenes 143

Macedonia and conquest of Greece 35, 55

Machimos, dystopia in Theopompus 45

Magnes in Theopompus 125

Mania, subsatrap 105

Mantinea, battle of 4, 7, 15, 19, 26, 94, 123, 180, 201; aftermath of 35; and closure 22; as false boundary 38; and Gryllus 253; and pessimism 38, 252

Mantinea, city of 207–208; and Cadmea 222; dioecism of 208; 'punishment' of 209; siege of 208; and Sparta 207–209

Marathon 22, 98

medizers 103

Meidias subsatrap 105, 107

mel–, and divine 227

Meleager 127

Melos 44, 218

Melon 229

memorialization and history 77, 140–141

Menon 67

Meropae 46

Messenia 4, 18